# THE MIDDLE EAST MILITARY BALANCE 1988-1989

## A Comprehensive Data Base & In-Depth Analysis of Regional Strategic Issues

Shlomo Gazit • Zeev Eytan
Edited by S. Gazit

**The Jerusalem Post**          **Westview Press**

Library of Congress Catalog Card Number:
86-50920

**Library of Congress Cataloging-in-Publication Data**

ISBN 0-8133-0961-1

Published for the Jaffee Center
for Strategic Studies
by
The Jerusalem Post
POB 81, Jerusalem 91000, Israel
and
Westview Press
Boulder, Colorado 80301, Frederick A. Praeger, Publisher

Printed in Israel at the Jerusalem Post Press

# JCSS Publications

JCSS Publications present the findings and assessments of the Center's research staff. Each paper represents the work of a single investigator or a team. Such teams may also include research fellows who are not members of the Center's staff. Views expressed in the Center's publications are those of the authors and do not necessarily reflect the views of the Center, its trustees, officers, or other staff members or the organizations and individuals that support its research. Thus the publication of a work by JCSS signifies that it is deemed worthy of public consideration but does not imply endorsement of conclusions or recommendations.

# Contents

# Preface

During the course of late 1988 and early 1989, research efforts at JCSS were concentrated upon our comprehensive study-group reports, *The West Bank and Gaza: Israel's Options for Peace* and *Israel and the West Bank: Toward a Solution*. This had two immediate implications. On the one hand, for some six months almost all work at the Center was focused on this study, and other tasks, such as the *Balance*, had to be postponed and reduced slightly in scope. On the other hand, we believe that this very special study should be considered as an important supplement to this year's *Balance*. All those who purchased the *Balance* through our Israeli distributor, *The Jerusalem Post*, received the study free of charge.

Our unusual time and resource constraints caused us to integrate all prose sections of the *Balance* into a single Part I, dealing with the major strategic developments in the Middle East. In 1988 these fit under two main headings: the Palestinian uprising, or *intifada* in the West Bank and Gaza Strip, and the ramifications of the ceasefire in the Iran-Iraq War. Each of these events is explored and analyzed from a variety of aspects. The opening chapter of Part I offers a general overview of last year's major strategic developments.

Part II this year provides, as always, an extensive and updated (April 1989) selection of data, figures and battle order information on all countries and armed forces in the region.

Finally, Part III offers updated reference material designed to facilitate the handling of the comprehensive figures: comparative tables, a glossary of weaponry, maps and a list of abbreviations. Here we have introduced an innovation: a chronology of the main political, military and strategic events in the area, updated to the end of June 1989.

A long list of persons deserves our thanks this year for their valuable contribution to the writing and production of the 1988-1989 *Balance*. First to be thanked is Dr. Mark A. Heller who wrote three chapters: Changes in PLO Posture, The Soviet Union in the Middle East, and Soviet Policy in the Gulf. Next comes Dr. Dore Gold, with two chapters: The US-PLO Dialogue, and Developments in US Policy in the Persian Gulf. Dr. Yehuda Ben Meir wrote on Political Developments in Israel, Dr. Efraim Karsh on Regional Strategic Implications of the Iran-Iraq War, Anat Kurz on Palestinian Terrorism in 1988 and Brig.Gen.(res.) Aryeh Shalev on The Uprising in Judea, Samaria and the Gaza Strip and its Ramifications.

While ultimate responsibility for the contents of this book lies with the authors of the individual papers, the *Balance* benefited from the comments of most other members of the Center – particularly the Head of Center, Maj.Gen.(res.) Aharon Yariv. It is also my pleasant duty to extend thanks to the Deputy Head of Center, Joseph Alpher, whose contribution in coordinating production cannot be overestimated.

Mrs. Miriam Cassuto and Ms. Gilla Berkovitz deserve special gratitude for wordprocessing the many drafts of this work. Finally, sincere thanks go to Reuven Danielli, who labored heroically to translate chapters written originally in Hebrew.

S.G.

July 1989

# PART I

# STRATEGIC DEVELOPMENTS IN THE MIDDLE EAST

# Introduction: Major Strategic Developments
## by Shlomo Gazit

The year 1988 and early 1989 will probably be remembered as a year of dramatic developments on both the international level and the local, Middle Eastern level. With historical perspective these developments may be seen to symbolize a turning point in the Arab-Israel conflict and the start of a process leading to a political settlement of the conflict. On the other hand, should there be no progress on the political front — should there be no inclination toward flexibility, dialogue and compromise — this process may lead, even in accelerated fashion, to a contrary trend of renewed military conflagration.

Three important spheres of development stand out: the *intifada*, the popular uprising of the Arabs inside the Israeli-Administered Territories; Soviet policy toward the third world; and the termination of the Persian Gulf conflict. In this chapter we shall outline developments in all three spheres, then summarize several additional strategic trends that characterized the Middle East during 1988-89.

## The Intifada

When it began — late 1987-early 1988 — the *intifada* occasioned much surprise. No intelligence estimate had envisioned the possibility of a spontaneous popular uprising by the inhabitants of the Administered Territories, one capable of sustaining a prolonged, unbroken struggle and encompassing a wide range of anti-Israel activities. With hindsight it has become evident that the *intifada* exposed Israel's Achilles' heel: despite its overwhelming superiority over the unarmed insurrectionists in the Territories, Israel was constrained from using its military capability to put down the *intifada*. Though some circles in Israel demanded that the uprising be crushed by extreme suppressive and punitive measures, the Israeli government and the minister of defense refrained from doing so. They were motivated by both ethical considerations — abstaining from taking steps repugnant to a large part of the Israeli populace — and pragmatic political considerations. It is thus of purely academic interest to note that, at least in the initial stages, the implementation of extreme measures might have served to terminate the *intifada*. By the Spring of 1989, with the uprising at an advanced stage and in its second year, one could begin to analyze its political and strategic achievements.

The *intifada* concurrently addressed itself to four different target groups. First and foremost, it operated within the Arab population of the Territories. After 20 years of military occupation, and in view of the lack of progress toward a political solution of their problem, the Arabs of the West Bank and Gaza found an outlet to express their accumulated frustration and desperation. We do not know whether any of the leaders of the uprising, wielding only rocks and petrol bombs and directing demonstrations, truly believed that they could eliminate Israel and the IDF from the Territories. But psychologically their achievement was immensely important. As a result of the uprising, each and every one of the 1.5 million inhabitants of the Territories was imbued with the feeling that he/she was no longer helpless before the Israeli occupation. Furthermore, the popular uprising made an important contribution toward the rehabilitation of Palestinian national pride and the consolidation of greater internal unity. This could prove important in creating conditions that would enable the Palestinian leadership to open a political dialogue with Israel in the future.

The second target group was Israel itself. Here the *intifada* tried to achieve two different goals: first, to exhaust Israel by forcing it to sustain the deployment of large forces to deal with the uprising, together with heavy economic damage; and secondly, to intensify the internal debate within Israel and strengthen and encourage those parties that favored an Israeli withdrawal from the Territories. Indeed, one of the *intifada*'s effects in Israel was to consolidate a wide-ranging, negative consensus regarding the routine that characterized the first 20 years of Israeli administration in the Territories: the status quo could no longer be maintained.

As the uprising progressed, hardly anything remained of the original policy in the Territories set out by Moshe Dayan. A basic tenet of this policy was that extensive Israeli-Palestinian coexistence could be developed and cultivated — albeit backed up by force and military rule — and could eventually lead to a normalization of relations. The uprising in the Territories eliminated all manifestations of coexistence; virtually nothing was left of the idea of integrating, at almost all levels, two peoples, two regions, and two economies fated to exist side by side. The *intifada* reinstated the "Green Line" border' that was so dramatically erased in 1967. To a lesser extent this held true of Jerusalem, too: the "reunited" city was divided once again, though along a different line of demarcation than the one prior to its conquest by Israel in 1967. After the Six-Day War in June 1967, there was a basic assumption in Israel that the inhabitants of the Administered Territories could themselves play no role either in the search for a settlement of the conflict or even in alleviating their own distress. The *intifada* made the inhabitants a central factor in any solution. Paradoxically, these developments in Israel concurrently strengthened the two poles of opinion with regard to the desired solution: the one calling for Israel's immediate withdrawal from the Territories; the other, calling for annexation and even "transfer," or deportation of the Arab population of the Territories.

The third target of the uprising was the international arena. Here the *intifada* had two central aims: first, to place the need for an immediate solution to the Palestinian problem on the world's political agenda; and secondly, to damage Israel politically by sullying its media image. In this regard the Palestinians exposed yet another Israeli Achilles' heel. The world had little sympathy for the sight of soldiers in action against civilians, and particularly women and children. Generally speaking the media projected a superficial picture, reporting each event while lacking the ability (still less, the will) to provide long explanations, background information and commentary. To a large extent Israel consciously refrained from closing the Territories or preventing media coverage of incidents, despite the resultant embarrassment. This reflected the paradox of a democratic regime whose only choice was to rule undemocratically, with everything that entails.

The last target group was the Arab world at large, and particularly the Palestinian establishment-in-exile (principally the PLO, of course). The *intifada* clearly signaled to the Palestinian exile leadership that the Arabs of the Territories were no longer willing to settle for promises and talk of a rosy future. They were the only ones suffering under the reality of enforced, hostile Israeli rule and the Palestinian leadership must take cognizance of it. The first to understand this was Arafat. Unilaterally, and with no concession (or promise of concession) on the part of Israel, he generated, in November-December 1988, a significant change in the basic Palestinian position. The decisions of the Palestinian National Council in November in Algiers — the Palestinian Declaration of Independence and the Council's Political Declaration — and Arafat's explanatory statements in Geneva one month later, all effectively canceled one of the central tenets of the Palestinian Charter of 1964 and 1968. Contrary to that Charter, the PLO now adopted resolutions acknowledging, at least implicitly, Israel's right to exist and the need for peaceful relations with it.

By the Spring of 1989 there was no irrefutable proof to indicate whether these steps were taken by the Palestinian leadership in good faith, with a genuine acceptance of the realities of the situation, or whether, in contrast, they were nothing but a tactical modification — a smoke screen meant to place Israel in a political and diplomatic quandary. Response to the steps in Israel reflected this uncertainty. On the one hand, some Israelis saw in the PLO's moves a substantial strategic change that merited Israeli acknowledgement and the initiation of a direct dialogue with the PLO. Yet others viewed them as a new and extremely dangerous tactic necessitating a hardening of positions and a categorical refusal to deal with PLO leaders on any terms.   The *intifada* in the Territories, in conjunct with the PLO's new diplomatic steps, placed a new challenge before Israel. As long as the Palestinian demand for the total annihilation (perhaps in stages) of Israel stood, it was easy to sustain a widespread national consensus in Israel against the Palestinian struggle: no one could expect Israel to adopt a policy of national suicide. But in the new situation which arose, Israel was forced to deal with a limited Palestinian objective, namely its withdrawal from Judea, Samaria and the Gaza Strip. The more clearly and unambiguously this limited Palestinian objective was defined, the greater the internal debate within Israel. By early 1989 the Palestinian position was still being articulated by disparate, contradictory voices, with the "sacred" Palestinian demand for the "right of return" of Palestinian refugees from 1948 to pre-1967 Israel's borders — implying, in effect, Israel's total annihilation — continuing to be enunciated from time to time.

We cannot conclude this short discussion of the *intifada* and its ramifications without pointing to the dangerous escalation of violent activities on the part of the Palestinians on the one hand, and Jewish extremists on the other, during the first half of 1989. As the number of violent incidents rose, Israel's security and governmental authorities concurrently were losing control over developments. If this process remained unchecked, matters could reach a dangerous impasse — a total disruption of Arab-Jewish relations and perhaps even violent altercations among Jews. Should this occur, it could generate an entirely new situation for all parties involved.

## Soviet Policy toward the Third World

During 1988 and early 1989 a number of key developments in the third world reached fruition, bearing upon the entire spectrum of international relations and inevitably influencing Middle East issues as well.

Undoubtedly, the key to these changes lay in the dramatic developments inside the Soviet Union and the international ramifications of Mikhail Gorbachev's policies of glasnost and perestroika. For the purpose of this analysis the main thrust of these policies lay in a calm Soviet foreign policy that sought to prevent and terminate conflicts and international crises that were liable to force the Soviet Union to take a stand or actively interfere in events — any such intervention being highly undesirable on its part. This attitude found expression in striking fashion during the discussions of the Communist Party Conference in Moscow in June 1988. The Conference recommended keeping Soviet foreign policy initiatives at a very low profile, with a view to allocating most national resources to domestic social and economic development.

This attitude was buttressed by an acknowledged change in basic assumptions. The Soviet Union was increasingly evidencing a loss of faith in the inevitability of communist victory and expansion, and as a result Soviet foreign policy was no longer directed toward serving the interests of the global class struggle. On the contrary, the guiding principle was now "coexistence," with inter-bloc rivalry manifesting itself at the level of economic interests, and free economic cooperation encouraged. Gorbachev backed away from the dichotomic view that posited total Soviet security at the price of total insecurity for the nations surrounding the Soviet Union. The new view was not absolutist but relativist, necessitating a search for compromise, cooperation, negotiation and "give and take."

These new trends had a direct and immediate bearing upon

Soviet policy toward third world nations, including those of the Middle East. An almost antithetic ideological view was slowly taking shape. Thus Andrei Kozyrev, who served as deputy head of the Department for International Institutions in the Soviet Foreign Ministry, wrote in the Summer of 1988: "The myth that the class interests of socialist and developing countries coincide in resisting imperialism does not hold up to criticism at all. The majority of developing countries already adhere or tend toward the western model of development and they suffer not from capitalism as from lack of it" (*Mezhddunarodnaya Zhin*, quoted in *IHT*, January 9, 1989).

Under these circumstances there occurred significant developments in third world countries once considered Marxist or counted among those with links solely to the Eastern Bloc. Angola, Ethiopia and PDRY all turned to the West for assistance. We also witnessed Moscow's negative reply to Damascus' request for economic assistance, investment in oil exploration and sophisticated equipment, referring the Syrians instead to the West. But the effects went further — the working model was no longer based on monopolistic relations between a superpower and its satellites. A reality of complex coalitions of different powers opened up, with a consequent vast responsibility for preventing unwanted reversals. It is against this background that we must consider a Soviet Union that encouraged American mediation in Lebanon and prodded the PLO into a dialogue with Washington, while on the other hand the United States did nothing to prevent Moscow's overtures toward Saudi Arabia, Jordan or Israel.

Yet this process appears to have had little effect on Soviet policy regarding the supply of advanced weapons systems to the states of the region. The economic and commercial importance of this export trade was greater than before; 1988 witnessed the supply of advanced armaments to Algeria, Libya and Iraq, the possible advent of an arms deal with Iran, and ongoing strategic supply to Syria too, even though in most cases this meant a greater risk of military conflagration in the region.

The year 1988 recorded dramatic progress in a long list of regional conflicts: Angola, Cambodia, Namibia, the two Koreas, the Persian Gulf, Afghanistan, Cyprus, the Western Sahara, and Libya-Chad. In this sense the Arab-Israel conflict stood out as one wherein no progress was made. The November 1988 elections to the Israeli Knesset were evidently an important factor in deterring the superpowers from dealing with the conflict until late in the year. Then the start of the American-PLO dialogue and Soviet Foreign Minister Edward Shevardnadze's visit to the region demonstrated that international activity in this sphere was imminent. It was the Soviet Union that encouraged and prodded the PLO into accepting American conditions. And it was the Reagan administration that displayed great flexibility when it agreed to accept Yasir Arafat's formulations regarding 242, terrorism and recognition of Israel. This made it unnecessary for the incoming Bush administration to deal with the question, thereby incurring, from Washington's standpoint, further delay.

It is impossible to discuss Soviet-US relations regarding the third world without considering one of the most important events, from the Soviet standpoint, of recent times: the withdrawal of Soviet forces from Afghanistan in February 1989. After more than nine years, the USSR came to terms with a stinging military defeat. From a strictly military viewpoint, there appeared to be little difference between this setback and that of the Americans in Vietnam; it offered additional proof that a regular army is unable to deal with a popular militia, especially when the regular army is fighting for a strategic goal of secondary importance. But in this case the global strategic ramifications could be of much greater importance. In Afghanistan, Islamic fundamentalist forces emerged victorious; it was a victory of fanatic religious fervor over one of the two greatest powers in the world. The near-term effects of this achievement could, perhaps, include the intensification of Muslim irredentist tendencies as part and parcel of the nationalist revival sweeping many of the Soviet Union's republics.

The dramatic changes in the Soviet Union did not automatically produce a totally new pattern of superpower relations, either globally or in the Middle East. True, the Reagan administration, in its last year in office, completely altered the tone of its relations with Moscow in the aftermath of the signing of the Intermediate Nuclear Forces (INF) Treaty and the accords on Afghanistan. In the Middle East, the Reagan-Shultz team formally dropped its opposition to an international peace conference on the Arab-Israel conflict, with Soviet participation. Yet the Bush administration in 1989 seemed far less influenced by the atmospherics of superpower summitry than its predecessor. The key buzzword for Bush's foreign policy team was "caution." The new team expressed considerable doubts about long-range Soviet intentions; in its view, Moscow's arms control initiatives were aimed at undermining the western alliance as much as they were intended to promote a more stable global order. Gorbachev's reforms, they maintained, were being undertaken for the purpose of creating a stronger, more efficient Soviet Union.

The State Department, under Secretary of State James Baker, argued that there was an uneven application of the "new Soviet thinking" in regional conflicts during the first months of 1989 — particularly in Central America and the Middle East. Baker, while not precluding the possibility of eventually holding an international peace conference on the Middle East, nonetheless felt that such a high visibility effort would have to await a considerable period of pre-negotiation and confidence-building. Baker also argued that the Soviets would have to earn their place as cosponsors of the peace process by first matching their rhetorical moderation with specific deeds: restricting the sale of sophisticated weapons to the Middle East, restoring full diplomatic relations with Israel, and joining the US and other western industrialized countries in restricting the transfer of ballistic missile technology to the third world.

Thus, while developments in the Soviet Union suggested the possible emergence of an entirely new pattern of superpower relations in the third world, mutual suspicions were still evident in 1989. They would have to be altered before competition could be replaced with cooperation.

## The End of Fighting in the Persian Gulf

After eight years of bloody fighting that inflicted grave losses upon both belligerents, a ceasefire in the Persian Gulf was finally accepted in the summer of 1988. As Iran and Iraq entered a post-war era, their actions would continue to influence the entire Middle East.

A basic assumption of both sides during the year that followed the ceasefire held that this was not the true end of the conflict. The war had come to a stop in a state of indecision, with Iran (the aggressed party) in an inferior position both militarily and in terms of morale. Under these circumstances both sides prepared, first to rebuild their armies in preparation for a new military faceoff, if and when it should occur, and secondly, to accelerate the restoration of their economies and national infrastructures, a necessary precondition for new military preparations. The inevitable consequence of these programs was heavy dependence on outside sources of supply for weapons and armaments, with purveyors from both the eastern and western blocs now considered legitimate for this purpose. A concomitant dependence upon foreign investments, particularly in oil production, arose.

At the military level the two countries were expected to continue a multipronged effort. For one, as long as neither country felt sure of a prolonged respite, both would attempt to maintain forces at a level only slightly below that which immediately preceded the ceasefire. Then too, both would seek speedily to rehabilitate units, restore weapons systems and equipment to combat condition, and supplement both by military acquisition and rearmament programs. In this regard, priority would be awarded to air forces and air defense. They would also be purchasing and deploying medium range (at least 500 kilometers) surface-to-surface missiles and chemical warfare systems. Iraq, for its part, would speed development of an independent nuclear power capability.

Negotiations between the two countries dragged on throughout the year following the ceasefire, with no result. In this sense, as long as no political accord was signed the possibility of renewed warfare always existed. In the short term, however, neither of the two Persian Gulf antagonists seemed likely to embark on a military adventure or adopt extremist policies that might involve it in immediate military challenges in the region. Furthermore, both had grave internal problems that suggested a moderate foreign policy, and both felt it incumbent to effect cooperation with neighbors and demonstrations of calm and stability that are considered a precondition for most western investment. Certainly, in view of Ayatollah Khomeini's anti-western legacy, the adoption of such a position in Iran could only take place gradually. By the late Spring of 1989 Iran had initiated contacts with the Soviet Union, with Soviet Foreign Minister Shevardnadze and Majlis Speaker Rafsanjani exchanging visits, and extensive economic and military cooperation deals signed. It had also put out feelers toward the United States; one manifestation was an attempt to broker the release of western hostages held by extremist Shi'ite elements in Lebanon.

The cessation of hostilities enabled Iraq to play a greater role in Lebanon. Here, Baghdad clearly intended to settle an old score with Hafez al-Assad's regime in Damascus. We recall that Syria, alone among the Arab states, supported Iran throughout the war.

Iraq saw its chance to retaliate in late 1988 by supporting Maronite Christian elements in Lebanon, mainly by supplying arms, with the aim of weakening Syria's attempt to establish hegemony in the country.

In view of this preoccupation, it was hard to see Iraq, or Iran for that matter (despite its having officially adopted the cause of the liberation of Jerusalem), taking any sort of military initiative against Israel. Nonetheless, as long as the ceasefire with Iran remained in force, and should an Arab-Israel war break out — even as a result of developments having nothing to do with Iraq — the latter would feel compelled to take part. Despite Iran's antagonism, Tehran was hardly likely to take advantage of Baghdad's involvement in a "holy" war against Israel to attack Iraq. The immense standing order-of-battle that Iraq continued to maintain after the end of the Gulf War would enable it to participate in an Arab-Israel war with a significant expeditionary force: 4-6 Iraqi divisions at the battle fronts, of which 2-4 would be armored and mechanized. Iraqi air contingents could also be expected to participate, both by advancing squadrons to airfields in Syria and Jordan and by launching direct sorties from forward airfields in Iraq itself. Iraq could also place part of its surface-to-surface missile array at the service of the Arab war coalition.

The participation of Iraqi forces in any future war with Israel has greater significance than the mere despatch of an expeditionary force — however larger than in the past — in and of itself. First, during eight years of warfare Iraq built an infrastructure of roads and a fleet of tank-transporters (approximately 2,800) that afford a level of mobility significantly greater than in 1980. The network of roads linking Iraq to Jordan was also significantly improved during the war years. Therefore the pace of arrival of Iraqi expeditionary forces would be quicker. Secondly, on a qualitative level, though Iraqi forces in the past were considered inexperienced in battle and therefore did not merit a major Israeli combat effort, the Iraqi Army of the 1980s would be a very different opponent. Indeed, Iraq's new land and air weapons systems, and the rich combat experience accumulated by Iraqi formations and their commanders, pose a serious challenge to any future enemy.

The only instance in which an independent Iraqi initiative against Israel appeared likely in the near term would be if Israel were to decide to take military steps to destroy Baghdad's nuclear capability — as happened in 1981, with Israel's air strike on the Osiraq reactor. Nearly ten years after Osiraq, Iraq would not let such a provocation go unanswered. Even if the Israeli attack did not generate the reemergence of a pan-Arab war coalition against Israel, Iraq could respond on its own with a surface-to-surface missile attack (and, with lesser probability, air attacks) against strategic targets in Israel. In early 1989 Iraq evinced great sensitivity to the possibility of such an Israeli initiative. This derived especially from the many disclosures, believed by the Iraqis to have emanated from Israel, concerning Iraq's progress in developing a nuclear weapon, and from a public warning by the IDF chief-of-staff that Israel might have to adopt a preemptive strike strategy calculated to disrupt and destroy the Arab military order-of-battle facing Israel.

## Proliferation of Nonconventional Weaponry and Means of Delivery

Developments in the Gulf War between Iran and Iraq, especially during the final year of fighting, bestowed a form of legitimacy upon the proliferation of advanced weapons systems in several other countries in the region. This trend took the form of the independent development and procurement of surface-to-surface missiles and weapons based on CWA (chemical warfare agents), otherwise described by the Arab states as "the poor man's nuclear weapon."

Iraq made liberal use of such weapons both against military targets in Iran and, perhaps more significantly, against Iranian and Kurdish civilian population centers. In the closing stages of the Gulf War Iraq launched approximately 200 surface-to-surface missiles that inflicted heavy losses and undermined Iran's fighting spirit. As such they were an important factor in Tehran's decision to accept a ceasefire.

The two dominant developments in this sphere were the Iraqi missile development program and Saudi Arabia's acquisition of surface-to-surface missiles. The Iraqi development effort focused on missiles of the El Hussein and El Abbas types. These are Soviet Scud missiles in which the warhead has been replaced with a lighter one, thereby increasing the Scud's original range to around 650 km for the El Hussein and 900 km for the El Abbas. Moreover, the Iraqis reportedly developed and successfully tested the FAW 1 anti-missile missile. Iraq's success in modifying these missiles surprised many who had underestimated Baghdad's scientific-technological capabilities.

The ambitious Iraqi weapons development program apparently extended to an improved surface-to-surface missile whose warhead and accuracy exceed those of the modified Scud, but was still within the 600-900 kilometer range. Concurrently Iraq most likely continued to develop and manufacture chemical warfare agents.

Iran, meanwhile, harbored similar aspirations, but remained behind Iraq in terms of capabilities.

The second important development was Saudi Arabia's procurement of Chinese-made CSS-2 surface-to-surface missiles, revealed in the Spring of 1988. The CSS-2 is an outmoded missile with only a conventional warhead but with a range of over 2,500 km. The surprise was twofold. First, this effort to acquire deterrent weapons as fast as possible reflected the depth of Saudi Arabia's strategic apprehensions regarding Iran and Iraq. Secondly, the deal was struck with the PRC. Surface-to-surface missiles are not off-the-shelf items. The number of countries involved in their development and manufacture is very small, and domestic and international constraints dictate that they are not usually sold in a hurry to anybody, not even to those with the means to pay.

Saudi Arabia may have sought surface-to-surface missiles in response to the threat posed by Iran and Iraq, but once in place they could be used against other targets in the Middle East, including Israel. Moreover, the Saudis were undoubtedly aware of the operational limitations of the CSS-2, and were likely to continue their efforts to procure a more advanced surface-to-surface missile.

In the chemical warfare field, Egypt has maintained an independent manufacturing capability for some 25 years. We recall that Egypt employed chemical warfare during its campaign in Yemen in the mid-1960s. Despite efforts by the United States to halt the process, in 1988-89 Egypt, in cooperation with Iraq and Argentina, proceeded with the development of a surface-to-surface missile, the Condor 2, with a planned range of 950 km. Unconfirmed reports indicated that the development program also included chemical warheads: Iraq, after all, had proved its technological capability in this regard and, no less important, its willingness to employ chemical warfare in the battlefield. Meanwhile Syria and Libya were also trying to achieve an independent capability in this field, with Brazilian help.

The proliferation of the manufacture and acquisition of chemical warfare agents could sooner or later lead to their falling into the hands of terrorist organizations — whether by legitimate procurement or by theft. Terrorist groups employing chemical warfare agents could considerably expand the scope of their exploits.

The dramatic entry of chemical warfare agents on the scene and the danger of their proliferation were formally discussed at an international conference convened in Paris in January 1989. The participating powers decided not to consider chemical warfare agents as non-conventional weapons on a par with nuclear weapons. They therefore refrained from initiating international legislation or implementing a watchdog mechanism like that which keeps tabs on nuclear weapons. Nevertheless, with the United States leading the way, it was decided to try to halt the proliferation of chemical warfare agents.

One development dating from late 1988 helped to alter the US attitude toward the problem: the report that a CWA manufacturing plant was being built in Libya with private western (especially West German) assistance. The availability of chemical warfare agents in Libya might pose a threat beyond their use in wartime; where Libya is concerned, there is always the possibility of the Qaddafi regime placing these weapons at the service of extremist elements, including terrorist organizations. Neither the disclosure of the affair, nor the American threat to destroy the Libyan installation (including an air incident in which Sixth Fleet planes downed two Libyan MiG-23s), nor yet the pressure on western states to restrain their firms from assisting in the development of installations that may be used to manufacture chemical warfare agents, appeared to affect CWA development and manufacturing activity in Libya. But in the short term these measures at least contributed to a sense of greater caution in the matter.

While Middle East regional efforts remained principally focused on the search for a non-nuclear weapon of mass-destruction such as CWA, early 1989 once again witnessed troubling reports about the possible emergence of a nuclear option.

According to reports published in the West (and evidently issuing from Israel), Iraq sought to renew its efforts to develop an independent nuclear capability. Naturally any such activity took place behind a shroud of secrecy and it was difficult to assess Iraqi progress. By conservative estimates an Iraqi nuclear weapon was at least 5-10 years away. Iraq's success in this field, coupled with its achievements in surface-to-surface missile technology, could add a new dimension to regional threats.

These reports worried Iran no less than they did Israel; we recall that the Iranian Air Force attempted to bomb and destroy the Osiraq reactor in Baghdad as early as October 1980, more than half a year before the Israeli attack. This is probably the principal explanation for the Iranian attempt to acquire nuclear installations "for civilian purposes" in France (it may be assumed that similar approaches were being made to other possible suppliers). By mid-1989 there were no indications of Iranian success in this field.

## Syria — An Independent Military Option

In the course of their military reorganization and procurement efforts over the past decade, Middle East states have given clear priority to their air forces and air defense. This is particularly striking in view of the budgetary constraints that have dictated cutbacks in most other military sectors throughout the region. Retrospective analysis of Arab efforts over the past ten years reveals that two thirds of the total investment in defense has been earmarked for air forces and air defense; this translates into procurement outlays of approximately $50 billion.

The leader in this field has been Syria. Damascus has yet to shake off the trauma it suffered in 1982 when Syrian air defenses in Lebanon were destroyed by the Israel Air Force. That blow totally erased the Arab advantage in this field acquired during the Yom Kippur War of 1973, and Syria once again found itself unable to counter an overwhelming Israeli air superiority.

The year 1988 saw the emplacement of additional SA-5 surface-to-air missile batteries in Syria, and a significant procurement effort in electronic warfare systems and other electronic subsystems. Further, the arrival in Syria of the Soviet MiG-29, whose operational capabilities are comparable with those of the American F-15, significantly improved Syria's position as regards the balance of forces in the air.

Syria was expected soon to take delivery of the Sukhoi-24, a two-seat bomber with capabilities comparable to those of the American F-111. The range of these planes, which enables them to cover all of Israel's territory, and the heavy payload of armaments they can carry (8 tons of bombs) combined to make them an important complement to Syria's Scud missiles.

Two other key strategic developments of 1988 in Syria did not directly involve procurement. The first of these was overall investment in the Syrian defense forces, which grew relative to 1987 despite the lack of any parallel improvement in Syria's economy and despite the need for additional overall reductions and austerity measures. Indeed, Syria deliberately conducted a policy of dissimulation on this issue, perhaps for reasons of internal policy, to lull public opinion while calling for real sacrifice on the part of the populace. Thus in 1988 it reported further reductions in the Syrian defense budget: the 1988 outlay was nominally the same as in 1987, but due to a yearly inflation rate of 25 percent this appeared to translate into a substantial reduction. In reality the extent of activities within Syria's armed forces during 1988 reflected a rise in both operational activities and expenditures in most fields.

The second development was the adoption of a new offensive profile in Syria's military training programs. Syrian land force maneuvers placed emphasis on breaching entrenched positions, with little attempt made to conceal the intended objective of recapturing the Golan Heights. In 1988 the Syrian Navy took part in joint maneuvers with units of the Soviet fleet, with some aspects indicating that a Syrian offensive capability at sea was presumably their goal.

Assuming no substantial change regarding these three developments in the near future, Syria appeared anxious to complete preparations for a possible independent military offensive option in the Golan Heights sometime toward 1990. However, beyond registering here the fact that Damascus might feel it held the operational capabilities for such an option, nothing could be inferred from this regarding Syria's political intentions.

## Developments in Israel

During 1988 the Israeli defense establishment had to deal with two sets of contradictory pressures: on the one hand, continued reductions in the defense budget, reflecting the country's ongoing economic crisis; and on the other, the need to meet the unexpected burden engendered by the *intifada*, both budgetarily and in the disruption of regular and reserve training programs and routine operations.

In mid-1987, when work on the Lavi development project (an

advanced fighter aircraft to have been produced by Israel Aircraft Industries) was halted, the defense establishment earmarked the funds saved thereby for the development of a line of advanced weapons systems for all arms of the military. Yet by early 1989 very little had been accomplished in this regard, as all residual funds were simply swallowed up by current operational costs. This held true, too, regarding funds earmarked by the defense establishment for new procurement orders from Israel's military industries.

Interesting statistical evidence regarding the effects of budgetary reductions could be found in the increase in the relative size of salaries as part of the defense budget, from 33.4 percent in 1987 to 36.6 percent in 1989. Moreover these figures did not include increased salary compensation for reservists, called up for duty in growing numbers to deal with the *intifada*; this was covered by National Insurance sources and was not included in the defense budget. At a minimum, the true meaning of these figures was a reduction of over three percent in the defense budget available for non-salary activities (procurement, training, etc.).

The cost of mounting an increased IDF deployment to counter the *intifada* in Judea, Samaria and the Gaza Strip was met only halfway by the government in the form of additional budgetary allotments. The IDF had to provide on its own for the urgent development and manufacture of protective equipment and arms adapted to specific new riot-control duties; and it dedicated significant intelligence efforts toward collecting and analyzing data on the uprising. These duties caused serious disruptions in training and operations, and, no less important, focused a considerable part of planning, intelligence, staff and command efforts on the urgent — yet, from a military standpoint, strategically marginal — problems of dealing with the *intifada*. Though the damage may be reversible as regards the IDF's standing order-of-battle, and regular army groups may be brought back to a satisfactory level of preparedness and alert without great difficulty, the same does not hold true for reserve units: these cannot be activated for unlimited periods to encompass both the requirements of the *intifada* and the training needed to maintain a level of preparedness and alert for war. Though many reservists' stint of duty in IDF field units grew to 60 days in 1988, little of this time was devoted to maneuvers. This meant that, as of the end of 1988, a growing number of reserve army formations had not had proper training and refresher exercises for an extended period.

The burden of dealing with the *intifada* also had its effect on morale. While the overall number of IDF soldiers who refused to serve in the territories was very small (from the start of the *intifada* in December 1987 until the end of March 1989, there were only 60 cases of refusal to serve, almost all involving reservists), this figure did not express the prevailing attitude among the great majority of soldiers called upon to perform such duties in the territories. The need to carry out difficult, "ugly" and troubling tasks left its mark on everybody involved, leading to political extremism in both directions.

One effort to alleviate this problem was to assign to policing duties special "dedicated" forces — principally by enlarging the Border Police's standing order-of-battle. A basic assumption was that a permanent force would be able to carry out its missions more effectively, would maintain economy of size and, most importantly, would free army reserves to deal with routine training and operational activities. Be that as it may, this process could only be implemented slowly.

Arab leaders were presumably cautious in drawing conclusions about the IDF's capabilities in war from its weakness in dealing with the uprising in the territories. Nevertheless, the many reports of budgetary reductions, damage to soldiers' morale, and a significant disruption of training programs did probably damage Israel's deterrent image. Under these circumstances Israeli deterrence might, in Arab eyes, rely increasingly on its ability to develop, manufacture and deploy sophisticated and unconventional weapons systems. Following upon the detailed reports about Israel's alleged nuclear capability circulated by Mordechai Vanunu, 1988 also witnessed Israel's successful launch of the Ofek-1 satellite, and Israeli-American cooperation within the framework of the "Star Wars" Program (SDI) to develop Israel's "Hetz" (Arrow) anti-missile missile. Within the Arab world these disclosures were thought to be deliberately instigated by Israel, with the intention of deterring the Arab armies from taking advantage of the IDF's perceived current weakness to launch a military offensive.

Another aspect of Israel's deterrence stemmed from strategic cooperation between Israel and the United States. This received relatively detailed publicity during 1988. For example, Defense Minister Yitzhak Rabin mentioned "at least 27 or 28 combined exercises" involving the IDF and the US Navy, Air Force and Marine Corps, in recent years.

## Other Regional Strategic Developments

The termination of fighting in the Persian Gulf in mid-1988 had immediate and severe economic ramifications for Jordan and Egypt. For Jordan, in particular, it meant the end of a period of economic prosperity, as the port of Aqaba had afforded Iraq a wartime land supply route through Jordan far preferable to the perilous naval route through the Gulf and the Emirate ports. This immediate loss of a major source of income was undoubtedly one of the factors contributing to the acute economic crisis that soon overtook the Hashemite Kingdom.

As for Egypt, throughout eight years of Gulf warfare it benefited from both the export of vital arms to Iraq and the employment of hundreds of thousands of Egyptian workers (some estimates reach one million) to replace conscripted Iraqi manpower. These two sources of income funneled badly needed foreign currency into the Egyptian economy. Although the termination of fighting curtailed the flow of arms from Egypt to Iraq, the latter's ongoing military rearmament program has engendered considerable collaboration between the two states that will span a longer period. A problem of a different sort was posed by the partial cutback in Iraq's need for imported labor. By early 1989 only relatively small numbers were involved, but the crunch was sure to come when Iraq commenced releasing a significant portion of its conscripted forces and reintegrating them into the local labor market.

Another by-product of the Iran-Iraq War appears to have been the process of consolidation of three economic pacts among Arab states. The first and most veteran is the Gulf Cooperation Council (GCC), which consists of the six Arab Gulf states, excluding Iraq. The second, formed in 1988, is the union of five North African states: Morocco, Algeria, Tunisia, Libya and Mauritania.

These developments spurred the formation in 1988 of a third pact. Here King Hussein was the driving force behind the establishment of the Arab Cooperation Council (ACC), a common market of four Arab states: Jordan, Egypt, Iraq and YAR (North Yemen). Hussein pinned his hopes on Jordan serving as a "middleman" for Egypt and Iraq; he also hoped to develop a new export market in North Yemen, a country of 7.3 million that had recently made promising oil strikes. Hussein hoped to see Amman chosen for the headquarters of this common market.

Only three countries remained outside these pacts: Sudan — thought to be a candidate to join the four-state ACC; PDRY (South Yemen); and Syria. The entire process appeared to deepen the political and strategic isolation of the latter two.

In early 1989, it was premature to discuss whether these developments offered a chance for viable political-economic development. Recent Middle East history is rich in attempts at political coalition-making, all of which fell apart sooner or later. Still, as long as these coalitions do exist they may have strategic ramifications. The ACC is a case-in-point: in view of the closer political and economic relations between Jordan, Egypt, Iraq and North Yemen, one might also expect more military cooperation among them. In this regard Jordan's central geographic position vis-a-vis Israel could generate an important role for Amman, especially for close intelligence coverage across the border.

Here Jordan's specific military efforts bear mention. Jordanian procurement continued in 1988 with a clearcut division between the acquisition of aircraft from the West and the purchase of air defense systems from the Soviet Union. Jordan would soon take delivery of the Tornado jet fighter and the Mirage 2000, while its air defense was based on the Gun Dish (ZSU short-range anti-aircraft gun), the SA-13, the SA-8, and the shoulder-launched SA-14 missile. Jordan also took its American HAWK missiles out of their permanent bases and redeployed them on mobile platforms, thereby breaking a promise made to the United States when the HAWK deal was authorized, according to which the missiles would be permanently based.

Another possible key strategic development in 1988 was Saudi Arabia's second "deal of the century." (We recall that the first such deal, finalized in 1985, involved the acquisition of advanced Tornado combat aircraft and HAWK and PC-9 trainers from Britain.) Based on partial disclosures, it appeared that the Saudis intended to buy arms and equipment mainly from Western European countries, especially Britain. Major transactions involved combat and training aircraft and helicopters, and would surely also include additional weapons systems and equipment. The deal, spread out over several years, was worth somewhere between 10 and 20 billion dollars.

Egypt continued to develop its armed forces in accordance with a long-term plan, unpressured by current military developments.

Egypt's peace accord with Israel enables development of its armed forces with little consideration for current defense constraints and according to a timetable fixed by the Egyptians themselves. By 1989 the Egyptians were at the start of their second five-year program. Of particular importance was the Egyptian program for the development of autonomous defense industries, including independent production of the French Mirage 2000 and the American M-1 battle tank.

These regional trends in arms procurement dovetailed with the unbridled competition among the powers (especially among the western countries themselves) for the arms export market to the Middle East. Gone were the old monopoly arms-commercial relationships between Great Powers and their regional clients. Even the Soviet Union now viewed arms as primarily a commercial export commodity, and Soviet decisions in this field were now based almost entirely on economic considerations.

Especially important developments in this field could be expected from Washington. If the new American administration acted in earnest to balance the United States' trade deficit, it would not easily concede major arms export deals to western competitors. More likely, all possible pressure would be exercised to win a lion's share of the arms export market. Under these circumstances it would be ever more difficult for Israel and its supporters in America to conduct lobbying campaigns on Capitol Hill and in the White House against the export of arms from the United States to Arab "front-line states." Indeed, the very lobbying effort itself might exacerbate Israeli-American relations.

# Section A. The Palestinian Uprising

In December 1987 a wave of spontaneous unrest broke out in areas administered by the Israeli government: Judea and Samaria (the West Bank), and the Gaza Strip. The unrest continued throughout the period under review, at times increasing and at times decreasing in violence, as the struggle of the inhabitants of the Territories against Israeli rule dominated the media and the political scene. A new type of Palestinian warfare against Israel had evolved.

Undoubtedly, the uprising is a central factor in any survey of strategic developments in the Middle East in 1988. Our analysis of this popular uprising (*intifada* in Arabic) will focus on the following aspects:

1.  a description of the uprising and its ramifications, by Brigadier-General (res.) Aryeh Shalev;
2.  changes produced by the *intifada* in the PLO stance, by Dr. Mark A. Heller;
3.  resultant political developments within Israel, by Dr. Yehuda Ben Meir;
4.  the new role of the US in the area, by Dr. Dore Gold;
5.  developments in Soviet policy in the area, by Dr. Mark A. Heller; and
6.  Palestinian terrorism, by Anat Kurz.

# 1. The Uprising in Judea, Samaria and the Gaza Strip and its Ramifications
## by Aryeh Shalev

In our coverage of the *intifada* in the *Middle East Military Balance 1987-88*, emphasis was placed on the reasons for the uprising and its initial characteristics. Here we shall focus on the state of the uprising and its ramifications to date, and shall seek to assess possible future developments.

## Violent Aspects

The Palestinian uprising which began on December 9, 1987 continued unabated, albeit with fluctuations in intensity, throughout the period under review. It expressed itself primarily in the form of acts of violence. The number of such acts in Judea, Samaria and Gaza in the period up to March 8, 1989 was (according to the figures of the IDF Spokesman) 28,232. While this figure did not include 1,516 incidents involving petrol bombs and 439 acts of arson, it still averaged out to a high rate of approximately 60 incidents per day.

The massive presence of IDF forces, including a large contingent of reservists, and the use of improved equipment and operational methods tailored to the problem did bring about a cessation of mass disturbances in which thousands of Palestinians gathered in one place. This reflected an IDF tactic whereby a military force would arrive upon the scene a short time after the commencement of violent activity, and would immediately disperse participants before their numbers could grow. This objective was more easily accomplished in the small area and short distances of the Gaza Strip than in the West Bank, which is almost 16 times larger than the Strip.

Increasingly successful use of tear gas, rubber bullets and plastic bullets also caused most of the violent activity to evolve toward the "hit and run" variety, carried out by small groups employing petrol bombs and stones with the assistance and cover of the local population.

There was, however, no decline in the total number of violent incidents; the peak months occurred toward the end of 1988 and not during the first months of the uprising. Indeed, in the very first month of the uprising a relatively large number of mass disturbances was recorded, but the total number of disturbances altogether (1,359 incidents) was relatively small. The two months in which the number of incidents (stone-throwing, tire-burning, erection of barriers, and rioting, but not including use of firearms or petrol bombs) in Judea, Samaria and Gaza was greatest (according to figures of the IDF Spokesman) were December 1988 and February 1989.

**Table I.     Judea, Samaria and Gaza: Incidents During Peak Months in 1988**

| Month | Judea and Samaria | Gaza | Total No. of Incidents |
|-------|-------------------|------|------------------------|
| Feb. 1988 | 1730 | 517 | 2248 |
| Sept. 1988 | 1594 | 817 | 2411 |
| Dec. 1988 | 2417 | 417 | 2834 |
| Jan. 1989 | 1939 | 500 | 2439 |
| Feb. 1989 | 2336 | 495 | 2827 |

A total of over 2,000 incidents per month was recorded five times. The smallest number of incidents per month occurred in April 1988 (1,319 incidents). Table I shows the number of incidents during the peak months. (The uprising having begun on December 9, 1987, all figures relating to specific monthly periods are calculated from the 9th of one month to the 8th of the next. Thus, for instance, the month of February designates the period between February 9 and the following March 8.)

These figures do not encompass violent activities in East Jerusalem: an average of 12-15 incidents per day (raising of the PLO flag, stone-throwing, roadblocks, tire-burning, petrol bomb incidents and acts of arson). During the course of 1988 there were 2,957 such incidents, of which 1,760 involved stone-throwing and 114 involved petrol bombs; there were an additional 1,229 acts of raising the PLO flag. The peak month during 1988 was December, with 657 incidents. Table II summarizes incidents in the Jerusalem area during 1988.

Throughout the period under review, the local activists involved in the riots and disturbances maintained their policy of abstaining from the use of firearms, and the PLO issued directives to the same effect. The populace was well aware that PLO terrorist operations had done little to advance the Palestinian cause, whereas the civilian uprising, symbolized by the stone, had registered successes. But this tactic also reflected fears of a highly asymmetrical armed confrontation with the IDF. Nevertheless as in previous years, and apparently irrespective of the uprising, up to March 8, 1989 the IDF Spokesman had reported 20 terrorist incidents involving shooting, 35 involving hand-grenades, 91 involving bombs and 51 involving knives and hatchets since the uprising began.

## Table II.   Incidents in the Jerusalem Area During 1988

| Stone Throwing | Road Blocks | Tire Burning | Petrol Bombs | Arson |
|---|---|---|---|---|
| 1,760 | 708 | 283 | 114 | 92 |

All told, acts of violence committed from the beginning of the uprising to March 8, 1989 (i.e., those acts detailed above together with acts of low-level violence forming part of the *intifada*, such as stone-throwing and incendiary bombs) resulted in the deaths of 14 Israelis (8 civilians, all of them in Judea and Samaria, and 6 soldiers, one of them in Jerusalem); 1,397 Israelis (including 493 civilians) were wounded. Most of the civilians were wounded in Judea and Samaria (450, as opposed to 43 in Gaza), while the number of soldiers wounded in Judea and Samaria was a little less than twice the number wounded in Gaza (583 as opposed to 321).

According to the figures of the IDF Spokesman, 307 local Palestinians were killed as a result of armed forces' activity from the start of the uprising until March 8, 1989. In contrast, on February 6, 1989 the minister of defense put the number of killed at 360. According to Palestinian sources, the total number of killed stood at 513 (347 shot by the IDF and Israeli settlers, 43 dead from beatings, 71 by tear gas overdoses, and 52 by other means). *HaOlam HaZe* weekly newsmagazine offered a mean figure of 414 killed; this appeared to be closest to reality.

One reason the number of killed reported by the IDF was not complete, was that it included only those killed while clashing with security forces; in some cases, Palestinians who died of their wounds in a hospital were not included. Similarly, according to the IDF Spokesman the number of wounded among the local Palestinian population up to March 8, 1989 was 4,812, while the minister of defense on February 6, 1989 put it at over 7,000. Rounding out all these figures, the average per day was about one killed and 12 wounded.

As of March 8, 1989 the number of those imprisoned from Judea, Samaria and Gaza came to 6,475, including 1,172 administrative detainees. The total number of those imprisoned from the start of the uprising until February 1989 was, according to the minister of defense, 27,000. In addition, 2,698 residents of East Jerusalem were imprisoned during 1988. Forty five Palestinians were deported to Lebanon (32 during 1988, and another 13 prior to March 8, 1989); 173 houses were demolished (129 in Judea and Samaria) and 72 were sealed (50 in Judea and Samaria). Economic activity was significantly reduced and the standard of living dropped by at least 30 percent, this due in great part to the 42 percent drop in the value of the Jordanian dinar. Employment declined: as a result of strikes, curfews and cordon and search operations, there was a 20-30 per cent reduction in the number of workdays in Israel put in by laborers from the Territories, with an attendant loss of income.

There is no direct correlation between the number of Israeli casualties and the number of Palestinian casualties. Even during months when Israeli casualties were relatively high, this generally had no effect on the behavior and response of the soldiers and did not result in an increase in local Palestinian casualties. Thus, for instance, in July 1988 local casualties (killed and wounded) were at their lowest level, while the number of Israeli casualties (soldiers and civilians) was almost at its peak. Likewise, in May 1988 the number of local casualties was relatively low while the number of Israeli casualties was high. The only exception was during March 1988, when the highest number of Israeli casualties was recorded and the number of local Palestinian casualties was also relatively high. Table III lists casualty figures as provided by the IDF.

For many years the prevalent view in Israel was that two particular forms of punishment — demolition of houses and deportation — constituted an especially effective deterrent. The *intifada* offers the possibility of examining the effectiveness of these punishments, by noting the presence or absence of a statistical correlation between the extent of the punishment invoked and a reduction in the level of violence.

## Table III.  Israeli and Local Casualties in Judea, Samaria and Gaza During Peak Months

| Month | Local Population | | | Israelis | | | | |
|---|---|---|---|---|---|---|---|---|
| | | | | IDF | | Civilians | | Total |
| | Killed | Wounded | Total | Killed | Wounded | Killed | Wounded | |
| 1988 | | | | | | | | |
| Jan. | 19 | 225 | 244 | 0 | 64 | 0 | 42 | 106 |
| March | 39 | 385 | 424 | 1 | 66 | 1 | 55 | 123 |
| April | 11 | 243 | 254 | 0 | 72 | 0 | 42 | 114 |
| May | 35 | 332 | 367 | 0 | 50 | 0 | 22 | 72 |
| July | 20 | 208 | 228 | 0 | 87 | 0 | 33 | 120 |
| Aug. | 16 | 327 | 343 | 0 | 71 | 1 | 28 | 100 |
| Sept. | 18 | 537 | 555 | 0 | 67 | 0 | 32 | 99 |
| Dec. | 26 | 441 | 467 | 2 | 58 | 1 | 33 | 94 |
| 1989 | | | | | | | | |
| Jan. | 27 | 417 | 444 | 0 | 41 | 1 | 18 | 60 |

As regards the demolition of houses, we found no correlation whatsoever between the number of houses demolished and the number of violent incidents recorded, or the number of Israeli casualties, or even the number of petrol bombs thrown, in the following month. This, despite the fact that, unlike deportation, demolition usually takes place soon after the discovery of the persons responsible and often hard upon the incident itself. All

# Table IV. House Demolitions and Ensuing Levels of Violent Incidents

| | House Demolitions | | | | Violent Incidents During The Following Month | | | Change |
|---|---|---|---|---|---|---|---|---|
| Month | Jud. & Sam. | Gaza | Total | Month | Jud. & Sam. | Gaza | Total | |
| **1988** | | | | | | | | |
| April | 21 | 2 | 23 | May | 1301 | 228 | 1529 | + 210 |
| June | 10 | 5 | 15 | July | 1019 | 391 | 1410 | - 152 |
| July | 10 | 6 | 16 | Aug. | 1637 | 215 | 1852 | + 442 |
| Aug. | 13 | 7 | 20 | Sept. | 1543 | 785 | 2328 | + 476 |
| Nov. | 17 | 7 | 24 | Dec. | 2381 | 409 | 2790 | +1195 |
| **1989** | | | | | | | | |
| Jan. | 15 | 0 | 15 | Feb. | 2287 | 481 | 2768 | + 396 |

told, 173 houses were demolished prior to March 8, 1989 — 129 in Judea and Samaria and 44 in Gaza. The peak months were April, August and November of 1988. Notably, during the first three months of the uprising (December 1987, January-February 1988) no houses were demolished or sealed.

Table IV lists those months in which 15 or more demolitions took place, in juxtaposition with the level of violent incidents for the month following, in order to evaluate the influence of the demolitions.

As Table IV shows, the demolition of houses had no immediate effect in reducing the levels of violent activity. Quite the contrary. Looking at two months in which a large number of houses were demolished, after the demolition of 23 houses in April 1988 the level of violent activity during the following month rose by 210 incidents; likewise, after the demolition of 20 houses in August, the number of violent incidents increased by 476.

Nor did the demolition of houses have any immediate effect, at least during the first nine months of the uprising, in reducing the number of petrol bombs thrown in Judea, Samaria and Gaza. During these months between 98 and 164 petrol bombs were thrown per month, and generally there was no reduction in the number of petrol bombs thrown in the course of the month after the demolition of a large number of houses. Thus, for example, after the demolition of 23 houses in April 1988 the number of petrol bombs thrown during the month of May rose to 163. Table V lists the incidence of petrol bomb attacks during the peak months in Judea, Samaria and Gaza.

In short, during the years prior to the uprising, the demolition of houses appears to have had a deterrent value. But under the conditions of the uprising, it was transformed into a stimulus to further escalation of resistance to Israeli rule. One explanation may be that during the uprising the PLO succeeded in smuggling funds to the owners of houses that had been demolished to enable them to build anew, so the severe hardship imposed on the family by demolition was only of short duration.

## Table V.    Petrol Bomb Attacks - Peak Months

| Month | Judea & Samaria | Gaza | Total |
|-------|-----------------|------|-------|
| Dec. 1987 | 62 | 47 | 109 |
| Jan. 1988 | 85 | 13 | 98 |
| Feb. | 121 | 43 | 164 |
| March | 126 | 26 | 152 |
| April | 83 | 36 | 119 |
| May | 138 | 25 | 163 |
| June | 94 | 27 | 121 |

The second form of punishment associated with deterrence over the years consists of deportation from Judea, Samaria and Gaza to an Arab country. Table VI shows the peak monthly figures of this form of punishment during the uprising, and the level of violence the next month (according to the IDF Spokesman).

We may conclude that there is a clear correlation between the number of residents deported — 45, all to Lebanon, prior to March 8, 1989 — and an ensuing increase in the number of violent incidents and Israeli casualties. Thus, for example, after the peak month of deportations (16 in April 1988) the number of violent incidents rose by 210, and after the 13 deportations in January 1989, the number of violent incidents rose by 396. Clearly the deterrent effect of deportation, which was previously considered by Israeli security authorities to be the harshest punishment in Palestinian eyes, must be questioned. Notably both deportation and the demolition of houses have been the subject of severe criticism abroad.

## Table VI. Deportations and Ensuing Levels of Violent Incidents

| No. of Deportations in Peak Months | | | | Violent Incidents During The Following Month | | | | Change |
|---|---|---|---|---|---|---|---|---|
| Month | Jud. & Sam. | Gaza | Total | Month | Jud. & Sam. | Gaza | Total | |
| **1988** | | | | | | | | |
| Jan. | 4 | 0 | 4 | Feb. | 1610 | 474 | 2084 | +315 |
| April | 11 | 5 | 16 | May | 1301 | 228 | 1529 | +210 |
| Aug. | 6 | 6 | 12 | Sept. | 1543 | 785 | 2328 | +476 |
| **1989** | | | | | | | | |
| Jan. | 7 | 6 | 13 | Feb. | 2287 | 481 | 2768 | +396 |

Another controversial policy concerned the closing of schools in Judea and Samaria and the Gaza Strip. In Judea and Samaria this was the primary means utilized by the Civil Authority (as distinguished from the military command) to attempt to restrain the uprising. In the Gaza Strip, in contrast, there were few cases of a comprehensive shut-down of the education system. All universities in Judea, Samaria and the Gaza Strip were closed at the beginning of the *intifada*, and remained so by mid-1989.

Elementary, junior high and high schools in Judea and Samaria were closed altogether in 1988 for eight months, and in 1989 throughout the first half of the year. They were first closed February 2, 1988, and reopened May 23. The authorities closed them again on July 21, reopened them during the first half of December, and on January 20, 1989 closed them again. All told, then, pupils lost over a year of studies. Yet the uprising continued.

Did the closing of the schools increase or decrease the number of disturbances in Judea and Samaria? Table VII attempts to correlate school closures with violent incidents. (Slight discrepancies between violent incident totals in Table VII and those in Table I are explained by differences in counting criteria.)

## Table VII.   Disturbances in Judea and Samaria Relative to Open/Closed Schools

| Open Schools | Closed Schools | Increase/Decrease of Incidents |
|---|---|---|
| Jan.-Feb.'88 | | Incidents in January increased by 366 (1487 in January compared with 1121 in December). This was one of the reasons for closing schools on February 2. |
| | Feb. 2-May 23 | In February the number increased (1773 in February versus 1487 in January). The number of incidents in the next three months decreased to the level before February (1537 in March, 1131 in April, and 1472 in May). One could therefore conclude that the closing was somewhat effective in restraining the intifada. |
| May 23-July 21 | | There was no increase in incidents after schools were opened; in July there was even a decrease (of 358 incidents) rendering that month the one with the lowest number of incidents. |
| | July 21 - mid-December | Schools were closed due to a rise in violent incidents in the schools (even though there was no overall rise in violence). After the closing there was a significant increase for two months (1750 in August and 1614 in September); afterwards, there was a decrease during October (1318) and November (1337). |
| Mid-Dec. - Jan. 22, '89 | | There was a significant increase in violence (from 1337 in Nov. to 2438 in Dec.); the number decreased in Jan. 1989 (to 1964). |
| | After Jan. 20, '89 schools remained closed. | A significant increase in incidents was recorded in Feb. and March (2353 in Feb. and the peak of 3007 in March). |

34

Table VII reveals the following: The first time the schools were closed (February-May 1988) there was a limited restraining effect on the number of incidents. Further, there was no increase in incidents when schools were opened for two months (May through June). Following the second closure, which lasted five months (July to December 1988), there was an increase in incidents for two months; then the number decreased. The second time the schools were reopened (the middle of December for a period of over a month), there was a significant increase in the number of incidents. The third time the schools were closed (January 1989) produced no moderating effect on the *intifada*. On the contrary, there was a significant increase in the number of incidents.

All told, the opening and closing of schools from early 1988 to early 1989 did not unequivocally affect the *intifada*. There was no increase in incidents after the first opening, though there was after the second. The first time schools were closed the situation calmed down; after the second time, there was an acceleration of incidents. By the end of January 1989 it seemed clear that closing down schools no longer reduced the number and extent of *intifada* incidents.

To summarize this survey of the violent aspects of the uprising and the efficacy of Israeli tactics, we may conclude that, despite IDF countermeasures such as reinforcement of security details, curfews and clampdowns, and use of riot batons, tear gas, rubber bullets, and on occasion live ammunition — the uprising was not quelled. By the beginning of 1989, the minister of defense and the high command of the IDF were forced to admit that they had no effective response against the stone-throwing. A more recent hope for a panacea — the use of plastic bullets, which by March 8, 1989 had resulted in the deaths of 55 Palestinians (37 in Judea and Samaria) — was no more effective in stopping the uprising.

## Civil Disobedience

A second phenomenon with severe ramifications for Israeli rule in the Territories was the gradual establishment by Palestinians of a mechanism for self-rule. This accorded with PLO objectives, and was facilitated in many ways by an extensive campaign of civil disobedience.

While in some ways Israeli rule had already been weakened before the uprising, the process gained momentum in the interim.

It was manifested in three principal ways. First, an organizational infrastructure was established from the lowest levels (street, neighborhood) to the general leadership. Local associations ("peoples councils") were established, largely in the name of the PLO, for the purpose of administering the daily life of the residents, directing the uprising, and posing an alternative to Israeli rule.

Secondly, an effort was made to build functional networks parallel to those of the civil administration and capable of replacing them in the future. By early 1989 success had been achieved primarily in the field of health care, with the establishment of a hospital in Jerusalem and private clinics in Judea and Samaria, and advances in private medical services.

Thirdly, even though by early 1989 most of the local residents employed by the civil administration (teachers, doctors, etc.) had not resigned their posts, in effect they no longer served the civil administration, and its status as an organ of rule was effectively undermined. The various civil servants considered themselves to be serving the Arab population and its nationalist aspirations rather than the Israeli administration.

The Palestinians in the Territories tended to assess that they had acquired effective rule in many fields and that, as a result of the uprising, they were on their way toward establishing a state of their own. Practically speaking, however, they had succeeded in establishing self-rule in only a limited number of fields. Yet the trend clearly favored the establishment of independent institutions, the augmentation, as far as possible, of their authority over the population, and the decline of Israel's rule.

The attempts to establish alternative Palestinian institutions were complemented and facilitated almost from the very beginning by a campaign of mass civil disobedience. The aim was to support the violent uprising by limiting Israel's civilian domination of the Palestinian population and reducing the latter's economic dependence on Israel. The scope of civil disobedience was limited in accordance with the recognized need not to create unmitigated havoc — the basic needs of the population had to be considered — but to involve the entire population in the struggle against Israel.

The civil disobedience campaign had a very mixed record of success and failure. The following are examples of successful aspects:

*General strikes.* The entire population was called upon, through printed leaflets and proclamations, to participate in a general strike during a certain day (or two or three) every week. The purpose of these strikes was to present a united front against Israel's rule and to demonstrate solidarity and support for the uprising. The call was heeded in full by the entire population.

*Commercial strikes.* In addition to the cessation of commerce during general strikes, all shops closed (in accordance with the directives of the *intifada* leadership) at twelve noon every day (after opening at nine). Shopkeepers strictly adhered to the directives, in part because of threats made against them. On the other hand, vendors' stalls were open throughout the day.

*Boycott of Israeli products.* In recognition of the population's economic dependence on Israel, the leadership of the uprising did not insist on a total cessation of trade, but it did order a boycott of Israeli products for which local alternatives were available — such as cigarettes, chocolate, soft drinks, plastic products and shoes. This directive was, on the whole, complied with, and youth gangs occasionally applied pressure and intimidation to ensure conformity. The director general of the Ministry of Commerce and Industry estimated that purchases of Israeli-made products by the residents of the Territories dropped 70 percent, from $850 million in 1987 to $250 million in 1988.

*Resignation of policemen.* Most local policemen resigned in accordance with the directives and demands of the *intifada* leadership. The small number of policemen who continued to report to work in effect refused to go on duty. Consequently, public order (which had been undermined by the violence in the first place) broke down, and the local judicial system functioned with reduced efficiency at all levels, from the civil courts to the high court. On the other hand, only eight policemen resigned in Jerusalem, and half of these eventually returned to their jobs.

*Resignation of tax collectors.* Many local tax collectors resigned, thereby generating a significant reduction in taxes paid to the administration. This reflected not only the directives of the leadership of the uprising, but also the financial crunch resulting from the overall drop in income.

Minister of Defense Rabin reported to the Knesset in July 1988 that revenue from tax payments in the Territories had dropped by 40 percent since the start of the uprising. Tax revenues later rose as a result of pressures applied by Israeli authorities (in regard to car license renewals, changes in license numbers, issuance of new identity cards, etc.), and figures for the entire year showed that during 1988 tax revenues totaled one-third less than originally anticipated.

In contrast, the civil disobedience campaign was unsuccessful in other aspects:

*Cessation of work in Israel.* The repeated demands of the leaflets in this regard were largely ignored. Because as many as half the male work force in Gaza and a third in Judea and Samaria relied on Israel for their livelihoods, the cessation of work in Israel would have meant mass unemployment and severe hardship. Nevertheless, there was a drop in the number of workers (and workdays) in Israel, and there were work stoppages due to strikes, curfews and cordon and search operations.

*Reopening of schools.* Universities and schools have long been centers of nationalist and violent activity in the West Bank. After the Israeli authorities closed the schools in order to contain the uprising, the *intifada* leadership called upon students, teachers and the local population to break into the schools and resume their studies. This did not occur, evidently because of teachers' fears of a direct confrontation with the authorities and the high risk of being fired. On the other hand, there were instances of studies being conducted in home circles. While the closing of the schools did not stop the uprising, it did restrict the organization of large scale violent activity by preventing students from gathering inside the schools in order to perpetrate large scale civil disorders.

*Resignation of Municipal Councils.* From February 1988 pressure was exercised by the leadership of the uprising upon members of municipal councils (especially those appointed by the civil administration rather than having been elected) to resign. This tactic was employed particularly in Ramallah, El Bira and Nablus. The *intifada* leadership had only limited success in this matter: most of the municipal councils and mayors did not resign (the mayor of El Bira was assaulted and wounded because of his refusal), although the mayor of Nablus did cease carrying out his functions.

All told, civil disobedience was limited, but this was by design. All the same, a self-image was created of a people fighting for its liberty through the utilization of all means, including civil disobedience. By early 1989 most of the local Palestinians employed by the civil administration continued on the job, but there were signs that cooperation was ebbing away. In effect, a local alternative administration dominated by the PLO was in the process of being established.

## Ramifications of the Uprising

*Social ramifications.* Concurrent with the uprising, and evidently as a consequence of it, several social upheavals took place within the population of the Territories that were certain to have long-term ramifications. For one, the status of the head of the family was decimated, as youth refused to bow to the traditional authority of their elders. While the social fabric had in general been increasingly strained since 1967, the actual rupture occurred as a direct result of the uprising. The younger generation was deeply critical of its parents and grandparents for living under Israeli occupation for 20 years and not fighting to liberate themselves. As the uprising developed, fathers became generally unaware of the activities of their sons, who independently decided if, where and how to demonstrate. As a result, family binds were replaced by ties of a nationalist-political nature. Still, the youngsters' nationalist struggle was not directed against their parents (despite the criticism), but against Israel, and with the general support of all the population.

Secondly, for the first time women gained a dignified position for themselves within Palestinian society — approaching the status of men. This was due primarily to the active role they played in the uprising. Women expressed fear that after the uprising ended they would be relegated — as happened after the Algerian rebellion — to their previous secondary status.

*Political ramifications within the Territories.* The uprising, which began spontaneously, gave rise to two conflicting internal political effects. On the one hand, there quickly evolved an indigenous leadership that initiated events and directed implementation. The leadership resided primarily in East Jerusalem, which since 1967 has been part of Israel, thereby imparting a measure of "immunity." A few of its members occasionally were arrested, but never the entire leadership, which consisted of a few dozen people. It performed its functions in cooperation with the PLO abroad, principally by means of tracts distributed within the Territories and broadcast by several radio stations: the "PLO Corner" on Baghdad Radio, Radio Monte Carlo, and Radio al-Quds in Syria. All the main factions that make up the PLO (Fatah, PFLP, DFLP and the Communist Popular Front) joined hands in directing the uprising. The Islamic Jihad also took part.

Secondly, during the uprising itself, a struggle developed between the PLO and the Islamic extremist *Hamas*. Though they had no differences regarding the tactical short-term aim of the uprising — the elimination of Israeli rule in the Territories — they were divided over the steps to be taken following the uprising. Supporters of the PLO took a relatively pragmatic approach that envisioned the establishment of a Palestinian state in all the territory of the West Bank, Gaza, and East Jerusalem. *Hamas*, in contrast, rejected the notions of political negotiation (including an international conference) and concessions, and argued that a holy war must be waged against Israel until the establishment of a Palestinian state within the entire territory of mandatory Palestine. *Hamas* successfully built up a power base in the Gaza Strip, and by early 1989 its power was growing in the West Bank, especially in Hebron and Nablus.

*External political ramifications.* The *intifada* generated three principal political ramifications for Palestinians beyond the geographical confines of Israel and the Territories. First, the local Palestinian population's standing vis-a-vis the PLO was strengthened. Because the local Palestinians bore the brunt of the struggle, the PLO was obliged to take into consideration, now as never before, the views of leaders inside the West Bank and Gaza, and to avoid making decisions without prior consultation with them.

Secondly, the Jordanian alternative disappeared. Jordan also reduced its direct day to day involvement in the Territories, and King Hussein proclaimed publicly on July 31, 1988 Jordan's disengagement from the West Bank, following up with a series of directives limiting contact between the West Bank and Jordan. The directives ordered cessation of payments (supplementary salaries) to civil service workers in the West Bank and the termination of financial assistance for municipalities (excepting funds for Waqf expenses and pension plans); in place of permanent passports, local residents were now issued temporary ones good for only a year or two; Jordanian government ministries no longer dealt with requests and applications on the part of West Bank residents; Jordanian imports from the Territories were limited to levels set by demand rather than by a policy of support for West Bank residents; and the number of West Bank students in Jordanian universities was significantly slashed.

The principal significance of Hussein's proclamation and the directives was political. They acknowledged Jordan's loss of status under the new state of affairs, yet without burning bridges or limiting future options. Jordan lost its central position in the peace process as a potential negotiator in regard to the Palestinian problem — either on its own or as the major principal in a joint delegation with the Palestinians. Unless some drastic change were to take place — such as an absolute defeat of the uprising and a steep decline in the PLO's status — Jordan could not return to represent the Palestinians. Consequently it could not, in the foreseeable future, be a leading partner in negotiations with Israel regarding the West Bank and Gaza.

Third, the PLO moderated its positions sufficiently to qualify for a dialogue with the United States. For 14 years the PLO had refused to accept US conditions (acknowledgement of Israel's right to exist, acceptance of UN Security Council resolutions 242 and 338, and the cessation of terrorist activities) for the start of a dialogue. Now, after less than a year of revolt and in response to demands from the West Bank and Gaza, the PLO changed its declarative stance, and registered what it regarded as a significant political victory in the form of a developing relationship with the United States. The countries of Western Europe, too, awarded the PLO greater recognition as a legitimate partner in negotiations. In short, the PLO commenced moving from armed conflict to political struggle under the favorable conditions created by the uprising. (These issues are explored in detail in Chapter 2, "Changes in PLO Posture," by Mark A. Heller, and Chapter 4, "The US-PLO Dialogue," by Dore Gold.)

*Ramifications For Israel.* For the first time, the Palestinian problem produced a growing polarity within Israeli public opinion. Most of the political parties continued to oppose negotiations with the PLO and the establishment of an independent Palestinian state in the West Bank and Gaza. But a political struggle intensified between those who held such views and those who came to believe that, with the Jordanian alternative gone and time working against Israel, there was no choice but to accept some sort of Palestinian alternative. This controversy was paralleled by a growing argument among Israelis over tactical policies regarding the Territories, and particularly security policy. (These issues are explored in detail in Chapter 3, "Political Developments in Israel," by Yehuda Ben Meir.)

## Conclusion

Despite the large proportion of refugees in the Gaza Strip (over half the population there) and their role in initiating the uprising in December 1987, within months the center of activity moved to Judea, Samaria and East Jerusalem. Here the principal struggle remained.

The IDF found no technical or technological solution, for example in the form of innovative weapons systems like the plastic bullet, to put down the uprising. For the *intifada* was a strategic development and could not be stopped by military means alone. Certainly the IDF could not eradicate the uprising as long as it continued operating under rules of conduct that prohibited indiscriminate firing upon demonstrators or mass deportation.

Israel thus conducted a military holding operation in the Territories. Generally, the initiative was in the hands of the local Palestinians. Despite Israeli retaliatory measures — arrests, trials and punishment, demolition of houses, deportations, and controlled use of firearms — the IDF's deterrent image was hurt by the struggle against the rioters.

Notwithstanding great difficulties incurred by the local population, the uprising appeared able to continue, with fluctuating intensity, as long as a political process failed to develop. The population had already paid a steep price in casualties and economic and social hardship; they were unlikely to countenance seeing their sacrifice made in vain.

By early 1989 the consensus opinion within Israel's governing leadership (the two major parties) against negotiating with the PLO had become unrealistic. Israel was losing one diplomatic card after another, particularly with the advent of dialogue between the United States and the PLO. In contrast, the PLO made political inroads in the United States and strengthened its position in

Western Europe. In a political sense, time was working against Israel and its position was weakening, unless Arafat and the PLO made some severe blunders — an unlikely hypothesis.

The PLO would presumably do everything to ensure that its dialogue with the United States did not fail. The dialogue was critical for the development of a political alternative both acceptable to the PLO and capable of being implemented. In this regard, there could develop a "moment of truth" in the relationship between the United States and Israel during the coming year, and Israel might have to change its position under American pressure.

Since the start of the uprising, the PLO's major strategic effort had turned from armed conflict to the political front. This trend was likely to continue, at least as long as the dialogue with the United States continued. Yet giving precedence to the political process did not necessarily imply that terrorism would be abandoned.

The uprising, despite and perhaps because of its violence and its success (from the Palestinian point of view), brought forward the option of political negotiation. Until significant negotiations began, the uprising would continue. If the value of the Jordanian dinar continued to fall, and if large sums were not sent to the Territories by the PLO, this too could influence the scope of the uprising.

# 2. Changes in PLO Posture

## by Mark A. Heller

If the *intifada* was a watershed in the post-1967 history of the West Bank and Gaza, positions taken by the PLO during 1988 constitute an equally dramatic shift in the diplomatic posture of that organization. In fact, there was an organic link between the two phenomena, since the *intifada* was largely, if not solely responsible for the changes in PLO posture during the period under review.

Since 1974, when the PLO adopted the "political struggle" as part of its overall strategy, Palestinian leaders have issued a variety of statements intended to convey the impression that the PLO was reconciling itself to a political settlement incorporating the continued existence of the State of Israel. Nevertheless, the overall spirit of PLO policy was ambiguous, to say the least: many positions were self-contradictory, accommodating statements by some were attacked by others, and individuals often denied their own pronouncements or attempted to balance them with others of a much more uncompromising nature. More importantly, the highest leadership levels tended to leave the work of diplomatic exploration to others, while the PLO, per se, refrained from committing itself unequivocally to the objective of peace with Israel.

Needless to say, such evasiveness did little to allay the conviction in Israel that any PLO flexibility was merely tactical maneuvering intended to improve the PLO's international standing and that any proposals it made were intended only to promote the ultimate liquidation of Israel at some subsequent date. As a result, the government of Israel continued to reject categorically any involvement of the PLO in the political process.

The United States was generally less dogmatic about the utility of official contacts with the PLO, but it stipulated a number of conditions before that could happen. The 1975 US-Israel Memorandum of Agreement ruled out US recognition of the PLO or negotiation with it as long as the PLO did not recognize Israel's right to exist and accept UN Security Council resolutions 242 and 338. The State Department considered renunciation of terrorism to be implicit in resolutions 242 and 338, and the 1987 Anti-Terrorism Act explicitly made contact with the PLO contingent on a presidential certification that the PLO had ceased to practice or support terrorism.

For many years, the PLO had been advised by critics as well as sympathizers to abandon the rhetorical obfuscation that characterized its policy statements and to meet American terms in the most unequivocal fashion possible. More recent pressure by the Soviet Union and Egypt had been particularly forceful. And after December 1987, West Bank and Gaza activists, desperate to translate the travails of the *intifada* into some tangible political achievement, added their voices to this chorus of encouragement. Moreover, events in the West Bank and Gaza created a propitious international environment for "responsible" Palestinian political demands, and there was room for concern that if the PLO did nothing to exploit this opportunity, its preeminence would be challenged by nationalist or religious elements from within the Territories.

While many in the leadership under Yasir Arafat appeared to recognize the necessity of such steps, actual change was slow and halting. Some factions within the PLO were opposed to any measures that would legitimize Israel's existence; others felt that unilateral concessions of this sort were premature and self-defeating; and Arafat himself was reluctant to provoke or further exacerbate divisions within the organization.

Nevertheless, developments during 1988 clearly pointed in this direction. In June, for example, Arafat adviser Bassam Abu Sharif circulated a paper entitled "PLO View: Prospects of a Palestinian-Israeli Settlement." The document endorsed a two-state settlement and emphasized its permanency. "We believe," said Abu Sharif, "that all peoples — the Jewish and the Palestinians included — have the right to run their own affairs, expecting from their neighbors not only non-belligerence but the kind of political and economic cooperation without which no state can be truly secure....The Palestinians want that kind of lasting peace and security for themselves and the Israelis because no one can build his own future on the ruins of another's....The key to a Palestinian-Israeli settlement lies in talks between the Palestinians and the Israelis."

The Abu Sharif document was noteworthy for at least two reasons. The first was the identity of the author. Bassam Abu Sharif had for many years been spokesman of the Popular Front for the Liberation of Palestine of George Habash. Abu Sharif himself lost an eye and was disfigured in 1972 by a letter-bomb widely suspected of having been sent as part of Israel's anti-terrorism campaign. The second was the behavior of Arafat following the publication of this document. Abu Sharif's statement evoked widespread criticism, even by Fatah stalwarts such as Faruq al-Qadumi. On previous occasions, a hostile response to "trial balloons" of this sort usually led Arafat to dissociate himself from the statement. This time, he refused to confirm its authenticity, but neither did he deny it, instead offering to provide clarifications to an American representative.

Two months later, a discussion paper advocating the declaration of Palestinian independence was unearthed in Jerusalem and leaked to the public (reportedly by Israeli security authorities). This paper was linked with Faisal al-Husseini, the head of the Arab Studies Society and one of the most prominent Palestinian personalities in the Territories. It had been circulating among Palestinian intellectuals and activists for some time and was presumably drafted in coordination with the PLO. The so-called "Husseini Document" was probably designed to influence the upcoming Palestine National Council to adopt measures that would place additional international pressure on the Israeli government. There may also have been some hope of generating domestic change through an appeal to the Israeli public, although the reference at the outset to the 1947 partition boundaries was bound to alienate even those Israelis not unalterably opposed to a Palestinian state. Nevertheless, the paper did stress that "the nature of the new state will confirm that it is not aggressive, and that the Palestinian people do not desire the annihilation of the state of Israel. Rather, they wish to live peacefully as its neighbor." The fact that even an "internal draft" contained such phrases reflects an important trend in Palestinian thinking.

In November, the Palestine National Council "intifada" session in Algiers produced authoritative evidence of further moderation. The most dramatic symbolic action of the PNC was a Declaration of Palestinian Independence, which made a tortured reference to the international legitimacy of the principle of partition. This formulation essentially overturned Article 19 of the Palestine National Covenant, which states, "The partitioning of Palestine in 1947 and the establishment of Israel is [sic] fundamentally null and void, whatever time has elapsed." While the Independence Declaration made no reference to boundaries, the Political Statement of the PNC explicitly called for Israeli withdrawal only from the Territories occupied since 1967 and conditionally accepted "the premise that the international conference convenes on the basis of Security Council Resolutions 242 and 338." It also rejected terrorism and conspicuously refrained from reaffirming the "armed struggle" which featured so prominently in all previous PNC resolutions. Perhaps most significantly, the PNC stripped rejectionists of their veto power when it discarded unanimity in favor of majority vote.

Professional analysts, immersed in the minutiae of the Palestinian debate and able to decipher codewords inserted and phrases omitted, could make a strong argument that the Palestinians' center of political gravity had shifted perceptibly in the direction of a political settlement with Israel. There were, however, still too many qualifications and reservations to satisfy the United States government, much less the government and people of Israel. The reference to partition, for example, was coupled with a description of UN Resolution 181 as an "historical injustice which was inflicted on the Palestinian Arab people." And the "rejection of terrorism in all its forms" was followed by a reiteration of the rignt to resist foreign occupation and struggle for independence and by praise for the "strike forces and the popular army" in the occupied Territories.

President Reagan and Secretary of State Shultz stressed that they were not going to be "suckers" for this kind of evasiveness, and it took an additional month of mediation by journalists, American Jews and Swedish diplomats before Yasir Arafat would say the "magic" words that made possible a dialogue with the United States. In early December Arafat met in Stockholm with a delegation from the International Center for Peace in the Middle East and issued a statement purporting to clarify the outcome of Algiers. The statement explained that the PNC, "affirming the principle incorporated in those UN resolutions which call for a two-state solution of Israel and Palestine," had "accepted the existence of Israel as a state in the region" and "declared its rejection and condemnation of terrorism in all its forms." On December 13, Arafat told a special UN General Assembly session on Palestine in Geneva that he condemned terrorism in all its forms and that UN Resolution 181, which decided on the establishment of two states in Palestine, "continues to meet the requirements of international legitimacy." He also repeated the PLO's adherence to the formula of an international conference for peace in the Middle East "on the basis of resolutions 242 and 338."

These formulations still fell a bit short in American eyes, and Arafat therefore issued further refinements in a press conference the following day. He repeated his references to UN Resolution 181 "as the basis for Palestinian independence" and to "our acceptance of Resolutions 242 and 338 as the basis for negotiations with Israel within the framework of an international conference." The PNC had accepted these three resolutions, Arafat said, and "it was clear that we mean our people's rights to freedom and national independence in accordance with Resolution 181 as well as the right of all parties concerned with the Middle East conflict to exist in peace and security, including — as I said — the state of Palestine, Israel and other neighbors in accordance with Resolutions 242 and 338." Arafat also repeated "for the record that we totally and absolutely renounce all forms of terrorism, including individual, group and state terrorism."

In many respects, the distance from Algiers through Stockholm to Geneva can be measured in microns. The difference between "we reject terrorism" and "we renounce terrorism" is not easily visible to the naked eye; the significance of saying "the right of all parties to exist in peace and security...including the state of Palestine, Israel and other neighbors" rather than affirming the principle of "a two-state solution of Israel and Palestine" is not self-evident. Nevertheless, these final adjustments were deemed necessary to satisfy American requirements, and after they were made, President Reagan announced that the US would enter into a substantive dialogue with the PLO.

Not unexpectedly, Israeli doubts about the credibility of PLO commitments and the sincerity of its intentions remained high. Nor was the subsequent record entirely unambiguous. Arafat's leadership in the PLO was apparently unchallenged, but some of his verbal concessions were condemned, not only by the rejectionist factions and *Hamas* (the Islamic fundamentalist movement based in the Gaza Strip), but also by elements that remained within the PLO, particularly PFLP leader George Habash, who claimed that Arafat's "clarifications" in Geneva deviated from the resolutions of the PNC and, as such, were unauthorized. Moreover, although Fatah refrained from launching any cross-border infiltration attempts after Algiers, Arafat was notably reluctant to condemn such efforts by other groups.

On balance, however, developments in 1988 reflected a significant change in the nature of the PLO's declared objectives and in the methods employed in pursuit of those goals. Particularly noteworthy was the increasing emphasis on direct appeals to Israeli public opinion. One example of this was a February 1989 videotaped address by Salah Khalaf (Abu Iyad) to a conference in Jerusalem, in which he called for peaceful coexistence on the land between two states, to be achieved through direct meetings at which everything could be discussed.

In the short run, the PLO would probably persist in this sort of political offensive, if only to preserve the diplomatic achievement of official contact with Washington, while seeking to prolong the *intifada*. In the longer run, however, the most likely PLO course of action was far from obvious. By early 1989, the PLO found itself in the position of having met the political terms of everyone except Israel, which refused to deal with it under any terms. The result was that, while the PLO had virtually no "military option" (and any attempt to use what did exist would be counterproductive), neither did it have anything else to fall back on if its "political option" failed to produce an Israeli response other than a demand for the PLO to endorse its own exclusion from any diplomatic process — thereby posing a high risk of institutional suicide. In these circumstances, PLO hopes would have to be pinned on one of two eventualities — coercive diplomacy by the United States, or a military initiative by the Arabs — neither of which appeared imminent.

# 3. Political Developments in Israel

## by Yehuda Ben Meir

The *intifada* came as a severe shock to Israeli society, under-mining its sense of complacency and security. The relative calm in the West Bank and Gaza that had existed for over 20 years and which was taken for granted by a generation of Israelis, was shattered. As weeks grew into months, and it became clear that the Arab uprising was not a mere passing phenomenon, many Israelis came to realize that they were facing a new and threatening situation. The day-to-day events of the *intifada* — the violence, the riots, the heavy death toll, massive civil disobedience, attempts at economic boycott; and their major strategic repercus-sions for Israel — a sharp increase in military reserve duty and the disruption of the regular army's training schedule, a severe drop in tourism, negative media coverage both within Israel and abroad, the response in the Arab world and in the international commun-ity, the Shultz initiative, King Hussein's disengagement from the West Bank, and finally the decisions of the PNC, Arafat's state-ment in Geneva and the opening of the American-PLO dialogue — all these dominated the Israeli scene in 1988.

In this chapter we shall examine the effects of the *intifada* on political developments in Israel. We will look first at the general elections of November 1988, examining the degree to which they were affected by the *intifada* and illuminating possible trends of strategic importance for the future. We will then describe the formation of the new National Unity Government, and consider possible consequences for future political developments. Finally, we will examine the political, social and economic effects of the *intifada*, trying to determine some of the possible directions in which Israel may be headed.

## The National Elections

The major political event of 1988 on the Israeli domestic scene was undoubtedly the general elections, held on the first day of November. Contrary to most expectations the National Unity Government that was established in late August 1984 had served its full constitutional term of office, and thus became the first government to do so since the Yom Kippur War in late 1973. The remarkable survivability and resilience of the National Unity Government, its detractors notwithstanding, may have been an omen of things to come.

The culmination of Israel's grand exercise in democracy was the reestablishment of a national unity government along lines very similar to those of its predecessor — in terms of both its political-parliamentary basis as well as its personal makeup — with a few significant differences. At the end of a hotly-contested election campaign, and after six weeks of intensive and exasperating coalition negotiations, Israel entered 1989 — and prepared to enter the 1990s — with essentially the same government, the same national leadership and the same basic political program that it had in previous years. Nevertheless, one can discern in the election results certain new trends of possible strategic import. A careful analysis of these results, as well as a close reading of key political decisions reached in the election aftermath, do suggest some interesting observations and conclusions, including the possibility of far-reaching changes both in Israel's system of government and in its internal political alignment.

The central feature of Israeli political life over the past two decades has been the great national divide regarding the future of the West Bank and Gaza. There exists no consensus in the country regarding this most important national issue facing the people of Israel, an issue of existential proportions: the final status of Judea, Samaria, the Gaza Strip, and the Golan Heights, and the nature of a permanent solution of the Arab-Israel conflict. While there is a broad consensus that Jerusalem and the Golan Heights should remain, for the most part, under Israeli rule, and while there was wide agreement that the Sinai should be returned to Egypt in return for peace — when it comes to the West Bank and Gaza, the country is split down the middle between the adherents of a Greater Israel who oppose any territorial withdrawal in Judea, Samaria and Gaza, and the supporters of territorial compromise who advocate, in return for peace with security, large-scale Israeli withdrawal from this area. True, over the years a negative consensus of sorts has emerged: no withdrawal without a negotiated settlement, no return to the 1967 borders, no Palestinian state, and no recognition of the PLO. Yet, as we shall see, the *intifada* and the political developments associated with it have brought even some elements of this negative consensus into question. In any case, negative consensus is no substitute for a positive course of action, and it presents no solution to the deadlock regarding the course of action to be preferred and pursued.

The elections of 1988 did nothing to solve this national deadlock. Like its predecessor and the election prior to that, this election too was billed abortively as Israel's most decisive ever — one that would, at long last, break the deadlock and determine the issue. In response to Foreign Minister Peres' campaign proposal to hold a national referendum on the territorial future of Judea, Samaria and Gaza, Prime Minister Shamir claimed repeatedly that the elections to the Knesset constituted the real referendum on the future of the Territories. If this was so, then one can only assess the result as a tie. The political Left, including the Arab vote, received 55 out of the 120 seats in the Knesset (46 percent), the political Right (including the hawkish National Religious Party) received 52 seats (43 percent), and the remaining 13 seats (11 percent) were won by three extreme Orthodox parties, whose position on the question of the Territories was unclear and equivocal. The formation of a renewed national unity government based on parity and incorporating a built-in deadlock between the Likud and Labor reflected this dire political reality.

The events of the *intifada* and their political repercussions formed the backdrop for the November 1988 elections. There was some expectation, based on most public opinion polls, that the net result of the *intifada*, in political electoral terms, would be further polarization of Israeli society and a definite shift to the Right. The first-hand experience of thousands of Israeli regular and reserve soldiers in dealing with violent Palestinian Arab hostility toward Israel and Jews, their deep sense of frustration with the orders limiting their response, and the growing despair of many Israelis at the chances for peaceful coexistence between Jews and Arabs in the Holy Land, were seen to be at the heart of this hawkish trend. It was thus predicted that both major parties would lose votes to the extreme parties on the Right, and to a lesser extent on the Left, and that the Likud and its natural allies would form the next government.

The election results presented a highly limited and only partial confirmation of the predictions. True, the decline of the two major parties, evidenced already in 1984, continued. The Likud and Labor declined from a combined vote of 74 percent and 95 seats in 1981 to a combined vote of only 61 percent and 79 seats in 1988 — a drop of close to 20 percent! But this time it was not the extreme hawks and doves who were the main beneficiaries of the windfall but, surprisingly, the extreme Orthodox parties. These doubled their vote — from 5.6 percent and seven seats in 1984 to 10.7 percent and 13 seats in 1988. This shift reflected less polarization or a shift to the Right, than grassroots religious revivalism and an abandonment of rationalism in favor of mysticism.

With the single exception of this important and intriguing phenomenon, the election results demonstrated once again the remarkable conservatism of the Israeli voter — a conservatism that withstood, to a large extent, even the shock and strain of the *intifada*. The extreme parties increased their relative representation, but in absolute terms their gain was quite minimal. The hawks increased their vote from five percent and six seats in 1984 to seven percent and seven seats in 1988. The Arab parties — representing the extreme dovish end of the political spectrum — received the same six seats this time as in the previous election, with their popular vote increasing from five percent to six percent. The Citizens Rights Party (RATZ), espousing a strong dovish image, almost doubled its vote — from 2.4 percent and three seats in 1984 to 4.3 percent and five seats in 1988. Thus the overall shift in favor of extreme hawkish and dovish parties did not exceed five percent of the electorate. In terms of actual political influence these parties remained a marginal phenomenon: none of them was included in the new national unity government.

Two observations are relevant regarding the extreme hawkish Right. The Israeli Supreme Court unanimously outlawed the Kach Party of Meir Kahana on the grounds that it was racist and negated the democratic character of the state. Simultaneously a retired IDF general established a party (Moledet) that called for the transfer "by democratic means" of Palestinians from the Territories to Arab countries. By adopting a style totally different from Kahane, this party achieved a certain degree of respectability, and received over two percent of the vote, entitling it to two seats in the Knesset.

As for the overall political balance, there was a shift to the Right, but not one of major proportions. If we count all the religious parties, including the ultra-orthodox, in the hawkish camp (a determination that is subject to some question), there is a shift, as a result of the current election, of 3.5 percent and five seats from the doves to the hawks. Given the fact that the previous elections had resulted in a perfect tie between the two blocs, each receiving

60 seats (51.5 percent of the popular vote went to the Right and 48.5 percent to the Left), even such a limited shift had significant political implications. Nevertheless, in absolute terms, a shift of 3.5 percent can hardly be seen as reflecting a major change in the political attitude of Israeli society. The shift to the Right was, most probably, primarily accounted for by a movement of 5 seats from Labor to Likud. However, this shift did not necessarily reflect a basic change in these voters' political attitudes. It might equally have represented a positive response to Likud's strong "centrist" appeal to the moderate vote. Some new Likud voters might also have been motivated by economic considerations.

The municipal elections held on February 28, 1989 — four months after the Knesset elections — strengthened these trends. The two large parties dominated the scene in the Jewish sector. The Likud achieved a number of dramatic victories and, for the first time in Israel's history, controlled at least as many municipalities as Labor. Whereas in most cases the causes behind the Likud's victory were local in nature, the results gave the Likud a grassroots political base it never had before, and strengthened its hand significantly.

Two additional comments on sectorial voting trends are in order. The first involves the soldiers' vote in the army, and the second the vote in the Arab sector. The soldiers' vote is traditionally seen as an indication of voting trends among the younger generation, and is thus of considerable value in predicting the results of future elections. In previous elections, support for hawkish parties was considerably stronger among the soldiers than in the general population, coupled with a consistent erosion in support for Labor and its allies on the Left. In 1988, after many years, the decline in support for the Left was halted. Any attempt to draw conclusions from changes in the army vote is, by its very nature, highly speculative, especially since the percentage of reservists on active duty was probably higher (because of the *intifada*) in 1988 than in previous elections. Nevertheless two facts seem to stand out quite clearly: the doves succeeded, after years of decline, in maintaining their level of support among the soldiers; and the size of the vote for the Labor bloc was at least as high in the army as it was in the country as a whole. Perhaps this is a sign that the Left reached a certain rock bottom in terms of decline in its popular support.

If the Jewish vote was expected to be affected by the *intifada*, one would certainly have expected the uprising to have a dramatic effect on the voting behavior of Israeli Arabs. The critical question here is whether the events of the *intifada* and their political repercussions indeed brought about a basic change in the attitude of Israeli Arabs toward the State of Israel, and in their self-image as citizens of Israel. There were claims that such a change had indeed been wrought, and that many Israeli Arabs who had previously accepted their status as citizens of Israel had become disillusioned with the Jewish state, and now identified themselves, first and foremost, as Palestinian Arabs. It was widely predicted that this change would manifest itself at the polls by a massive protest vote against the Zionist parties in favor of the radical Arab parties: the Communists, the Progressive List for Peace, and the Independent Arab List.

In this sense the results of the Arab vote offered the second big surprise of the election. There was a definite shift in favor of the Arab parties, but its scope was far less than had been expected. The shift in the Arab vote was in the vicinity of seven percent: support for the Jewish Zionist parties dropped from 46 percent in 1984 to 40 percent in 1988, while the vote for the Arab parties increased from 51 percent to 58 percent. Interestingly, the Likud actually increased its vote from five percent to seven percent; Labor — strongly identified with Defense Minister Rabin, who symbolized for Israeli Arabs the use of force to suppress the *intifada* — received 17 percent of the vote (down from 23 percent in 1984); even the hawkish NRP maintained most of its traditional support in the Arab sector (three percent of the vote versus four percent in 1984); and the most radical Arab party — the Progressive List for Peace — actually declined, from 18 percent in 1984 to 14 percent in 1988. These results would seem to indicate that while Israeli Arabs identified with their Palestinian brethren across the Green Line and supported their quest for an independent state, they themselves had no intention of joining the *intifada*, and were not willing to jeopardize their status as Israeli citizens.

In contrast, the results of the municipal elections in the Arab sector did indicate a certain extremist trend. Interestingly, Arab voter turnout for these elections exceeded that of the Knesset elections, whereas in the Jewish population it was less than two-thirds of the level of participation in the Knesset elections. This might indicate that some Israeli Arabs boycotted the general elections — no doubt, for nationalistic reasons — and, even more important, that many Israeli Arabs look upon their locally-elected leadership (the Arab mayors) as the core of a potentially autonomous leadership. In any event, the most dramatic development in the Arab municipal sector was the rise of the Islamic Movement. Its candidates won the mayoralty contests in five municipalities, including one city and one Bedouin township. These results have been heralded as signifying a growing fundamentalist trend among Israeli Arabs, and posing a cause of concern for the Israeli leadership. In contrast, the moderate behavior and restraint demonstrated by the Israeli Arab population during its general strike on Land Day (March 30, 1989) seemed to imply that it was still unwilling to cause a major confrontation with the authority of the State.

## The New Government

In 1984 neither of the two major parties was able to form a coalition; in 1988 the Likud was theoretically able to do so, with the support of 61-65 members of Knesset. This would have required the participation in the government of many of the small parties, especially the ultra-orthodox. The latter had thus in effect acquired immense power, beyond all proportion to their actual gains at the polls. The moment the election results were known, Labor and the Likud began a no-holds-barred race for the favor of the ultra-orthodox until, eventually, these religious parties overplayed their hand, causing a tremendous public backlash, bordering on actual revulsion at the cynical and at times almost ludicrous coalition negotiations.

The spectacle of the unsavory coalition game dragging on for weeks on end generated widespread public recognition that there was a basic flaw in Israel's electoral system that endangered Israeli democracy. There had always been broad public support for electoral reform, but as a direct result of the events of November and December 1988 the entire issue took on much greater urgency.

For both Likud and Labor a moment of truth had arrived in the post-election autumn of 1988. The Likud had to decide whether to grasp the opportunity of forming its own government, but only by bowing to the almost unbelievable ideological and practical demands of seven small parties. The alternative was to form a national unity government with Labor, the price being a genuine sharing of power down the line — a parity government and ideological compromise. Many within the Likud preferred the first option. These forces were led by former Defense Minister Ariel Sharon and former Finance Minister Yitzhak Modai, and probably enjoyed the support of the majority of the Likud's central committee. But Prime Minister Shamir and his supporters (including Foreign Minister Arens, Deputy Prime Minister David Levy, Justice Minister Dan Meridor and former Prime Minister Begin's son, Benjamin Begin) opted for the latter alternative, and they carried the day. In retrospect it seems likely that Yitzhak Shamir, noting the results of the elections, may never have intended to form a narrow coalition: from the beginning he may have been determined, at almost any price, to reestablish a national unity government together with Labor. The dramatic advent of a US-PLO dialogue in mid-December may have strengthened Shamir's zeal to form a broad-based national unity government. All told, Shamir's ultimate decision, taken together with his new appointments to the government — many of them young leaders, strong personal supporters of the prime minister, and noted for their relative moderation — can be seen as reflecting a desire to present the Likud as a party of the political Center.

Labor, on the other hand, had to decide whether to preserve its ideological purity and lead a strong parliamentary opposition to a Likud-led right-wing government, or to join a Likud-led national unity government under the leadership of Yitzhak Shamir, without rotation in the prime ministership — a government in which the Likud would be in charge of foreign affairs. Here, too, a fierce struggle ensued. Labor leaders Shimon Peres and Yitzhak Rabin opted for the latter alternative, claiming that as a responsible party Labor could not forego an opportunity to share power and to prevent the rise of a right-wing government — and they, too, carried the day. The decision by a majority of two-thirds of Labor's central committee to join the national unity government can also be seen as a victory for a moderate, centrist approach versus the more dovish segments of the party.

On December 22, 1988, seven weeks after the elections, the national unity government was presented to and approved by the Knesset. Its basic guidelines were quite similar to those of the previous government, as was its personal makeup: Shamir continued as prime minister, Peres as vice prime minister, and Rabin as defense minister. There were two significant departures from the immediate past: no rotation in the post of prime minister — Shamir would hold this position for the government's full four-year term of office; and an exchange between Labor and Likud of the foreign and finance ministries — the foreign ministry going to Arens of the Likud (replacing Peres) and finance going to Peres (instead of Nissim). The agreement called for the establishment of a 12-member Inner Cabinet on the basis of parity — six members each for the Likud and Labor. This body would, in effect, constitute the real government of the country, just as in the former unity government (1984-1988).

## Political, Economic and Social Effects of the Intifada

The effects of the *intifada* could increasingly be felt throughout the fabric of Israeli life. In many ways Israel underwent a process of reassessment in which basic tenets of faith were questioned and assumptions commonly accepted for over twenty years were reevaluated and reexamined. Three key developments of 1988 and early 1989, related to the *intifada*, were the major causes for this reassessment.

First, *the extent and duration of the intifada.* More and more Israelis became convinced that the *intifada* could not be suppressed by force. This perception was reinforced by the oft-stated position of the IDF high command: namely, that within accepted political and moral limitations there was no military solution to the *intifada.* Israeli hawks argued that decisive action by the government could put a quick end to the *intifada*; their claim was backed up by proposals for draconian steps that would supposedly achieve this end. Many Israelis do believe that had the government and the army acted more decisively in December 1987, the *intifada* would have been nipped in the bud. But the evident willingness of the Palestinian Arabs to suffer casualties and economic hardship over a long period of time eventually also convinced a large segment of Israeli public opinion that it was too late for such countermeasures. A corollary of this perception was that the absence of a political settlement, or at least some political movement, meant an indefinite continuation of the *intifada*, with all its negative consequences for Israel.

Secondly, *Jordan's disengagement from the West Bank.* The "Jordanian Option" was for years the favorite approach of Israeli mainstream doves. The Labor leadership had, in the past, been as adamant as the Likud in rejecting an independent Palestinian state, as well as any negotiations with the PLO. Its proposed partner in a territorial compromise agreement was always Jordan, under King Hussein. But Hussein's decision of July 1988 to cut all formal ties between Jordan and the West Bank cut the ground out from under Labor. This left the mainstream doves with no partner and no coherent or feasible program. As it became clear that Hussein's action was not a new ploy, and that, given the post-*intifada* realities of the Arab world, Hussein could no longer be the sole partner to a settlement in the West Bank — the disarray in the moderate camp increased.

Lastly, *the PLO peace offensive.* Arafat's declaration in Geneva in November 1988, and the subsequent American decision to open a dialogue with the PLO were, by early 1989, the major political achievements of the *intifada.* Their repercussions reinforced those circles in Israel that espoused a Palestinian solution for the West Bank and Gaza and advocated negotiations with pro-PLO Palestinians.

These developments generated a number of key strategic consequences and implications for Israel. One of these was, for the first time, a growing polarization within Israeli society with regard to the Palestinian question. True, most of the political establishment, including Labor and Likud, remained opposed to an independent Palestinian state and to direct negotiations with the PLO — indeed, these positions were embodied in the basic guidelines of the national unity government. But cracks began to appear. Some Israelis were impressed with repeated statements by PLO leaders calling for a two-state solution and advocating political accommodation with Israel. Many more, though, were influenced by the growing international recognition of the PLO and the demise of the Jordanian option, to believe in the inevitability of the Palestinian option. For the first time, members of Knesset belonging to Zionist parties (including left-leaning Labor members) and establishment academicians participated in international conferences together with leading members of the PLO. Ezer Weizman, a maverick but a Cabinet member for Labor nonetheless, openly called for negotiations with the PLO and expressed his readiness to meet with Yasir Arafat. What was once taboo and tantamount to treason became the focus of an increasingly intense debate. This was clearly demonstrated in mid-March 1989 by the leak of a top-secret national intelligence estimate purporting to state that no authoritative Palestinians would be ready to engage in a dialogue with Israel without PLO approval, that there could be no end to the *intifada* without such a dialogue, and that the mainstream PLO leadership declared its support for political accommodation with Israel.

Traces of these developments could be found in public opinion polls. Initial indications pointed to a slight dovish trend. A number of opinion polls taken in the early months of 1989 showed that while less than one-fifth of Israeli Jews (15-20 percent) supported immediate talks with the PLO, a majority (53-58 percent) supported talks with the PLO on the basis of Arafat's Geneva declaration and on condition that the PLO did indeed refrain from all acts of terrorism.

Similar data could be found in the continuing survey of the Israel Institute of Applied Social Research. The institute found a slow increase in support for a Palestinian state over a ten year period, from 13 percent in the aftermath of Camp David to 23 percent in January 1989. And while absolute support for immediate talks with the PLO and for a Palestinian state remained quite low, a *New York Times* survey conducted in Israel in early 1989 found that 62 percent of Israeli Jews believed that talks with the PLO were inevitable in the ensuing five years, and that the establishment of a Palestinian state in the West Bank and Gaza was inevitable in the next 10-20 years.

This development was paralleled by a growing realization in the Israeli government of the need for an Israeli peace initiative. Within days after the formation of the new government, both Prime Minister Shamir and Foreign Minister Arens declared that the prime minister would soon put forth new ideas on moving the peace process forward. This recognition of the strong need for an Israeli initiative based, at least partially, on some new ideas, was clearly a result of both internal and international pressures. It also stemmed from a growing awareness — perhaps even shared by Shamir and Arens — that time was not in Israel's favor and that the continuation of the status quo constituted a serious strategic disadvantage for Israel.

First to come forward with a clear-cut proposal was Defense Minister Rabin. His plan was an elaboration of the guidelines presented by Peres and Rabin before the November 1, 1988 elections. It called for a temporary halt to the *intifada*, to be followed by general elections throughout the West Bank and Gaza, then negotiations between Israel and the democratically elected representatives of the Palestinians, to determine interim autonomy arrangements. Finally, at the end of three years, negotiations would be held over a final settlement. Prime Minister Shamir, during his visit to Washington in the first week of April, in effect adopted this plan. In May Shamir officially presented it as an Israeli peace proposal.

Many questions remained open regarding various aspects of the central feature of this plan: namely, the elections in the West Bank and Gaza. One key element would presumably be a concentrated American effort to mediate indirectly between Israel and the PLO — as agreement by both was clearly a sine qua non for such elections. Shamir for his part intimated that Israel would recognize and negotiate with the elected Palestinian representatives, even if they were identified with and supported by the PLO, and that he could conceive of joint Israeli-Palestinian supervision of such elections, possibly even with American observers.

A third key strategic consequence of developments in 1988 was a growing confrontation between the Jewish population living on the settlements in Judea, Samaria and Gaza on the one hand, and the army, the authorities and the government on the other hand. Throughout 1988 and early 1989 the confrontation grew in scope and in intensity. It reflected the ascendancy of a number of perceptions among settlers.

First, the settlers came to see themselves as being increasingly isolated. One consequence of the *intifada* was to recreate, in effect, the "Green Line" — the pre-1967 border between Israel and the West Bank and Gaza Strip, which was effectively erased during the years 1967-1987. Many Israelis, fearing for their safety, hesitated to travel in the Territories, even to visit relatives and friends living in these areas. There was even a considerable drop in the number of Jews visiting or traveling through East Jerusalem. Then, too, settlers felt that their personal safety was being compromised. The IDF could not guarantee their absolute security, and here and there Jews were injured and even killed by Arab attacks — mainly stone and firebomb ambushes against Jewish traffic on public roads. Further, the settlers began to suspect that the Israeli government, including Shamir and Arens, was slowly but surely moving toward a political compromise with the Palestinians — a compromise totally unacceptable to them.

One could hardly expect the settlers and their supporters to stand by idly while the Israeli government worked out some political accommodation with the Palestinians. To the degree that the new Israeli initiative moved forward and a political process got underway, one could surely anticipate that the confrontation with the settlers and their supporters would become more intense, perhaps even violent, resulting in a sharp increase in the polarization of Israeli society. By mid-1989 calls among the settlers for retaliation, vigilantism and underground activity were increasing.

Turning to the economic effects of the *intifada*, it is almost impossible to arrive at an accurate estimate of the total cost of the uprising for Israel. The direct cost is easier to assess; it is far harder to reach an agreed upon figure for the indirect costs. The most direct expenditure is the cost of IDF operations in the West Bank and Gaza. Yet even here the differences between the ministries of defense and finance are significant. The army asked for over $200 million in additional funds for 1988/89 and about half that sum for 1989/90, to compensate it for additional expenditures incurred as a result of the uprising; it received an additional budget of close to $90 million for 1988/89 and about $50 million for 1989/90. In mid-1989 it requested an additional $140 million as a supplementary budgetary allocation to cover costs of the *intifada*. These sums did not reflect the loss of many thousands of man-hours in the civilian sector as a result of the increase in military reserve duty. In many instances, reservists served as many as 60 days in 1988 — double that of the previous year.

Another direct economic consequence of the *intifada* for Israel was a decline in tourism. It decreased by 15 percent in 1988 (down from over 1.5 million in 1987 to 1.3 million in 1988), generating a direct loss to the Israeli economy of a quarter of a billion dollars. Another direct loss resulted from a significant diminishing of economic ties between Israel and the Territories. Israel's trade surplus in goods and services with the West Bank and Gaza dropped by two-thirds — from $174 million in 1987 to only $56 million in 1988 — a loss of $120 million. To this must be added the indirect loss resulting from a decline in production as a result of the drop in the number of Arabs from the Territories working in Israel. Government sources estimated that 90,000 laborers from the Territories were still working in Israel in 1989 as compared with 114,000 in the last quarter of 1987. Yet many of these 90,000 worked fewer days per month than previously, due to strikes and boycotts associated with the *intifada*.

In 1988 Israel's Minister of Economy, Gad Yaacoby, estimated the economic cost of the *intifada* at between $600-700 million — roughly equivalent to 2 percent of Israel's Gross Domestic Product. Whatever the cost, it is clear that the economic toll exacted by the *intifada* was a limited one, and the economic factor remained of secondary importance for Israel. A number of textile companies might have gone out of business as a result of the loss of markets in the West Bank, and a number of building firms presumably faced serious difficulties due to a shortage of Palestinian laborers. But the Israeli man or woman in the street hardly felt the economic effects of the *intifada*, and the Israeli economy was robust enough to deal with any economic disruptions or dislocations caused by the uprising. Rather, the truly serious effects of the *intifada* for Israel were in the political, social and moral realms.

Nowhere was this truer than in the IDF itself, as its standing force and reserves bore the brunt of policing and quelling riots in the Territories. We have already noted that the defense establishment was constrained by receiving only partial financial compensation for the costs of the *intifada*. But the major repercussions for the IDF were evident in other areas.

First, reservists were required to serve 60 days in 1988. This immediate measure taken by the General Staff caused hardship to the citizen-soldier, and disrupted IDF routine training and exercises. As a corollary, the efforts of the senior military command to handle the *intifada* to a large extent disrupted the main defense effort: deterrence, preparing for war, and providing early warning of enemy attack.

Finally, morale was affected. While conscientious objection to serving in the Territories was limited, the impact on values and morale was far more serious, with more and more soldiers aware of conflicting emotions. Meanwhile criticism — from both directions — of the political leadership threatened the national consensus regarding the goals of military service.

# 4. The US-PLO Dialogue

## by Dore Gold

The decision of the Reagan administration to open a substantive dialogue with the PLO was a product of both remote and proximate causes. During the Reagan years American policy on the issue of Palestinian representation in the peace process had evolved subtly. The principal governing document that Reagan inherited from his predecessors was the 1975 Memorandum of Agreement between Henry Kissinger and Yigal Allon, according to which the US undertook not to recognize or negotiate with the PLO as long as it did not recognize Israel's right to exist and accept UN Security Council Resolutions 242 and 338. Even were the PLO to meet these conditions, the 1975 MOA further stipulated that the subsequent participation of any additional state or organization in the Geneva Peace Conference required the prior agreement of all the initial participants in the conference (including Israel). The renunciation of terrorism was added as a third American precondition by Congress in 1985.

In the 1978 Camp David Accords, Israel acquired virtual veto power over the issue of Palestinian representation. In Part A of the agreements, the "Framework for Peace in the Middle East," the modalities for establishing a self-governing authority for the West Bank and Gaza were to be negotiated by Israel, Egypt and Jordan. While Palestinians from the Territories could be included in the negotiations within the delegations of either Arab party, the inclusion of "other Palestinians" (i.e. diaspora Palestinians) required the mutual agreement of all, including Israel.

As a matter of national policy neither the Ford nor Carter administrations totally rejected the concept of a Palestinian option involving the PLO — in the event that the organization made the changes that the 1975 MOA called for. Constant low level contacts — both covert and through third parties — were thus maintained with the PLO in order to evaluate its policy toward different initiatives and to convince it to accept the conditions for a US dialogue laid out in the 1975 MOA. But despite these attempts to reach some mutual understanding over the peace process, American policy remained consistent with its treaty commitments and did not seek to involve the PLO as a partner in the international diplomacy of the Arab-Israel peace process.

President Reagan reaffirmed his commitment to the 1975 MOA and the Camp David Accords at the time his September 1982 plan was announced. Moreover, the Reagan Plan strengthened the American preference for a Jordanian-based solution for the Territories; it called for self-government by the Palestinians "in association with Jordan." Again, a Palestinian option was not entirely ruled out, as evidenced by the administration's own attempts to feel out the organization through private American initiatives. Nonetheless the US did not swerve from its Jordanian preference.

In 1985, however, some subtle changes became apparent in the administration's attitude toward the issue of Palestinian representation. The February Hussein-Arafat agreement and the subsequent Mubarak initiative were the occasion for an accelerated American effort to initiate discussions between Israel and a joint Jordanian-Palestinian delegation. During the detailed negotiations over the question which Palestinians might join the delegation and meet with US representatives, Secretary Shultz established a distinction between the PLO and the Palestinian National Council (PNC); accordingly, he stated that it was possible to find in the PNC Palestinians who were not members of the PLO and who were "dedicated to non-violence." The US did not recognize Israel's veto power in the matter of "other Palestinians" and was prepared to accept PLO-selected PNC members in the joint delegation. In the end, however, the Americans did not meet with a Jordanian-PNC delegation because the latter refused to meet with Israel outside of the framework of an international conference. The net effect of the initiatives in 1985 was an erosion of the 1975 and 1978 American commitments.

A second occasion for further American involvement in the issue of Palestinian representation in the peace process came during the Shultz Initiative of 1988, which itself was largely a result of the Palestinian uprising in the Territories. First Shultz, appearing at the American Colony Hotel in East Jerusalem, read a statement intended for West Bank and Gaza Palestinians — who boycotted any meeting with him outside the framework of the PLO — in which he stated that "Palestinians must be active participants in negotiations to determine their future." The US appeared interested in upgrading the Palestinian political role at all stages of the peace process.

A second development in this regard was Shultz's explicit

support for "the political rights of the Palestinians" that began to enter the American lexicon during his visit to the Middle East in June 1988. American spokesmen were vague about the difference between past support for legitimate rights, and this new reference to political rights; it is instructive to recall that Jordan proposed in 1985 US support for Palestinian self-determination in the framework of a confederation as a precondition for PLO acceptance of 242. "Political rights" may have been as far as Shultz was willing to go toward the PLO, in the expectation that it would now finally accept 242, renounce terrorism, and thereby make itself a party to the international conference that lay at the heart of his plan.

Third, in August 1988, after King Hussein had announced that he was cutting legal and administrative links with the West Bank, US policymakers began more seriously to consider a Palestinian alternative to the Jordanian option. Some of Shultz's closest advisors concluded that the time had come for seeking a way for the US to deal with the PLO. The latter had proven to Washington that it was a factor in the Middle East peace equation whose influence could not be ignored. Moreover, with Jordan out of the game, were the US to refuse to consider a Palestinian option, the peace process would effectively come to an end.

The more proximate causes of the US-PLO dialogue were related to events surrounding the PNC meeting in Algiers in November. Initially the US appeared to be a passive party in the process of the PLO's declaratory moderation; it was not actively involved in the selection of the language used in the PNC political document in Algiers. While the State Department noted positive elements in the PNC decisions — "the outcome of the PNC session in Algiers produced signs that there are Palestinians who are trying to move the PLO in a constructive way" — it found the language to be too ambiguous to merit the opening of a dialogue.

Former Secretary of State George Shultz, moreover, felt that the November 1985 Cairo Declaration was an insufficient basis for the PNC's condemnation of terrorism; because of the repeated involvement since that time of PLO elements, including Fatah units of Force 17 and those of Colonel Hawari, in "more than 30 instances" of international terrorism (11 operations in Europe and 22 in Israel), Shultz decided on November 26 to deny PLO Chairman Arafat an entry visa into the US to address the United Nations General Assembly. The PNC statement on terrorism, in Shultz's view, required that the US test PLO intentions over time: "We must take the attitude that we will have to watch and see what happens, whether the new declaration has a more restrictive effect on terrorism than the prior one did."

Shultz insisted on denying Arafat entry into the US even though one day earlier he had received a delegation from Sweden bearing the text of an agreed joint statement secretly negotiated by an American Jewish delegation and Arafat's political advisor, Khalid al-Hassan, that was far more explicit about answering American preconditions for a dialogue. But after the 154 to 2 decision of the General Assembly, on December 2, to move its debate on the Middle East to Geneva, the US found itself isolated regarding its hard-line attitude toward the PLO. Again it was the continuing Swedish diplomatic initiative that sought to bridge the gap between the US and the PLO; Sweden's ambassador to the US, Count Wilhelm Wachtmeister, asked Shultz on behalf of his foreign minister what explicitly Arafat would have to say to fulfill the American preconditions for a dialogue. The ensuing exchange led to a presidential decision on December 6 that if Arafat made his newest statements in public, the US would initiate a "substantive dialogue." The notion of a period of testing the PLO on the terrorism issue appeared to have been dropped.

According to later comments by Swedish Foreign Minister Sten Andersson, the statement read by Arafat at the Geneva news conference on December 14 also did not fully correspond to what the US had requested. Yet, despite these imperfections, the US nonetheless decided that the conditions of its 1975 memorandum had been met.

Several reasons explain the American move. First, from the American perspective the US had laid out conditions for negotiating with the PLO for 13 years. By and large the PLO had now met these conditions. Failure to respond to the PLO's efforts might have signaled a certain unreliability concerning American commitments. As Arafat's statements came closer to the text required by the Department of State, had the US continued to hold that its conditions for a dialogue had not yet been met, American trustworthiness would have become increasingly suspect. Thus a member of the Bush transition team explained at the time that the US "would have devalued its word" if it had not opened talks with the PLO after the organization had met the American conditions; the US could not "establish conditions and then change the ground rules when they are met." For Shultz's top advisers, many of whom would stay on for the incoming Bush administration, establishing the dialogue in the last days of the Reagan period would spare the new administration political fallout from taking a similar step during its first year in office.

Then too, prior to Shultz's rejection of Arafat's entry visa, the differences between US views on the PLO and those of its allies in Europe and the Middle East were essentially dormant. The visa rejection put the PLO issue at the top of the international agenda. The vote to shift General Assembly discussions to Geneva revealed just how isolated the American position had become. US diplomacy appeared to be increasingly conservative in the view of the European allies, especially in the wake of the December conventional arms control initiatives of Soviet leader Mikhail Gorbachev. Refusal to open the US-PLO dialogue because of minute points of language would only have reinforced the image of inflexible American diplomacy, especially if the US had no adequate response to Soviet arms control suggestions.

Finally, as with the Shultz initiative, failure of the US to meet the PLO's diplomatic challenge would possibly have shifted the Middle East peace process away from American control and increasingly put it under the auspices of the Western Europeans or the USSR. The Soviet Union, long a strategic ally of the PLO, was already in the process of upgrading its diplomatic relations with Israel; Moscow would soon be in a position of having ties with both parties to the conflict that the US did not share. Thus American preeminence in the peace process was assured through its new dialogue with the PLO.

Moreover, the forces that might have resisted the American-PLO dialogue were in a condition of total disarray. Congress was in recess; organized American Jewry was totally preoccupied by the "Who is a Jew" issue that arose in connection with the Israeli coalition talks with the religious parties. American Jewry was in no position to oppose a Secretary of State who had, over the years, built up considerable credibility with the American Jewish community.

## The Terms of the Initial US-PLO Dialogue

The 1975 Memorandum of Understanding between the US and Israel governing US diplomatic contacts with the PLO stated that, as long as its preconditions were not met, the US would not recognize or negotiate with the organization. Thus, once the State Department judged that the PLO had fulfilled the preconditions at Geneva, the US conceivably could have extended some sort of diplomatic recognition to the PLO or to its role as a representative of the Palestinian people. Moreover, the US could equally have concluded that the PLO was now a full party to the next stage of the Middle East peace process. Instead Washington's response to the PLO was minimalistic:

— the US opened with the PLO a "substantive dialogue," but did not yet recognize the organization as a party to peace negotiations. State Department Spokesman Charles Redman explained that: "the question of which parties participate in negotiations is not for the United States to decide unilaterally. That is up to the parties, Arabs and Israelis alike to decide." Thus, in the American view, both Jordan and the Palestinians of the West Bank and Gaza remained potential participants in the peace process.

— Washington confined the US-PLO dialogue to one authorized channel: the US ambassador to Tunisia.

— The US reiterated that by opening a diplomatic channel to the PLO, it was not recognizing the independent Palestinian state that the PNC had declared at Algiers in November. Washington underlined its view that the status of the West Bank and Gaza could not be determined by unilateral acts of either side. The US at this point did not alter its view of the preferred outcome of a settlement on the West Bank and Gaza: self-government by the Palestinians of the Territories in association with Jordan.

— State Department officials stated that they would closely monitor Yasir Arafat's adherence to his renunciation of terrorism. President Reagan said that the US would "certainly break off communications" with the PLO if the organization committed terrorist acts in the future. Secretary Shultz suggested that the first item of business in the dialogue would be the issue of terrorism; Undersecretary of State Michael Armacost summarized the Reagan administration view: "if terrorism persists, and if they're accountable for it, then we would be unable to move forward in our dialogue. If attacks occur, and it appears to be the responsibility of elements that are close to the PLO, we would expect [it] to denounce them, to disassociate from them, certainly to expel any elements that are involved in this from the PLO."

Tactically, it made sense for the US to grant the PLO the most minimal diplomatic concessions in exchange for Arafat's statements. Thus the US could use further concessions to draw the organization toward greater moderation. Nonetheless the US official response to Arafat was less than enthusiastic. Washington appeared to have been forced by circumstance, and not at a timing of its choice, to live up to its 1975 Memorandum.

In the first 90-minute meeting between the US and the PLO on December 15 in Tunisia wide differences of opinion were apparent. According to a protocol of the session leaked to the Egyptian weekly *Al-Mussawar*, the US focused initial discussion on the issue of international terrorism, demanding that the PLO clear its ranks of "those who embrace terrorism." While no specific reference was made to persons whom the US wished to see removed from the PLO, Secretary Shultz had earlier referred to the presence of Abu Abbas on the PLO Executive Committee as well as the ongoing operations of Force 17 and the Hawari group as the active terrorist elements in the PLO that had caused him to deny Arafat a visa during November. Presumably the US was now targeting these groups. Subsequent reports in the Arab press stated that the US was demanding the liquidation of Force 17, the expulsion of Abu Abbas and other terrorist leaders from the PLO, and an increased commitment to confederation with Jordan as preconditions for endorsing a PLO role in the peace process.

The PLO for its part maintained the view that neither the *intifada* nor military actions directed against Israel could be defined as terrorism. The US reiterated that it understood terrorism as including "all Palestinian military action against Israel, whether against Israeli targets, installations or people." The US did not distinguish between military actions undertaken by Palestinians inside the Territories or outside the Territories. According to the public record, however, the US never made a blanket judgment defining the *intifada* as terrorism. The State Department's own review of international terrorism for 1988 only established that "the Intifada should be viewed primarily as civil insurrection that contains elements of terrorism in specific instances."

The two sides also took different approaches to the format for peace negotiations. The US preferred direct negotiations, stating that eventually direct Israeli-PLO talks could be held in Washington. In all events direct preliminary talks without outside interference had, in the American view, to precede any international conference. The PLO stressed the need to have an authoritative international conference in which all parties participated on an equal basis along with the five permanent members of the UN Security Council. The "international presence," according to the PLO, had to be involved in all negotiations with Israel. And it insisted on "compulsory adoption" of the outcome of the conference. Subsequently Yasir Abd-Rabu, PLO Executive Committee Member from the Democratic Front for the Liberation of Palestine and the PLO delegation head during the talks with the US in Tunis, further clarified his organization's differences with the Americans on issues of procedure: "We made it clear that the question of bilateral negotiations between us or other Arab countries and the Israelis was out of the question. The negotiating has to take place in the context of an international conference."

## The Bush Administration and the PLO

The incoming Bush administration's general attitude of caution toward the Soviet Union in some degree affected its attitude toward the PLO as well. Immediately upon becoming secretary of state, James Baker faced several tests with the new US-PLO relationship. First, the PLO wanted to see whether its new dialogue had altered the American approach to Israel at the UN; through a non-aligned ally in the Security Council it proposed a resolution condemning Israel's handling of the Palestinian uprising. The US took care to reject even a subdued condemnation so as not to signal any dramatic shifts in US policy toward the Arab-Israel conflict because of the new US-PLO dialogue.

A second test came about because of the military activities of Arafat's internal opposition within the PLO. The Bush team was forced to consider its policy on the dialogue with the PLO at a very early stage due to increasing numbers of infiltration attempts along the Israeli-Lebanese border by constituent organizations of PLO-Tunis that did not fully agree with the line of policy developed by Yasir Arafat. After such an infiltration attempt on February 5 by a joint PFLP-PLF (Tal'at Ya'aqub) squad, Secretary Baker established that the US was not about to cut off its new dialogue with the PLO: "we are not prepared to say at this time that this constitutes an action by the PLO which would cause us to break the dialogue. We made the point (to the PLO in Tunis) that such actions as this directed against civilian or military targets inside or outside of Israel was something that gave us trouble."

While National Security Advisor Brent Scowcroft explained that before any high-level meeting might be arranged between a member of the Bush administration and PLO Chairman Arafat, it was necessary to better understand Arafat's intentions, the Bush-Baker team, unlike Reagan and Shultz, clearly refused to establish conditions for ending the US-PLO dialogue, in the event of persistent terrorism. This basic American position was not altered by another attempted infiltration conducted by Nayif Hawatmah's DFLP at the end of the month, aimed at the Israeli civilian settlement of Moshav Zar'it. Indeed, even as the credibility of Arafat's renunciation of terrorism came into question, the Bush administration began to send signals that the US-PLO dialogue was not threatened; rather, Washington hinted that the dialogue might lead ultimately to Israeli-PLO negotiations at a later stage of the peace process. On March 14 Secretary Baker told a House Appropriations Subcommittee that "if you can't have direct negotiations that are meaningful that do not involve negotiations with the PLO, we would then have to see negotiations between Israelis and representatives of the PLO." The following day, before the Senate Appropriations Committee he repeated the same idea: "You're not going to have peace without direct negotiations between Israelis and Palestinians. If that can be accomplished through a dialogue between Israelis and Palestinians in the occupied Territories, that would be, of course, a preferred approach. But we ought not rule out categorically, absolutely and unequivocally consideration of going beyond that if it's necessary to move toward peace in the Middle East." In subsequent Congressional testimony on March 21, Baker clarified his remarks, stating that while it might be desirable for Israel to negotiate with the PLO, the US was not advocating that course or trying to force it on Israel: "we have not made a policy statement that we are going to recommend that they negotiate with the PLO."

Baker appeared to be saying that while Israeli-PLO negotiations were not inevitable, nonetheless he would not rule out the PLO as a possible party to negotiations at a later stage of the peace process. His complicated presentation made sense when taken in the context of the Bush administration's emerging three-stage strategy for easing Israeli-Palestinian tensions in the West Bank and the Gaza Strip.

In the first "confidence-building" stage of the plan, Israel would be asked to release some Palestinian prisoners, end or limit administrative detention, and reopen schools; the PLO and the Palestinians would be asked to halt violent demonstrations, block anti-Israel raids from Lebanon, and stop the distribution of inflammatory leaflets. At the second stage, Israel would be expected to conduct negotiations with Palestinians of the Territories over an interim settlement; the PLO would be asked not to interfere in these negotiations.

Only at the third stage, assuming the first two were executed successfully, did the US envisage a negotiating role for the PLO in final-status talks with Israel; but even at this point the US did not envision that the PLO would be the sole representative of the Palestinians. The administration appeared willing to test this strategy quietly with the parties to the conflict. But it was not willing to present its ideas in the form of a public doctrine – a "Baker Plan." Neither the president nor his secretary of state were willing to risk their reputations in Washington over the Middle East. Growing congressional frustration with ongoing PLO cross-border infiltration attempts, and hardline remarks by PLO spokesmen, did not make the administration's task in defending its Middle East strategy any easier. Yet without a firm declaratory position, the degree of commitment of the administration to its emerging strategy was not entirely clear.

The US forwarded some of these ideas regarding its Middle East peace strategy to the PLO on March 22, during the first official session of the dialogue held under the Bush administration. The PLO delegation reportedly did not reject the American confidence-building proposals out of hand, though PLO delegation head Yasir Abd Rabu implied that formal recognition of the Palestinians' right to self-determination and an independent state, and a concomitant Israeli withdrawal from the Territories, would be prerequisites for any confidence-building program. The PLO did however somewhat relax its formal demand for an international conference as the exclusive framework for negotiations – its delegates expressed a readiness for direct preparatory talks with Israel before the conference was actually convened.

Still, wide differences remained on many issues. The PLO claimed that it alone could designate participants in talks with

Israel; it thus rejected the use of elections in the Territories as a means of choosing Palestinian representatives for peace talks with Israel. The PLO did not indicate that it was willing to halt cross-border attacks from Lebanon on a unilateral basis. The US appeared to understand that the PLO had a long way to go before it could become a full partner in the peace process; yet Washington seemed determined to achieve such a transformation of the organization. The US would not rule out the possibility of upgrading the dialogue to a higher level if its confidence-building program of easing tensions was accepted.

While doubts remained about PLO intentions, Washington had clearly set a course of ultimately bringing the organization into the Arab-Israel peace process. By May 1989, with the Bush administration supporting Prime Minister Shamir's election proposal, US Middle East diplomacy began moving along two parallel tracks: the election proposal and the US-PLO dialogue. The US perhaps hoped that it could integrate the two processes: a "green light" from the PLO in Tunis was viewed as a necessary condition for moving the election proposal in the Territories forward, although it was unclear what the US would precisely offer the PLO in order to obtain its agreement to the Shamir initiative. Nevertheless the administration allowed that the pace of introducing the PLO into negotiations would be set in the Middle East, and by the parties themselves. The US was interested in encouraging an Israeli-Palestinian dialogue, but it did not see its role as one of coercing the parties into agreements that they themselves had no interest in achieving.

# 5. The Soviet Union in the Middle East

## by Mark A. Heller

Soviet Middle Eastern policy in 1988 was marked by a steady implementation of the principles of "new thinking." Since the accession to power of Mikhail Gorbachev in 1985, Soviet foreign policy, in general, has tended to reflect a more modest appreciation of the political utility of regional conflicts and growing skepticism about the need for aggressive and expensive Soviet involvement in the third world. Rather than an opportunity to make gains at the expense of the West, third world conflicts are increasingly viewed as irritants and potential dangers which should be removed from the superpower agenda — through negotiated settlements — in order to facilitate improved Soviet-American relations.

This sort of "new thinking," if carried to its logical conclusion, would mean Soviet retrenchment or disengagement from the third world, and some published Soviet commentary has appeared to advocate precisely that. For example, Igor Malashenko, writing in *New Times*, argued that improving domestic living standards was far more important for national security "than the course developments may take in some exotic country that many of us can barely find on the map of the world."

The Soviet Union, of course, was not about to retreat into isolationism in 1988. There was no indication whatsoever that the Soviets intended to relinquish the influence and presence appropriate to their status as a superpower, and Soviet diplomats were, if anything, becoming more visible and peripatetic. But Soviet policy was marked by a decreasing emphasis on military means, a growing reluctance to provide diplomatic and material support for a narrow circle of "radical" allies or clients, and a corresponding increase in efforts to cultivate better relations with the local or regional rivals of those allies or clients. In short, the Soviet Union continued to diversify its foreign relations, with the apparent purpose of projecting a more "constructive" and "even-handed" image in order to promote settlement of regional conflicts. The theme that guided Soviet proposals for conflict resolution was the "balance of interests" of all parties.

The single most dramatic manifestation of this underlying purpose in 1988 took place, not in the heartland of the Middle East, but on its periphery — in Afghanistan. The agreement signed in Geneva in April called for an end to all foreign interference in Afghanistan and thereby permitted the Soviets to claim that the ostensible objective of their military intervention in 1979 had been accomplished. But this was a transparent artifice, a fig-leaf for what amounted to unilateral Soviet withdrawal. Soviet spokesmen were remarkably candid in their retrospective assessment that the invasion had been a mistake; they attributed it to the flawed decisionmaking processes of the Brezhnev regime, especially the tendency of a narrow coterie of top leaders to pursue an excessively militarized foreign policy based on ideology rather than on facts and reality, i.e., on information and analysis provided by professional advisers.

The Soviet pull-out began in May 1988 and was completed, on schedule, on February 15, 1989. But while the departure of the last Soviet soldier from Afghanistan symbolized the abandonment of the Brezhnev Doctrine, the logic of new thinking had begun to inform Soviet behavior in the Middle East several years before. This trend continued during the period under review.

In the Arab-Israel arena, the substance of Soviet policy — support for a political settlement to provide for Palestinian self-determination, one that would be secured through an international conference of all interested parties and the five permanent members of the United Nations Security Council — had been in place for a long time. However, the elements of this policy were now being pursued with increasing dexterity and sophistication. Soviet diplomats forcefully argued that a military solution to the conflict was unattainable, and they recognized that a political settlement required greater sensitivity to the interests and concerns of all parties, particularly Israel. The Soviets accepted that they could not coerce Israel into accepting their terms, or those of their Arab allies; nor could they even play a constructive role in the politics of the Arab-Israel conflict without Israel's approval. Consequently, they placed a much greater emphasis on reassuring Israel and enticing it to modify its stated positions. This objective was carried forward through bilateral contacts as well as through efforts to encourage various Arab parties, especially the PLO and Syria, to adopt more flexible and realistic positions.

At the bilateral level, perhaps the most noteworthy event was the reestablishment of an Israeli diplomatic presence in Moscow, in the form of a consular mission operating out of the Israel "Interests Section" of the Dutch Embassy. This mission, which arrived at the end of July 1988, was the counterpart of a Soviet mission sent to Tel Aviv in September 1987. Both missions had originally been described as short-term operations (the diplomats had been issued two- or three-month visas) and charged with purely technical responsibilities such as inspecting property and visa procedures. However, the terms of the missions were repeatedly extended and the scope of their activities was gradually broadened to include political discussions as well. This process was given additional momentum in late 1988 by two unanticipated events: the hijacking of a Soviet airliner to Israel and a massive earthquake in Soviet Armenia. Israeli assistance in both cases created the need (and the opportunity) for more high-level contact between the missions and host governments; in December the head of the Israeli consular delegation was received by Soviet Foreign Minister Shevardnadze, who thanked him for Israel's cooperation during the hijacking but took advantage of the meeting to ask whether Israel could propose some alternative to the international conference.

These direct contacts were part of an ongoing process of dialogue, usually involving higher-level meetings on neutral ground. In May 1988 Israeli Foreign Minister Peres met with the Soviet Ambassador in Washington, Yuri Dubinin, who presented a verbal proposal which reportedly went to great lengths to accommodate Israeli concerns — stressing that a peace conference would be "non-coercive," emphasizing Israeli withdrawal from "Territories" rather than "the Territories," and intimating that Palestinian self-determination might be achieved in some framework other than a fully independent state. In June, Shevardnadze held a highly publicized discussion with Prime Minister Shamir at the United Nations; he met twice with the new Israeli Foreign Minister, Moshe Arens, in early 1989 — first in Paris, and then in Cairo.

These meetings were supplemented by a series of reassuring Soviet declarations over the year. Senior Soviet officials, including Gorbachev himself, repeatedly insisted that the Soviet Union bore no hostility to Israel or to its legitimate security requirements. Hints were dropped that Israel did not necessarily have to accept the Soviet version of an international conference and that Palestinian interests might not have to be represented by a separate PLO delegation.

At the same time, relations on other issues continued to intensify at an accelerating pace. Jewish emigration increased substantially and the last refuseniks were released. Conditions for Jews remaining in the Soviet Union were reported to have eased; the jamming of Israeli radio broadcasts ceased and a Jewish Cultural Center was opened in Moscow in early 1989. Representatives of Aeroflot and El Al met to discuss a commercial agreement, because the volume of Soviet-Israel air traffic had risen so much (25,000 passengers in 1988, including several thousand Soviet tourists) that the absence of direct flights was denying both airlines a lot of business. In January 1989 the Deputy Head of the KGB, Vitali Ponomarev, announced that he was interested in anti-terrorist cooperation with foreign intelligence agencies, including the Mossad. Cultural and sports exchanges were stepped up; theater companies and basketball teams planned or carried out reciprocal visits, and even Alla Pugachova, a leading Soviet rock star, made a concert appearance in Israel.

Perhaps most revealing of all, there was a steady erosion in the Soviet terms for the resumption of diplomatic ties. Since 1967, the Soviet position had consistently been that relations had been broken because Israel occupied Arab territories; relations could not be restored until the occupation ended. This condition was considerably softened after Gorbachev's assumption of power, and by early 1988 the resumption of relations had been made contingent only on the convening of an international conference. But during the course of the year, the Soviet position became even more elastic. In September, Soviet Deputy Foreign Minister Vladimir Petrovsky was quoted in *Izvestia* as having told Shimon Peres that normalization would occur "with the start of work on an international conference," and in January 1989 Ambassador Dubinin, speaking to a group of American Jewish leaders, expressed the hope that ties would be restored "in the course of the peace process."

Some analysts argued that Soviet-Israeli rapprochement was propelled by a common concern about the spread of Islamic fundamentalism. While both parties undoubtedly felt threatened by this phenomenon, it is not altogether clear how cooperation between them would help ward off the danger, and any evidence of Soviet understanding for Israeli interests would only provide additional fuel to the anti-Soviet sentiment characteristic of radical Islamic forces. It is true that a political settlement of the Arab-Israel conflict might eventually eliminate one of the factors that heightens the receptiveness to fundamentalist appeals in the Arab world, but even that might only be a longer-term consequence of peace; the immediate impact of a settlement – meaning significant ideological concessions to Israel — could well be to inflame Muslim sensitivities. In any event, there is nothing to indicate that concern about fundamentalism is a major determinant of Soviet policy toward Israel in particular, or regarding the Middle East in general. Were that the case, the Soviets would certainly have provided much stronger backing for Iraq in its long war with Iran.

Instead, developments during the period under review suggest that the Soviets were gradually but quite clearly working toward restoration of diplomatic relations with Israel as part of a broader policy aimed at promoting a political settlement of the conflict, on terms that fell far short of maximal Arab demands. Indeed, the obverse of their dealings with Israel was a consistent effort to disabuse their closest Arab partners — Syria and the PLO — of the illusion of a military option and to persuade them to moderate their positions.

Soviet-Syrian tensions had occurred in the past, both before and after Gorbachev's rise to power. These tensions, however, were usually related to inter-Arab disputes, especially to Syrian conflicts with the PLO. But since 1987, reports of serious policy differences over the Arab-Israel conflict have become fairly common. The most publicized incident took place during Syrian President Assad's visit to Moscow in April 1987, when he was told by Gorbachev that there was no military solution to the conflict and that the absence of ties between the Soviet Union and Israel was not normal. The Soviets continued to communicate this message during 1988, and they demonstrated their seriousness at least twice by refusing to provide certain advanced weapons systems requested by Syria. The first occasion came during another visit by Assad in March, when he was also advised not to rely on an international conference for an imposed settlement. The second refusal was made to Syrian Defense Minister Mustapha Tlas during a visit at the end of October; on that occasion, Tlas was informed that Syria (unlike Egypt) would not be allowed to reschedule its outstanding debts for previous arms supplies, and he was strongly encouraged to curtail Syrian hostility to the PLO, especially in Lebanon.

The PLO also came in for its share of political advice during the course of the year. Much of this focused on the need for the PLO to adopt a more realistic and flexible program that took Israeli concerns into account. In April, during his visit to Moscow, Yasir Arafat was told by Gorbachev that any settlement would have to be based on a balance of interests of all parties, and he was encouraged to provide the recognition of Israel that the Soviets felt was a prerequisite to further diplomatic progress; in June, the message was repeated by Deputy Foreign Minister Vorontsov in Algiers, just prior to the Arab summit conference. In the fall, in anticipation of the upcoming Palestine National Congress session, PLO leaders were urged to refrain from taking steps, including the formation of a government-in-exile and the unilateral declaration of a state, that might have an adverse impact on Israeli and American opinion. While not all of this advice was heeded, the Soviets were obviously well informed about PLO deliberations. In a meeting in late August with the Israeli foreign minister's policy adviser, the deputy head of the Soviet Foreign Ministry's Middle East Department predicted that there would soon be an historic shift in PLO policy (an assessment which the Israeli side did not share). In any event, the more moderate posture assumed by the PNC in November, along with the failure of the Popular Front and the Democratic Front to break from the PLO, may be attributed, at least in part, to Soviet intervention.

In addition to these direct approaches, there were some developments within the Soviet Union that could be interpreted as indirect measures to reinforce the message. Perhaps the most curious of these was an October article in the Moscow newspaper *Moskovskoye Novosti* that blamed the Arabs for preventing implementation of the 1947 UN partition resolution and called for the immediate resumption of Soviet-Israel relations. This may have simply been a "trial balloon" or part of a campaign to prepare domestic Soviet opinion for a subsequent decision on ties with Israel, but it could also have been a subtle way of signaling to some Arab actors that continuing Soviet support for elements of their policy should not be taken for granted.

Notwithstanding such actions, there were clear limits to Soviet influence and to Soviet room for maneuver. There was never any indication that the Soviets had become so exuberant about their developing relations with Israel that they were prepared to stretch their ties with the Syrians and Palestinians to the breaking point. The Soviets did not endorse Syrian aspirations for "strategic parity" but they did remain committed to supporting Syria's defensive needs, at least as understood by Soviet leaders. Some new weapons systems, particularly the MiG-29, were supplied for the first time in 1988. Other forms of Soviet-Syrian military cooperation continued, including a joint naval exercise and high-level visits by Soviet military figures (most notably, the chief of the Soviet Army Chemical Weapons Development Department, who came to Syria in March). There were even reports that the Soviet military presence in Syria was enhanced through the acquisition of expanded base rights in Tartus (whatever the accuracy of these reports, the US Department of Defense acknowledged that the average number of Soviet ships in the Mediterranean on any given day declined to about 30 from 40-45 during the previous year).

Similarly, any Soviet-PLO differences that may have emerged over political strategy did not imply a Soviet willingness to abandon the PLO, or to risk being abandoned by it. The Soviets continued to endorse the basic PLO position with respect to Palestinian representation and the central focus of a settlement, and though their initial response to the PNC proceedings was not overly enthusiastic, they ultimately recognized the Palestinian state declared contrary to Soviet counsel.

Furthermore, the "erosion" in Soviet conditions for a renewal of diplomatic relations with Israel appeared to stop during Foreign Minister Shevardnadze's visit to Cairo in February 1989. Speaking to the ruling National Democratic Party of Egypt, Shevardnadze not only made further progress toward a resumption of full-scale diplomatic relations contingent on Israeli acceptance of an international conference; he also added the requirement that Israel agree to a dialogue with the PLO.

This more stringent declarative posture stood in apparent contradiction to the agreement to proceed with de facto normalization, and Shevardnadze may have felt that it was necessary to palliate Arab criticism. In any event, the statement certainly conformed with the generally apologetic tone adopted by Soviet officials regarding emerging ties with Israel. In conversations with Arab interlocutors, these officials downplayed the extent of Soviet Jewish emigration and pointed out that most Soviet Jews did not end up in Israel. They insisted that the more rapid development of relations between Israel and the Eastern European governments, especially Poland, Hungary and Bulgaria, was en-tirely the result of independent decisions by those governments (this claim, echoed by East European officials, struck many observers as somewhat disingenuous). And they stressed that the exchange of consular missions was a purely technical matter that did not necessarily foreshadow diplomatic relations. The vote against accepting Israel's credentials at the United Nations General Assembly in October, subsequently excused by the Soviet Foreign Ministry spokesman as just "tradition," was probably another element in the effort to allay Arab suspicions.

Notwithstanding this defensiveness, however, the Soviet Union was clearly attempting to move away from exclusive identification with the more radical elements in the Arab-Israel political arena. This was evident, not only from the evolution of Soviet-Israel relations, but also from the cultivation of ties with Jordan (Shevardnadze's visit to Amman in February 1989 was the first ever by a high-ranking Soviet official) and from Soviet behavior in Lebanon. There, a new ambassador attempted to promote national reconciliation by pursuing visible contacts with all factions, including those, like the Lebanese Forces, previously shunned by Soviet emissaries.

This logic also underlay the accelerating rapprochement with Egypt. During the course of 1988 and early 1989, the Soviet Union began again to supply arms and spare parts to Egypt, new Soviet cultural centers and consulates were opened, Egypt's debt to the Soviet Union was rescheduled on easy terms, and new agreements on trade, technical, and scientific cooperation were signed. Senior officials from the Communist Party Central Committee and the Soviet Foreign Ministry visited Cairo at the beginning of the year to discuss these issues, and political consultation became more visible during the May visit of the Egyptian foreign minister to Moscow. By February 1989 Egypt almost seemed to have regained its pride of place in Soviet Middle Eastern diplomacy. Not only did the Soviet foreign minister have a lengthy meeting with President Mubarak; he also found Cairo to be the most congenial place on his Middle East itinerary to host (separately) Moshe Arens and Yasir Arafat.

For many years, only the United States had been capable of carrying on this kind of nimble diplomacy based on comprehensive contacts with the actors in the Arab-Israel arena. Soviet flexibility stemming from the logic of new thinking meant that the peace process was no longer an exclusive American preserve. But the same logic also implied that the Soviet Union would no longer view the Middle East simply as an arena of competition or seek to enhance its regional status as a way to make cheap gains at the expense of the United States. Instead, there were grounds for concluding that Soviet leaders, while hardly oblivious to influence and presence as ends in themselves, were primarily interested in promoting a process for settling the Arab-Israel conflict that served the larger aims of perestroika. Continued Soviet dexterity increased the likelihood that active Soviet-American cooperation would become a central element in this process.

# 6. Palestinian Terrorism in 1988

## by Anat Kurz

This review covers three interrelated arenas of Palestinian terrorist activity: attacks originating in Israel and the Territories, cross-border assaults, and international terrorism. The nature of the Palestinian uprising and the political processes it intensified created a new frame of reference for the conduct of terrorism in all arenas. It focused upon Israel and the Administered Territories as the core of the Palestinian struggle, and related to the border and international arenas as substitutes for the limited feasibility of conducting an escalated armed struggle within. Indeed, the activities conducted in the latter arenas demonstrated the differences among Palestinian organizations regarding the use of terrorism as a means to advance their cause.

## The Political Backdrop

The volume and major features of Palestinian terrorist activity during 1988 must be considered against the backdrop of the first year of the popular uprising in the Israeli Administered Territories, and its ramifications for the Palestinian national struggle.

Palestinian organizations — rejectionists and PLO mainstream groups alike — have viewed armed struggle as an inseparable part of the comprehensive framework of the struggle itself. For the more pragmatic elements that are affiliated with the mainstream Palestine Liberation Organization, the issue has also involved the persistent dilemma of adjusting the course of terrorism to immediate and long-term political goals.

Actual engagement in or association with terrorist activity, especially attacks perpetrated in the international arena, have consistently seemed to lower the PLO's prospects for joining a Middle East political process as the representative of the Palestinian people. In addition, an explicit negation of terrorism as a mode of warfare to advance the Palestinian cause had been put forth since 1975 by the United States as one of several preconditions for the opening of direct contacts between the administration and the PLO. In December 1988, after he addressed the UN General Assembly in Geneva, Yasir Arafat recognized Israel's existence and renounced "terrorism in all forms." Had he not done so, he would have risked losing the political advantages that appeared to be inherent in the *intifada*.

The resultant official American acceptance of the PLO as a partner for a dialogue in December 1988 provided the organization with a long-desired interim gain. This development, albeit limited to the establishment of a formal procedure for the US to communicate with the PLO, was a high point in the history of the Palestinian national struggle in general, and in the *intifada* in particular.

The perceived impact of Palestinian terrorism, however, remained a constant source of concern for the leadership of the politically oriented stream of the PLO. Violent activities, carried out by Palestinian rejectionist groups and particularly by PLO member groups, have always posed a threat to the organization's international prestige. While world opinion and many governments have apparently become aware of the differences regarding precepts and tactical preferences between the PLO's mainstream and Palestinian radical groups, terrorist assaults perpetrated by any Palestinian elements could still harm Arafat's efforts to consolidate the PLO's image as a responsible partner for political negotiations.

This appeared to be true concerning Palestinian terrorism in all arenas, including Israel and the Administered Territories, and along Israel's borders. Yet incidents perpetrated in the international sphere seemed likely to be the least tolerable and most politically costly, while the negative effects of violence in the Territories proved to be minimal compared with the overall impact of the uprising, due to the legitimacy attributed in world opinion to the popular protest against the Israeli occupation.

Thus PLO spokesmen repeatedly stressed that the *intifada*, considered a legitimate course of struggle against Israel and therefore excluded from the tactics renounced by Arafat, would continue and even be expanded. "The intifada and the armed struggle against the occupation are not terrorism," said Salah Khalaf, deputy head of Fatah, in Tunis on March 25, 1989.

In fact, even infiltration attempts into Israel across the border carried out by PLO radical factions — George Habash's Popular Front for the Liberation of Palestine (PFLP) and Naif Hawatmeh's Democratic Front for the Liberation of Palestine (DFLP) — and attempted cross-border attacks by Palestinian rejectionists, appeared to pose but a minor diplomatic problem for the PLO. "The PLO is not prepared to condemn operations that any

Palestinian organization or faction undertakes," said the head of the PLO's Political Department, Farouk Kaddoumi. While this course of activity indeed reflected intra-PLO disputes, the organization's mainstream, headed by Arafat, recognizing its limited ability to control the radical factions and to maintain PLO unity at the same time, confronted the dilemma publicly by defending the border activity. In any event, the US administration appeared unlikely to rely upon formal definitions of terrorism as a pretext for halting the dialogue with the PLO. Rather, it was considerations related to the broader context of the political process that would determine the continuation and direction of the contacts.

The most acute challenge to the PLO leadership would be the inclination of radical Palestinian groups to respond to political developments regarding the Palestinian issue by carrying out blatant terrorist campaigns in the international arena. Such assaults could well jeopardize the organization's growing political prestige. International attacks perpetrated by rejectionist groups might result in growing opposition in Israel and elsewhere to a political solution involving the PLO as a partner, and might erode the PLO position within the Palestinian community if simultaneously its political orientation failed to bear fruit. Moreover, doubts would be raised, if not concerning the PLO's genuine peaceful intentions, then at least regarding its ability to control extremists and to guarantee peaceful implementation of an agreement.

## Terrorist Activity in Israel and the Administered Territories

The declared policy of the PLO leadership during the first year of the uprising was marked by self-imposed restrictions on the use of firearms by the masses. Explicit orders were issued by the PLO to the population in the Territories to refrain from the use of arms. On October 23, 1988, shortly before the Knesset elections in Israel, Arafat said: "We will continue not to use arms...," and an official PLO statement that followed a deadly petrol bomb attack against an Israeli bus in Jericho in late October stressed a denunciation of "acts of violence against civilians (on both sides)."

This attempt to maintain the insurrection within the bounds of unarmed civil resistance was mainly motivated by the wish to preserve its popular image. This would prove crucial in augmenting the political achievements gained by the PLO in the international arena. And it dovetailed with the goal of not providing Israeli authorities with a justification for quelling the *intifada* by reliance on unbridled force. Leaflets issued by the PLO-backed United National Leadership of the Uprising repeatedly stressed calls for protest, while at the same time ordering the population of the West Bank and Gaza Strip to refrain from the use of firearms. This policy still prevailed by mid-1989.

By and large, then, the disturbances inside Israel and the Territories were indeed civilian and unarmed in nature. Nevertheless the inclination toward terrorism — the actual or attempted carrying out of violent attacks against persons or property objectives against the backdrop of nationalist or political motives — dramatically increased. Tables VIII, IX and X clearly attest to an acceleration in rates of terrorist incidents perpetrated since the start of the *intifada*, compared with previous years. This trend encompassed all parts of Israel and the Territories. And while terrorist assaults perpetrated in the West Bank and Gaza Strip were initiated by local elements, activity in Israel within the Green

## Table VIII. Distribution of Terrorist Incidents by Region and Tactics

| | Small Arms | Hand Grenades | Expl. Charges | Knives, Hatchets, etc. | Sabotage | Arson | Petrol Bombs | Total |
|---|---|---|---|---|---|---|---|---|
| **West Bank** | | | | | | | | |
| 1985 | 39 | 12 | 26 | 7 | 13 | 60 | 239 | 391 |
| 1986 | 19 | 8 | 19 | 13 | 8 | 31 | 131 | 229 |
| 1987 | 6 | 9 | 37 | 9 | 9 | 59 | 230 | 359 |
| 1988 | 25 | 12 | 31 | 129 | 75 | 399 | 1170 | 1841 |
| **Jerusalem** | | | | | | | | |
| 1985 | 3 | - | 27 | 5 | - | 3 | 15 | 53 |
| 1986 | 6 | 3 | 24 | 3 | 1 | 3 | 14 | 60 |
| 1987 | 1 | 1 | 8 | 3 | - | 7 | 27 | 47 |
| 1988 | 2 | - | 8 | 5 | 3 | 100 | 122 | 240 |
| **Gaza Strip** | | | | | | | | |
| 1985 | 9 | 9 | 19 | 6 | 2 | 11 | 16 | 72 |
| 1986 | - | 12 | 6 | - | - | 6 | 45 | 69 |
| 1987 | 1 | 6 | 23 | 3 | - | 21 | 91 | 145 |
| 1988 | 5 | 7 | 52 | 12 | 1 | 43 | 316 | 436 |
| **Israel** | | | | | | | | |
| 1985 | - | - | 62 | 3 | 3 | 4 | 3 | 75 |
| 1986 | - | - | 46 | 3 | 3 | 4 | 5 | 61 |
| 1987 | - | 3 | 51 | 5 | 1 | 3 | 6 | 69 |
| 1988 | 2 | 3 | 20 | 14 | 26 | 96 | 49 | 210 |

Line primarily reflected growing militancy among Israeli Arabs, inspired by the unrest in the Territories. Correspondingly, the increased volume of Palestinian terrorist activity during 1988 resulted in growing rates of casualties, both Jewish and Arab. Note that the statistics in Table X referring to Arabs victimized by terrorist activity reflect only intra-Palestinian militancy, and do not include casualties inflicted by Jewish vigilante activity or Israeli security forces.

## Table IX.  Jewish Victims of Palestinian Terrorist Activity
### (W-wounded; K-killed)

| | Cross-border Attacks Sec. Forces | | Civilians | | Gaza Strip Sec. Forces | | Civilians | | West Bank Sec. Forces | | Civilians | | Jerusalem Sec. Forces | | Civilians | | Israel Sec. Forces | | Civilians | | Total Sec. Forces | | Missing | Total Civilians | |
|---|---|---|---|---|---|---|---|---|---|---|---|---|---|---|---|---|---|---|---|---|---|---|---|---|---|
| | W | K | W | K | W | K | W | K | W | K | W | K | W | K | W | K | W | K | W | K | W | K | | W | K |
| 1983 | - | - | - | - | - | - | - | 2 | 5 | - | 1 | 2 | - | - | 46 | 6 | 1 | - | 17 | 5 | 6 | - | | 64 | 15 |
| 1984 | - | - | - | - | 5 | - | - | - | 1 | 1 | 23 | 2 | 2 | - | 67 | 1 | 2 | 2 | 20 | 3 | 10 | 3 | | 110 | 6 |
| 1985 | 5 | - | 1 | - | 3 | - | 6 | - | 7 | 4 | 21 | 3 | 3 | - | 18 | 1 | 2 | 3 | 27 | 8 | 20 | 7 | | 73 | 12 |
| 1986 | 16 | 5 | 3 | - | 6 | - | 2 | 3 | 1 | 1 | 8 | 3 | 42 | - | 36 | 3 | 2 | 1 | 50 | 1 | 67 | 7 | 2 | 99 | 10 |
| 1987 | 7 | 6 | - | - | 2 | 2 | 8 | 2 | 2 | - | 8 | 4 | 12 | - | 6 | - | - | 2 | 17 | - | 23 | 10 | | 39 | 6 |
| 1988 | 32 | 17 | 1 | - | 8 | - | 7 | - | 12 | 3 | 39 | 10 | - | - | 14 | 1 | 2 | - | 48 | 5 | 55 | 20 | | 109 | 16 |
| Jan 1-May 31, 1989 | - | - | - | - | - | - | 1 | - | 8 | 1 | 7 | 1 | - | 1 | 3 | 2 | 1 | 2 | 3 | 1 | 2 | 4 | 1 | 14 | 4 |

This overall increase in terrorist activity evident in Israel and the Territories since the eruption of the uprising was linked with the growing use of relatively unsophisticated methods. These included petrol-bomb attacks, arson, sabotage and assaults with knives, hatchets and the like. Choice of tactic, however, could not be seen as a sole indicator of the nature of the perpetrating element or a sole means of differentiating organized from unorganized activity: stone-throwing and petrol bomb attacks, considered the most popular violent manifestations of the uprising, were quite often organized by strike-forces affiliated with known organizations. In contrast, there was no substantial increase in the use of tactics usually associated with organized activity that is based on enhanced logistical capabilities and infrastructure, e.g., bombing.

By mid-1989 radical elements by and large remained rather cautious in openly defying the PLO mainstream's strategy, and confined their opposition to total verbal rejection of political moves and gestures. Calls for escalating terrorism were issued by extreme nationalists and also by Muslim fundamentalist groups that gained prominence during the uprising, mainly in the Gaza Strip. Yet systematic association between active cells and parent organizations in most cases could not be established; as in the several years preceding the *intifada*, the major part of terrorist activity was attributed to cells not belonging to any group. Most terrorist cells whose organizational affiliation was known, however, belonged to Fatah, attesting to the brcad popular basis the organization had in the Territories. Other active organizations were the PFLP and the fundamentalist Islamic Resistance Movement (*Hamas*).

The predominance of locally organized cells was the outcome of growing unrest among the Territories' residents. The accompanying increased use of home-made or improvised arms was the result of logistical limitations. These had been considered crucial in determining the volume and characteristics of terrorist activity in Israel prior to the eruption of the *intifada*, and apparently did not undergo any radical change by mid-1989. The increase in activity of locally organized units and unaffiliated individuals was also linked to the authorities' success in constraining organizational recruiting activities. Thus, the scope and volume of terrorist activity in the Territories in 1988 apparently reflected the efforts of unaffiliated individuals and cells to exhaust all available means, against a backdrop of scarce resources and heavy security pressures imposed by Israeli authorities. Political constraints, such as those advocated by the PLO, were apparently of limited restrictive value within this context, if at all.

Threats to escalate were nevertheless also made by the PLO. These were seen as attempts to prepare a possible response to a failure to create a process that would afford the Palestinians political achievements, or as a potential retaliatory response for an Israeli crackdown in the Territories. On November 6, 1988, for example, Salah Khalaf said that the PLO was planning to escalate the "armed struggle" in the Territories in anticipation of an Israeli crackdown there following the elections. Pledges to continue the uprising, though without specifying tactics, were explicitly made by PLO spokesmen following the renunciation of terrorism by

# Table X. Arab Victims of Palestinian Terrorist Activity

### (W-wounded; K-killed)

|  | Gaza Strip | | West Bank | | Jerusalem | | Israel | | Total | |
|---|---|---|---|---|---|---|---|---|---|---|
|  | W | K | W | K | W | K | W | K | W | K |
| 1985 | 9 | - | 27 | 7 | 21 | 2 | 22 | 6 | 79 | 15 |
| 1986 | 9 | 2 | 31 | 3 | 80 | 2 | 16 | - | 136 | 7 |
| 1987 | 4 | 3 | 24 | 3 | 16 | 1 | 23 | 2 | 67 | 9 |
| 1988 | 22 | - | 71 | 9 | 17 | 1 | 59 | 3 | 169 | 13 |

Arafat in December 1988. "Our decision was and has been to continue the *intifada* until the occupier is pushed from the Territories...," said Arafat.

One may question the probable influence of a future call from the uprising's leadership to intensify violent acts, and particularly the use of arms, upon the inclination toward extremist activity. Such a policy shift would likely be associated with dynamics and events that would in any event precipitate increased militancy. Hence it would be difficult to differentiate background processes and atmosphere in the Territories, from the response to them by the *intifada*'s leadership.

## Cross-Border Palestinian Terrorism Against Israel

The Palestinian organizations' need to achieve spectacular gains, coupled with the limited feasibility of conducting terrorist campaigns within Israel, prompted them to carry out cross-border attacks against Israel. This persistent drive grew even more urgent during 1988 against the backdrop of the ongoing popular uprising in the Territories. As in the years preceding the *intifada*, most of the attempted attacks were launched from Southern Lebanon, where Palestinian organizations enjoyed a relatively high measure of freedom of action, as compared with other border arenas.

Infiltration attempts were designated to demonstrate solidarity with the residents of the West Bank and Gaza Strip. Border activity also expressed the competition among the various organizations over the leadership of the struggle, and pressures on Fatah, in this vein, were especially heavy. The PLO's self-imposed and unprecedented restrictions on the course of activity inside Israel actually intensified Fatah's need to show its devotion to the armed struggle elsewhere.

Intensified attempts to carry out cross-border attacks were already evident during the early stages of the *intifada,* and this

**Table XI.  Distribution of Infiltration Attempts and Cross-Border Attacks for the Period January 1988-April 1989, by Perpetrating Organizations\*\***

| | 1988 | | | | | | | | | | | | | 1989 | | | | |
| | Jan | Feb | Mar | Apr | May | Jun | Jul | Aug | Sep | Oct | Nov | Dec | Total | Jan | Feb | Mar | Apr | Total |
|---|---|---|---|---|---|---|---|---|---|---|---|---|---|---|---|---|---|---|
| Fatah | 1 | 2 | 2 | 1 | | | | | 1 | 1 | | | 8 | | | 1* | | 1 |
| JI | | | | | | | | | | | | | | | | 1* | | 1 |
| DFLP | | 1 | | 1 | | | | | 1 | 1 | | | 4 | | 1 | 1 | | 2 |
| PFLP-GC | | 1 | | 1 | | | | | | | | | 2 | | | 1 | | 1 |
| PFLP | | | | 1 | | 1 | | | | 1 | 1 | | 4 | | 1 | 1 | | 2 |
| PLF | | | | 1 | | | | | | 1 | | 1 | 3 | | 1 | 1 | | 2 |
| FRC | | | | 1 | | | | | | | | 1 | 2 | | | | | |
| PPSF | | | | | | | | | | | 1 | 1 | 2 | | | | 1 | 1 |
| Fatah Rebels | | | | | | | | 1 | | | | | 1 | | | 1 | | 1 |
| Hamas | | | | | | | | 1 | | | | | 1 | | | | | |
| A-Saiqa | | | | | | | | | | | 1 | | 1 | | | | | |
| Unknown | | | | | 1 | | | | | | | | 1 | | | 1 | 1 | 2 |
| TOTAL | 1 | 4 | 2 | 6 | 1 | 1 | - | 2 | 2 | 4 | 3 | 3 | 29 | - | 2* | 7* | 2 | 11* |

*Two infiltration attempts carried out in early 1989 were joint operations by more than one organization: one by Fatah/Islamic Jihad, the other by a joint PLF-PFLP team.

\*\*   Organizations surveyed:
A-Saiqa
DFLP - Democratic Front for the Liberation of Palestine
Fatah
Fatah Rebels/ Abu Musa
FRC - Fatah Revolutionary Council/ Abu Nidal
Hamas - (Gaza-based) Islamic Resistance Movement
JI - (Gaza-based) Islamic Jihad
PFLP - Popular Front for the Liberation of Palestine
PFLP-GC - PFLP/General Command
PLF - Palestine Liberation Front
PPSF - Palestinian Popular Struggle Front

trend continued in waves throughout 1988 and early 1989. In all, 29 cross-border attempts were made during 1988, compared to a total of ten recorded during 1987 and eight recorded the previous year. Three attempts to infiltrate the Israeli-Egyptian border were conducted — two by Fatah cells and one by a member of *Hamas*; only two of these involved actual attacks, including a Fatah-perpetrated barricade-hostage incident in March in the Negev. One attempt by a cell whose organizational affiliation remained unclear was intercepted at the Israeli-Jordanian border. The remaining 25 infiltration attempts were carried out from Southern Lebanon; all were foiled. Four of these were seaborne attacks, and the others were intercepted within the security zone in Southern Lebanon, or at the Israeli-Lebanese border fence.

Divided into waves, this activity clearly shows the prominent role played by PLO mainstream groups during the first half of 1988. During the period January-June, they were responsible for nine incidents, while only five were perpetrated by radical groups, operating mainly in Syrian-controlled areas in the eastern sector of Southern Lebanon. No infiltration attempt was recorded in July; from August onward, both streams shared an equal volume of activity, with seven attempts perpetrated by each. During late 1988 and the first half of 1989, the role of opposition groups within the PLO in carrying out infiltration attempts increased, while Fatah, with one apparent exception (a Sinai-Negev joint infiltration), ceased all cross-border activity.

The escalating activity of groups operating under Syrian auspices toward the end of 1988 attested to their opposition to the diplomatic moves carried out by the PLO in advance of the convening of the Palestine National Congress in Algiers, and to the further gestures made by Arafat afterward. A principal motive behind this course of activity in Southern Lebanon during the period under review apparently was a Syrian-radical Palestinian wish to strengthen extremist elements within Fatah, and to entangle Fatah in confrontations with Israel in the Security Zone or through continuation of the infiltration drive. Provoking Israeli military operations or retaliatory raids in the region would probably make it even more difficult for Fatah to refrain from action. Fatah tread a fine line in this respect. A statement allegedly made by Arafat in late November 1988 calling for a halt to attacks against Israel from Lebanon was neither officially confirmed nor denied by PLO sources.

Unlike the Syrian-sponsored Palestinian organizations that enjoyed relative freedom of movement in the Syrian-controlled areas in Southern Lebanon, Fatah was forced to coordinate its activities with local forces. Cooperation between Fatah and Hizballah that began in 1987 was intended to enhance Fatah's operational capabilities there, and several infiltration attempts, including two perpetrated in early 1988, were indeed coordinated with that organization. In late 1988, however, an accord was signed between Fatah and the Shi'ite militia Amal, formerly its bitter enemy. Fatah intended to take advantage of the agreement to strengthen its strongholds in the western and central sectors of Southern Lebanon. There, along with Amal, it would be able to lead a concerted campaign against the Israeli military presence and the SLA in the security zone. Such a course would provide it with a pretext to lower, at least temporarily, the profile of the cross-border drive.

Official Fatah statements further stressed the organization's intention to enforce its policies in the region over all Palestinian groups — particularly those of the radical Salvation Front — using the advantages accruing from the accord with Amal. Yet Fatah's ability to control its Palestinian rivals apparently remained limited. The agreement, a tactical move by the Fatah, might also afford Syria, through its links with Amal, another opportunity to influence Fatah's activity in the area.

Activities conducted by radical PLO factions in early 1989 following the renunciation of terrorism by Arafat in December 1988 in Geneva, attested to disputes within the organization regarding the scope and operational meaning of political concessions made in order to gain international recognition. During the period January-April 1989, 11 infiltration attempts into Israel were made. Five of the nine attempts that were intercepted in Southern Lebanon were carried out by factions affiliated with the PLO, yet opposing Arafat's line. The DFLP was involved in two attempts. The PFLP was also responsible for two, one of which was carried out jointly with Tal'at Ya'aqub's Palestinian Liberation Front, which was also responsible for an additional independent attempt.

Two attempts made during the first half of 1989 took place in other border arenas. One was carried out from Sinai, near Rafah, by a two-man Islamic Jihad team in association with Fatah. The other, an armed attack against an IDF patrol south of the Dead Sea, was perpetrated by a Jordanian-originated terrorist team affiliated with the Fatah splinter organization of Abu Musa.

The Southern Lebanon arena in particular was transformed by activities perpetrated by PLO radical groups — the PFLP and the DFLP — into a testing ground for the credibility of Arafat's public promise to avoid terrorism. Infiltration attempts directed by these groups threatened to demonstrate the PLO mainstream's limited control over extremist member organizations that did not consider themselves committed to Arafat's political concessions made in Geneva. George Habash, leader of the PFLP, vowed to continue the armed struggle from Lebanon. Renouncing terrorism was an effort "to call an end to the military struggle against the Zionist enemy," maintained an official PFLP statement following the interception of a PFLP infiltration attempt (conducted in cooperation with the PLF) in Southern Lebanon in early February 1989. Calling Arafat a traitor, Habash promised to step up attacks from across the border. Speaking at a news conference in Damascus on March 7, he said, "there is no resolution (by the PNC)...providing for a truce in South Lebanon between us and the Israelis."

These infiltration attempts perpetrated by PLO radical factions in early 1989 indeed embarrassed the PLO's mainstream leadership. Following a brief attempt to formulate a diplomatic reply to American pressure to practice control, the PLO leadership elected to defend this course of activity. The alternative — denouncing it — was apparently perceived as a concession bound to culminate in a split within the PLO. The organization's mainstream was evidently also reluctant to make any new far-reaching commitments that it clearly could not fulfill, since this would further damage its international prestige as well as its standing among Palestinians. Thus, to project internal consensus, an official PLO spokesman from Tunis defended infiltration attempts carried out by the PFLP and Abu al-Abbas' PLF in early 1989. The statement argued that the intercepted teams were on a military mission that did not violate Chairman Arafat's renunciation of terrorism in Geneva in December.

The Israeli-Lebanese border zone, therefore, was likely to remain active in the foreseeable future, and infiltration attempts would probably be intensified in advance of any further moves toward a negotiated settlement of the Israeli-Palestinian conflict. While the motives of rejectionist groups could be expected to remain unchanged, it would probably require a new freeze in the political process to generate greater pressure on the PLO's mainstream groups to participate in new border attacks.

## Palestinian International Terrorism

The 35 incidents carried out by Palestinian terrorists in the international arena during 1988 marked an increase in volume, compared with the previous year's total, when 13 international terrorist incidents were attributed to Palestinian elements. Yet a more remarkable feature was the recurrence of indiscriminate, mass assaults. In terms of tactics and choice of targets, these resembled the attacks that in 1986 resulted in retaliatory measures by the affected states against Syria and Libya — the primary sponsors of the perpetrating organizations. These retaliatory moves had in turn been instrumental in bringing about the low-profile that characterized international terrorist activity of Palestinian groups in the subsequent period. Now, a series of attacks perpetrated after April 1988 heralded a spectacular comeback of Palestinian radical elements to the international scene:

— On April 15, the second anniversary of the US air raid on Libya, an explosive charge went off near a club frequented by US Navy personnel in Naples, Italy. The incident, in which ten people were killed, was carried out by the Anti-Imperialist International Brigades (AIIB) — a group affiliated with the Japanese Red Army and the PFLP.

— A premature explosion in a carbomb on May 11 in Nicosia, Cyprus, apparently foiled a plan of Abu Nidal's FRC to attack the Israel Embassy there.

— Four days later, on May 15, the FRC carried out simultaneous attacks on a club (an armed assault) and a hotel lobby (where a bomb went off) in Khartoum, Sudan, Seven people, all British citizens, were killed in these incidents.

— A Greek cruiser was attacked by an FRC unit in the Aegean Sea on July 11. Eighty persons on the ship — Greek, French, Swedish and West German tourists — were injured, and nine were killed. The attack was carried out after a premature explosion that occurred a few hours earlier in a car in Athens allegedly foiled a scheme to hit a US Navy ship in Piraeus.

- The interception of a three-man FRC team on July 17 in Lima, Peru, allegedly foiled a plot to attack the Israeli, Belgian and British embassies and the American consulate there.
- Another planned operation was probably foiled when a 14-man team of Ahmed Jibril's PFLP-GC was captured in November in Frankfurt, West Germany. The team was in possession of barometric fuses and charges of the Czech-made explosive Semtex, of the types used in the December 27 explosion aboard a Pan Am airliner over England that killed 259 passengers and crew, and 11 persons on the ground.
- The organizational affiliation of the perpetrators of the Pan Am incident had not been established definitively by early 1989. Though the possible involvement of Shi'ite extremists was not ruled out, Palestinian extremists remained the prime suspects. Among those who appeared to have a motive, the PFLP-GC was still held the most probable perpetrator, due to its past record in carrying out such highly sophisticated attacks.

With the Pan Am explosion included, the PLFL-GC was responsible for three incidents perpetrated in the international arena in 1988. Seven incidents were attributed to the AIIB. The major perpetrating group, which was responsible for 12 incidents, was the FRC.

Sixteen states formed the venues for the incidents, of which 16 were carried out in the Middle East, 10 in Western Europe, five in Asia, two in Africa, one in Latin America and one in the USA.

The USA formed the most preferred target: nine incidents targeting American citizens and objectives were carried out, and an additional six were foiled. Israel was targeted in five instances, including three intercepted attempts and two minor incidents.

The 1988 spate of international terrorism was in effect one aspect of the ongoing intra-Palestinian struggle over strategy for advancing the cause, with the *intifada* as a direct pretext. The less cautious conduct of rejectionist Palestinian groups may be interpreted as a show of intent to resort to extremes in order to disrupt a process that might lead to a negotiated solution. Further attacks could be expected in advance of future political moves — with Israel, additional states involved in the process, and pragmatic Palestinians as the most likely targets.

Barring unexpected dramatic developments, PLO-affiliated groups seemed likely to refrain from association with terrorist activity in the international arena. Even before events culminated in the December 1988 pledge given by Arafat regarding the PLO attitude toward terrorism, the organization was reluctant to provide the other parties to the political process with excuses to negotiate a solution without it. These considerations apparently prevailed even in the face of what might have been perceived as direct provocations — such as the assassination, allegedly by Israeli forces, of Fatah's military chief, Khalil al-Wazir (alias Abu Jihad) in Tunis in April 1988.

However, if the political momentum were to slow down or to offer few prospects for independent PLO participation, then reaction by Fatah's radical elements might involve international terrorism. Terrorist incidents would probably be perpetrated even if unauthorized by the higher echelons of the organization, with the aim both to demonstrate the PLO's indispensability for peace talks, and of expressing Palestinian disappointment and frustration. Another cause for impatient elements associated with the PLO mainstream to activate their international terrorist infra-structure might be linked with shifts in the balance of power within the Palestinian national movement. Were, say, a new Palestinian leadership from within the Israel Administered Territories to acquire international recognition as well as growing influence among the Palestinian people at the expense of the PLO, then the more extreme elements of Fatah or the PLO as a whole might feel obliged to defend their historical position, and might conclude that they had little to lose in terms of international political credibility, by relying on international terrorism.

By mid-1989 prospects for such developments seemed remote. The political opportunities offered to the PLO as the representative of the Palestinian people appeared to be far from exhausted.

# Section B: In the Aftermath of the Iran-Iraq War

The fighting in the Persian Gulf lasted for eight years. The carnage, the cruel and ugly atrocities committed by both parties, and certainly the ceasefire of July-August 1988, had important ramifications that went far beyond their direct significance to either Iraq or Iran. There were ramifications for all countries bordering the conflict area; ramifications concerning the strategic balance between Israel and its neighbors; and there were global ramifications, first and foremost involving the two superpowers, but also projecting directly on global oil production and international oil traffic.

The second grouping of articles in this year's survey of strategic developments describes and assesses these developments. It includes:

7.  an assessment of the regional strategic implications of the war, by Dr. Efraim Karsh;
8.  a look at developments in US policy in the Persian Gulf, by Dr. Dore Gold;
9.  an assessment of Soviet policy in the Gulf, by Dr. Mark A. Heller; and
10. a review of Shi'ite terrorism in 1988, by Anat Kurz.

# 7. Regional Strategic Implications of the Iran-Iraq War

## by Efraim Karsh

## The Belligerents

The Iran-Iraq War ended in August 1988, a month before its eighth anniversary. It was a struggle over power and ideas between two mutually exclusive regimes. For Tehran, unlike Baghdad, it was also a war for absolute stakes. If the Iraqis had ever entertained thoughts of undermining the revolutionary regime in Iran, by 1988 they had long since relinquished them. In contrast, the Islamic Republic displayed an unshakable commitment to the concept of "war until victory" (which implied the overthrow of the Ba'th regime) up to the very last days of the actual fighting.

It is for this reason that Iran's announcement on July 18 of its readiness to accept Security Council Resolution 598 took the international community by surprise. After all, the announcement came only four months after the specter of a major Iranian breakthrough in Kurdistan drove the apprehensive Iraqis to employ gas on an unprecedented scale against the Kurdish town of Halabja. And yet, although surprising, the Iranian move was not a rash decision taken in a moment of despair; rather it was the culmination of a prolonged and painful process of disillusionment that had been eroding Iran's resolve at all levels for quite some time.

Judged from a short-term perspective, Iran's acceptance of a ceasefire was a reaction to the impressive chain of Iraqi military successes during the Spring and the Summer of 1988. In April 1988, after nearly six years in a defensive posture, Iraq moved to the offensive, and in 48 hours of fierce fighting (April 17-18) recaptured the Fao Peninsula that had been under Iranian occupation since February 1986. A major psychological victory for Iraq (the occupation of Fao had been Iran's most tangible territorial gain during the war), the recapture of Fao signaled a shift in the fortunes of the war. It was soon followed by other significant advances: in late May Iraq drove the Iranians out of their positions in Salamcheh (east of Basrah), and a month later dislodged them from the Majnoon Islands, held by Iran since 1985. In early July Iraq launched a major offensive in Kurdistan that resulted in the capture of several strategic heights, and in mid-July Iraq gained a modest strip of Iranian territory in the Dehloran-Mehran area in the central front.

These severe setbacks were compounded by Iran's growing difficulties in the Gulf, primarily the intensification of the American (and other western) naval presence there. For most of the war's duration, direct American involvement in the conflict had been surprisingly meager; it manifested itself in diplomatic and limited military support for the Gulf Arab states. From 1984 onward the US sought to compel Iran to accept a ceasefire by severing it from any weapons sources (Operation Staunch), but in 1985-86 Washington deviated from its own strategy and secretly sold arms to Iran in return for the release of US hostages held in Lebanon. The embarrassing exposure of the Iran-Contra Affair drove the US to more vigorous efforts to contain the war. While the most visible manifestation of this change of tack was undoubtedly the administration's agreement to reflag (and protect) 11 Kuwaiti tankers, Washington's efforts to terminate the war had a diplomatic component as well, namely, the engineering of Security Council Resolution 598 of July 1987 and the orchestration of the so-called "second resolution" which called for a UN-enforced arms embargo on Iran for its failure to abide by Resolution 598.

The American arrival in the Gulf in the summer of 1987 was viewed by Iran with the utmost alarm. It confronted Tehran with an omnipotent foe that threatened to tie its hands in the ongoing Tanker War, while leaving Iraq free to attack Iranian-bound shipping. Hence, notwithstanding a measure of muscle-flexing, Iran sought to avoid a direct confrontation with the United States and to signal its interest in deescalation. And indeed, with the exception of a brief American-Iranian exchange in September-October 1987 following the Iran Air incident, a direct collision between the two countries was avoided until April 1988. The April clash, following the holing of a US frigate by an Iranian underwater mine, could not have come at a more inopportune time for Iran: it coincided with the dislodging of Iranian forces from Fao. The result was an Iranian attempt at retaliation, and the subsequent loss of a significant portion of Iran's naval force — two (out of three) frigates.

The final straw for Iran appears to have been the (mistaken) downing of an Iranian airbus by the USS Vincennes on July 3, 1988, in which 290 Iranian civilians were killed. Whether or not the Iranians believed that the shooting of the airbus was a premeditated attack, this tragic event was apparently used by the advocates of a ceasefire (who portrayed it as part of an overall design to subdue Iran) both to divert attention from military setbacks on the Iraqi front and to mobilize widespread support for termination of the war.

But if the devastating setbacks on the battlefield and the incapacitating American presence in the Gulf constituted the immediate reasons for Iran's acceptance of a ceasefire, the roots of the decision lie in the more distant past. In fact, opposition to continuation of the war surfaced as early as mid-1982, when a loose coalition of political and military figures began to question the logic of taking the war into Iraq. Chief among this coalition were most of the military leadership, who doubted the armed forces' ability to carry out such an enterprise. The military leaders were supported in their judgment by several leading politicians, such as Prime Minister Mir-Hussein Mussavi and President Sayyed Ali Khamenei, who rejected the invasion on grounds of its high human, material and political costs.

That this skeptical view was overwhelmingly overruled could be inferred from the course of the war after the summer of 1982. However, as the edifice of Iran's morale became increasingly permeable to material and human privations, the regime could not afford to remain completely insensitive to the public mood, and the moderates became increasingly influential. In 1984, for example, they succeeded in ending the "first war of the cities" despite the opposition of the hardliners; more importantly, they brought about the reversal of the costly war strategy of human-wave attacks in favor of a more conventional and orderly tactic. The power of the moderates was further enhanced in the ensuing years by the gradual erosion of the public's sense of purpose. This was reflected in serious manifestations of discontent, such as large-scale demonstrations against the war and the government (most notably those of Spring and Summer 1985), and a significant drop in the number of volunteers from late 1984 onwards, which assumed alarming proportions in 1987 and 1988.

Yet four additional years of bloody and futile war were required for the moderates to be able to persuade Ayatollah Ruhollah Khomeini to agree to a ceasefire. And it was not before the total collapse of public morale manifested itself in the breakdown of military morale — with its consequent series of military disasters — that the aged Ayatollah became fully convinced that unless brought to a swift termination, the war would lead to the complete alienation of the Iranian people from the revolutionary regime.

Iran's acceptance of Security Council Resolution 598 was therefore no tactical matter but rather a decision of the highest strategic order: the war was brought to an end in order to preserve the very revolution that had given birth to it. Indeed, it is arguable that in announcing its readiness to end the war and enter into peace negotiations with Iraq, Iran's regional worldview had now come full circle: from the revisionist dream of shaping the Gulf along Islamic lines, to acquiescence in the regional status quo established by the Shah in 1975; from the vision of "the permanent revolution" to the notion of "Islam in one country." True, Khomeini's vision of an Islamic *umma* did not disappear from the Iranian vocabulary. But the far-reaching goal of subverting the regional order had succumbed to eight years of futile conflict, giving way to the conventional "rules of the game" to which the Islamic Republic had been so adamantly opposed.

Emerging from the war a crippled nation, Iran faced the Sisyphean task of reconstructing its devastated social, economic and military systems. The ceasefire was followed by a heated debate among the clerics whether to allow greater room for the private sector in the reconstruction effort and to accept foreign aid to this end. By and large the pragmatists, who advocated greater openness of the Iranian economy, appeared to have the upper hand over the more doctrinaire faction, although their position apparently suffered a certain setback following the Salman Rushdie affair.

No less alarming from the pragmatists' point of view was the setback in Iran's international standing following Khomeini's call in February 1989 for Rushdie's execution. Until that month, Iran's vigorous attempts to break its international isolation and return to the mainstream of international politics had met with considerable success on both the regional and the international levels. With the threat of Islamic fundamentalism apparently receding, the Arab monarchies of the Gulf, Iraq's staunchest supporters throughout the war, had begun to distance themselves from overt animosity toward Iran: in late September 1988 Kuwait reestablished diplomatic relations with Iran, and a fortnight later Bahrain and Iran agreed to upgrade diplomatic relations. Even Saudi Arabia, which severed diplomatic relations with Iran in April 1988, reacted favorably to Iranian overtures: on October 25, in response to a conciliatory statement by Speaker of the Parliament Hashemi-Rafsanjani, King Fahd ordered the state-controlled media to halt propaganda attacks on Iran.

In the international sphere Iran virtually discarded the ideological precept of "neither East nor West" which guided the revolution from its very inception, in favor of a pragmatic policy of courting both East and West. Relations with the Soviet Union, which plunged to their lowest ebb in 1983 following the suppression of the *Tudeh* Party, began warming in 1986 with the reactivation, after a six-year suspension, of the bilateral Permanent Commission for Joint Economic Cooperation. This improvement gained considerable momentum from mid-1987 onward as Iran saw in the USSR a major counterbalance to the growing US naval presence in the Gulf.

The end of hostilities also enabled Iran to mend fences with the western powers following the severe setback of 1987: diplomatic relations with France were restored in June 1988, with Canada a month later, and with Britain in December. Relations with West Germany, already warmer than with the rest of the West European powers, intensified with a visit by Hans Dietrich Genscher to Iran in November 1988. This renewed honeymoon was abruptly curtailed, however temporarily, as a result of the Rushdie affair, and by early 1989 Iran appeared to be heading toward a new collision with the West, and particularly with Britain. Yet even at this moment of mounting passions Iran did not abandon caution, and displayed a measure of restraint. Thus, for example, Khomeini's call for Rushdie's execution was paralleled by milder voices indicating possible ways for crisis aversion (e.g., a demand for Rushdie's and/or Britain's apology). Also, Iran sought to signal to the West the undesirability of confrontation by promptly warming relations with the Soviet Union, best illustrated by the cordial reception given to Soviet Foreign Minister Edward Shevarnadze on his visit to Tehran in February 1989.

In sharp contrast to Iran's subdued reaction to the ceasefire, Iraq loudly praised this development. Indeed, Baghdad's vociferous approval led not a few analysts and observers to crown Iraq as the victor of the eight-year war. At first glance, this view seems quite comprehensible: did not the ceasefire come in the wake of a

104

long chain of Iraqi successes that brought Iran to its knees? Did not Khomeini in person define the decision to stop fighting as worse than taking poison? Moreover, the war did have positive results from the standpoint of the Ba'th regime, primarily in contributing to the crystallization of Iraqi nationalism. Since the mid-1970s the Ba'th had made a sustained effort to create a new and specifically Iraqi identity out of the disparate elements of Iraq's population. Without seeking to divorce Iraq from the Arab world, it emphasized Iraq's unique Mesopotamian heritage in order to create a "new Iraqi man." This approach was pursued into the war with a fairly good measure of success, as the enormous pressure put by the Iranians on the Iraqi people reinforced its cohesiveness and created a strong sense of shared destiny.

Yet, notwithstanding the Iraqi gains — the very survival of the Ba'th regime can be considered a real achievement in view of Tehran's determination to overthrow it — Iraq undoubtedly paid a far higher price than Saddam Hussein had anticipated in 1980. The Ba'th regime might well rejoice at its alleged victory, but the real victim of the war was the Iraqi people, who bore the consequences of the ambitions of its leaders.

Hence the termination of hostilities did not necessarily augur calm on the Iraqi domestic front. As long as the war was raging, Saddam Hussein could well demand complete submission to his will by waving the frightening specter of an Iranian victory as a Sword of Damocles over the head of the Iraqi people; once the unmistakable Iranian military threat was removed in July-August 1988, Saddam could no longer hope to rely on unquestioned submission to his absolutism, but rather was doomed to continue his ceaseless fight for personal survival. It was hardly surprising, therefore, that the ceasefire was followed by the purging of several high-ranking officers who gained a measure of prestige during the war (e.g., the Commander of the Seventh Army, Lt.-General Maher Abd al-Rashid). This precautionary move, nevertheless, did not prevent a reported abortive coup against Saddam in February 1989.

This state of affairs made economic reconstruction no less crucial for the survivability of the Iraqi Ba'th regime than it was for the revolutionary regime in Tehran. Since the maintenance of an artificially high standard of living was one of the major buttresses of Iraqi morale during the war, the Ba'th would have to find adequate ways to keep the public satisfied in the postwar era, in view of an already visible diminution in Arab financial support. And since the success of Iraq's reconstruction programs would apparently be largely dependent on foreign investments, Baghdad would likely be responsive to the wishes of its potential supporters; this, in turn, was bound to inject a measure of moderation into Iraqi foreign policy.

Moreover the ending of the war, however coveted a goal of Saddam's for nearly eight years, weakened Baghdad's bargaining position on both the regional and the global levels. During the war years Iraq managed to rally international support for its cause by making skilful use of what is often called the "power of the weak," its major asset being the Gulf monarchies' fear and superpowers' reluctance to see an Iranian victory — which appeared imminent on several occasions. This situation changed drastically following the termination of hostilities. On the one hand, Iraq lost its major bargaining chip, vulnerability. On the other, it remained highly dependent on its neighbors and the two superpowers for its survival: it needed a continued substantial influx of Soviet weaponry to counter the (however latent) Iranian threat, and it required Arab and western economic aid for its ambitious reconstruction programs. Above all, the support of both East and West would be crucial for Iraq to extract a satisfactory peace agreement from Iran.

This precarious balance of weakness on both sides was likely to keep Iran and Iraq largely preoccupied with domestic affairs — the consolidation of political power, and economic, social and military reconstruction. Furthermore, the termination of the war on the basis of the 1980 status quo ante, with neither victor nor vanquished, had left the core of the conflict unresolved if not exacerbated. Certainly the eight-year war did very little to cultivate mutual trust and benevolence between the two countries, and with both regimes remaining intact, however bloodied, another conflagration could not be ruled out.

Indeed, it was the awareness of this danger that accounted, by and large, for the ensuing deadlock in the peace talks between the two countries. Fully cognizant of its fundamental geopolitical and demographic inferiority to Iran, Iraq appeared to be adamant on obtaining the widest security margins through the nullification of the 1975 Algiers Agreement. This demand was of course, unacceptable to Tehran, if only because it could not allow Baghdad to emerge from the eight-year war with such a visible gain. Hence, even if one or both parties were to deviate from their intransigence, thereby paving the way for an agreement, the mutual grim recognition that at some point in the future they might well have to fight again was likely to keep the two protagonists largely absorbed in each other. Hence they would retain a fairly high level of mobilization and maintain significant military forces along, or near, the joint border.

## Regional Implications

Viewed from a regional point of view, the ending of the war was by and large a highly positive development. Not only did Iran fail to topple the Ba'th regime and thus set in train a wave of fundamentalism throughout the Gulf, but its vision of an Islamic order was widely spurned by most Sunni fundamentalists. Only in Lebanon did Iran's version of Islamic fundamentalism appear to have left an impact, but even there it was severely constrained by domestic and external factors. It would be no exaggeration to argue that with the confinement of the revolution to Iran's boundaries the Middle Eastern state-system had withstood one of the gravest ideological challenges to its existence.

True, the victory of the status quo powers over this formidable force of revisionism was incomplete: Islamic fundamentalism was subdued but not completely eradicated. Rooted essentially in a broader third world trend of seeking refuge in religion from the alienating forces of modernization, fundamentalism did not originate in the Islamic republic, nor was it likely to die due solely to developments in Iran. However, as long as Iran adhered to a pragmatic regional course, the fundamentalist trends would remain largely controllable.

Neither was Iraq now likely to rock the edifice of Middle Eastern politics. Notwithstanding the loud voices emerging from Baghdad in the wake of the ceasefire, Iraq's aspirations for Arab and Gulf hegemony — a rather chilling vision for not a few regional actors — had been sharply constrained by the war. With the two great hegemonic powers of the Gulf interlocked for the foreseeable future in mutual suspicion and fear, the rest of the region could readily look forward to a more relaxed period.

And yet not all the countries of the Middle East unequivocally welcomed the ending of the war. Turkey, for example, had few reasons to rejoice over the ceasefire given its substantial gains from the war. In the economic sphere, a significant increase in Turkish trade with both belligerents immeasurably improved the outlook of its crisis-ridden economy. Strategically, Turkey's importance in the region, already boosted following the Iranian revolution and the consequent loss of western strategic assets there, was further enhanced by the war in general, indeed by the very thought of an Iranian victory. For Turkey, therefore, the postwar era harbored diminishing gains and new challenges.

Nor was the attitude of the Arab Gulf states toward the ceasefire one of unqualified satisfaction. True, these countries reacted to the end of hostilities with a deep sigh of relief. Given their military weakness and proximity to the theater of war, the conservative Gulf states suffered the most from the ongoing war, and would have been the first victims of either an Iranian or an Iraqi victory. Although according to the Iranian claim a victory over Baghdad was merely the first step on the road to Jerusalem, the conservative Arab monarchies feared that the Iranians would make a short "detour" in the Gulf before proceeding west toward the Holy Land. An Iraqi victory, on the other hand, unlikely as it seemed until the Spring of 1988, would have established Baghdad as the leading power in the Gulf, an equally undesirable development from the Gulf states' standpoint.

On the other hand, the postwar era entailed new risks for these countries in the economic sphere. To be sure, the ceasefire might have heralded a measure of economic relief in the sense that Gulf financial support for Iraq would probably cease, or at least be reduced sharply. However, as Iraq and Iran were likely to increase their oil quotas in order to revive their devastated economies, these "savings" for the Gulf states might well be offset by the deepening of the oil glut, and depressed prices which would ensue as a consequence of far higher Iraqi and Iranian production.

But the major loser from the ending of the war was undoubtedly Iraq's neighbor to the west, Syria. Animosity between the Syrian and Iraqi ruling Ba'th parties predated the outbreak of the Gulf War and manifested itself in mutual subversive and terrorist activities, as well as harsh propaganda campaigns; on several occasions in the mid- and late 1970s the two countries had come close to war. During the Gulf War Syria became Iran's staunchest ally, curtailing Iraq's war effort to some extent: in April 1982, for example, Syria closed its border with Iraq and cut off the flow of Iraqi oil to its Mediterranean terminal at Banias, thus temporarily reducing Iraq's expected oil revenues by $US 5 billion, and forcing Saddam Hussein to announce the imposition of economic austerity.

Even though Syrian-Iraqi relations improved somewhat in 1987-88 as a result of Jordanian and Soviet pressures, Saddam Hussein neither forgot nor forgave Syria's role during the war; once hostilities were over he stated his intention to settle the account with Damascus. However, since Saddam's high rhetoric did not blind him to strategic realities, he chose to harass Syria through an indirect approach: Lebanon. Accordingly the closing months of 1988 witnessed the evolution of substantial Iraqi support, in the form of money and arms, to the Christian Maronites who only a few years earlier had been Israel's close ally. Simultaneously, Iraq reportedly established close contacts with non-aligned Shi'ites and PLO representatives in Lebanon. While it was highly questionable whether Iraq could pose a real challenge to the Syrian position in Lebanon given Syria's immediate proximity to that country and extensive military presence there, there was little doubt that this display of Iraqi activism was most unwelcome to President Assad. (Iranian involvement in Lebanon is also described in Chapter 10, "Shi'ite Terrorism in 1988," by Anat Kurz.)

Interestingly, the Israeli reaction to the Iranian-Iraqi ceasefire was far milder than might have been expected. To be sure, by engaging two hostile states and their allies in a deadly conflict for eight years, the war had given Israel a much needed "strategic breather;" indeed, the ceasefire was followed by loud cautions that Iraq, now free of Iranian pressure, might direct its formidable military might against Israel. These voices of alarm, nevertheless, remained in a marked minority. During the last two years of the war, particularly following the Iran-Contra Affair in 1985-1986 and the impressive Iraqi chain of military successes in 1988, decisionmakers in Jerusalem were gradually driven to the assessment that the war had outlived its usefulness as far as Israeli interests were concerned; all its possible benefits had by that time been exhausted, whereas its prolongation entailed considerable risks.

In the first place, contrary to the economic dislocation occasioned by the war, the military capabilities of both belligerents (and especially those of Iraq) had become far more formidable. The Iraqi Army, for example, had increased its numbers fourfold from the beginning of the war: from 200,000 troops (12 divisions employing some 2,750 tanks) in September 1980 to some 955,000 (50 divisions and around 6,000 tanks) in late 1988. The Iraqi Air Force, during the same period, increased from 332 combat aircraft to 500. Moreover, reliance on an extensive defensive system and unquestioned material superiority had enabled Iraq from 1982 onwards to defend its territory at a relatively low direct military cost.

The Iranian Army, though incapacitated by material privations, had also improved significantly. The high command of the Imperial Army was replaced (albeit in a brutal process) by an imaginative and dedicated officer corps that gained abundant first-hand experience during lengthy years of fighting. Once arms supplies to Iran were restored in full and its two main military arms, the professional army and the Revolutionary Guards (*Pasdaran*) were incorporated into an effective unified command (this might turn out to be a less remote goal than was commonly assumed), Tehran would regain a high regional military profile. Under these circumstances, the prolongation of hostilities could hardly be expected to erode Iraqi or Iranian military power. On the contrary, a few more years of continued fighting could have only presented Israel with stronger, far more experienced and better equipped potential foes.

Another major reason for the diminution in Israel's enthusiasm for the persistence of the war was that in its latter stages, the conflict seemed to be spawning a new and dangerous Middle East arms race, involving missiles and chemical weapons, that affected the longterm Arab-Israel military balance. This, together with the twin dangers of an Iraqi victory and friction with the United States (which by that time had become anxious to see the termination of hostilities), served to reverse the conventional wisdom in Jerusalem regarding the desirability of the war's persistence.

Last but not least, the war had borne a highly positive, albeit often ignored, fruit for Israel, one that could only be maximized in the postwar era: it had apparently moderated the Iraqi position on the Arab-Israel conflict, and created a potential convergence of interests between the two countries. Prior to the war, Iraq had been one of the most vocal members of the "rejectionist front" which totally rejected Israel's right to exist. In the course of the war, as Iraq realized in the most painful way that the major threat to its existence came from Tehran rather than from Jerusalem, a gradual dissociation from its notorious rejectionist radicalism began to evolve. This was manifested in the voicing of public support, however limited, for peace negotiations between Israel and the Arabs, and in reported signals to Israel regarding Iraq's interest in establishing a tacit dialogue with that country.

Several factors reinforced this change in the Iraqi position. First, during the war Iraq drew closer than ever to the moderate bloc of pro-western Arab states, particularly Jordan, Egypt, Morocco and Saudi Arabia, and this very process exerted a moderating impact on its radical zeal. Also, the strengthening of the moderate camp implied the further isolation of Syria in the Arab world, a longstanding objective of Iraqi foreign policy. Then too, by distancing itself from the rejectionist camp Iraq hoped to kill two birds with one stone in its relations with the two superpowers: to consolidate its bilateral relations with the United States, which recovered during the war from the low ebb to which they had descended following the 1967 Six-Day War; without at the same time alienating Moscow, which unequivocally supports Israel's right to exist and would view Iraqi moderation and the consequent growing Syrian isolation as useful constraints in its persistent attempts to bring Syria into the Arab-Israeli peace process. Finally, Iraq's moderation was apparently motivated, at least in part, by its anxiety to forestall Israeli military support for Iran.

That all these factors might remain valid in the postwar era was evidenced by Baghdad's attitude to the peace initiatives of the PLO. Not only did Iraq not oppose the Algiers declarations and Arafat's statements in Geneva late in 1988, but it apparently was a major sponsor, together with Egypt, of this process: were it not for Saddam's readiness to shield the PLO from the wrath of Assad, the Palestinians' political maneuverability would have been severely constrained.

Above all, it was Iraq's acrimony toward Syria that, perhaps, constituted the major incentive for possible future Iraqi-Israeli rapprochement. For just as the Syrian-Israeli conflict improved Iraq's standing vis-a-vis Syria, so did Iraqi-Syrian hostility widen Israel's security margins. A potential arena for the evolution of cooperation, however tacit, was provided by Iraq's growing intervention in Lebanon. Indeed, in November 1988 Saddam Hussein stated his readiness to cooperate even with Israel for the "liberation of Lebanon."

Given this intricate web of considerations — Iraq's war fatigue, its growing dependence on both the moderate Arab camp and the superpowers, its ingrained hostility against Syria and above all, the continued Iranian threat — Iraq was unlikely to strive energetically to revive the "eastern front" against Israel. However, were an Arab-Israeli war to break out, Iraq could be expected to dispatch, albeit unenthusiastically, an expeditionary force (4-6 divisions) to the battlefront, as it did in previous conflicts. In addition Iraq could support the Arab war effort by launching surface-to-surface missile attacks and/or air raids against Israeli targets. Here one must take into account the possible highly improved performance of Iraqi forces after ten years of battlefield experience in the Gulf War.

If the ending of the Gulf war did not increase the likelihood of another Arab-Israeli conflagration, it certainly raised the potential level of violence in such a war, should it erupt. The Gulf War eroded several crucial thresholds and "red lines" in inter-state conflicts: it was the first conflict since World War I to witness the operational employment of gas on a fairly wide scale; and it involved the most intensive campaign against non-belligerent shipping, and perhaps the harshest attacks on population centers and economic targets, since World War II. Given the exceptionally mild international reaction to the use of chemical weapons by the Iraqis during the war (only when Iraq resorted to an extremely widespread employment of gas against its civilian Kurdish population in late 1988, several months after the war, did the United States and other states organize an effective protest), every army facing the possibility of war would now have to take into consideration that the international accords barring the use of chemical weapons in war were apparently of little binding value. This grim outlook was further compounded by a significant acceleration in the already alarming arms race in the region following the war. Of particular significance were the purchase of long-range Chinese surface-to-surface missiles by Saudi Arabia, and reliable reports that Libya and Syria were developing chemical warfare capabilities in addition to their continuing interest in procuring more surface-to-surface missiles.

## Superpower Reactions

Like most of the regional actors, the two superpowers — indeed the international community at large — welcomed the ceasefire between Iran and Iraq. Both the United States and the USSR had followed the war with grave apprehensions, but had also sought to exploit it to their benefit; both deemed the expansion of the war to be highly detrimental to their interests and neither desired to see a decisive victory by either combatant. Once things appeared to be getting out of control, both were anxious to see the war end.

This mirror-image superpower judgment of the possible implications of the war contrasted sharply with customary Soviet-American practice in regional conflicts. Unlike previous interstate wars in the post-World War II epoch (e.g., Korea, Vietnam, Arab-Israeli wars, Ethiopia-Somalia) where the two superpowers tended to adopt a "zero-sum" approach according to which a gain for one was necessarily a loss for the other, this time the conflict was viewed as a "mixed-motive game." True, elements of a zero-sum game were undoubtedly evident, as manifested by each power's anxiety to exclude the opposing power from the Gulf. These were nevertheless overshadowed by shared common interests and goals which, in turn, led to a measure of responsiveness to each other's perceived needs and even to the evolution of tacit cooperation between the two. Indeed, it is no exaggeration to argue that the two superpowers saved Iraq from total collapse and enabled it to tip the scales of war in its favor: the USSR by providing Baghdad with the necessary weapons and war materiel at critical times; the United States, by withholding from Iran any sustained supply of offensive arms. And even though Iran managed to secure alternative sources of arms with which to continue to prosecute the war, it failed to reconstruct and reorganize its forces to the extent that would enable it to prevail over Iraq.

Broadly speaking, the United States was one of the major beneficiaries of the Iran-Iraq War. If in September 1980 US relations with both Iran and Iraq were at a low ebb, the war enabled Washington to rebuild relations with Iraq, obtain a potential strategic opening, however tenuous, to Iran, and reinforce its partnership with the conservative Gulf states. And considering that the years of massive reconstruction awaiting the two protagonists would require substantial western investments and support, the prospects for the future looked rather promising. In short, a decade after its humiliating expulsion from the Gulf following the Iranian Revolution, the United States was back in the region, and well-poised to meet future events. (This topic is further developed in Chapter 8, "Developments in US Policy in the Persian Gulf," by Dore Gold.)

Nor did the eight-year war damage the USSR's regional position in any meaningful way. True, the war was one the USSR did not welcome, mainly because of the fear (which was to be fully vindicated later) that it would enable the United States to return to the Gulf. Also, the war initially eroded Soviet-Iraqi relations following Moscow's objection to Baghdad's war initiatives and its subsequent avoidance of supporting the Iraqi offensive. But it should be borne in mind that the Iraqis had never been subservient allies and had always tried to keep their distance from Moscow. And in any event, once Iraq was forced onto the defensive the USSR provided it with the necessary military backing to ward off Iranian pressure; this in turn, generated a significant improvement in Soviet-Iraqi relations. Moreover, not unlike the United States, Moscow did see in the war an opportunity to expand its relations with Iran and the Arab states of the Gulf and, no less important, to legitimize its role as a major actor in Gulf affairs. (This topic is further developed in Chapter 9, "Soviet Policy in the Gulf," by Mark A. Heller.)

# 8. Developments in US Policy in the Persian Gulf

## by Dore Gold

American military involvement in the Persian Gulf from the end of 1987 until the Iran-Iraq ceasefire in August 1988 proved to be one of the most successful applications of US force projection in the postwar period. Yet at the time the US Joint Task Force Middle East (JTFME) actually began its mission of convoying reflagged Kuwaiti tankers in July 1987, there were significant reasons for suspecting that it would ultimately prove to be problematic.

The administration could not rely on a clear consensus of support in Congress for the enlarged American role in the Gulf. Moreover, the American retreat from Lebanon no doubt affected the initial propensity of local Gulf states to take any risks of visibly assisting the American military effort: America's Arab allies in the region recalled the American disengagement from Lebanon in 1984 once US forces became embroiled in a local Middle Eastern conflict and became the victims of terrorist attack.

Yet any reluctance on the part of the Gulf states to assist the US effort would be coming at a time when Washington was increasingly aware of the need to cut the federal budget deficit. Accordingly, the US was voicing its interest in greater "burden sharing" regarding most American overseas defense responsibilities. Congressional sensitivity to this issue also related to the responsibilities that Japan and the NATO allies were expected to assume in the Gulf, given their greater dependence than the United States on Middle Eastern oil.

Indeed, the extensive American deployment in the Gulf region — by the fall of 1987 it had reached some 35 combat ships as well as a little over a dozen support vessels — was not inexpensive to maintain. The US Navy was forced to draw down the number of ships it deployed in other vital regions; by the end of 1987 it was spending about $20-30 million a month in operating expenses in the Gulf. In short, the potential for domestic and external political controversy over the Gulf mission was ever present.

Part of the reason for the success of the US Gulf mission was the continuing determination of the American military command in 1988 to respond firmly but proportionately to any Iranian challenges. Thus, after an American frigate, the USS Samuel B. Roberts, while escorting a Kuwaiti tanker, struck a newly laid Iranian mine in the central Gulf on April 14, the US carefully calibrated its retaliatory response. As in the case of the US Navy's retaliatory attacks in October 1987, when two Iranian offshore oil platforms were destroyed, it avoided responding with overwhelming firepower. Again, two offshore oil platforms were targeted; however, this time one of the platforms, Sirri, was one of Iran's main sources of oil production.

Only when the Iranians countered with attacks against a helicopter from the USS Simpson and against the USS Wainright — both of which were involved in the Sirri operation — and with a desperate naval attack against an American surface action group in the Straits of Hormuz, did the US fully engage the Iranian Navy. Six Iranian ships, including two frigates, were either sunk or disabled. Washington showed its readiness selectively to punish Iranian assaults against the US escort mission in the Gulf, and to resist all attempts to bring about an American retreat.

American determination appeared to be even more heavily underlined within two weeks of the US-Iranian naval engagements when President Reagan announced an expansion of the American naval role in the Gulf. On April 29 the US Navy was ordered to extend American naval protection from ships flying the US flag to all neutral, non-communist shipping. Previously, some critics of the president's reflagging and convoying policy, like Senate Armed Services Committee Chairman Sam Nunn (D-Ga), had noted that by restricting American protection to US-flagged ships the US might simply cause the Iranians to shift their attacks to all other Gulf shipping.

In fact, for most of 1987 the US had failed to deter Iranian attacks on non-American flagged vessels; if in 1986 there were ten Iranian attacks on Kuwaiti-bound neutral shipping, by 1987 the number had increased to about 40. Since the 11 reflagged Kuwaiti tankers carried only about one-sixth of Kuwait's oil exports, the initial limited American protection policy did not even meet the stated American goal of assuring "the unimpeded flow of oil" to the western industrial countries. The added protection of non-American neutral shipping in 1988 meant that US military policy now more closely conformed to Washington's strategic interests. It also indicated to Iran that in the face of a direct military challenge, the US was not going to curtail its military involvement.

The success of the American mission in the Gulf was not a function of American determination alone. The US Navy succeeded in maintaining its posture in the Gulf by careful planning and by fine-tuning the extent of its deployment. Instead of using the growing American commitment in 1988 to further build up the US fleet in the Gulf itself and in the northwest Indian Ocean, the Navy actually trimmed back its force posture. As noted earlier, in October 1987 the Gulf force reached a high point of 35 combat ships; successive force cutbacks were instituted throughout the first half of 1988 — 32 combat ships were deployed in January, 28 in February, and 26 by July, despite the expansion of the Navy's mission at the end of April. Thus even before the August 20 ceasefire between Iraq and Iran, the US Navy managed to slash the number of combat ships it committed to Gulf operations by some 25 percent. A little over six months after the ceasefire, in March 1989, the American naval task force in and around the Gulf stood at 20 combat ships.

The US Defense Department, moreover, constantly sought ways to streamline the Gulf command structure. During 1987 the problem of the Gulf mission being divided by two separate US unified operational commands — the US Central Command (USCENTCOM) with its Bahrain-based US Middle East Force within the Straits of Hormuz, and the carrier and battleship battle groups of the US Pacific Command (USPACOM) in the Gulf of Oman and the Indian Ocean beyond the Straits of Hormuz — had been alleviated by the unification of the two naval groupings under a single joint task force linked only to CENTCOM. In 1988 a single two-star admiral took command of a unified structure that encompassed both the forces in the Gulf and the task force as a whole.

The main exception to the American success story in the Persian Gulf during 1988 was the accidental downing, on July 3, of an Iran Air Airbus carrying 290 civilians, by an anti-aircraft missile fired from the Aegis cruiser USS Vincennes. This was followed by an attempt to explain the circumstances of the incident in terms that ultimately proved to have little basis in fact: that the airliner had been outside of the prescribed air corridor between Bandar Aḥbas and its destination in Dubai; that the airliner transmitted electronic signals generally produced by Iranian F-14s; and that the airliner was descending toward the Vincennes in an attack profile so that, having been misidentified as an F-14, it could be assumed to have "hostile intent" and therefore was a legitimate target according to the US Navy's rules of engagement in the Persian Gulf following the USS Stark tragedy.

The US Navy's report of inquiry on the incident established that the Iranian airliner was, in fact, within the civilian air corridor — though it did not strictly follow along the mid-line of the corridor as most Iran Air pilots were known to do. Due to human error, the airliner's transponder was mistakenly interpreted by the Vincennes crew as sending out the signal associated with military aircraft. Similarly, a mistaken judgment was given that the aircraft was descending when that apparently had not been the case. On the other hand, the Iranian airbus received repeated warnings which it failed to acknowledge. Moreover, it had taken off from Bandar Abbas airport just minutes after a sea battle between the Vincennes and Iranian gunboats — only a few months earlier, on April 18, Iranian fighter aircraft, using the same airport, entered a naval battle against the US Navy in support of Iranian naval forces.

In short, the airline incident could not be attributed to faulty technology or military planning. Nor did it result from the US Navy being overburdened with more extensive responsibilities, though formally the Vincennes moved into the position from which it attacked the airliner because it was coming to the aid of a non-American flagged Danish supertanker that had been under attack.

It was established that the primary cause for the tragedy was human error on the part of US personnel. Had Iran, shortly thereafter, not decided to accept UN Security Council Resolution 598 and the ceasefire in hostilities that it entailed, domestic pressure may then have built up in the US for a reassessment of America's Gulf commitments. Ironically, the Iranians themselves linked the downing of the Iran Air Airbus with their decision to stop the war, though this connection was probably established largely for internal propagandistic purposes — to help the Iranian leadership explain its policy reversal regarding the war.

Besides the Vincennes affair, several other questions stood out regarding the otherwise well-executed US naval mission in the Gulf. While American perseverance indeed corrected the damage caused to American credibility among the GCC states by the Lebanon withdrawal, and US relations with Saudi Arabia and the shaykhdoms reached unprecedented levels especially in the military-strategic sphere, it was not entirely clear whether the same degree of cooperation would continue into the post-war period. With the direct threat to their security lowered, there was little reason for the Gulf states to continue to permit the US its wartime level of access to their territories. Symbolizing the changing threat environment in this regard was the decision to withdraw four US Air Force AWACS aircraft from Saudi Arabia that had been deployed in the kingdom since the outbreak of the Iran-Iraq War in 1980. The last two of the four AWACS left Saudi Arabia on April 15, 1989.

Certainly, emerging post-war relationships between the US and each of the belligerents did not hold out much promise for the foreseeable future. While the deepening American involvement in the Gulf effectively placed the US on the side of Iraq by the time the war drew to an end, there were clear constraints on the growth of US-Iraqi relations. Iraq's widespread use of chemical weapons, especially against its own Kurdish citizenry, caused the US repeatedly to distance itself from the Iraqi regime; in September 1988 the Senate passed with an overwhelming margin the "Prevention of Genocide Act" that contained economic sanctions against Iraq in protest against its chemical attacks upon its Kurdish population. Ultimately these sanctions did not go into effect as they became tied to other legislation that was not as generally approved. Nevertheless, congressional awareness of Iraqi atrocities would cloud the development of full economic and military ties between Washington and Baghdad in the near future.

Nor was there any visible improvement in US-Iranian relations in the wake of the Iran-Iraq ceasefire. The war's end did not bring about a rapid release of American hostages held by pro-Iranian groups in Lebanon. Indeed, repeated US-Iranian confrontations at sea actually helped improve the environment for Soviet-Iranian relations. With the completion of the Soviet withdrawal from Afghanistan in February 1989, one of the major impediments to closer ties between Moscow and Teheran was removed. A vastly improved state of relations between Iran and its traditionally-feared northern neighbor was expressed in the unusually high-level visit made by the Soviet foreign minister early in the year. On the whole, then, the war's end left the US in an inferior diplomatic position to that of the USSR in both Iran and Iraq.

The reflagging and convoy mission probably left a long term impact on overall US military strategy in Southwest Asia. The operation had underlined the nature of the changing threats to US interests at the end of the 1980s in comparison to the beginning of the decade. In March 1980, when the US Department of Defense established the Rapid Deployment Joint Task Force (RDJTF), the main threat to US interests was thought to be posed on land, by Soviet divisions deployed in the southern USSR along the Iranian border. The RDJTF and its successor, USCENTCOM, planned on stopping the Soviet invasion along a line in the Zagros Mountains in southwestern Iran with rapidly deployed US ground forces.

By the end of the decade, the direct Soviet threat had diminished; it was Iran that threatened western shipping; and ultimately it was the US Navy with the support of US Air Force units in Saudi Arabia that protected America's interest in the free flow of oil. It was not surprising therefore that at the end of 1988, CENTCOM's commander in chief, General George B. Crist, announced that the US was dropping its ambitious Zagros Mountain Strategy and opting for holding a more southern line at the head of the Gulf itself, in the unlikely event of a Soviet or Iranian attack. The reduced sense of urgency concerning the Soviet threat, and its replacement with local Middle Eastern threats, would clearly shift most of the US power projection mission back to the Navy and Air Force and perhaps even allow for some cuts in the US Army's future force structure in the deficit conscious Department of Defense of the 1990s.

# 9. Soviet Policy in the Gulf

## by Mark A. Heller

If there was relatively little innovation in 1988 in Soviet policy on the Iran-Iraq War, it is only because the main elements of established policy — efforts to bring the war to a close, to cultivate good relations with both belligerents, and to resist a Pax Americana — were not inconsistent with the logic of perestroika. Unlike in the Arab-Israel conflict, the Soviets here did not have to overcome the burden of longstanding identification with one side only. On the other hand, the theater was closer and more threatening to the Soviet Union, and the American challenge (in the form of a large naval presence in the Gulf) was more pronounced. Consequently Soviet policy, though not without elements of new thinking, resembled the past more closely than in the Arab-Israel arena.

During the first half of 1988 Soviet concerns focused on two issues: implementation of UN Security Council Resolution 598 calling for a ceasefire in the war, and the large American naval buildup that took place following the reflagging of Kuwaiti tankers. The Soviets had voted for the resolution in 1987 at a time when Iraq was much more eager than Iran to stop the fighting; they were reluctant, however, to approve a follow-on resolution applying sanctions against the side — Iran — that resisted the ceasefire. In part, this posture stemmed from Soviet unwillingness to alienate Iran as completely as the Americans had done. Since the exposure of the Iran-Contra scandal in late 1986, the United States had essentially identified itself with Iraq; in an effort to regain the confidence of the Arab Gulf states, the United States had revived "Operation Staunch" (the arms embargo on Iran), had intensified its economic sanctions against Iran, and had clashed several times with Iranian forces. Soviet endorsement of sanctions now would be tantamount to supporting the American lead.

Even though this would have entailed some damage to Soviet-Iranian relations, the Soviets might have been willing to cooperate politically with the US if their offer of military cooperation — meaning a Gulf naval presence of equal status — had not been rebuffed. But the United States rejected Soviet proposals for an international or UN-sponsored flotilla in the Gulf. Instead, the naval intervention to protect maritime traffic was a unilateral

American action or, at best, a western operation (following the appearance of contingents from other NATO members). That it was motivated in large part by the desire to exclude the Soviet Union from the Gulf seemed to follow from the history of the intervention: in early 1987, the United States had initially rejected a Kuwaiti request to reflag tankers and had reversed its position only after the Soviets responded positively to a similar request. As a result, the Soviets called for the removal of all foreign naval forces from the Gulf, a position that obviously converged with Iran's strategic interest.

To avoid risking their tenuous position in Iran, the Soviets attempted to promote an end of the war through less forceful means. Soviet "even-handedness" did not stem from a more sanguine attitude about the character of the Iranian regime. If anything, domestic unrest in the Central Asian republics, often with Islamic fundamentalist overtones, meant that Iran was a more direct political threat to Soviet than to American security, and some Soviet officials complained publicly that Iranian broadcasts were having an "extremely negative influence" on the people.

Still, Iran's deteriorating military position made the prospects of an Iranian victory increasingly remote. As this primary danger receded, the Soviets apparently calculated that there was little to be gained, and much to be lost, by overt complicity in an American campaign to compel Iran to surrender. The alternative approach might secure the Soviets a privileged position in Iran and the possibility of influencing Iranian policy in more desirable directions. Indeed, there were indications in 1987 and early 1988 that such expectations were well-founded; several high-level visits took place and a number of commercial agreements were signed.

In March, however, the Soviets suffered a setback. Iraqi attacks with extended-range surface-to-surface missiles had inflicted damage and casualties in Tehran and caused considerable panic among the civilian population, and Iranian opinion assumed that the upgraded technology had been supplied by the Soviet Union. As a result, mobs stormed the Soviet Embassy in Tehran and the consulate in Isfahan, and Iranian officials and media vilified Soviet behavior, placing the Soviet Union in the same class as the United States.

This contretemps, though serious, was short-lived. Soviet protestations of innocence, along with a proposal to end attacks on civilian targets (which objectively favored Iran and was rejected by Iraq), permitted the resumption of mediation efforts. Moreover, the Soviet decision to withdraw from Afghanistan eliminated a major irritant to Soviet-Iranian relations. In July, Deputy Foreign Minister Yuli Vorontsov met with Iranian President Khamene'i and offered to hold Iran-Iraq peace talks in a Soviet "Muslim" city. Though the offer was not accepted, the visit itself signified a normalization of bilateral ties, and this process was accelerated following the ceasefire at the end of July. In November, political and economic relations were again the subject of discussions in Tehran, this time between First Deputy Foreign Minister Bessmertnykh and Parliament Speaker Rafsanjani, and by January 1989 relations had evolved to the point where Gorbachev himself received Ayatollah Khomeini's personal emissary when he came to urge Gorbachev to recognize the evident failure of communism. A month later, Shevardnadze brought Gorbachev's reply to Tehran. In the first audience granted to a visiting foreign minister by Ayatollah Khomeini, Shevardnadze defended the Soviet system as the right choice for the Soviet people. He also heard Iranian calls for cooperation against the "devilish" acts of the West and he raised the prospect of social and cultural collaboration between the two states.

This "tilt" toward Iran could have been expected to have an adverse impact on Soviet relations with Iraq and its Arab allies in the region. Indeed, Soviet spokesmen were sensitive to Arab criticism and constantly minimized their own role while highlighting the assistance given by Israel and other "agents of American imperialism" to Iran's war effort.

Nevertheless, the practical impact appears to have been minor. Iraq itself maintained a reserved attitude toward Soviet activities, but this was consistent with a long-term trend rather than a significant reorientation; for several years, Iraq had already been drifting westward in its search for foreign capital, technology and even weaponry. At the same time, as long as hostilities continued or threatened to reerupt on short notice, Iraq was far too dependent on continuing arms and spare parts supplies to risk a serious rupture with the Soviet Union.

Meanwhile, the other Arab states in the Gulf were becoming, if anything, even more receptive to new or improved relations with the Soviet Union. In July, for example, Kuwait agreed to purchase several hundred million dollars worth of Soviet military equipment, though this may just have been a show of displeasure at the US Senate's recent rejection of a proposed sale of Maverick missiles. In any event, the Soviet Union had a longstanding (and profitable) military supply relationship with Kuwait.

Since 1985, Soviet diplomacy in the Gulf had been guided by the same general goals that inspired policy elsewhere: avoid exclusive identification with "progressive" states or political forces and develop at least some ties with all parties in a given system or region. A less threatening image of the Soviet Union, coupled with diminished domestic threats from communists and other secular troublemakers, produced a more congenial environment for these objectives, and diplomatic relations were quickly established with Oman and the United Arab Emirates.

However, Saudi Arabia, the most important of the Gulf states, remained wary for several more years. Something resembling a breakthrough did not occur until 1988 and that, ironically enough, was largely due to the influence on Iran that the Soviets were presumed to have because of the "pro-Iran" policy. In February, following several Saudi ministerial visits to Moscow, the head of the Foreign Ministry's Middle East Department, Vladimir Poliakov, made the first visit of a high-ranking official to Saudi Arabia since World War II. During these meetings the Saudis urged their Soviet counterparts to apply the sanctions against Iran then under consideration. Although Soviet compliance was not forthcoming, the issue that created the incentive for sustained political contact did not pose an obstacle to expanded relations, because it became moot at the end of July when Iran decided, even without the prod of Soviet sanctions, to accept a ceasefire.

These early discussions also touched on the terms of a settlement in Afghanistan, as did a subsequent meeting in Riyadh between Deputy Foreign Minister Vorontsov and King Fahd himself. Afghanistan was a serious impediment to any Soviet demarche toward Saudi Arabia; like sanctions against Iran, it was essentially removed from the Soviet-Saudi agenda by a political development: the April 1988 Agreement that cloaked the Soviet decision to withdraw. Following completion of the Soviet withdrawal in February 1989, little else stood in the way of formal diplomatic relations. Were these to be renewed, they would symbolize the achievement of Soviet respectability and legitimacy in the Gulf.

One final dimension of Soviet involvement in this part of the

Middle East is noteworthy: the absence of any visible superpower cooperation regarding the Iran-Iraq War. Although the war was discussed in the periodic meetings between Assistant Secretary of State Richard Murphy and Vladimir Poliakov, including those held in March and August of 1988, there appears to have been little in the way of a coordinated effort to end the war or address the underlying conflict. However, the second of these meetings did address a particularly worrisome byproduct of the war: the proliferation and use in the Middle East of longer-range missiles and chemical weapons. That this was a source of common concern was already acknowledged at the Moscow Summit in June; Secretary of State Shultz and Foreign Minister Shevardnadze had agreed then that joint efforts should be made to prevent the further spread of such weapons, and the Murphy-Poliakov talks presumably dealt with the operational implications of this basic coincidence of interests. If the talks actually produced concrete decisions, these were not made public.

Nevertheless, the mere fact that an attempt was made to address this issue was an additional indication of the inclination to pursue interests and avoid dangers common to both superpowers. This inclination, which appeared to be a central feature of evolving Soviet third world policy under Gorbachev, might eventually have momentous consequences for a wide range of issues in the Middle East.

# 10. Shi'ite Terrorism in 1988

## by Anat Kurz

Shi'ite terrorism has been linked with organizations motivated by fundamentalist zealotry and inspired by Iran. Besides Iranian interests, local factors have also influenced the scope and magnitude of terrorist attacks, as well as the selection of objectives for operations. The attitudes of local and foreign forces toward the challenge put forward by Iranian-sponsored terrorism have obviously also played a dominant role.

For the purpose of this discussion, Shi'ite terrorism is divided into several spheres, relating to the different political contexts that inform its activities. These are the Southern Lebanon scene, the ongoing affair of foreign hostages held in Lebanon, the Western European arena, and terrorist activity against interests of Gulf states.

## Shi'ite Terrorist Activity in Southern Lebanon

Shi'ite terrorist activity in Lebanon in 1988 was organized under the umbrella of Hizballah, and was quite distinct from that of other groups contributing to the internal chaos in that country. Unlike Lebanese organizations and militias that fought in the name of specific ideologies and communal interests, even if supported by foreign states, Hizballah operated to a large extent as a proxy of an external power: Iran. Hizballah strove to promote Iranian interests throughout the Arab world, particularly in Lebanon, where it aimed ultimately to establish a Muslim fundamentalist state.

Massive Iranian support was crucial in making Hizballah a significant political factor in Lebanon — one that posed a threat to Amal's claim for dominance over the Shi'ite population there. During 1988, the rivalry between Hizballah and the Amal mainstream militia intensified, and Beirut and Southern Lebanon witnessed fierce battles between the two.

On May 28, 1988 some 4,500 Syrian troops were deployed in the southern suburbs of Beirut, following three weeks of clashes between Amal and Hizballah in which the latter gained the upper hand. These clashes had been preceded by Amal victories over its rival in Southern Lebanon, that led to the expulsion of Hizballah fighters from villages in the western section of that region.

These internecine clashes resulted in a decrease in the volume of Hizballah activity against the IDF and the Israeli-backed SLA (Southern Lebanese Army) in Southern Lebanon. This trend was further buttressed by the SLA's improved operational capabilities, and by IDF counter-terrorism activities aimed primarily at curbing Hizballah efforts to escalate assaults in the area, particularly against the Christian enclave in the eastern section of the security zone.

In 1987 Hizballah had intensified its drive to gain control over the region linking its strongholds in the Beqa'a Valley and in Southern Lebanon. Large-scale attacks characteristic of guerrilla warfare were carried out then against SLA positions by units of up to 150 fighters. In June and July 1988 Hizballah carried out two similar attempts to take over SLA posts. These assaults, however, were in the central sector of the security zone, and by smaller units. Both were repulsed. They were apparently part of a demonstration of force conducted by Hizballah following an unprecedented IDF raid on its strongholds in the area of Maidun in the eastern sector of the security zone in early May.

The major part of the organization's activity during 1988 involved firing and artillery shelling on SLA positions and SLA and IDF patrols. In a number of instances several posts were attacked simultaneously. The most intensive attack was conducted on February 20, when for several hours Hizballah units bombarded over a dozen SLA posts along the entire length of the security zone, from the coast to the area of Jezin.

In two instances, however, Hizballah's attacks utilized preferred tactics of the previous years. It was responsible for the August 19 explosion of a roadside charge that hit an IDF patrol on the Hardaleh Bridge inside the security zone, injuring three soldiers. Two months later, on October 19, Hizballah carried out a spectacular suicide attack against an IDF convoy north of Metula. A car laden with some 150 kg of explosives went off near the convoy, killing eight soldiers. In both cases, responsibility for the attack was claimed by the Islamic Resistance, a name used by Hizballah when operating in the region.

All told, the IDF and SLA formed the target for about 85 terrorist attacks in Southern Lebanon in 1988. Most of the incidents were armed attacks, with several bombings. About 50 percent of the total were carried out by Hizballah, which was probably also responsible for at least some of the 24 additional incidents recorded during the year whose perpetrators' organizational affiliation remained unclear. Amal, the Lebanese Communist Party, the pro-Syrian Nasserite Organization and the Lebanese National Resistance Front (FNRL) were responsible for a few incidents each.

There have been profound differences between Amal and Hizballah regarding the focus of their struggle in Southern Lebanon. Hizballah has attempted to escalate terrorist campaigns, culminating in its large-scale assaults in 1987. Amal, on the other hand, has advocated low-intensity but continuous war, to be concentrated against the SLA and IDF within the security zone so as not to provoke Israel into large-scale military retaliation or drag it into deeper involvement in the area.

Pressure exerted by Amal on Hizballah in 1988 helped bring about two shifts of focus in the latter's activity. One concerns the firing of Katyusha rockets from the security zone on the Galilee — a tactic that was not exclusive to Shi'ite militants. Though the dramatic decline in Katyusha firings may also be attributed to Israeli and SLA countermeasures and Hizballah's preoccupation with the intra-Shi'ite conflict, Amal's preventive efforts were also apparently instrumental. Thus while 28 Katyusha firings on targets within Israel were recorded in 1987, only 12 such attacks occurred the following year, and most of these caused no damage.

One apparent exception to this pattern occurred on December 29, 1988, when Katyushas were fired by Amal on the Galilee Panhandle. The firing, like many Katyusha attacks, was in retaliation for an IDF raid in Southern Lebanon: a helicopter attack on Amal headquarters in Sultaniya, following a Palestinian infiltration attempt into Israel that allegedly had been assisted by Amal extremists. A few days later Amal ordered its units to restore the previous policy of carrying out attacks within the boundaries of the security zone only. Notably, the Shi'ite elements assisting the Palestinian unit on its way to Israel belonged to the "Believers' Resistance," a pro-Iranian splinter of Amal headed by Mustafa Dirani, which started to operate independently in early 1988.

Amal's pressure on Hizballah also brought about a decline in tensions related to the presence of UNIFIL soldiers in the area. While UN troops were involved in several incidents during 1988 —

including the February 17 abduction in Tyre of Lt. Col. William Higgins, chief of the Truce Supervision Organization's Observers group (UNTSO) in Lebanon — the overall low volume of clashes with UN troops may be attributed mainly to an understanding reached in 1987 between Amal and Hizballah leaders.

Further difficulties that presumably constrained Hizballah's freedom of action in Lebanon, and particularly in Southern Lebanon, derived from the status of the organization's relations with Iran.

Factions within Hizballah differed over the extent to which they should adhere to Tehran's line. In 1988 Iran attempted to tighten its control over Hizballah following instances of alleged defiance of its policy; Tehran ordered the replacement of several Hizballah military leaders in Southern Lebanon. Iran was also confronted with difficulties concerning the hostages affair, when elements within Hizballah refused to release hostages they were holding or made demands upon Iran in return for their release, thereby interfering with Iranian intentions to fulfill international commitments it had made. Iran's mid-1988 acceptance of the ceasefire in the Gulf War reportedly lowered morale among the organization's members. Internal power struggles within the Iranian regime might also have exacerbated its relations with Hizballah.

Yet all Iranian factions presumably retained a primary interest in maintaining close links with Hizballah. Future difficulties in controlling Hizballah elements might be associated with the reduction of financial assistance granted to the organization by Iran due to the state of its economy. This in turn could cause more factionalism within Hizballah, and might result in recruiting difficulties.

Were Hizballah's operational capabilities to deteriorate, this would be focused mainly in the areas where it faced intensive military pressure by the Syrian-backed Amal. Indeed, the Syrian factor was likely to grow in importance against the backdrop of increasing friction between Hizballah and Iran. In order to maintain direct links with Hizballah on Lebanese soil, and to keep its Revolutionary Guards there, Iran has been dependent on Syria. In May 1988 Iran agreed to Syrian military moves to implement a ceasefire between Amal and Hizballah in Beirut, thus enhancing the Syrian capability of controlling Hizballah activities.

Iran's aspiration to turn Lebanon into a Muslim state has in fact challenged the Syrian claim for patronage over the country. Open antagonism between Hizballah and Syria erupted as early as 1984, and peaked in February 1987 when Syrian troops entered the Shi'ite section of West Beirut. A major motive behind that deployment, which was also allegedly one of the considerations that led Syria to enter the southern suburbs of Beirut the following year, was the issue of the western hostages held by Hizballah — the most visible and provocative feature of Shi'ite international terrorism.

## The Hostages Affair

As of the beginning of 1989, 17 foreigners were held hostage in Lebanon, 12 of whom had been abducted by Hizballah. Ten kidnapping incidents involving 15 victims were carried out in Lebanon during 1988. Hizballah carried out five of these, Abu Nidal's FRC was responsible for two, and an additional abduction was associated with both organizations. Two other kidnappings were perpetrated by the Shi'ite "Believers Resistance."

The two hostages taken in 1988, who remained in captivity in early 1989, were apparently held by Hizballah. They were an American UN officer and a Belgian citizen. Two other incidents — the abductions of a West German citizen and of two Swedish journalists mistaken for West Germans — were concluded within a short period of time, with the release of the West German citizen allegedly secured through Syrian mediation. Also during 1988 Hizballah released three French citizens held since 1985 and an Indian professor of the American College in Beirut, held since January 1987.

That no additional French hostages remained in Lebanon indicated that France and Iran appeared to have settled all significant differences. On June 16, 1988 the two countries restored diplomatic relations. Moreover, the final French-Iranian hostage-release deal reputedly comprised the repayment of the remainder of funds that Iran claimed France owed it (France denied the allegations), as well as a French promise to consider the case of jailed Fatah member Anis Naccash, and the payment of up to $30 million in ransom to Hizballah. Additional rumors alleged that France would soon begin shipping arms to Iran, via Syria, and that it would reduce arm sales to Iraq. The release in France in March 1988 of Muhammad Mujaher, a Hizballah leader apprehended there the previous year, was also probably linked to the French hostage release.

The Indian professor (with American resident alien status) was released in October 1988, shortly before elections in the US. At that time it was expected that one of the four hostage professors of the American College would be released, yet only the Indian was freed. Official Indian statements linked Syrian mediation to the move.

Syria's reported efforts to mediate the release of hostages held by Hizballah had dramatically intensified in 1986, within the framework of moves by Damascus to enhance its international prestige following that year's disclosures concerning its involvement in international terrorism. But the major benefactor of agreements concluding abduction episodes continued to be Iran, whose demands were met with concessions made by the governments involved. Iran's acceptance of the truce in the Gulf War in July 1988, and Tehran's ensuing moves to ease tensions with western countries, created high expectations for further gestures related to the hostages affair. These, however, did not materialize. By late 1988 and early 1989 there were presumably elements in Damascus, as well as among pragmatic circles within the Iranian regime, that would have liked to bring to an end a continuing crisis that appeared to have lost a great deal of its extortionate political power. Yet disputes between Tehran and the kidnappers apparently perpetuated the deadlock over the hostages. Thus while western governments were making concessions to Iran in return for the release of their abducted citizens, Iran was forced to concede to the terrorists' demands, and apparently became increasingly dependent on their good will. With the affair liable to disrupt Iranian efforts to restore international links, further pressures by Iran on Hizballah could be expected. Syria, for its part, was likely to continue playing an active role in cooperating with Iran to secure the release of hostages, for the sake of its own Lebanese interests as well as its international concerns.

The decrease in the volume and international impact of the Shi'ite kidnapping campaign against foreigners in Lebanon in 1988 reflected a more general reduction in Shi'ite international terrorism. Whereas Iranian agents and Iranian-sponsored terrorists were responsible for 54 incidents perpetrated in the international arena during 1987, only 30 attacks were recorded in 1988, including 13 in Lebanon.

# Western Europe

Western Europe was the site of three incidents. Two minor attacks, apparently perpetrated by Shi'ite militants, targeted Jewish objectives in Denmark and in West Germany. Another, also carried out in West Germany, targeted a Saudi objective.

The Shi'ite terrorist infrastructure in Western Europe had apparently been weakened by the uncovering of Hizballah cells and the interceptions of planned attacks in Britain, Italy, France and West Germany during 1987. Western European governments and security agencies took a firm stand in combatting the Iranian-inspired terrorist drive. The reduction in terrorist activity that followed, however, was also associated with Tehran's desire to prevent further deterioration of its links with the West, and to avoid another affair like the 1987 "war of the embassies" involving Tehran and Paris. The broadening of the geographical scope of the Shi'ite terrorist infrastructure to the Far East and Africa (see below) in 1988 may therefore be related to self-imposed restrictions on activities on Western European soil.

# The Gulf States

The Gulf states, with their pro-Iraqi stance during the Iran-Iraq War, remained a preferred target for Iranian-sponsored insurgency and Shi'ite terrorism. During 1988 Saudi Arabia, which severed its ties with Iran in April, was the most frequent target for assaults perpetrated by Iranian agents and Hizballah. The Saudi ambassador to Ankara was assassinated by Hizballah on October 25, and Saudi diplomats were assaulted and injured in Lagos, Nigeria in March, apparently by Iranian agents. Other incidents targeting Saudi missions and facilities took place in West Germany, Turkey, Kuwait and Pakistan.

The most spectacular attack perpetrated by Hizballah within the context of the Shi'ite campaign against Gulf states was the April 1988 hijacking of a Kuwaiti airliner. The plane was commandeered while on a flight from Bangkok to Kuwait. It landed in Algiers after stopovers in Iran and Cyprus. The hijackers demanded the release of 17 Shi'ite terrorists imprisoned in Kuwait — a demand consistently raised as a precondition for the release of persons held hostage by Hizballah. The episode lasted for 15 days, during which two of the 112 passengers aboard were killed. When it was over, the hijackers left for Libya and from there were flown to Beirut. Kuwait, however, maintained its policy of no concession to terrorist demands, and apparently did not commute the sentences of the jailed Shi'ite terrorists.

The operation was allegedly directed by extremists in Tehran, who sought to heighten tensions in the Gulf in advance of Iran's parliamentary elections. An offer of political refuge in return for the release of the hostages, made to the hijackers by Speaker of Parliament Rafsanjani, presumably reflected the desire of the more pragmatic faction in Tehran to terminate the affair. Yet even the granting of asylum would have attested to Iran's involvement in the case.

Terrorist warfare, along with other forms of insurgency, remained a principal method employed by Iran to advance its regional interests and its commitment to export the Islamic revolution in 1988. The relative reduction in activity evident during 1988 and early 1989, including that aimed at destabilizing Arab regimes in the Gulf, appeared to reflect short term political considerations, and particularly the truce in the war and the political situation inside Iran.

There are two exceptions to this trend: one quite clear, the other a matter of speculation. First, in February 1989 ideological zealotry once again proved to play a key role in directing Iranian international policies. The publication in Britain of *The Satanic Verses* by Salman Rushdie generated a call by Khomeini to execute the author of the book. The affair created an international furor and temporarily halted the process of rehabilitating Iranian links with the West. Secondly, the perception of a relatively low profile of terrorist activity by Shi'ite elements in the international arena in 1988 would be changed radically, were allegations linking Iran to the explosion of a Pan Am airliner in December 1988 over Scotland to be confirmed.

In any event, in early 1989 it seemed likely that the future course of Iranian-inspired international terrorism would be associated primarily with the outcome of the power struggle within the regime in Tehran between pragmatic factions advocating rapprochement with the West, and the militant, more ideologically oriented stream.

# PART II

# REGIONAL
# MILITARY FORCES

## Introductory Note

In Parts II and III the definition of high quality tanks includes the following tanks (mentioned in the text): T-72/improved T-72; Chieftain in Jordan and Oman (but not Chieftain Mk.5 in Iran and Kuwait); M-60 A3; Merkava. Similarly, the high quality interceptors include F-14, F-15 and MiG-25. High quality strike and multi-role aircraft include F-16, Mirage 2000, Tornado, MiG-29 and Su-24. Short range SAMs include all models which normally fulfill the task of providing air defense to ground forces, though the same weapons system may also be part of the Air Force or Air Defense Force. As in previous years, defense expenditure figures include foreign military grants; numbers of weapons systems mentioned include systems in service and in storage; and bombers are included in numbers of total combat aircraft.

## Acknowledgements

In addition to my colleagues at JCSS, I wish to thank a number of persons for their comments and assistance during the process of collecting and collating the data for Part II: Ofra Bengio, Uzi Rabi and Yehudit Ronen of the Dayan Center for Middle Eastern and African Studies, Tel Aviv University; and JCSS researchers and research assistants whose aid was particularly valuable--Ariel Merari, Anat Kurz, David Tal, Ehud Kadim, Sofia Kotzer, Yael Traiber, Orit Zilka, Maskit Burgin, Heda Rechnitz-Kijner, and especially Tamar Polani, Orly Geva, and Michal Harel.

Daniel Leshem, who served as principal research assistant to the JCSS Military Balance Project, deserves a very special word of praise and thanks.

Withal, I alone bear responsibility for any inaccuracies.

Z.E.

# 1. ALGERIA

BASIC DATA
  Official Name of State: Democratic and Popular Republic  of
    Algeria
  Head of State:  President  Chadli  Benjedid  (also  Supreme
    Commander of the Armed Forces and Defense Minister)
  Prime Minister: Kasdi Merbah
  Chief of General Staff: Brigadier General Khalid Nezzar
  Commander of the Ground Forces:  Brigadier  General  Lamine
    Zeroual (also Deputy Chief of the General Staff)
  Commander of the Air Force and Air Defense Forces:  Colonel
    Muhammad al-Mukhtar Bouteimine
  Commander of the Navy: Commodore Abd al-Majid Targhit
  Area: 2,460,500 sq. km.
  Population:                                    23,100,000
    ethnic subdivision:
      Arabs                    18,134,000           78.5%
      Berbers                   4,481,000           19.4%
      Europeans                   231,000            1.0%
      Unknown                     254,000            1.1%
    religious subdivision:
      Sunni Muslims            22,869,000           99.0%
      Christians and Jews         231,000            1.0%
  GDP:
    1984--$52.2 billion
    1985--$57.5 billion
  Balance of Payments (goods, services & unilateral  transfer
    payments):
    year    income          expenditure          balance
    1985    $13.96 bil.     $12.94 bil.       +$1.02 bil.
    1986    $ 9.64 bil.     $11.87 bil.       -$2.23 bil.
  Defense Expenditure:
    1986--$1.1 billion
    1987--$1.2 billion
  Foreign Military Aid Received:
    financial aid from:
      USA--$50,000 grant (financing of military education and
      training)
    military training:
      foreign   advisors/instructors   from--Bulgaria;   Cuba
        (unconfirmed); GDR, Pakistan, USSR (1000)
      trainees   abroad   in--Britain   (pilots   for   civilian
        aircraft),  Egypt  (unconfirmed),   France,   Tunisia
        (exchange of trainees), USSR
    arms transfers from:
      Brazil (ARVs); Britain ( radars, target drones); Canada
        (aircraft  training  simulators);   France   (helicopters,

137

ARVs, ATGMs); Italy (engines for Soviet helicopters); Netherlands (transport aircraft); PRC (combat aircraft); USA (air traffic control equipment, radars); USSR (tanks, combat aircraft, missile corvettes, submarines, ASW vessel, SAMs)
Foreign Military Aid Extended:
    financial aid to:
        PLO--grant
    military training:
        advisors/instructors in--Kuwait; POLISARIO
        foreign trainees from--ETA (Spanish Basque separatists); Kuwait; Moroccan anti-government groups (unconfirmed); PLO-affiliated organizations; POLISARIO; Tunisia (part of an exchange program); Amal Lebanese militia
    arms transfers to:
        Burkina Faso (Soviet-made fighter aircraft); POLISARIO
    facilities provided to:
        Palestinian organizations (training camps); Chad anti-government groups (camps); POLISARIO (training, camps and operational facilities)
Cooperation in Arms Production/Assembly with:
    Britain (naval vessels); Italy and Tunisia (diesel engines); France (trucks); Czechoslovakia (light transport aircraft)

INFRASTRUCTURE
    Road Network:
        length:                                          80,000 km
            paved roads                                  60,000 km
            gravel, crushed stone and
                earth tracks                             20,000 km
        main routes:
        Algiers--Oran
        Algiers--Sidi-bel-Abbes
        Oran--Oujda (Morocco)
        Sidi-bel-Abbes--Bechar--Tindouf--Atar (Mauritania)
        Bechar--Adrar--Gao (Mali)
        Algiers--Laghouat--Tamenghest    (Tamanrasset)--Agadez
            (Niger)
        Algiers--Setif--Constantine
        Constantine--Biskra--Touggourt
        Constantine--Tebessa--Sousse (Tunisia)
        Algiers--Annaba--Tunis (Tunisia)
        Annaba--Tlemcen
    Railway Network:
        length:                                           3,890 km
            standard gauge                                2,632 km
            narrow gauge                                  1,258 km

# ALGERIA

main routes:
  Algiers--Mostaganem--Oran
  Mostaganem--Sidi-bel-Abbes--Bechar--Kenadsa
  Sidi-bel-Abbes--Oujda (Morocco)
  Algiers--Constantine--Annaba--Tunis
  Algiers--Laghouat
  Constantine--Biskra--Touggourt
  Annaba--Tebessa--Tunis

Airfields:    145
  airfields by runway type:
    permanent surface airfields    54
    unpaved fields and usable airstrips    91
  airfields by runway length:
    2440--3659 meters    29
    1220--2439    73
    under 1220    43
  international airports: Algiers, Annaba, Constantine, Oran
  major domestic airfields:
    operational--Adrar, In Amenas, Bechar, Biskra, Borj Omar Driss, Ghardaia, El Golea, Laghouat, Ouargla, El Oued, Illizi, In Salah, Tamenghest, Timimoun, Tindouf, Touggourt
    under construction--Ayn Guezzem, Batna, Bordj Bajdi Mokhtar, Setif

Airlines:
  companies: Air Algerie (international and domestic);
  aircraft:
    Airbus A-310-200    2
    Boeing 737-200/737-200C    13
    Boeing 727-200    10
    Fokker F-27/F-27-400M/F-27-600    8
    Lockheed L-100-30    3

Maritime Facilities:
  harbors--Algiers, Annaba, Arziw, Bejaia, Beni Saf, Ghazaouet, Mostaganem, Oran (Wahran), Skikda (Philippeville)
  anchorages--Cherchell, Collo, Dellys, Jijel, Nemours, Tenes (Port Breira)
  oil terminals--Algiers, Annaba, Arzew, Bejaia, Oran, Skikda

Merchant Marine:

| vessel type | number | DWT |
|---|---|---|
| LPG carrier | 2 | 11,361 |
| products tanker | 6 | 155,199 |
| LNG carrier | 6 | 353,506 |
| general cargo | 13 | 155,954 |
| tanker | 6 | 24,831 |
| bulk carrier | 4 | 93,500 |
| ro/ro | 12 | 37,244 |

139

| | | |
|---|---|---|
| bunkering tanker | 5 | 11,241 |
| ferry | 5 | 11,487 |
| general cargo/container | 14 | 104,344 |
| chemical tanker | 2 | 9,150 |
| TOTAL | 75 | 967,817 |

Defense Production:
  army equipment:
    production under license--diesel engines (with Italy and Tunisia); trucks (in collaboration with France)
  air force equipment:
    production under license--Czech ten-passenger transport aircraft and four passenger light aircraft
  ships:
    tugs constructed; landing craft & gunboats under construction (under license from Britain) at Mers el Kebir

ARMED FORCES
  Personnel:
    military forces--

| | regular | reserves | total |
|---|---|---|---|
| army | 170,000 | 150,000 | 320,000 |
| air force | 12,000 | - | 12,000 |
| navy | 8,000 | - | 8,000 |
| TOTAL | 190,000 | 150,000 | 340,000 |

  para-military forces--

| | |
|---|---|
| gendarmerie | 30,000 |

Army:
  major units:

| unit type | brigades | independent battalions |
|---|---|---|
| armored/tank | 4 | 3 |
| infantry, mechanized & motorized infantry | 16 | 28 |
| airborne/special forces | 1 | 4 |
| TOTAL | 21 | 35 |

  small arms:
    personal weapons--
      9mm MAT 49 SMG
      9mm Vigneron SMG
      9mm Uzi SMG
      7.62mm AK-47 (Kalashnikov) AR
      7.62mm AKM AR
      7.62mm SKS (Simonov) SAR
    machine guns--
      14.5mm ZPU 14.5x4 HMG (employed in anti-aircraft role)
      12.7mm D.Sh.K. 38/46 (Degtyarev) HMG
      7.62mm SG-43/SGM (Goryunov) MMG
      7.62mm RPD (Degtyarev) LMG

```
   7.62mm PK/PKS (Kalashnikov) LMG
   7.62mm (0.3") BAR LMG
  light and medium mortars--
   82mm M-43
  light ATRLS--
   RPG-7
tanks:
  model                                     number
   high quality
    T-72                                      150
   medium quality
    T-62                                      200
    T-55                                  335-350
                          (sub-total   535-550)
   low quality
    AMX-13                                     50
    T-54                                      150
                          (sub-total     200)
  TOTAL                                   885-900
APCs/ARVs:
  model                                     number
   high quality
    BMP-2 (number unconfirmed)               150
    BMP-1                                     650
    Engesa EE-9        (unconfirmed)          50
                          (sub-total      850)
   others
    AML-60                                     50
    BRDM-2                                    150
    BTR-40/50/60                             600
    BTR-152                                  100
    M-3 (Panhard)                             50
                          (sub-total      950)
  TOTAL                                      1800
```

```
artillery:
  self propelled guns and howitzers--      number
   122mm M-1974 SP howitzer                  70
   122mm ISU SP gun
   100mm SU-100 SP
  towed guns and howitzers--
   152mm howitzer                            50
   130mm howitzer
   122mm D-30 howitzer                      100
   122mm M-1938 howitzer                     40
   85 mm M-1945/D-44 field/ AT gun
  mortars, over 160mm--
   160mm M-43 mortar                          +
  mortars, under 160mm, but excluding light and
   medium--
```

```
    120mm M-43 mortar
    TOTAL                                                    500
  MRLs--
    240mm BM-24                                              20
    140mm BM-14-16                                           20
    122mm BM-21                                              60
    TOTAL                            (unconfirmed)          100
anti-tank weapons:
  missiles--
    AT-1 (Snapper)
    AT-3 (Sagger)
    AT-4 (Spigot)
    AT-5 (Spandrel; unconfirmed)
    AT-6 (Spiral)
    BRDM-2 carrying AT-3 (Sagger) SP
    MILAN
  guns--
    85mm M-1945/D-44 field/AT gun
    76mm AT gun
    107mm B-11 recoilless rifle (unconfirmed)
surface-to-surface missiles and rockets:
  model                                               launchers
    FROG-7
    FROG-4
    TOTAL                                                    25
army anti-aircraft defenses:
  missiles--                                          launchers
    SA-6  (Gainful)                                          18
    SA-7  (Grail)
    SA-8  (Gecko)
    SA-9  (Gaskin)                                          10
    SA-13 (Gopher, unconfirmed)
    SA-14 (Gremlin, unconfirmed)
  short-range guns--
    57mm ZSU 57x2 SP
    23mm ZSU 23x4 SP (Gun Dish)                            130
    23mm ZU 23x2
    57mm M-1950 (S-60)
    37mm M-1939
Air Force:
  aircraft--general:                                    number
    combat aircraft                                        341
    transport aircraft                                      55
    helicopters                                            128
  combat aircraft:
    interceptors--
      high quality
        MiG-25 A/B/U (Foxbat)                               26
      others
        MiG-21 MF/bis/U (Fishbed)                          115
```

```
Total                                               141
strike and multi-role aircraft--
   medium quality
      MiG-23/27 (Flogger B/D);
      MiG-23MF (Flogger G, unconfirmed)              70
      Su-17/20 (Fitter C)                            30
                              (sub-total        100)
   others
      MiG-17 (Fresco), MiG-15
         and F-4 Shenyang                            80
      Su-7 BM/U (Fitter A)                           20
                              (sub-total        100)
   Total                                            200
transport aircraft:
   An-12 (Cub)                                         6
   An-24 (Coke)/An-26(Curl)(possibly civilian a/c)  a few
   Beechcraft Queen Air                               5
   Beechcraft King Air                                2
   Beechcraft Super King Air T-200T
      (employed in maritime patrol role)             6
   C-130H & C-130H-30 Hercules                       17
   Fokker F-27 Mk 400/Mk 600
      (employed in maritime patrol role)             3
   Gulfstream III                                     3
   IL-76 (Candid)                                     4
   IL-18 (Coot)                                       4
   IL-14 (Crate)                                      4
   Mystere Falcon 20                                  1
   TOTAL                                             55
training and liaison aircraft:
   Beechcraft T-34C (Turbo Mentor)                    6
   CM-170 Fouga Magister                             20
   L-39 Albatross                                    16
   Yak-11 (Moose)                                    16
   TOTAL                                             58
on order: 16 L-39 Albatross
helicopters:
   attack--
      Mi-24/Mi-25 (Hind)                             37
   heavy transport--
      Mi-6 (Hook)                                    10
   medium transport--
      Mi-4 (Hound)                                   30
      Mi-8/Mi-17 (Hip)                               40
      SA-330 Puma                                     5
                              (sub-total         75)
   light transport--
      Alouette II/III                                 6
   TOTAL                                            128
   on order: French helicopters
```

```
advanced armament:
  air-to-air missiles--
    AA-2 (Atoll)
    AA-6 (Acrid, unconfirmed)
    AA-7 (Apex, unconfirmed)
anti-aircraft defenses:
  long-range missiles--
    model                                    batteries
      SA-2 (Guideline)/SA-3 (Goa)                  41
  long-range guns--
    100mm
    85mm
military airfields:                                  7
  Algiers,  Bechar,  Biskra,  Boufarik,  Oran,  Ouargla,
  Tindouf
aircraft maintenance and repair capability:
  for all models
```

Navy:
```
  combat vessels:                              number
    submarines--
      K class (Kilo)                               2
      R class (Romeo)                              2
      TOTAL                                        4
    MFPBs--
      Ossa I                                       2
      Ossa II                                     10
      Total                                       12
    missile corvettes
      Nanuchka II class/Bulgarian-Algerian Nanuchka  4
    ASW vessels--
      Koni class frigate                           3
      SO-1 large patrol craft                      6
      Total                                        9
    mine warfare vessels--
      T-43 class minesweeper                     1-2
    gunboats/MTBs--
      Kebir class (Brooke Marine)                  6
    patrol craft--
      Baglietto Mangusta                           6
      Baglietto 20 GC  (possibly
        with Coast Guard)                         10
      P-802 (possibly with customs service)        2
      P-1200 (possibly with customs service)       3
      Zhuk class                                   1
      Total                                       22
    on order: 3 Kebir class
  landing craft:
    Polnochny class LCT                            1
    Brooke Marine 2,200 ton LSL                    2
    Total                                          3
```

auxiliary vessels:
| | |
|---|---|
| armed fishing | 6 |
| Niryat diving tender | 1 |
| Poluchat I class torpedo collecting | 1 |
| tankers | 4 |

on order: one 180 ton research vessel from the
  Netherlands
advanced armament:
  surface-to-surface missiles--
  SS-N-2 Styx
  surface-to-air missiles--
  SA-N-4

naval bases:                                                    3
  Algiers, Annaba, Mers el Kebir
ship maintenance and repair capability:
  3 slipways belonging to Chantier Naval de Mers el Kebir
  at Oran; 4 x 4,000-ton dry docks at Algiers; small
  graving dock at Annaba; small dry dock at Beni Saf.

# 2. BAHRAIN

BASIC DATA
Official Name of State: State of Bahrain
Head of State: Emir Isa ibn Salman al-Khalifa
Prime Minister: Khalifa ibn Salman al-Khalifa
Minister of Defense: Major General Khalifa ibn Ahmad al-Khalifa (also Deputy Commander in Chief of the Armed Forces)
Commander in chief of the Armed Forces: Shaykh Hamed ibn Isa al-Khalifa (also heir apparent)
Chief of the General Staff: Brigadier General Abdullah ibn Salman al-Khalifa
Commander of the Air Force: Major Mohanna Fadel al-Naime
Commander of the Navy: Brigadier General Khalil al-Rahman (Pakistani)
Area: 676 sq.km. (estimate, including 32 small islands)
Population:                                                   430,000

| ethnic subdivision: | | |
|---|---|---|
| Arabs | 314,000 | 73.0% |
| Persians | 39,000 | 9.0% |
| Southeast Asians, Europeans | 77,000 | 18.0% |
| religious subdivision: | | |
| Shi'ite Muslims | 301,000 | 70.0% |
| Sunni Muslims | 129,000 | 30.0% |
| nationality subdivision: | | |
| Bahrainis | 271,000 | 63.0% |
| Alien Arabs | 43,000 | 10.0% |
| Alien non-Arabs | | |
| Southeast Asians | 56,000 | 13.0% |
| Iranians | 34,000 | 8.0% |
| Others | 27,000 | 6.0% |

GDP:
1985--$4.5 billion (estimate)
Balance of Payments (goods, services & unilateral transfer payments):

| year | income | expenditure | balance |
|---|---|---|---|
| 1986 | $3.33 bil. | $3.34 bil. | -$ 10 mil. |
| 1987 | $3.30 bil. | $3.62 bil. | -$320 mil. |

Defense Expenditure:
1986--$134.8 million
1987--$137.5 million (unconfirmed)
Foreign Military Aid Received:
military training:
foreign advisors/instructors/serving personnel from--Britain, Egypt, France, Jordan, Pakistan, USA
trainees abroad in--Britain, France, Egypt, Jordan, Saudi Arabia, USA
arms transfers from:
Britain (patrol craft, trucks); France (ARVs); FRG

(MFPBs, helicopters); Italy (helicopters); Sweden
(SAMs, via Singapore); USA (ATGMs, combat aircraft,
helicopters, tanks)
Foreign Military Aid Extended:
  financial aid to:
    Syria, Palestinian military organizations
  facilities provided to:
    USA (naval facilities & intelligence installations)
  forces deployed abroad in:
    Saudi Arabia (part of GCC rapid deployment force)
Joint Maneuvers with:
  GCC (members: Bahrain, Kuwait, Oman, Qatar, Saudi Arabia,
  UAE)

INFRASTRUCTURE
  Road Network:
    length:                                          475 km
      paved roads                                    250 km
      earth tracks                                   225 km
    main routes:
      al-Manamah--Muharraq (airport)
      al-Manamah--Sitrah (oil terminal)
      al-Manamah--Budaiyah
      al-Manamah--Isa Town--Awali
      al-Manamah--Dhahran ( Saudi Arabia ); 25 km bridge
        causeway
      Awali--al-Zallaq
      Awali--Ras al-Yaman
  Airfields:                                              2
    airfields by runway type:
      permanent surface field                            1
      unpaved field                                      1
    airfields by runway length:
      over 3660 meters                                   1
      1220--2439                                         1
    international airport: Bahrain (Muharraq)
  Airlines:
    companies:
      Gulf Air (international)--jointly owned by Bahrain,
      Oman, UAE and Qatar, with headquarters in Bahrain
    aircraft:
      Boeing 767-300ER                                   2
      Boeing 737-200                                     8
      Lockheed L-1011-200 Tristar                        3
      Lockheed L-1011-100 Tristar                        5
      Lockheed L-1011-1 Tristar                          3
      on order: 4 Boeing 767-300ER (delivery mid-1989)
  Maritime Facilities:
    harbors--Mina Sulman; Sitrah (ALBA aluminum terminal);
    Mina Manamah

```
    oil terminal--Sitrah
  Merchant Marine:
    vessel type                      number                    DWT
      bulk carrier                      1                   20,003

ARMED FORCES
  Personnel:
    military forces--
      army                                                     2300
      air force                                                 200
      navy                                                      700
      TOTAL                                                    3200
  Army:
    major units:
      unit type      brigade      battalion        independent
                                                       company
        mechanized        1              1
        armored                                            1
        TOTAL             1              1                  1
    small arms:
      personal weapons--
        9mm Model 12 Beretta SMG
      machine guns--
      light and medium mortars--
        81mm L-16 A1
    Tanks:
      model                                                number
        high quality
          M-60 A3                                              54
    APCs/ARVs:
      model                                                number
        others
          M-3 (Panhard)                                        90
          AML-90
          AT-105 Saxon
          Ferret
          Saladin
        TOTAL                                                 200
    artillery:
      towed guns and howitzers--
        105mm howitzer                                          8
      on order: 155mm M-198 A1 howitzer
    anti-tank weapons:
      missiles--                                         launchers
        BGM-71C Improved TOW                                   60
      guns--
        120mm BAT L-4 recoilless rifle
    army anti-aircraft defenses:
      missiles--                                         launchers
        FIM-92A Stinger (unconfirmed)                          70
```

```
        RBS-70                                        40-50
        on order: FIM-92A Stinger SAM
Air Force:
   aircraft--general:
      combat aircraft                                    12
      transport aircraft                                  1
      helicopters                                     24-25
   combat aircraft:
      strike and multi-role aircraft--
         medium and low quality
         F-5E/F                                          12
         on order: 16 F-16C/D
   transport aircraft:
      Gulfstream II                                       1
   helicopters:                                      number
      maritime attack--
         AS-365 Dauphin                                 1-2
      medium transport--
         AB-212                                          10
         Bell 412                                         2
                              (sub-total               12)
      light transport--
         500 MG                                           2
         MBB BO-105                                       9
                              (sub-total               11)
      TOTAL                                           24-25
   advanced armament:
      air-to-air missiles--
      AIM-9 Sidewinder
   military airfields:                                    1
      Muharraq; a second AFB is under construction at Suman
   anti-aircraft defenses:
      on order: MIM-23B Improved HAWK SAMs; Cossor  SSR  and
         Plessey  Watchman  air  traffic  control  radars  for
         civilian and military use
Navy:
   combat vessels:                                   number
      MFPBs--
         Lurssen TNC-45                                   4
      missile corvettes--
         Lurssen 62 meter                                2
      gunboats/MTBs--
         Lurssen FPB-38 gunboat                           2
      patrol craft--
         Cheverton 50 ft. (15.3 meter)                   1
         Cheverton 27 ft. (8.2 meter)                    3
         Tracker                                          3
         Fairey Marine Sword                             4
         Swift FPB-20                                     2
         Wasp 30 meter                                    1
```

|                                       |    |
|---------------------------------------|----|
| Wasp 20 meter                         | 2  |
| Wasp 11 meter                         | 3  |
| Total                                 | 19 |

landing craft:

|                                       |    |
|---------------------------------------|----|
| 150 ton Fairey Marine LCM             | 1  |
| Tropmire Ltd. hovercraft              | 1  |
| Loadmaster 60 ft. (18 meter) LCU      | 1  |
| Swiftships 390 ton LCU                | 1  |
| Total                                 | 4  |

on order: 14 British landing craft

advanced armament:
  surface-to-surface missiles--
    MM-40 Exocet
    RGM-84A Harpoon

naval bases:
  Jufair

ship maintenance and repair capability:
  Arab Shipbuilding & Repair Yard (ASRY), a 500,000 DWT drydock engaged in repairs and construction (mainly supertankers; jointly owned by Bahrain, Kuwait, Qatar, Saudi Arabia, UAE--each 18.84%, Iraq--4.7% and Libya-- 1.1%)

# 3. EGYPT

BASIC DATA
Official Name of State: The Arab Republic of Egypt
Head of State: President Muhammad Husni Mubarak
Prime Minister: Dr. Atif Sidqi
Minister of Defense and War Production: Major General Youssuf Sabri Abu Talib
Chief of the General Staff: General Saffi al-Din Abu Shenaf
Commander of the Air Force: Lieutenant General Allah al-Din Barakat
Commander of the Air Defense Forces: Lieutenant General Mustafa Ahmad al-Shazli
Commander of the Navy: Vice Admiral Muhammad Sharif al-Sadiq
Area: 1,000,258 sq. km.
Population:                                              50,700,000
  ethnic subdivision:
  | | | |
  |---|---:|---:|
  | Arabs | 49,889,000 | 98.4% |
  | Bedouin | 101,000 | 0.2% |
  | Nubians | 50,000 | 0.1% |
  | Greeks, Italians, Armenians | 406,000 | 0.8% |
  | Others | 254,000 | 0.5% |

  religious subdivision:
  | | | |
  |---|---:|---:|
  | Sunni Muslims | 47,658,000 | 94.0% |
  | Copts, other Christians | 3,042,000 | 6.0% |

GDP (figures unreliable, calculated according to the official exchange rate of 1.4286 per US dollar. In reality there are four exchange rates, giving a much lower value to the Egyptian pound than the official rate)
1986--$54.60 billion
1987--$62.93 billion
Balance of Payments (goods, services & unilateral transfer payments):

| year | income | expenditure | balance |
|---|---|---|---|
| 1986 | $ 8.91 bil. | $10.78 bil. | -$1.87 bil. |
| 1987 | $10.85 bil. | $11.17 bil. | -$320 mil. |

Defense Expenditure:
1987--$4.6 billion (unconfirmed; could be higher due to Arab aid)
1988--$4.0 billion (unconfirmed)
Foreign Military Aid Received:
  financial aid from:
    USA--$1.3 billion grant; Italy--$50 million grant or loan (unconfirmed); Arab aid (unconfirmed)
  military training:
    foreign advisors/instructors from--Brazil, France, USA
    trainees abroad in--Brazil, Britain, France, FRG, USA

# EGYPT

(over 500 men)
arms transfers from:
   Belgium (mobile shelters for repair of artillery, tank fire control systems, LMGs); Brazil (trainer aircraft); Britain (ATGMs, helicopter parts, radio transceivers, tank guns, torpedoes); France (combat aircraft, ATGMs, helicopters, AAMs, SAMs, radar for AAGs, and night vision devices for tanks); FRG (mobile shelters, trucks); India (spare parts for Soviet aircraft); Italy (helicopters, ECM, shipborne SAMs, air defense systems); North Korea (spare parts for Soviet arms); Romania (spare parts for tanks, artillery); PRC (combat aircraft, missile frigates, SAMs, submarines); Spain (APCs, trucks); Switzerland (AAGs, air defense systems); USA (APCs, ATGMs, combat aircraft, early warning aircraft, radars, SAMs, tanks, target drones, fire control systems for submarines); USSR (spare parts for Soviet made weapons)
construction aid by:
   USA (upgrading of airfields and dry docks)
maintenance ⌄f equipment in:
   FRG (fighter and transport aircraft)
maintenance aid by:
   USA (aircraft)
Foreign Military Aid Extended:
   financial aid to:
      Sudan ($42 million grant, given in arms, figure unconfirmed)
   military training:
      advisors/instructors in--Bahrain, Djibouti, Iraq, Jordan (unconfirmed), Kuwait; Morocco (unconfirmed), Oman, Qatar, Somalia, Sudan, UAE, YAR; Zaire
      foreign trainees from--Algeria (unconfirmed), Bahrain, Chad, Djibouti, France, Iraq (400), Jordan, Kuwait, Morocco (unconfirmed), Nigeria, Oman, Pakistan, Qatar, Senegal, Somalia, Sudan, Tanzania, Tunisia, UAE, YAR, Zaire
   arms transfers to:
      Afghan rebels (small arms until August 1988); Chad (small arms); Djibouti (ATGMs, unconfirmed); Iraq (ammunition, trainer aircraft, helicopters, spare parts, APCs, SAMs, artillery, tanks, combat aircraft, MRLs); Kenya (type unknown); Kuwait (APCs); (Lebanon (miscellaneous); Morocco (mortars, APCs); Oman (APCs); Qatar (APCs, MRLs); Sudan (APCs, ATGMs); Tunisia (Brazilian designed trainer aircraft, unconfirmeJ); UAE (APCs, air defense systems, unconfirmed); Uganda (type unknown, unconfirmed); YAR (unconfirmed); Zaire (APCs)
   maintenance of equipment for:
      Iraq (aircraft)

facilities provided to:
  USA (airfields at Cairo West, Qena, Inshas; facility at Ras Banas--construction frozen); Iraq (naval vessels)
Cooperation in Arms Production/Assembly with:
  Argentina and Iraq (development and production of SSM); Brazil (trainer aircraft); Britain (ATGMs, electronics); France (aircraft, electronics, helicopters, SP AAGs); FRG (APCs; companies involved in SSM production); Iraq (spares for Soviet arms); Italy (AAGs, unconfirmed); North Korea (SSMs); Romania (jeeps); Spain (planned assembly of trucks); USA (APCs, ammunition, electronics, trucks, plans for tank assembly)
Joint Maneuvers with:
  France, Italy, Jordan, USA

INFRASTRUCTURE
  Road Network:

| | |
|---|---:|
| length: | 29,000 km |
| paved roads | 12,300 km |
| gravel and stone roads | 2,500 km |
| improved earth roads | 14,200 km |

    main routes:
    Cairo--Alexandria
    Cairo--Tanta--Alexandria
    Cairo--Isma'iliya
    Cairo--Suez
    Alexandria--Marsa Matruh--Tobruk (Libya)
    Alexandria--al-Alamein--Siwa (oasis)
    Marsah Matruh--Siwa (oasis)
    Isma'iliya--Bir Gafgafah--Beer Sheva (Israel)
    Kantara--al-Arish--Ashkelon (Israel)
    Sharm al-Shaykh--Eilat (Israel)
    Suez--Isma'iliya--Port Sa'id
    Cairo--al-Mansura--Damietta
    Cairo--al-Fayum
    Cairo--Asyut--Qena--Aswan
    Asyut--al-Kharga
    Suez--Hurghada--Ras Banas--Port Sudan (Sudan)
    Qena--Safaga
  Railway Network:

| | |
|---|---:|
| length: | 4,857 km |
| standard gauge | 4,510 km |
| narrow gauge (0.75m.) | 347 km |

    main routes:
    Cairo--Tanta--Alexandria
    Tanta--Damietta
    Cairo--Zagazig--Isma'iliya
    Cairo--Suez
    Suez--Isma'iliya--Port Sa'id

```
        Alexandria--Marsa Matruh--Salum
        Cairo--Asyut--Aswan
        Zagazig--al-Salahiya
Airfields:                                              85
   airfields by runway type:
      permanent surface fields                          63
      unpaved fields and usable air strips              22
   airfields by runway length:
      over 3660 meters                                   2
      2440--3659                                        45
      1220--2439                                        22
      under 1220                                        16
   international airports: Cairo, Aswan, Alexandria, Luxor
   major domestic airfields: Abu Simbel, Asyut, Hurghada,
      Port Sa'id, Sharm al-Shaykh
Airlines:
   companies: Egyptair (international); Misr Overseas
      Airways (international, charter and cargo); ZAS
      (Zarakani Aviation Services, cargo); Air Sinai
      (domestic, and to Israel); Petroleum Air Service
      (domestic, to oil fields); North African Airways
      (charter)
   aircraft:
      Airbus A-300 B4                                    7
      Boeing 767ER                                       3
      Boeing 747-300 combi                               2
      Boeing 737-200                                     8
      Boeing 707-320C                                   12
      DC-9-51                                            1
      DHC-7 (Dash-7)                                     5
      Fokker F-27-500                                    4
      Lockheed Jetstar                                   2
   helicopters:
      Bell 212 (including on lease)                     11
      Bell 206B/206-L3                                   8
   on order: 2 Boeing 767-200ER, 2 MD-83
Maritime Facilities:
   harbors--Adabiya, Alexandria, Damietta, al-Dikheila
      (under construction, partly operative), Port Sa'id,
      Safaga, Suez
   anchorages--Abu Zneima, Kosseir, Marsa al-Hamra
      (al-Alamein), Marsa Matruh, Nuweiba, Ras Banas, Sharm
      al-Shaikh, al-Tur
   oil terminals--Ras Gharib, Ras Shukeir , Wadi Fieran, Abu
      Qir
Merchant Marine:
```

| vessel type | number | DWT |
|---|---|---|
| general cargo | 89 | 503,066 |
| crude carrier | 1 | 38,177 |
| oil tanker | 6 | 150,298 |

| | | |
|---|---|---|
| bulk carrier | 14 | 565,067 |
| passenger/cargo | 2 | 2,654 |
| ro/ro | 8 | 37,951 |
| general cargo/container | 7 | 49,859 |
| multipurpose | 2 | 25,200 |
| ferry | 4 | 3,581 |
| reefer | 3 | 16,591 |
| bunkering tanker | 6 | 14,731 |
| TOTAL | 142 | 1,407,103 |

Defense Production:

army equipment:

manufacture--120mm mortars; 122mm Saqr 10/18/30 MRLs; Saqr 80 surface-to-surface rockets; ammunition for artillery, tanks and small arms; mines; rifles; short-range SAMs; conversion of 122mm D-30 howitzers to SP howitzers; APCs; conversion of 23mm AAGs to Sinai 23 SP AAGs; add-on armor to M-113 APCs; toxic gas (unconfirmed, with assistance from a Swiss company)

production under license-- BGM-71D TOW, Dragon III ATGMs, (under development); 130mm artillery pieces; British tank guns; tank tracks; upgrading of Soviet tanks (with British, USA and Austrian assistance); trucks and jeeps(with USA); jeeps (with Romania); APCs (with FRG components and assistance); Soviet design AAGs, MGs and small arms; tank (with USA, under development); APCs (with Yugoslavia)

assembly--short-range SAMs, APCs, AAGs, trucks

air force equipment:

production under license--CBUs (US design); anti-runway bombs; parts for F-16; parts for Mirage 2000; aircraft fuel pods; aerial bombs

assembly--Alpha Jet trainers; SA-342 Gazelle helicopters; Embraer EMB-312 Tucano

ships:

assembly--6 US Swiftships patrol boats

electronics:

production under license--AN/TPS-63 radars (assembly, with 30% of components locally produced); radio transceivers (in collaboration with France and Britain); SAM electronics (in collaboration with Britain)

optronics:

night vision devices, laser range-finders

ARMED FORCES

Personnel:

military forces--

| | regular | reserves | total |
|---|---|---|---|
| army | 320,000 | 600,000 | 920,000 |

| air force | 27,000 | 15,000 | 42,000 |
| air defense | 80,000 | 70,000 | 150,000 |
| navy | 20,000 | 15,000 | 35,000 |
| TOTAL | 447,000 | 700,000 | 1,147,000 |

para-military forces--
  coast guard--7,000
  frontier corps--6,000

Army:
  major units:

| unit type | army corps HQ | divisions | independent brigades/ groups |
|---|---|---|---|
| all arms | 2 | | |
| armored | | 4 | 3 |
| mechanized | | 7 | |
| infantry | | 1 | 11 |
| airborne | | | 2 |
| special forces | | | 3 |
| TOTAL | 2 | 12 | 19 |

  small arms:
    personal weapons--
      9mm Aqaba SMG
      9mm Carl Gustaf Model 45 SMG
      9mm Port Sa'id SMG
      7.62mm AK-47 (Kalashnikov) AR
      7.62mm AKM AR
      7.62mm Rashid SAR
      7.62mm SKS (Simonov) SAR
    machine guns--
      14.5mm KPV HMG
      14.5mm ZPU 14.5x4 HMG (in anti-aircraft role)
      12.7mm D.Sh.K. 38/46 (Degtyarev)
      12.7mm (0.5") Browning M2 HMG
      7.62mm MAG (FN) LMG
      7.62mm RPD (Degtyarev) LMG/Suez LMG
      7.62mm SG-43/SGM (Goryunov) MMG/Aswan MMG
    light and medium mortars--
      82mm M-43
      60mm (Hotchkiss-Brandt)
    light ATRLs--
      RPG-2
      RPG-7

tanks:

| model | number |
|---|---|
| high quality | |
|   M-60 A3 | 850 |
| medium quality | |
|   T-62 | 600 |
|   T-55 | 950 |
| (sub-total | 1550) |

```
      TOTAL                                    2400
   on order: 555 M-1 A1 tanks
APCs/ARVs:
   model                                     number
      high quality
         BMP-1                                  200
         M-113 A2                              1700
                           (sub-total         1900)
      others
         BMR-600                                250
         BRDM-2
         BTR-40/50/60/152
         Fahd
         OT-62
                           (sub-total         2200)
      TOTAL                                    4100
   on order: about 680 M-113  A2;  Fahd;  Cadillac  Gage
   Commando Scout ARV
artillery:
   self propelled guns and howitzers--         number
      155mm M-109 A2 SP howitzer                 144
   towed guns and howitzers--
      180mm S-23 gun (possibly phased out)
      152mm M-1943 (D-1) howitzer (possibly  phased  out)
      130mm M-46 gun/Type-59 gun                 440
      122mm D-30 howitzer
      122mm M-1938 howitzer (possibly phased out)
      100mm M-1955 field/AT gun
   mortars, over 160mm--
      240mm mortar
      160mm mortar
   mortars, under 160mm, but excluding light and medium--
      120mm M-43 mortar
      107mm (4.2") M-30 SP mortar  (on M-106 A2 carrier)
      TOTAL                                    2200
   on order: 122mm D-30 SP (still under development)
   MRLs--
      122mm BM-21
      122mm BM-11
      122mm Saqr 10/18/30
   on  order:  AN/TPQ-37  artillery  and   mortar-locating
   radar
engineering equipment:
   Bar mine-laying system
   EWK pontoon bridges
   GSP self-propelled ferries
   M-123 Viper minefield crossing system
   MT-55 bridging tanks
   MTU-55 bridging tanks
   mine-clearing rollers
```

```
PMP folding pontoon bridges
PRP motorized bridges
armored recovery vehicles:
  M-88 A1
AFV transporters:                                          1000
anti-tank weapons:
  missiles--                                          launchers
    AT-3 (Sagger)
    BGM-71C  Improved  TOW
    BRDM-2 carrying AT-3 (Sagger)
    M-901 ITV SP (TOW under Armor)
    MILAN
    Swingfire
    TOTAL                                           1600-1800
    on order: 180 BGM-71D TOW II launchers
  guns--
    107mm B-11 recoilless  rifle  (possibly phased out)
surface-to-surface missiles and rockets:
  model                                              launchers
    FROG-7
    SS-1 (Scud B)
    TOTAL                                                    24
on order: Saqr 80, Badr 2000 (still under development)
army anti-aircraft defenses:
  missiles--                                          launchers
    Ain al-Saqr
    Crotale                                                 12
    MIM-72A Chaparral                                       26
    SA-6 (Gainful)                                          48
    SA-7 (Grail)
    Skyguard AA system (missiles  and  guns; Egyptian
      designation: Amoun)                                   18
  short-range guns--                                      number
    57mm ZSU 57x2 SP
    35mm Oerlikon-Buhrle 35x2 GDF-002
    23mm ZSU 23x4 SP (Gun Dish)
    23mm ZU 23x2
    Skyguard AA system (missiles,  radars  and  guns;
      Egyptian designation: Amoun)
    TOTAL                                                 2500
  on order: 8 additional Skyguard AA systems; Sinai 23 AA
    systems
CW capabilities:
  personal protective equipment, Soviet type
  decontamination units
  stockpile of gases
Air Force:
  aircraft--general:                                     number
    combat aircraft                                         542
    transport aircraft                                       34
```

**EGYPT**

```
helicopters                                              198
combat aircraft:
 interceptors--
  high quality
    F-16A/B/C/D (multi-role, employed as
       interceptor)                                        79
    Mirage 2000 (multi-role, employed as
       interceptor)                                        19
                                  (sub-total               98)
  medium and low quality
    F-7 Shenyang                                           60
    F-6 Shenyang/FT-6                                      80
    MiG-21 MF/U (Fishbed)                                 150
                                  (sub-total              290)
    Total                                                 388
 strike and multi-role aircraft--
  medium quality
    F-4E Phantom                                           33
    Mirage 5                                               71
                                  (sub-total              104)
  others
    MiG-17 (Fresco) & MiG-15 (limited serviceability)
                                                           50
    Total                                                 154
 on order: 40 F-16 C/D; 20 Mirage 2000
transport aircraft (older models partly grounded):
 Boeing 707                                                 2
 C-130H Hercules (including ELINT)                         20
 DHC-5D Buffalo                                             9
 Mystere Falcon 20                                          3
 TOTAL                                                     34
training and liaison aircraft:
 al-Gumhuriya                                             100
 Alpha Jet and Alpha Jet MS-2                              43
 Embraer EMB-312 (Tucano)                                  40
 L-29 (Delfin)                                            100
 PZL-104 Wilga 35/80                                       10
 Yak-18 (Max)                                              35
 TOTAL                                                    328
 on order: 14 EMB-312
helicopters:
 attack--
   SA-342 L/M Gazelle                                      80
 heavy transport--
   CH-47C Chinook                                          15
   Westland Commando Mk.2                                  25
                                  (sub-total               40)
 medium transport--
   Mi-8 (Hip)
   Mi-4 (Hound)
```

```
                                    (sub-total        55)
    light transport--
      Hiller UH-12E                                   18
    ASW--
      Westland Sea King Mk.47                          5
    TOTAL                                            198
    on order: 2 UH-60A Black Hawk
  maritime surveillance aircraft:
    Beechcraft 1900C                                   6
  miscellaneous aircraft:
    Aerospatiale CT-20 target drone
    Beech AQM-37A target drone
    Beech MQM-107B target drone
    Skyeye R4E-50 mini RPV                            48
    E-2C Hawkeye AEW                                   5
    Teledyne Ryan model 324 Scarab                   29
    on order: 70 TTL BTT-3 Banshee target drones
  advanced armament:
    air-to-air missiles--
      AA-2 (Atoll)
      AIM-7F/7M Sparrow
      AIM-9 Sidewinder; AIM-9L; AIM-9P
      R-550 Magique
      R-530D Super
    air-to-ground missiles--                      number
      AGM-65 Maverick                               1100
      AM-39 Exocet (unconfirmed)
      AS-1 Kennel
      AS-5 Kelt
      AS-30L
      HOT
    bombs--
      CBU-7A
    on order: 282 AIM-7M AAMs
  aircraft shelters:  in  all  operational  airfields,  for
    combat aircraft
  military airfields:                               21
    Abu Suweir,  Alexandria,  Aswan,  Beni  Suef,  Bilbeis,
    Cairo West,  Fayid,  Hurghada,  Inshas,  Janaklis,  Kabrit,
    Luxor, al-Maza, al-Minya, Mansura, Marsah Matruh, Qena,
    Ras Banas, Tanta, 2 additional
  aircraft maintenance and repair capability:
    for all models
Air Defense Force:
  radars:
    AN/TPS-43 (unconfirmed)
    AN/TPS-59                                          4
    AN/TPS-63                                          9
    Spoon Rest (P-12)                                  +
    Tiger S (TRS-2100)                                12
```

```
   on order: AN/TPS-63 (to  complete  total  to  42); an
     additional AN/TPS-59
   long-range missiles:
     model                                        batteries
       MIM-23B Improved HAWK                             12
       SA-2 (Guideline) & SA-3 (Goa)                    120
       TOTAL                                            132
Navy:
   combat vessels: (some older Soviet vessels
     may no longer be operational)                   number
     submarines--
       R class (Romeo)/Chinese R class                   8
       W class (Whiskey)                                 2
       Total                                            10
     MFPBs--
       Hegu (Komar, made in PRC)                         6
       October                                           6
       Ossa I                                            7
       Ramadan                                           6
       Total                                            25
     gun destroyers--
       Z class                                           1
     missile frigates--
       Descubierta class                                 2
       Jianghu class                                     2
       Total                                             4
     mine warfare vessels--
       T-43 class minesweeper                            3
       T-301 class minesweeper                           2
       Yurka class minesweeper                           4
       Total                                             9
     gunboats/MTBs (older vessels  of  limited
       serviceability)--
       Hainan class                                      8
       Shanghai II                                       4
       Shershen class MTB                                6
       Total                                            18
     patrol craft--
       Bertram class 28 ft. (8.5 meter)                  6
       Timsah class                                     12
       de Castro 110 ton (Nisr class)                    3
       Crestitalia 70 ft. (21 meter)                     6
       Swiftships 28.4 meter                             9
       Total                                            36
     on order:  2 Tripartite minesweepers (delayed for  lack
       of funds)
   landing craft:
     LCM                                                10
     Polnochny class LCT                                 3
     SMB-1 class LCU                                     2
```

```
SRN-6 hovercraft                                      3
Vydra class LCU                                       9
TOTAL                                                27
auxiliary vessels:
  Niryat diving support                               2
  Okhtensky (tug)                                     2
  Poluchat II torpedo recovery                        2
  training (1 Sekstan, 1 4650-ton
    and 1 other)                                      3
advanced armament:
  surface-to-surface missiles--
    Hai Ying-2 (HY-2)
    OTOMAT Mk.2 (also used for coastal defense)
    RGM-84A Harpoon
    SS-N-2 Styx
  surface-to-air missiles--
    Aspide
  advanced torpedoes--
    Stingray anti-submarine
coastal defense:                           launchers
  SSC-2B Samlet coastal defense missile (probably  no
  longer in service)
  OTOMAT coastal defense missile
  SSN-2 Styx converted to coastal defense role
  Total                    (unconfirmed)            30
special maritime forces:
  divers and frogmen
naval bases:                                          8
  Abu Qir (naval academy), Alexandria, Hurghada, Marsa
  Matruh, Port Sa'id, Safaga, Suez; Berenice (Ras Banas)
ship maintenance and repair capability:
  Alexandria (including construction up to 20,000 DWT),
  Port Sa'id
```

# 4. IRAN

BASIC DATA

Official Name of State: Islamic Republic of Iran

Supreme Religious and Political National Leader: Hojatoleslam Ali Khamenei (succeeded Ayatollah Khomeini in June 1989)

Head of State (subordinate to national leader): President Hojatolislam Ali Khamenei--until August 1989

Prime Minister: Mir Hossein Moussavi

Minister of Defense: Colonel Mohammad Hussein Jallali

Acting Commander in Chief of the Armed Forces: Hojatolislam Ali Akbar Hashemi Rafsanjani

Commander of the Ground Forces: Brigadier General Hussein Hassani-Saadi (Official title: Head of the Joint Command of the Armed Forces of the Islamic Republic of Iran.)

Commander in Chief of the Islamic Revolution Guards Corps (IRGC): Mohsen Rezai

Commander of the IRGC Ground Forces: Ali Shamkani

Commander of the Air Force: Brigadier General Mansour Sattari

Commander of the IRGC Air Arm: Ali Sahnadat

Commander of the Navy: Captain Muhammad Hoseyn Malekzadegan

Area: 1,647,240 sq. km.

Population: 51,250,000

| | | |
|---|---|---|
| ethnic subdivision: | | |
| Persians | 36,285,000 | 70.8% |
| Azeris | 8,713,000 | 17.0% |
| Arabs | 2,921,000 | 5.7% |
| Kurds | 1,589,000 | 3.1% |
| Bakhtiaris | 721,000 | 1.4% |
| Lurs and others | 1,025,000 | 2.0% |
| religious subdivision: | | |
| Shi'ite Muslims | 47,662,000 | 93.0% |
| Sunni Muslims (incl. Kurds) | 2,563,000 | 5.0% |
| Christians, Zoroastrians, Jews, Bahais and others | 1,025,000 | 2.0% |

GDP:

1984--$166.9 billion

1985--$168.1 billion

Balance of Payments (goods, services & unilateral transfer payments):

| year | income | expenditure | balance |
|---|---|---|---|
| 1983 | $22.84 bil. | $18.47 bil. | +$4.37 bil. |
| 1984 | $18.16 bil. | $18.57 bil. | -$410 mil. |

Defense Expenditure:

1988--$6-8 billion (unconfirmed)

1989--$8.5 billion (unconfirmed)

Foreign Military Aid Received:

163

military training:
  foreign advisors/instructors/serving personnel from--
    USSR, GDR, Bulgaria (unconfirmed), Cuba
    (unconfirmed), Libya (unconfirmed), North Korea
    (unconfirmed), PRC, Syria
  serving personnel from--Afghanistan (dissidents)
  trainees abroad in--France, GDR, North Korea, Pakistan
    (nuclear scientists), PRC, USSR; Cuba (unconfirmed)
arms transfers from:
  Algeria (Soviet-made arms); Austria (artillery pieces
  via Libya; AAGs, unconfirmed); Argentina (small arms,
  ammunition, high explosives, land mines); Belgium
  (small arms); Brazil (APCs, MRLs, unconfirmed); Britain
  (workshops, spare parts for tanks and ARVs, landrovers,
  radars); Ethiopia (US-made combat aircraft); France
  (spare parts for MFPBs, artillery ammunition, rubber
  boats, trucks); FRG (trucks); Greece (details unknown);
  Hong Kong (American aircraft spares and miscellaneous
  items); Italy (AAGs, optronics, ammunition,
  helicopters, land mines, artillery pieces, spare parts
  for aircraft, naval guns, construction of harbor, naval
  mines via intermediaries); Libya (Brazilian-made APCs
  and ARVs, Soviet-made naval mines, Soviet-made SSMs);
  North Korea (tanks, artillery pieces, AAGs, small arms,
  naval mines, midget submarine, SSMs); Portugal
  (ammunition); PRC (artillery pieces, coastal defense
  SSMs, combat aircraft, SAMs, tanks; SSMs, unconfirmed);
  South Africa (artillery pieces, unconfirmed; other
  weapons); South Korea (aircraft spare parts, SAMs,
  unconfirmed); Sweden (explosives, patrol boats, trucks;
  SAMs via Singapore); Switzerland (trainer aircraft;
  AAGs and fire control, unconfirmed); Syria (Soviet-made
  small arms and ATGMs, AAGs, ammunition); Taiwan
  (artillery ammunition, mortars, small arms; US-made
  tanks, unconfirmed); USSR & Soviet bloc (AAGs, APCs,
  artillery pieces, small arms); Vietnam (US-made
  aircraft, helicopters, tanks, APCs, artillery
  pieces--war booty)
use of facilities abroad:
  Syria (unconfirmed use of airfields); Turkey (use of
  supply routes)
Foreign Military Aid Extended:
  financial aid to:
    opposition groups in Bahrain, Iraq, Saudi Arabia--
    grants; Hizb Allah militia in Lebanon--grant; al-Amal
    movement in Lebanon--grant (unconfirmed); Syria--grant
    (free oil); Palestinian organizations (Abu Musa
    faction)--grant; Afghan anti-government rebels;
    POLISARIO (unconfirmed); Tunisian anti-government
    fundamentalists--grant (unconfirmed); Egyptian

anti-government fundamentalist groups--grant
military training:
foreign trainees from--Lebanon (Shi'ite militias);
Iraq, Bahrain, Saudi Arabia (opposition groups);
ASALA (Armenian Secret Army for the Liberation of
Armenia); Afghanistan (rebels); Egyptian
anti-government fundamentalist groups; POLISARIO
(unconfirmed)
advisors/instructors in--Algeria (POLISARIO units);
Lebanon (with Hizb Allah, IRGC men)
arms transfers to:
Afghan rebels; POLISARIO (via Algeria, type unknown)
facilities provided to:
Afghan rebels (training camps near Mashhad); radar
facilities to USSR (unconfirmed)
forces deployed abroad in:
Lebanon--1000-2000 revolutionary guards with Hizb
Allah
Cooperation in Arms Production/Assembly with:
Czechoslovakia (artillery, ammunition, unconfirmed);
companies from FRG (cooperation in production of toxic
gas, unconfirmed)

INFRASTRUCTURE
Road Network:
| | |
|---|---|
| length: | 136,400 km |
| paved roads | 40,066 km |
| gravel and crushed stone roads | 46,866 km |
| improved earth tracks | 49,468 km |

main routes:
Teheran--Qom--Yazd--Kerman--Zahedan
Kerman--Shiraz--Bushehr
Shiraz--Ahwaz--Abadan
Bandar Khomeini--Ahwaz
Qom--Isfahan--Shiraz
Qom--Arak--Dezful--Ahwaz--Abadan
Qom--Hamadan
Teheran--Hamadan--Kermanshah--Ilam--al-Kut (Iraq)
Abadan--Basra (Iraq)
Kermanshah--Qasr-i Shirin--Baghdad (Iraq)
Dezful--Shahabad--Qasr-i Shirin
Shahabad--Kermanshah--Zanjan
Teheran--Zanjan--Tabriz--Jolfa--Nakhichevan (USSR)
Tabriz--Ardabil--Astara--Lenkoran (USSR)
Teheran--Mashhad
Mashhad--Ashkhabad (USSR)
Mashhad--Zahedan--Chah Bahar
Zahedan--Quetta (Pakistan)
Mashhad--Herat (Afghanistan)
Kerman--Bandar Abbas

```
Railway Network:
  length:                                            4,601 km
    standard gauge                                   4,509 km
    1.676m gauge                                        92 km
  main routes:
    Teheran--Qom--Isfahan--Yazd--Kerman
    Qom--Arak--Dezful--Ahwaz--Abadan
    Ahwaz--Basra (Iraq)
    Teheran--Zanjan--Tabriz--Jolfa--Nakhichevan (USSR)
    Teheran--Semnan--Mashhad
    Mashhad--Ashkhabad (USSR)
    Zahedan--Quetta (Pakistan)
    Tabriz--Malatya (Turkey)
Airfields:                                               146
  airfields by runway type:
    permanent surface fields                             80
    unpaved fields and usable airstrips                  66
  airfields by runway length:
    over 3660 meters                                     16
    2440--3659                                           17
    1220--2439                                           68
    under 1220                                           45
  international airports: Teheran, Abadan
  major domestic airfields: Abu Musa, Ardabil, Bandar
    Abbas, Bushehr, Chah Bahar, Gorgan, Isfahan, Kerman,
    Mashhad, Rasht, Sanandaj, Shiraz, Tabriz, Yazd,
    Zahedan
Airlines:
  companies: Iranair (international), Iranian Assaman
    Airlines (domestic)
  aircraft:
    Aerocommander/Turbocommander/Strike Commander        15
    Airbus A-300 B2                                       5
    Boeing 747-200F/SP/100B/200B                         13
    Boeing 737-200                                        1
    Boeing 737-200C                                       2
    Boeing 727-200                                        5
    Boeing 727-100                                        2
    Boeing 707-320C                                       5
    Britten Norman BN-2 Islander                          2
    Fairchild FH-227B                                     3
    Fokker F-28-4000                                      2
    Islander                                              2
    Mystere-Falcon 20F                                    4
    Piper Chieftain                                       2
Maritime Facilities:
  harbors--Bandar Abbas, Bandar Anzelli, Bandar Lengeh
    (Lingeh), Chah Bahar, Khorramshahr (not in use due to
    war), Bandar Khomeini (formerly Bandar Shahpur; also
    referred to as Bandar Imam)
```

oil terminals--Bandar Abbas, Bushehr, Bandar Khomeini, Bandar Lengeh, Ganaveh, Kharg Island, Larak Island, Sirri Island

Merchant Marine:

| vessel type | number | GRT |
|---|---|---|
| general cargo | 40 | 381,000 |
| tanker | 15 | 651,000 |
| TOTAL | 55 | 1,032,000 |

(note: tanker figures do not include leased storage tankers)

Defense Production:

army equipment:

rifles (Heckler & Koch G-3 AR, under license); machine guns (MG-1A1, under license); artillery; MRLs, copy of a Soviet and Chinese design; SSMs (unconfirmed); small arms, mortars, and artillery ammunition; spare parts; trucks (assembly); toxic gas; gas masks; ATRLs (uncomfirmed); ATGMs (uncomfirmed)

air force equipment:

light aircraft (probably still under development); spare parts for aircraft

electronics:

radio transceivers (copy of USA model)

ships:

250 ton LCU, (Foque 101), PBs, mines, 8.4 meter hovercraft

ARMED FORCES

Personnel:

military forces--

| | regular | reserves | total |
|---|---|---|---|
| army | 300,000 | 350,000 | 650,000 |
| IRGC | 300,000 | 895,000 | 1,195,000 |
| Baseej | 100,000 | | 100,000 |
| air force | 35,000 | -- | 35,000 |
| navy | 20,000 | -- | 20,000 |
| TOTAL (including IRGC and Baseej): | | | |
| | 755,000 | 1,245,000 | 2,000,000 |

para-military forces--

| | | |
|---|---|---|
| Baseej (militiamen/boys) (estimate) | | 900,000 |
| gendarmerie | | 75,000 |

Army:

major units (including IRGC now integrated into Army; some units not fully organized):

| unit type | army corps | divisions | independent brigades |
|---|---|---|---|
| all arms | 3 | | |
| mechanized | | 1 | |
| armored | | 6 | |
| infantry | | 35 | |
| paratroop/ | | | |

```
    special forces              1              3
    airborne                                   2
    TOTAL               3              43      5
    (some divisions undermanned; about 13 army divisions,
      30 IRGC divisions)
small arms:
  personal weapons--
    11mm (0.45") M-3 A1 SMG
    9mm Uzi SMG
    7.62mm G-3 (Heckler & Koch) AR
    7.62mm M-1 Garand SAR
    7.62mm AK-47 (Kalashnikov) AR
  machine guns--
    12.7mm D.Sh.K. 38/46 (Degtyarev) HMG
    12.7mm (0.5") Browning M2 HMG
    7.62mm MG 1A1 LMG
    7.62mm (0.3") Browning M-1919 MMG
    7.62mm MAG (FN) (unconfirmed)
    7.62mm PK/PKS (Kalashnikov) LMG
  light and medium mortars--
    81mm M-29
    60mm M-19
  light ATRLs--
    3.5" M-20
    RPG-7
tanks:
  model                                      number
    high quality
      T-72 (unconfirmed, captured)           a few
    medium quality
      Chieftain Mk.3/Mk.5
      T-62                                     150
      M-60 A1
      T-55/Type 69/Type 59
    low quality
      M-48/M-47
      Scorpion
    TOTAL   (limited serviceability due to lack of  spare
      parts)                                 600-700
    on order: Type 69 (unconfirmed)
APCs/ARVs:
  model                                      number
    high quality
     M-113
      BMP-1
      Engesa EE-9
    others
      BTR-40/50/60
      BTR-152
      Fox
```

```
      Ferret
      TOTAL                                                1000
artillery:
  self propelled guns and howitzers--
    203mm M-110 SP howitzer
    175mm M-107 SP gun
    155mm M-109 SP howitzer
  towed guns and howitzers--
    203mm (8") M-115 howitzer
    155mm G-5 gun/howitzer
    155mm GHN-45 howitzer                                   140
    155mm M-114 howitzer
    130mm M-46 gun/Type 59 gun
    105mm M-101 howitzer
  mortars less than 160mm, but excluding light and
    medium--
    120mm M-65 mortar
    107mm (4.2") M-30 mortar
    TOTAL                                               800-1000
    (approximately 2/3 high quality including  about   200
    SP guns & howitzers)
  MRLs--
    230mm Oghab
    180mm SS-40 Astros II (unconfirmed)
    130mm Type 63
    122mm BM-21
    107mm
engineering equipment:
  pontoon bridges
  light infantry assault boats
  self-propelled pontoons
anti-tank weapons:
  missiles--                                           launchers
    AT-3 (Sagger)
    BGM-71A TOW
    M-47 Dragon
    SS-11/SS-12
  guns--
    106mm M-40 A1C recoilless rifle
surface-to-surface missiles and rockets:
  SS-1 (Scud B)                                             3+
  Iran-130 (unconfirmed)
army anti-aircraft defenses:
  missiles--                                           launchers
    FIM-92A Stinger (with IRGC)                           a few
    Rapier                                                  45
    RBS-70                                                  10
    SA-7 (Grail)
    Tigercat                                                15
  short-range guns--
```

```
        57mm ZSU 57x2 SP
        57mm
        40mm Bofors L-70 (unconfirmed)
        37mm
        35mm Contraves Skyguard ADS (unconfirmed)
        35mm Oerlikon - Bhurle 35x2 GDF-002
        23mm ZSU 23x4 SP (Gun Dish)
        23mm ZU 23x2
      on order: RBS-70 short-range SAMs (unconfirmed)
    CW capabilities:
        personal protective equipment for part of  the  armed
        forces
        stored gas (unconfirmed)
        decontamination units
Air Force:
    aircraft--general:                                    number
      combat aircraft (about 60% serviceable)                163
      transport aircraft                                     120
      helicopters                                            250
    combat aircraft:
      interceptors--
        high quality
          F-14A Tomcat (limited serviceability)               15
        others
          F-7 (unconfirmed)                                   18
        Total                                                 33
      strike and multi-role aircraft--
        medium quality
          F-4 D/E/RF Phantom (limited serviceability)         50
        others
          F-5 A/B/E                                           40
          F-6                                                 40
                                        (sub-total            80)
        Total                                                130
      on order: 32 F-7
    transport aircraft:
      Aero Commander 690                                       2
      Boeing 747                                              12
      Boeing 737-200                                           3
      Boeing 707 & KC-135 tanker
        (refuelling; including
        Boeing 707s in electronic
        surveillance/EW/CEW role)                             14
      C-130 E/H Hercules (including 2-3 in
        electronic surveillance role)                         50
      Cessna 310                                               5
      Fokker F-27-400 M                                       17
      Fokker F-27-600                                          8
      Mystere Falcon 20                                        9
      TOTAL                                                  120
```

```
training and liaison aircraft:
  Beechcraft Bonanza F-33                             50
  Cessna 185                                          45
  Pilatus PC-7 Turbo-Trainer                          35
  T-33                                                 9
  TOTAL                                              139
  on order: 15 EMB-312 (unconfirmed)
helicopters:
  attack--
    AH-1J Cobra
  heavy transport
    CH-47C Chinook                                    60
    CH-53D
    SA-321 Super Frelon
  medium transport--
    AB-214A
    AB-205                                            75
    AB-212                                            11
    HH-34F (S-58, unconfirmed)
  light transport--
    AB-206 JetRanger
ASW--
  SH-3D                                               32
  TOTAL            (limited serviceability)          250
  on order: 12 AS-61, 18 AB-212, attack helicopters  from
    Italy via  intermediaries  (unconfirmed);  13  CH-47C
    Chinook from Italy
maritime surveillance aircraft:
  P-3 Orion (unconfirmed)                              2
advanced armament:
  air-to-air missiles--
    AIM-54A Phoenix (possibly not serviceable)
    AIM-9 Sidewinder
    AIM-7 Sparrow
  air-to-ground missiles--
    AGM-65 Maverick
    AS-12
anti-aircraft defenses:
  radars--
    AR-3D
  long-range missiles--                         batteries
    HAWK / MIM-23B Improved HAWK                      17
    SA-2 (Guideline)                                  1
    HQ-2J                                             4
    TOTAL                                            22
  aircraft shelters--
    in some of the operational airfields
military airfields:                                  13
  Bandar Abbas, Bushehr,  Ghaleh-Marghi,  Isfahan,  Jegi,
  Kharg Island, Khatami, Mehrabad, Murgeh, Qeshm, Shiraz,
```

# IRAN

```
      Tabriz, Teheran
Navy:
   combat vessels:                                     number
    MFPBs--
       Combattante II (Kaman) class                      10
    missile destroyers--(possibly no longer in service)
       Battle class                                       1
       Sumner class                                       2
       Total                                              3
    missile frigates--
       Vosper Mk.5                                        3
    gun corvettes--
       PF-103 class                                       2
    mine warfare vessels--
       MSC 292 & MSC 268 class minesweepers               3
       Cape class minesweeper                             2
       Total                                              5
    patrol craft--
       PGM-71 (improved) class                            3
       Cape (US coastguard)                               3
       Peterson Mk.II 50 ft. (15 meter)                  56
       Sewart 40 ft. (12 meter)                           6
       Boghammar (13 meter; IRGC)                        51
       Bertram 30.4 ft. and 20 ft.                       12
       Total                                            131
   landing craft:
    BH-7 (Wellington) class hovercraft                    5
    SRN-6 (Winchester) class hovercraft                   8
    Hengam class landing ship                             4
    750 ton LCT                                           3
    LST (South Korean)                                    3
    US LCU 1431                                           1
    250 ton LCU                                           1
    TOTAL                                                25
   auxiliary ships:
    Amphion class repair ship                             1
    Cargo Vessel (765 DWT)                                5
    harbor tanker (1700 ton full load)                    1
    Luhring Yard 3,250 DWT supply ship                    2
    Mazagon Docks 9430 ton water tanker                   2
    Swan Hunter replenishment ship                        1
    YW-83 class 1250 ton water tanker                     1
    Jansen research vessel                                1
    on order: 2 1350 ton maintenance ships from Japan
   advanced armament:
    surface-to-surface missiles--
       RGM-84 Harpoon
       Seakiller
       C-801 (unconfirmed)
    surface-to-air missiles--
```

```
    Standard
    Seacat
coastal defense:                          launchers
  HY-2 (Silkworm) SSMs                        100
  C-801 SSM                                   100
special maritime forces:
  frogmen and divers
  A 30 ton midget submarine (made in North Korea)
naval bases:                                   8
  Bandar Abbas, Bandar Anzelli, Bandar Khomeini,  Bandar
  Lengeh,  Bushehr,  Chah Bahar,  Farsi  Island,   Kharg
  Island
IRGC naval bases:                              9
  Abadan oil terminal,  Abu  Musa  Island,  al  Fayisiyah
  Island,  Cyrus  oilfield,  Halul  Island  platform
  (unconfirmed),  Larak  Island,  Rostam  Island  oilfield,
  Sir Abu Nu'air, Sirri Island
ship maintenance and repair capability:
  1 MAN Nordhaman 28,000 ton floating dock
```

# 5. IRAQ

BASIC DATA
Official Name of State: The Republic of Iraq
Head of State: President Saddam Hussein (also Prime
Minister and Supreme Commander of the Armed Forces)
Defense Minister: General Abd al-Jabbar Shanshal (also
Deputy Supreme Commander of the Armed Forces)
Chief of the General Staff: Lieutenant General Nizar Abd
al-Karim al-Khazraji
Commander of the Air Force: Lieutenant General Hamid
Sha'aban al-Takriti
Commander of the Navy: Rear Admiral Rhaib Khassoun Rhaib
Area: 438,446 sq. km.
Population: (not including 1.5-2 million Arab nationals
working in Iraq)                               17,050,000

| ethnic subdivision: | | |
|---|---|---|
| Arabs | 12,532,000 | 73.5% |
| Kurds | 3,683,000 | 21.6% |
| Turkmens | 409,000 | 2.4% |
| Others | 426,000 | 2.5% |
| religious subdivision: | | |
| Shi'ite Muslims | 10,230,000 | 60.0% |
| Sunni Muslims (inc. Kurds) | 6,309,000 | 37.0% |
| Christians | | |
| Yazidis and others | 511,000 | 3.0% |

GDP:
1981--$31.36 billion (estimate)
Balance of Payments (goods, services & unilateral transfer
payments):

| year | income | expenditure | balance |
|---|---|---|---|
| 1981 | $10.53 bil. | $7.90 bil. | +$2.63 bil. |

Defense Expenditure (figures unreliable)
1986--$10 billion (unconfirmed)
1987--$6-8 billion (unconfirmed)
Foreign Military Aid Received:
financial aid from:
Kuwait, Qatar and UAE--grants and loans; Saudi
Arabia--$2 billion grants and loans (amount
unconfirmed)
military training:
foreign advisors/instructors from--Britain (30-40),
Brazil (50 Engesa employees), Egypt, France, Jordan,
Morocco, USSR and the Soviet Bloc (1000,
unconfirmed)
trainees abroad in--Britain, Egypt (400), France,
Italy, Britain, Jordan, Turkey (unconfirmed), USSR
and the Soviet bloc
arms transfers from:

Austria (artillery pieces, via Jordan); Belgium (ammunition); Brazil (APCs, ARVs, trucks, MRLs, trainer aircraft via Egypt); Britain (electronic equipment, land rovers); Chile (aerial bombs); Egypt (ammunition, Soviet-made combat aircraft, ATGMs, small arms, tanks, APCs, SAMs, MRLs, mortars, trainer aircraft, helicopters); Ethiopia (second-hand arms); France (combat aircraft, artillery pieces, ATGMs, SAMs, AGMs); FRG (tank transporters); Greece (artillery ammunition); Italy (missile frigates and corvettes, aircraft electronics, artillery pieces, radars, helicopters, small arms, land mines, spare parts; chemicals for production of gas by private firms, unconfirmed); PRC (tanks, artillery pieces, combat aircraft; anti-ship AGMs, unconfirmed); Morocco (second-hand arms); Philippines (second-hand arms); Portugal (ammunition); Saudi Arabia (US-made artillery pieces, ammunition); South Africa (artillery pieces and ammunition, unconfirmed); Spain (mortar ammunition); Spain/FRG (helicopters); USA (allegedly civilian helicopters); USSR and the Soviet bloc (combat aircraft, tanks, SSMs, helicopters, artillery pieces, ammunition, SAMs); Yugoslavia (small arms)
support forces from:
volunteers serving with the Popular Army and Army--Arab nationals working in Iraq; volunteers from YAR, until December 1988, serving with the Army
use of facilities abroad:
Jordan (use of supply routes and harbor); Kuwait (use of harbors, overflight rights for combat aircraft); Saudi Arabia (use of harbors); Turkey (use of supply routes); Egypt (facilities for use by naval vessels)
construction aid by:
Belgium, India (railway construction), Yugoslavia (highways, power plant), Poland (highway construction)
maintenance of equipment in:
Egypt (aircraft)
Foreign Military Aid Extended:
financial aid to:
PLO (al-Fatah, Abu al-Abbas faction of PLF, ALF); Iranian anti-government groups, including Mujahedeen Khalq
arms transfers to:
PLO (ALF--small arms); non-government militias in Lebanon (Sunni and Lebanese forces, including artillery, MRLs and tanks); Sudan (artillery pieces, ammunition, small arms) Jordan (tanks captured from Iran)
facilities provided to:
Palestinians (a camp for ALF, 15th May organization,

unconfirmed; PLO--headquarter facilities; PLA forces)
Cooperation in Military Operations with:
Turkey (against Kurdish rebels in Northern Iraq)
Cooperation in Arms Production/Assembly with:
Egypt (production of spares for Soviet arms);  Egypt  and
Argentina (development of SSM); companies  from  FRG
(involved in SSM production); France (electronics);  USSR
(small arms, ammunition); Italy (ammunition); Yugoslavia
(small arms, ammunition); companies from Italy,  FRG  and
other countries (assistance in toxic gas production)


INFRASTRUCTURE
  Road  Network:
    length:                                    13,720 km
    paved roads                                 8,190 km
    improved earth roads                        5,530 km
    main routes:
      Baghdad--Kirkuk--Mosul
      Baghdad--Mosul--al-Qamishli (Syria)--Diyarbakir(Turkey)
        /Mosul--al-Hasakah (Syria)
      Baghdad--al-Hadithah--Qusaybah--Dir e-Zor (Syria)
        /Qusaybah--Palmyra (Syria)
      Baghdad--al-Rutbah--Damascus (Syria)
      Baghdad--H-3--Mafraq (Jordan)
      Baghdad--al-Hillah--al-Najaf--al-Samawah--Basra
      Baghdad--al-Kut--al-Nasiriyah--Basra/al-Kut--al-Amarah
        --Basra
      Basra--Abadan (Iran)
      Basra--Kuwait
      al-Najaf--Rafha (Saudi Arabia, on  TAPline road leading
        also to Jordan)
  Railway  Network: (some  temporarily  inoperative  due  to
    Iran-Iraq War)
    length:                                     2,710 km
    standard gauge                              2,205 km
    narrow gauge                                  505 km
    main routes:
      Baghdad--Mosul--al-Qamishli--Aleppo
        (Syria)/Mosul--al-Qamishli--Ankara (Turkey)
      Baghdad--Kirkuk--Arbil
      Baghdad--al-Nassiriya--Basra
      Baghdad--al-Ramadi--al-Haditha--al-Qaim (Syrian border
        near Abu Kemal)
      Kirkuk--al Hadithah
      Baghdad--Mussayib--Karbala--Najaf--Kufa--Samawah--Basra
        --Umm Qasr

  Airfields:                                         96
    airfields by runway type:
      permanent surface fields                       65

```
    unpaved fields and usable airstrips            31
    airfields by runway length:
      over 3660 meters                              7
      2440--3659                                    48
      1220--2439                                    12
      under 1220                                    29
    international airports: Baghdad, Basra
    major domestic airfields: Arbil, H-3, al-Haditha, Kirkuk,
      Mosul
Airlines:
    companies: Iraqi Airways (international and domestic);
      Arab Air Cargo, owned jointly with Jordan (cargo,
      aircraft listed under Jordan)
    aircraft:
      Antonov An-12                                 5
      Antonov An-24                                 3
      Boeing 747-200C                               3
      Boeing 747-SP                                 1
      Boeing 737-200C                               2
      Boeing 727-200                                6
      Boeing 707-320C                               2
      Ilyushin IL-76                               30
      Lockheed Jetstar II                           6
      Mystere Falcon 50                             4
      Mystere Falcon 20F                            2
      Piaggio P-166                                 4
Maritime Facilities (temporarily inoperative due to war):
    harbors--Basra, Umm Qasr
    oil terminals--Khor al-Amaya, Faw (in Iranian hands  from
      February 1986 to March 1988), Mina al-Bakr
Merchant Marine (flag carrying,  operating  from  non-Iraqi
    ports due to war):
```

| vessel type | number | DWT |
|---|---|---|
| crude carrier | 14 | 1,377,700 |
| small tanker | 2 | 17,083 |
| general cargo/container | 4 | 14,222 |
| general cargo | 9 | 96,062 |
| training/cargo | 1 | 12,650 |
| ro/ro | 3 | 11,955 |
| reefer | 1 | 9,247 |
| ferry | 1 | 1,223 |
| barge | 4 | 6,648 |
| product tanker | 2 | 16,388 |
| TOTAL | 41 | 1,563,178 |

```
Defense Production:
    army equipment:
      manufacture--small arms and artillery ammunition (with
        Soviet, Yugoslav and Italian assistance); electronics
        (with French assistance); toxic gas: mustard, tabun,
        sarin; biological weapons (unconfirmed);  SSM  under
```

development (in cooperation with Argentina and
Egypt); upgrading of Soviet designed Scud B SSMs
(with assistance from Egypt and companies from FRG)
production under license--ATRLs, rifles
aircraft armament:
production under license--Chile-designed Cardoen aerial
CBU (unconfirmed); aerial bombs

## ARMED FORCES
### Personnel:
military forces--

| | regular | reserves | total |
|---|---|---|---|
| army | 555,000 | 480,000 | 1,035,000 |
| air force | 40,000 | | 40,000 |
| navy | 5,000 | | 5,000 |
| TOTAL | 600,000 | 480,000 | 1,080,000 |

para-military forces--
Popular Army--650,000-800,000 (about one quarter
currently mobilized; slow demobilization in effect
since December 1988); security troops; 15,000 pro-Iraqi
Iranians of the Iranian National Liberation Army,
organized and based in Iraq

### Army:
major units: (some units not fully organized)

| unit type | army corps HQ | divisions | independent brigades |
|---|---|---|---|
| all arms | 9 | | |
| armored | | 7 | |
| mechanized | | 3 | |
| infantry/ | | | |
| special forces | | 45 (unconfirmed) | 14 |
| TOTAL | 9 | 55 | 14 |

small arms:
personal weapons--
7.62mm P.P.Sh. SMG
7.62mm AK-47 (Kalashnikov) AR
7.62mm SKS (Simonov) SAR
5.45mm AK-74 (Kalashnikov, unconfirmed) AR
machine guns--
14.5mm KPV HMG
14.5mm ZPU 14.5x4 HMG (in anti-aircraft role)
12.7mm D.Sh.K. 38/46 (Degtyarev) HMG
7.62mm SGM (Goryunov) MMG
7.62mm RPD (Degtyarev) LMG
7.62mm PK/PKS (Kalashnikov) LMG
light & medium mortars--
82mm M-43
light ATRLs--
RPG-7
tanks:

| model | | number |
|---|---|---|
| high quality | | |
| T-72 | | 1000 |
| medium quality | | |
| T-62 | | 1200 |
| T-55/Type 59/Type 69/M-77 | | 3600 |
| | (sub-total | 4800) |
| low quality | | |
| PT-76 | | 200 |
| TOTAL | | 6000 |

APCs/ARVs:

| model | | number |
|---|---|---|
| high quality | | |
| BMP-1 | | 600 |
| YW-531 | | + |
| Engesa EE-9/11 | | 300 |
| | (sub-total | 1800) |
| others | | |
| AML-90/60 | | |
| BRDM-2 | | |
| BTR-40/50/60 | | |
| FUG-70 | | |
| M-3 (Panhard) | | |
| OT-62/OT-64 | | |
| MT-LB (an artillery prime-mover, employed also as APC) | | |
| | (sub-total | 3200) |
| TOTAL | | 5000 |

on order: EE-3/9/11/17

artillery:
  self propelled guns and howitzers--
    155mm M-109 SP howitzer (captured)
    155mm GCT SP howitzer                                85
    152mm M-1973 SP howitzer
    122mm M-1974 SP howitzer
    100mm SU-100 SP gun
  towed guns and howitzers--
    155mm G-5 howitzer/gun                              100
    155mm GHN-45 howitzer/gun
    155mm M-114 A1 howitzer
    152mm M-1943 howitzer
    130mm M-46 gun/ 130mm Type 59 gun
    122mm D-30 howitzer
    122mm M-1938 howitzer
    105mm M-56 Pack howitzer
    85mm field/AT gun
  mortars, over 160mm--
    160mm mortar
  mortars, under 160mm, but excluding light and medium--
    120mm M-43 mortar

```
    TOTAL                                          4500-5000
  artillery ammunition carriers--
    MT-LB (some MT-LB used as artillery prime-movers,
    command post vehicles, mortar carriers, MRL carriers
    and other tasks)
  MRLs--
    300mm SS-60 (unconfirmed)
    262mm Ababil (unconfirmed)
    180mm SS-40 Astros
    132mm BM-13
    130mm
    127mm SS-30 Astros/SBAT-127
    122mm BM-21/BM-11
  on order: 155mm GCT SP howitzers; 300mm SS-60
engineering equipment:
  MTU-55 bridging tanks
  GSP self propelled ferries
  mine-clearing rollers
  PMP pontoon bridges
  Soviet-model tank-towed bridges
AFV transporters:                                    2800
anti-tank weapons:
  missiles--                                      launchers
    AT-3 (Sagger)
    AT-4 (Spigot)
    BGM-71A TOW
    BRDM-2 (carrying AT-3 Sagger) SP
    M-3 (carrying HOT) SP
    VCR/ TH (carrying HOT) SP                        100
    MILAN
    Swingfire
    TOTAL                                           1500
  guns--
    107mm B-11 recoilless rifle
    73mm SPG-9 recoilless gun
surface-to-surface missiles and rockets:
  model                                           launchers
    FROG-7                                            24
    SS-1 (Scud B)                                     24
    al-Hussein (Iraqi   modified   SS-1)               +
    TOTAL                                            48+
  on order: al-Abbas, Badr 2000
army anti-aircraft defenses:
  missiles--                                      launchers
    SA-6  (Gainful)
    SA-7  (Grail)
    SA-8  (Gecko)                                     20
    SA-9  (Gaskin) SP
    SA-11 (Gadfly, unconfirmed)
    SA-13 (Gopher)
```

```
      SA-14 (Gremlin)
      Roland                                              90-100
    short-range guns--                                    number
      57mm ZSU 57x2 SP
      57mm
      37mm
      23mm ZSU 23x4 SP (Gun Dish)
      23mm ZU 23x2
      TOTAL                              (estimate) 1000
  CW capabilities:
    personal protective equipment
    Soviet type unit decontamination equipment
    gas: mustard, sarin, tabun
    biological warfare capabilities:
    biological weapons and toxins (unconfirmed)
Air Force:
  aircraft--general:                                      number
    combat aircraft                                       705
    transport aircraft                                    86
    helicopters                                           585
  combat aircraft:                                        number
    interceptors--
      high quality
        MiG-25 (Foxbat)                                   30
        MiG-29 (Fulcrum; multi-role aircraft
          employed in interceptor role;
          quantity unconfirmed)                           26
                                  (sub-total              56)
      others
        MiG-21 MF/bis/U (Fishbed)/F-7                     170
        MiG-19/F-6                                        30
                                  (sub-total              200)
      Total                                               256
    strike and multi-role aircraft--
      high quality
        Su-24 (Fencer C)                                  15
      medium quality
        MiG-23 B (Flogger)/MiG-27                         90
        Mirage F-1B/EQ5/EQ2/EQ4                           72
        Su-20/22 (Fitter C/H)                             150
        Su-25 (Frogfoot)                                  40
                                  (sub-total              352)
      others
        F-6                                               30
        Su-7B (Fitter A)                                  30
                                  (sub-total              60)
      Total                                               427
    on order: additional MiG-29 (Fulcrum); 60  additional
        Su-25; Mirage 2000 (unconfirmed); Su-24 (Fencer C)
    bombers--
```

```
    Tu-22 (Blinder)                                8
    Tu-16 (Badger)/H-6 (B-6D)                     14
    Total                                         22
transport aircraft:
  An-2 (Colt)                                     10
  An-12 (Cub, some converted
    to refuelling a/c)                            10
  An-24 (Coke)                                     6
  An-26 (Curl)                                     9
  IL-76 (Candid)                                  24
  IL-14 (Crate)                                   13
  Mystere Falcon 20                               12
  Tu-124A/Tu-134 (Crusty)                          2
  TOTAL                                           86
  on order: 6 L-100 (unconfirmed)
training and liaison aircraft:
  Embraer EMB-312 (Tucano)                        80
  L-29 (Delfin)                                   42
  L-39 (Albatross)                                75
  MBB-223 Flamingo                                16
  Pilatus PC-7                                    52
  Pilatus PC-9 (unconfirmed)                      19
  Yak-11 (Moose)                                  10
  TOTAL                                          294
  on order: Alpha Jet (unconfirmed)
helicopters:                                   number
  attack--  (part of Army Aviation)
    Alouette III (armed)                          25
    Mi-24 (Hind)                                  45
    SA-342 Gazelle                                60
    MBB BO-105                                     30
                            (sub-total          160)
  heavy transport--
    AS-61                                          6
    SA-321 Super Frelon (also employed in
      maritime attack role)                       10
    Mi-6 (Hook)                                   12
                            (sub-total           28)
  medium transport--
    Mi-8/Mi-17 (Hip)                             220
    Mi-4 (Hound)                                  15
    SA-330 Puma                                   10
    Bell 214                                      40
    Mi-2 (Hoplite)                                10
                            (sub-total          295)
  light transport--
    Alouette III                                  22
    Hughes 500D                                   28
    Hughes 300C                                   28
    Hughes 530F                                   24
```

# IRAQ

```
                              (sub-total         102)
ASW--
  AB-212 (unconfirmed)
TOTAL                                            585
on order: 6 AS-332 Super Puma; BK-117; 6 AS-365 Dauphin
   2
advanced armament:
  air-to-air missiles--
    AA-2 (Atoll)
    AA-6 (Acrid, unconfirmed)
    AA-7 (Apex, unconfirmed)
    R-530
    R-550 Magique
  air-to-ground missiles--
    AM-39 Exocet
    Armat (anti radar)
    AS-2 Kipper (unconfirmed)
    AS-4 Kitchen
    AS-5 Kelt
    AS-6 Kingfish
    AS-7 Kerry
    AS-9
    AS-10 (laser-guided)
    AS-12
    AS-30L (laser-guided)
    Hai Ying-2 (HY-2, Silkworm, air launched anti-ship
      version)
    LX anti-ship missile (unconfirmed)
    X-23 anti-radiation missile (unconfirmed)
  bombs--
    Belouga CBU
    Cardoen CBU
anti-aircraft defenses:
  long-range missiles--
    model                                    batteries
      SA-2 (Guideline)/ SA-3 (Goa)                  60
  long-range guns--(possibly phased out)
    model                                       number
      100mm
      85mm
      TOTAL (estimate)                            200
  aircraft shelters--
    for all combat aircraft
mililtary airfields:                              20
  Arbil, Balad, Basra, H-2, H-3, Habbaniyah, Kirkuk, Kut
  el-Amarah, Mosul, al Nassiriya, al-Rashid (Baghdad),
  Shu'aiba, 8 additional
aircraft maintenance and repair capability:
  repair of main models, with assistance from Soviet,
  Egyptian, and French technicians
```

**IRAQ**

```
Navy:
  combat vessels:                                    number
    MFPBs--
      Ossa I
      Ossa II
      Total                                             8
    ASW vessels--
      SO-1 large patrol craft                           3
    mine warfare vessels--
      Nestin class minesweeper                          3
      T-43 class minesweeper                            2
      Yevgenia class coastal minesweeper                3
      Total                                             8
    gunboats/MTBs--
      P-6 MTB                                           6
    patrol craft--
      Niryat II                                         4
      PO-2 class                                        3
      Poluchat I                                        2
      SO-1                                              3
      Thornycroft 100 ft. (PB-90, 30.5 meter)           3
      Thornycroft 36 ft. (10.9 meter)                   8
      Thornycroft 21 ft. (6.4 meter)                    4
      Zhuk class                                        5
      Total                                            32
    on order: 4 Lupo class missile frigates and 6 Assad
      class missile corvettes (formerly Wadi class)--
      mostly ready for delivery, but held in Italy
  landing craft:
    Polnochny class LCT                               2-3
    SRN-6 (Winchester) hovercraft                       6
    Total                                             8-9
    on order: 3 3500 ton LSTs (completed and available in
      Denmark)
  auxiliary vessels:
    training frigate, 1850 ton (can carry SSMs)         1
    746 ton harbor craft (former royal yacht)           1
    Stromboli class support ship (held in Egypt)
    advanced armament:
    surface-to-surface missiles--
      SS-N-2 Styx
      on order: OTOMAT Mk.2
  coastal defense:
    Hai Ying-2 (HY-2, Silkworm)
  naval bases:                                          3
    Basra, Um Qasr , Faw (all damaged during the war)
  ship maintenance and repair capability:
    one 6,000 ton capacity floating dock (held in Egypt)
```

# 6. ISRAEL

BASIC DATA
Official Name of State: State of Israel
Head of State: President Haim Herzog
Prime Minister: Itzhak Shamir
Minister of Defense: Itzhak Rabin
Chief of the General Staff: Lieutenant General Dan Shomron
Commander of the Air Force: Major General Avihu Ben-Nun
Commander of Ground Forces HQ: Major General Uri Sagui
Commander of the Navy: Rear Admiral Micha Ram
Area: 20,325 sq. km. including East Jerusalem and vicinity annexed in 1967 (not including Golan Heights, 1,100 sq. km., to which Israeli law was applied in 1981)
Population:                                              4,404,000
  ethnic subdivision:
    Jews                             3,611,000            82.0%
    Arabs, Druze, and
    others (Armenian,
      Circassian, European)            793,000            18.0%
  religious subdivision:
    Jews                             3,611,000            82.0%
    Muslims                            617,000            14.0%
    Christians                         101,000             2.3%
    Druze and others                    75,000             1.7%
GDP:
  1986--$29.4 billion
  1987--$34.7 billion
Balance of Payments (goods, services & unilateral transfer payments):
  year       income           expenditure          balance
  1986       $17.07 bil.      $15.61 bil.          +$1.46 bil.
  1987       $18.60 bil.      $19.60 bil.          -$1.00 bil.
  (These figures include special emergency economic aid grants from the USA in the amount of $750 million for 1986. Israel's surplus would otherwise have been $501 million in 1986.)
Defense Expenditure:
  1987--$4.6 billion
  1988--$5.1 billion
Foreign Military Aid Received:
  financial aid from:
    USA--$1.8 billion grant (1988)
  military training:
    trainees abroad in--USA, Britain, France, FRG
  arms transfers from:
    USA (tanks, SP artillery, naval SSMs, combat aircraft, attack helicopters, tank transporters); Belgium (LMGs); Britain (spare parts); France (spare parts, via intermediaries); FRG (tank transporters, trucks); Italy

(helicopters, naval guns)
Foreign Military Aid Extended:
  financial aid to:
  South Lebanon militia--$20 million
  military training:
    advisors / instructors / technicians in--Colombia*
    (unconfirmed), Ecuador*, Liberia, Singapore*, South
    Lebanon (SLA militia), Sri Lanka* (unconfirmed), USA,
    Zaire
    foreign trainees from--Colombia*, Lebanon (various
    militias), Liberia, Papua New Guinea, Sri Lanka*,
    Zaire
  arms transfers tɔ:
    militias in Lebanon (small arms, tanks, artillery
    pieces); Argentina (aircraft sub-components, AAMs,
    aircraft radars, MRLs); Australia (conversion of Boeing
    707 aircraft into aerial tankers); Brazil* (naval
    SSMs); Belgium* (naval tactical training center);
    Cameroon* (combat aircraft, transport aircraft); Canada
    (ammunition, mine clearing rollers); Chile* (AAMs,
    AAGs, tanks, MFPBs); Colombia* (combat aircraft, small
    arms; combat aircraft on order); Ecuador* (AAMs, combat
    aircraft); El Salvador* (transport aircraft); FRG
    (ammunition, electronic equipment, ECMs, mini-RPVs on
    order); Guatemala (rifles); Haiti (Uzi SMGs); Honduras*
    (transport aircraft); Ireland (ballistic helmets;
    communications equipment, unconfirmed); Italy (tank
    ammunition); Kenya (naval SSMs); Liberia (transport
    aircraft); Mexico (transport aircraft); Papua New
    Guinea (patrol craft, transport aircraft); Paraguay
    (transport aircraft); Singapore* (SSMs, AAMs, naval
    tactical training center); Peru (ARVs, helicopters,
    patrol boats, unconfirmed); South Africa* (MFPBs, SSMs,
    rifles, refuelling aircraft); Spain* (tank guns, tank
    fire control systems, optronics and range finders); Sri
    Lanka* (patrol boats, small arms); Swaziland*
    (transport aircraft); Switzerland (mini-RPVs, tank
    ammunition); Taiwan* (SSMs); Thailand (transport
    aircraft, mini-RPVs); UNITA* (Angolan anti-government
    rebels; captured Soviet arms, unconfirmed); USA (parts,
    mini-RPVs, light AT rockets, tactical air-launched
    decoys, combat aircraft on lease, mine ploughs for
    tanks); Venezuela (MRLs); Zaire (small arms)


*According to foreign and Israeli publications

forces deployed abroad in:
  Lebanon--observation units on a small scale in the
  security zone in South Lebanon (about 1000 men)
Cooperation in Arms Production/Assembly with:
  Argentina* (tank components, unconfirmed); Chile*
  (assistance in upgrading combat aircraft in Chile;
  provision of AAGs and turrets for Chilean-made SP AAG
  vehicle); Colombia* (assistance in upgrading combat
  aircraft in Colombia); FRG (joint production in FRG of
  Israeli mini-RPVs); South Africa* (joint production of
  a South African fighter aircraft, unconfirmed);
  Switzerland* (cooperation in upgrading fighter
  aircraft, unconfirmed; cooperation in production of
  mini RPVs in Switzerland); USA (aircraft, electronics,
  naval vessels, tank guns, terminal guidance bombs)
Joint Maneuvers with:
  USA


INFRASTRUCTURE
  Road Network:
    length (paved):                         4,760 km
    main routes:
      Tel Aviv--Jerusalem
      Tel Aviv--Hadera--Haifa
      Tel Aviv--Ashdod--Beer Sheva
      Hadera--Afula--Tiberias/ Afula--Amiad--Rosh-Pina
      Haifa--Tiberias
      Haifa--Nahariya--Naqura (Lebanon)
      Acre--Safed--Rosh Pina/Acre--Amiad
      Tiberias--Metula--Marj Ayoun (Lebanon)
      Beer Sheva--Eilat
      Rafah (Rafiah)--Nitsana--Eilat
      Eilat--Sharm al-Shaykh (Egypt)
      Beer Sheva--Nitzana--Isma'iliya (Egypt)
      Tel Aviv--Gaza--Kantara (Egypt)
      Jerusalem--Hebron--Arad/Beer Sheva
      Jerusalem--Nablus--Afula
      Jerusalem--Allenby Bridge--Amman (Jordan)
      Jerusalem--Jericho--Beit Shean/Jericho--Eilat
  Railway Network:
    length (standard gauge):              767 km


*According to foreign and Israeli publications

```
main routes:
  Tel Aviv--Haifa
  Haifa--Nahariya
  Tel Aviv--Jerusalem
  Tel Aviv--Beer Sheva--Oron
  Kiryat-Gat--Ashkelon--Ashdod
  Tel Aviv--Lod--Ashdod
  Tel Aviv--Lod--Gaza (serviceable as far as Rafah)
  Lod--Haifa
```

Airfields: 56

```
  airfields by runway type:
    permanent surface fields                          26
    unpaved fields and usable airstrips               30
  airfields by runway length:
    2440--3659 meters                                  6
    1220--2439                                        11
    under 1220                                        39
  international airports: Ben Gurion (Tel Aviv), Eilat
  major domestic airfields: Beer Sheva,  Haifa,  Jerusalem,
    Rosh Pina, Tel Aviv, Massada
```

Airlines:

companies:  El  Al  (international);  CAL  (cargo);
Arkia/Kanaf-Arkia (domestic and charter); Nesher (taxi
and charter); Sun d'Or (charter); Shahaf (domestic  and
charter); ICS (charter,  subsidiary  of  Sun  d'Or  and
Arkia)

aircraft:

| | |
|---|---|
| Boeing 767/767ER | 4 |
| Boeing 757 | 3 |
| Boeing 747-300B/200F/200B Combi/100F | 9 |
| Boeing 737-200 | 2 |
| Boeing 707-320B/320C | 4 |
| Britten-Norman BN-2 Islander | 1 |
| DHC-6 Twin Otter | 1 |
| DHC-7 (Dash 7) | 3 |
| Piper Navajo/Chieftain | 5 |

on order: 1 Boeing 757; 1 Boeing 747-200; 1 DHC-6  Twin
Otter

Maritime Facilities:

```
  harbors--Ashdod, Eilat, Haifa
  anchorages--Tel Aviv-Yaffo
  oil terminals--Ashkelon, Eilat, Haifa
  coal terminal--Hadera
```

Merchant Marine:

| vessel type | number | GRT |
|---|---|---|
| general cargo, including container | 63 | 654,000 |
| bulk carrier | 22 | 580,000 |
| other | 17 | 885,000 |
| TOTAL | 102 | 2,119,000 |

Defense Production:
  army equipment:
    manufacture--
      artillery pieces; small arms; ATGMs; ATRLs; electronic equipment; heavy, medium and light mortars; MRLs; mortar and small arms ammunition; mines; mine-clearing rollers; MRLs; tanks; tank guns; artillery ammmunition; SP AAGs (Soviet gun, USA carrier); tread width mine ploughs for tanks (TWMP)
  aircraft and air ammunition:
    manufacture--
      AAMs; CBUs; TV and laser terminal guidance bombs; combat aircraft; light transport aircraft; naval patrol aircraft; mini RPVs; ultra-light aircraft; operational flight trainer systems; radars; upgrading of combat aircraft
    production under license--
      helicopter parts
  ships and naval ammunition:
    manufacture--
      LCTs; MFPBs; patrol boats; SSMs
    production under license--
      patrol boats; torpedo components
  electronics:
    manufacture--
      radars; direction finders; ELINT equipment; EW jammers; radio transceivers; audio/video microwave transceivers; radio voice scramblers and encryption units
  optronics:
    manufacture--
      night vision devices, laser rangefinders and target designators

ARMED FORCES
  Personnel:
    military forces--

|  | regular | reserves | total |
|---|---|---|---|
| army | 130,000 | 365,000 | 495,000 |
| air force | 30,000 | 55,000 | 85,000 |
| navy | 10,000 | 10,000 | 20,000 |
| TOTAL | 170,000 | 430,000 | 600,000 |

    para-military forces--
    Nahal--7,500
    border police--6,000
  Army:
    major units (including reserves):

| unit type | divisions | independent brigades |
|---|---|---|
| armored | 12 | |

```
    mechanized/infantry/
      territorial                                20
    airborne                                      5
    TOTAL                         12             25
small arms:
  personal weapons--
    9mm Uzi SMG
    7.62mm AK-47 (Kalashnikov)
    7.62mm FAL/FN SAR
    7.62mm Galil sniper rifle
    7.62mm M-14 SAR
    5.56mm Galil AR
    5.56mm M-16 Al & A2 AR
  machine guns--
    12.7mm (0.5") Browning M2 HMG
    7.62mm (0.3") Browning M-1919 Al MMG
    7.62mm MAG (FN) LMG
    5.56mm Minimi (FN) LMG
  automatic grenade launchers--
    40mm Mk.19
  light and medium mortars--
    81mm Soltam
    60mm
    52mm IMI
  light ATRLs--
    M-72 LAW
    RPG-7
tanks:
  model                                      number
    high quality
      Merkava MK.I/MK.II*                       660
      M-60 A3/upgraded M-60                     550
                            (sub-total         1210)
    medium quality
      Centurion/upgraded Centurion            1100
      M-60/M-60 Al                             850
      M-48 A5                                  400
      T-62                                     150
      T-55 (upgraded)                          100
                            (sub-total         2600)
    TOTAL                                      3810
  on order: Merkava MK.III
APCs/ARVs:
  model                                      number
    high quality
      M-113 (various marks)
      Nagmashot*                               100
```

*According to foreign and Israeli publications

190

```
    RBY
                              (sub-total      5100)
    others
      M-2 & M-3 halftrack
      BTR-50
      OT-C2
      BRDM-2
                              (sub-total      3000)
    TOTAL                                     8100
artillery:
    self propelled guns and howitzers--
    203mm M-110 SP howitzer
    175mm M-107 SP gun
    155mm M-109 A1 & A2 SP howitzer
    155mm L-33 SP howitzer (SOLTAM)
    155mm M-50 SP howitzer
    towed guns and howitzers--
    155mm M-71 howitzer
    130mm M-46 gun
    122mm D-30 howitzer
    mortars, over 160mm--
    160mm SP mortar
    mortars, under 160mm, but excluding light and medium
    120mm mortar                              250
    TOTAL                                    1300
  artillery/mortar-locating radars--
    AN-TPQ-37
    AN-PPS-15
  MRLs--
    290mm MAR 290
    240mm
    140mm
    122mm BM-21
engineering equipment:
  Gilois motorized bridges
  M-123 Viper minefield crossing system
  M-69 A1 bridging tanks
  mine-clearing rollers
  mine layers
  Pomins II portable mine neutralization system*
  tank-towed bridges
  TLB (trailer launched bridge)
  Tread width mine ploughs (TWMP)
AFV transporters:
```

*According to foreign and Israeli publications

```
anti-tank weapons:
  missiles--
    AT-3 (Sagger)
    BGM-71A TOW and BGM-71C Improved TOW
    M-47 Dragon
    Mapats SP
    Israeli BGM-71C Improved TOW SP
surface-to-surface missiles and rockets:
  model                                       launchers
    MGM-52C (Lance)                               12
    Jericho Mk. I/II SSM (acc. to foreign publications)
army anti-aircraft defenses:
  missiles--                                  launchers
    MIM-72A Chaparral                          ca. 50
    MIM-43A Redeye
    SA-7 (Grail)
  short-range guns--                           number
    40mm Bofors L-70
    37mm
    ZU 23x2
    20mm M-163 Al Vulcan SP
    20mm TCM-20 Hispano Suiza SP
    20mm Hispano Suiza
  TOTAL                                          900
CW capabilities:
  personal protective equipment
  unit decontamination equipment
Air Force:
  aircraft--general:                           number
    combat aircraft (including 70 in storage)    635
    transport aircraft                            91
    helicopters                                  220
  combat aircraft:
    interceptors--
      high quality
        F-15 Eagle                               48
        F-16A/B/C (multi-role,
          employed as interceptor)              123
      Total                                     171
    strike and multi-role aircraft--
      high quality
        F-16D                                    24
      others
        F-4E/RF-4E Phantom                      145
        A-4 Skyhawk                             125
        Kfir C-2/TC-2/C-7/TC-7                  100
                            (sub-total          370)
        Kfir and A-4 Skyhawk (in storage)    ca. 70
      Total (including aircraft in storage)     464
```

```
on order: 5 F-15D, 60 F-16C/D
transport aircraft:
  Arava                                          10
  Beechcraft Queen Air                           12
  Boeing 707                                      8
  Boeing 707 tanker (refuelling)                  2
  C-130H Hercules                                24
  DC-3 Dakota (C-47)                             20
  Dornier Do-28                                  10
  KC-130 tanker (refuelling)                      2
  Westwind 1124                                   3
  TOTAL                                          91
training and liaison aircraft:
  Cessna U-206 (Stationair-6)                    41
  CM-170 Fouga Magister/Tzukit                   90
  Piper Cub                                      35
  TOTAL                                         166
helicopters:
  attack--
    AH-1G/1S Cobra                               42
    500MG Defender                               35
                                   (sub-total   77)
  naval attack/search & rescue--
    HH-65A Dolphin                                2
  heavy transport--
    CH-53                                        35
    SA-321 Super Frelon                           8
                                   (sub-total   43)
  medium transport--
    Bell-212                                     58
  light transport--
    AB-206 JetRanger/Bell-206L                   40
  TOTAL                                         220
  on order: 24 AH-64 Apache
maritime surveillance aircraft:
  Seascan (Westwind 1124N)                        5
miscellaneous aircraft:
  Beech AQM-37A target drone
  Beech BQM-107B target drone
  Boeing 707 ELINT and Boeing 707 EW aircraft
    (according to foreign publications)
  E-2C Hawkeye AEW                                4
  Mastiff (Tadiran) Mini-RPV
  MQM-74C Chukar II RPV
  Pioneer Mini-RPV
  Scout (IAI) Mini-RPV
  Teledyne Ryan 1241 RPV
  Samson tactical air-launched decoys
advanced armament:
  air-to-air missiles--
```

```
    AIM-9 Sidewinder; AIM-9L
    AIM-7 Sparrow
    Python 3
    R-530 Matra
    Shafrir
  air-to-ground missiles--
    AGM-78D Standard ARM
    AGM-65 Maverick
    AGM-62A Walleye
    AGM-45 A/B Shrike
  bombs--
    CBU
    runway-penetration bombs
    Pyramid TV terminal-guidance bombs
    Guillotine laser terminal-guidance bombs
  on order: AIM-9M AAM
EW and CEW equipment:
  chaff for combat aircraft
  on order:  20  AN/ALQ  131  electronic  countermeasures
    systems
anti-aircraft defenses:
  radars--
    Elta
    FPS-100
    AN/TPS-43
  long-range missiles--
    model
      HAWK
      MIM-23B Improved HAWK
  aircraft shelters--
    in all operational airfields, for combat aircraft
military airfields:                                      11
  Haifa, Hatzerim, Hatzor, Lod, Nevatim, Palmachim, Ramat
  David, Ramon, Tel Aviv, Tel Nof, Uvda
aircraft maintenance and repair capability:
  maintenance  on  all  models  in  service,  partly  in
  airfields,  partly  at  Israel  Aircraft  Industries
  facilities
Navy:
  combat vessels:                                  number
    submarines--
      IKL/Vickers Type 206                              3
    MFPBs--
      Dvora                                             2
      Sa'ar 2 and 3 class                              10
      Sa'ar 4 class (Reshef)                            8
      Sa'ar 4.5 class (Aliyah)                          4
      Total                                            24
    missile-armed hydrofoils--
      Flagstaff                                         2
```

```
patrol craft--
  Dabur class                                       37
  Kedma class (with Police Force)                    4
  PBR--Yatush                                        6
  Total                                             47
```
on order: 3 Sa'ar 5 missile corvettes (delivery in 1993-95); additional Dvora patrol craft without missiles
naval attack helicopters and maritime surveillance aircraft--listed under Air Force
landing craft:
```
  Ash class LCT                                      6
  Bat-Sheva class LST                                1
  LSM 1 class                                        3
  Sealand Mk III hovercraft                          2
  US type LCM                                        3
  TOTAL                                             15
```
auxiliary vessels:
```
  support ship                                       1
```
  swimmer delivery vehicles
advanced armament:
  surface-to-surface missiles--
    Gabriel 2 & 3
    RGM-84A Harpoon
  anti-missile guns--
    20mm Vulcan-Phalanx radar-controlled anti-missile gun
  advanced torpedoes--
    Mk.37 anti-submarine torpedoe
  on order: NT-37E anti-submarine torpedo, Barak anti-missile missile
special maritime forces:
  frogmen and divers
```
naval bases:                                         3
```
  Ashdod, Eilat, Haifa
ship maintenance and repair capability:
  repair and maintenance of all naval vessels in Haifa, partly in conjunction with Israel Wharves
Note: maritime surveillance aircraft and naval attack helicopters listed under Air Force

# 7. JORDAN

BASIC DATA
 Official Name of State: The Hashemite Kingdom of Jordan
 Head of State: King Hussein Ibn Talal al-Hashimi
 Prime Minister: Sharif Zaid Ben Shaker (also Defense Minister)
 Chief of the General Staff: General Fathi Abu Talib
 Commander of the People's Army: Major General Abd al-Majid al-Halaila
 Commander of the Air Force: Major General Ihsan Shardum
 Commander of the Air Defense Forces: Lieutenant General Khalid al-Trauna
 Area: 90,700 sq. (excluding West Bank; Jordan renounced all claims to this territory in July 1989)
 Population: 2,850,000
  ethnic subdivision:

| | | |
|---|---:|---:|
| Arabs | 2,759,500 | 98.0% |
| Circassians & Armenians | 91,000 | 2.0% |

  religious subdivision:

| | | |
|---|---:|---:|
| Sunni Muslims | 2,668,000 | 93.6% |
| Greek Orthodox & other Christians | 157,000 | 5.5% |
| Others | 25,000 | 0.9% |

 GDP:
  1986--$4.69 billion
  1987--$4.98 billion
 Balance of Payments (goods, services & unilateral transfer payments):

| year | income | expenditure | balance |
|---|---|---|---|
| 1986 | $3.51 bil. | $3.55 bil. | -$ 40 mil. |
| 1987 | $3.62 bil. | $3.98 bil. | -$360 mil. |

 Defense Expenditure:
  1986--$735 million
  1987--$745 million ( unconfirmed; including Arab aid)
 Foreign Military Aid Received:
  financial aid from:
   USA--$26.5 million, grant; Saudi Arabia--grant; Inter-Arab aid--$454 million grant (mostly from Saudi Arabia and Kuwait); Japan--$100 million loan, for road construction
  military training:
   foreign advisors/instructors from--USA, USSR (about 25-40); Egypt
   trainees abroad in--Britain, Egypt, France, FRG, Pakistan, Saudi Arabia, USA, USSR
  arms transfers from:
   Australia (tank targets); Belgium (tank fire control systems); Brazil (APCs); Britain (combat engineering equipment, radars); France (combat aircraft,

196

helicopters, advanced aerial weaponry, Artillery fire
control systems, ATRLs); Spain (transport aircraft,
trainer aircraft); USA (tanks, SP artillery, terminally
guided artillery shells, ATGMs, AAGs, SAMs,
helicopters); USSR (SAMs, AAGs, APCs)
maintenance of equipment in:
FRG (transport aircraft)
Foreign Military Aid Extended:
military training:
advisors/instructors in--Bahrain, Iraq, Kuwait, Oman,
Qatar, UAE
foreign trainees from--Bahrain, Iraq, Kuwait, Lebanon,
Oman, PLO, Qatar, Saudi Arabia, Sudan, UAE, YAR
arms transfers to:
Iraq (ammunition); Badr unit of the PLA (small arms);
Sudan (surplus obsolete arms)
facilities provided to:
Iraq (use of harbor, airfields and supply route); PLA
(camp for Badr unit)
maintenance of equipment for:
Sudan (civil aircraft)
Cooperation in Arms Production/Assembly with:
Britain and USA (tank upgrading)
Joint Maneuvers with:
USA (Special Forces, Air Force); Egypt; Britain

## INFRASTRUCTURE
Road Network:
| | |
|---|---:|
| length: | 7,500 km |
| paved roads | 5,500 km |
| gravel and stone roads | 2,000 km |

main routes:
Amman--Ramtha--Dar'a (Syria)
Amman--Mafraq--Baghdad (Iraq)
Amman--Ma'an--Tabuk (Saudi Arabia)/Ma'an-- Aqaba
Amman--Allenby Bridge--Jerusalem (Israel)
Amman--al-Salt--Damiah Bridge--Nablus (West Bank)
Railway Network:

| | |
|---|---:|
| length (narrow gauge): | 619 km |

main routes:
Amman--Ramtha--Dar'a (Syria)
Amman--Ma'an--Aqaba/Ma'an--Haret Ammar (Saudi Arabian
border)

| | |
|---|---:|
| Airfields: | 19 |
| airfields by runway type: | |
| permanent surface fields | 14 |
| unpaved fields and usable airstrips | 5 |
| airfields by runway length: | |
| over 3660 meters | 2 |
| 2440--3659 | 14 |

```
1220--2439                                                  1
under 1220                                                  2
```
international airports: Amman (Queen Alia), Aqaba
major domestic airfields: Amman (Marka), Mafraq, Zarqa,
    Ma'an, H-5
Airlines:
  companies: Royal Jordanian Airline (international and
    domestic); Arab Air Cargo, owned jointly with Iraq
    (cargo, aircraft listed here); Arab Wings (charter;
    subsidiary of Royal Jordanian)
  aircraft:

| | |
|---|---|
| Airbus A-310-300 | 3 |
| Boeing 727-200 | 3 |
| Boeing 707-320C | 4 |
| L-1011-500 Tristar | 7 |

  on order: 6 A-320 Airbus (delivery 1990); 3 additional
    A-310 (delivery 1989-90); 5 A-340 Airbus
Maritime Facilities:
  harbors--Aqaba
  oil terminals--Aqaba
Merchant Marine:

| vessel type | number | DWT |
|---|---|---|
| Ro-ro | 1 | 3,878 |
| bulk carrier | 2 | 43,832 |
| TOTAL | 3 | 47,710 |

ARMED FORCES
  Personnel:
    military forces--

| | regular | reserves | total |
|---|---|---|---|
| army | 80,000 | 60,000 | 140,000 |
| air force | 9,700 | -- | 9,700 |
| navy | 300 | -- | 300 |
| TOTAL | 90,000 | 60,000 | 150,000 |

    para-military forces--
    People's Army--40,000
  Army:
    major units:

| unit type | divisions | independent brigades |
|---|---|---|
| armored | 2 | |
| mechanized | 2 | |
| infantry | | 2 |
| airborne/ special forces | | 1 |
| TOTAL | 4 | 3 |

    para-military forces--
    one brigade of General Security Forces (gendarmerie)
  small arms:
    personal weapons--

```
7.62mm AK-47 (Kalashnikov) AR
7.62mm G-3 (Heckler & Koch) AR
5.56mm M-16 Al AR
machine guns--
  12.7mm (0.5") Browning M2 HMG
  7.62mm (0.3") Browning M-1919 MMG
  7.62mm MAG (FN) LMG
  7.62mm M-60D GPMG/LMG
light and medium mortars--
  81mm M-29
light ATRLs--
  APILAS
  3.5" M-20 (being phased out)
  LAW-80
```

tanks: (including some in storage)

| model | number |
|---|---|
| high quality | |
|   Chieftain (Jordanian designation Khalid) | 275 |
|   M-60 A3 | 100 |
| (sub-total | 375) |
| medium quality | |
|   Centurion (improved, Jordanian designation Tariq) | 290 |
|   M-60 Al | 100 |
|   Chieftain (from Iran, captured by Iraq, in storage, not yet serviceable) | 90 |
| (sub-total | 480) |
| low quality | |
|   M-48 Al (in storage, not operational) | 260 |
| TOTAL | 1115 |

APCs/ARVs:

| model | number |
|---|---|
| high quality | |
|   BMP-2 | 25 |
|   M-113 A1/A2 | 1240 |
|   Engesa EE-11 (with Security Forces) | 100 |
| (sub-total | 1365) |
| others | |
|   Ferret | 140 |
|   Saracen/Saladin (obsolete, in storage) | 60 |
| (sub-total | 200) |
| TOTAL | 1565 |

```
artillery:
  self propelled guns and howitzers--
    203mm M-110 A2 SP howitzer
    155mm M-109 A2 SP howitzer
    155mm M-44 SP howitzer
  towed guns and howitzers--
    203mm (8") M-115 gun
    155mm M-59 (Long Tom) gun
```

```
    155mm M-114 howitzer
    105mm M-52 SP howitzer
    105mm M-102 A1 howitzer
  mortars, less than 160mm, but excluding light and
    medium
    120mm mortar
  TOTAL                                              600
PGM--
  100 155mm Copperhead projectiles (CLGP)
engineering equipment:
  bridges (British model)
  British mine-clearing ploughs and dozers attached to
  Chieftain and Centurion tanks
AFV transporters:              (unconfirmed)        200
anti-tank weapons:
  missiles--                               launchers
    BGM-71A TOW/BGM-71C Improved TOW
    M-47 Dragon
    M-901 ITV SP (TOW under armor)
  TOTAL                                              550
army anti-aircraft defenses:
  missiles--                               launchers
    MIM-43A Redeye                              300
    SA-8  (Gecko)                                20
    SA-13 (Gopher) SP
    SA-14 (Gremlin)
  short-range guns--                          number
    40mm M-42 SP                                   +
    23mm ZSU 23x4 SP (Gun Dish)                  16
    20mm M-163 A1 Vulcan SP                     100
  on order: Mistral SAMs (unconfirmed), 35mm 35x2 AAG
    (unconfirmed)
CW capabilities:
  personal protective and decontamination equipment
Air Force:
  aircraft--general:                          number
    combat aircraft                            107
    transport aircraft                          14
    helicopters                                 69
  combat aircraft:
    strike and multi-role aircraft--
      medium quality
        Mirage F-1 C/E                          34
      others
        F-5 E/F                                 73
      TOTAL                                    107
      on order: 12-20 Mirage 2000
  transport aircraft:
    Boeing 727                                   1
    C-130 Hercules                               6
```

```
CASA C-212                                              2
Mystere Falcon 50                                       3
Sabreliner 75A                                          2
TOTAL                                                  14
on order: C-130; 1 CASA C-212; 2 CASA/Nurtanio CN-235
training and liaison aircraft:
AS-202 Bravo (unconfirmed)                             20
CASA C-101                                             16
Cessna 318 (T-37)                                      10
BAe-SA-3-125 Bulldog                                   19
TOTAL                                                  65
helicopters:
  attack--
    AH-1G/1S Cobra                                     24
  medium transport--
    S-76                                               18
    UH-60A Black Hawk                                   3
    AS-332 Super Puma                                  12
                                    (sub-total         33)
  light transport--
    Alouette III                                        1
    500 MG                                              8
    MBB BO-105            (with Police)                 3
                                    (sub-total         12)
TOTAL                                                  69
on order: AS-332 Super Puma (unconfirmed)
advanced armament:
  air-to-air missiles--
    AIM-9B/E/J/N/P Sidewinder
    R-550 Magique
  bombs--
    Belouga CBU
    Durandal anti-runway bombs
anti-aircraft defenses:
  radars--
    model                                           Units
      AN/TPS-43
      AN/TPS-63
      Marconi S711                                      5
    on order: Marconi radars (Britain)
  long-range missiles--
    model                                       batteries
      MIM-23B Improved HAWK                            14
  aircraft shelters--
    for all combat aircraft
military airfields:                                     6
  Amman (Marka), Azrak, H-4, H-5, Ja'afar, Mafraq
aircraft maintenance and repair capability:
  repair and maintenance of all models, possibly with
  French/American technical help
```

## JORDAN

```
Navy:
  combat vessels:                            number
    patrol craft--
      Bertram class (Enforcer)
        38 ft. (11.6 meter)                      4
    on order: 3 30 meter patrol boats from Vosper
      Thornycroft
  special maritime forces:
    a few divers
  naval base:
    Aqaba
```

# 8. KUWAIT

BASIC DATA
Official Name of State: State of Kuwait
Head of State: Emir Jabir al-Ahmad al-Sabah
Prime Minister: Sa'ad Abdullah al-Sabah (also Crown Prince)
Minister of Defense: Nawaf al-Ahmad al-Jabir al-Sabah
Chief of the General Staff: Major General Mizyad Abd al-Rahman al-Sani
Commander of the Ground Forces: Lieutenant General Youssuf Abd al-Rahman al-Rashid
Commander of the Air Force and Air Defense Forces: Brigadier General Daud al-Ghanim
Area: 24,280 sq. km.

| Population: | | 1,870,000 |
|---|---|---|
| ethnic subdivision: | | |
| Arabs | 1,629,000 | 87.1% |
| Persians | 93,000 | 5.0% |
| Southeast Asians | 40,000 | 2.1% |
| Europeans | 39,000 | 2.1% |
| Others | 69,000 | 3.7% |
| religious subdivision: | | |
| Sunni Muslims | 1,029,000 | 55.0% |
| Shi'ite Muslims | 561,000 | 30.0% |
| Christians, Parsis, Hindus and others | 280,000 | 15.0% |
| nationality subdivision: | | |
| Kuwaitis | 729,000 | 39.0% |
| Aliens | | |
| other Arabs | 729,000 | 39.0% |
| Southeast Asians | 168,000 | 9.0% |
| Iranians | 76,000 | 4.0% |
| Others | 168,000 | 9.0% |

GDP:
  1985--$19.68 billion
  1986--$17.12 billion
Balance of Payments (goods, services & unilateral transfer payments):

| year | income | expenditure | balance |
|---|---|---|---|
| 1986 | $16.38 bil. | $11.39 bil. | +$4.99 bil. |
| 1987 | $15.22 bil. | $10.81 bil. | +$4.41 bil. |

Defense Expenditure:
  1985--$1.83 billion
  1987--$1.40 billion (unconfirmed)
Foreign Military Aid Received:
  military training received:
    foreign advisors/instructors from--Algeria, Britain, Egypt, France, FRG, India, Jordan, Pakistan, USA,

## KUWAIT

USSR
  trainees abroad in--Algeria, Britain, Egypt, France,
    FRG, Jordan, Saudi Arabia, USA, USSR
arms transfers from:
  Austria (small arms); Britain (APCs, tanks, trainer
  aircraft, naval patrol craft, landing craft, trucks);
  Egypt (APCs); France (radars, combat aircraft,
  helicopters, SP artillery, ATGMs); FRG (AFV
  transporters, MFPBs); Hungary (electronics, probably in
  collaboration with USSR); Japan (tugs); USA (APCs,
  patrol boats, SAMs); USSR (surface-to-surface rockets,
  SAMs, AAGs)
construction aid by:
  Japan (naval base)
Foreign Military Aid Extended:
  financial aid to:
    Iraq--grants and loans; Jordan; Palestinian
    organizations--grants; Syria; Tunisia
  facilities provided to:
    Iraq--use of harbors, overflight rights for Iraqi
    aircraft
Joint Maneuvers with:
  GCC (members: Bahrain, Kuwait, Oman, Qatar, Saudi Arabia,
  UAE)

INFRASTRUCTURE
Road Network:
  length:                                        2,600 km
  paved roads                                    2,300 km
  gravel and improved earth roads                  300 km
  main routes:
    Kuwait--al-Jahrah--Raudhatain--Basra (Iraq)
    Kuwait--al-Jahrah--Hafar al-Batin (Saudi Arabia)
    Kuwait--al-Ahmadi
    Kuwait--Fahaheel--Mina al-Ahmadi--Mina Saud--Ras Tanura
      (Saudi Arabia)
Airfields:                                              4
  airfields by runway type:
    permanent surface fields                           4
  airfields by runway length:
    2440--3659 meters                                  4
  international airport: Kuwait
  major domestic airfields: al-Ahmadi
Airlines:
  companies: Kuwait Airways (international)
  aircraft:
    Airbus A-300 C4-600                                1
    Airbus A-310-200                                   5
    Boeing 767-200ER                                   3
    Boeing 747-200 combi                               4

```
    Boeing 727-200                                          3
    Gulfstream III                                          2
    on order: 4 Boeing 767-200ER
Maritime Facilities:
  harbors--Shuwaikh (Kuwait City); Shuaiba, Mina al-Ahmadi
  anchorage--Khor al-Mufatta
  oil   terminals--Mina   al-Ahmadi/Sea   Island;   Mina
    Abdullah; Mina Saud (Zour)
Merchant Marine:
```

| vessel type | number | DWT |
|---|---|---|
| crude carrier | 2 | 176,101 |
| gas tanker (LPG) | 1 | 61,401 |
| product tanker | 7 | 306,270 |
| asphalt tanker | 1 | 4,225 |
| bunkering tanker | 1 | 18,949 |
| chemical tanker | 1 | 4,925 |
| general cargo/container | 16 | 379,091 |
| container | 5 | 155,471 |
| livestock carrier | 6 | 148,195 |
| TOTAL | 40 | 1,254,028 |

ARMED FORCES
  Personnel:
    military forces--

| | |
|---|---|
| army | 16,000 |
| air force | 2,200 |
| navy | 1,800 |
| TOTAL | 20,100 |

  Army:
    major units:

| unit type | brigades |
|---|---|
| armored | 1 |
| mechanized | 2 |
| tactical reserve brigade | 1 |
| TOTAL | 4 |

```
    small arms:
    personal weapons--
      9mm Sterling Mk.4 SMG
      7.62mm CAL/FAL (FN) SAR
      7.62mm SSG-69 sniping rifle
    machine guns--
      7.62mm Browning M-1919 MMG
      7.62mm MAG (FN) LMG
    light and medium mortars--
      81mm
    tanks:
```

| model | number |
|---|---|
| medium quality | |
| Chieftain | 165 |
| Centurion | 40 |

```
        Vickers Mk.1                                      70
     TOTAL                                               275
APCs/ARVs:
  model                                             number
    high quality
      M-113
      V-150 Commando
    others
      AT-105 Saxon
      Saladin/Saracen/Ferret
      Fahd
    TOTAL                                               480
    on order: 100 Fahd, 245 BMP-2
artillery:
    self propelled guns and howitzers--
      155mm M-109 A2 SP howitzer                         18
      155mm Mk. F-3 (AMX) SP howitzer                    40
    TOTAL                                                58
  MRLs--
    on order: Soviet MRLs (unconfirmed)
AFV transporters:                                        30
anti-tank weapons:
  missiles--
    AT-4 Spigot (unconfirmed)
    BGM-71A Improved TOW
    HOT
    M-901 ITV (TOW under Armor)                          56
    M-47 Dragon
    Vigilant
surface-to-surface missiles and rockets:
  model                                            launchers
    FROG-7                                             4
army anti-aircraft defenses:
  missiles--                                       launchers
    SA-7 (Grail)
    SA-8 (Gecko)                                        4
    SA-9 (Gaskin)
  short-range guns--
    40mm Bofors L-70/L-60
    35mm Oerlikon-Buhrle 35x2 GDF-002
    23mm ZSU 23x4 SP (Gun Dish)
    20mm Oerlikon GAI
  on order: Crotale SAMs (unconfirmed); 10 Skyguard
    (Amoun) air defense systems (unconfirmed); additional
    23x4, SA-14
CW capabilities:
  personal protective equipment
  decontamination units
Air Force:
  aircraft--general:                                 number
```

```
  combat aircraft                                           60
  transport aircraft                                         7
  helicopters                                               44
combat aircraft:
  strike and multi-role--
    medium quality
      Mirage F-1B/C                                         30
    others
      A-4 KU/TA-4 KU Skyhawk II                             30
    TOTAL                                                   60
    on order: 40 F-18
transport aircraft:
  Boeing 737-200                                             1
  C-130-30 Hercules/L-100-30                                 4
  DC-9                                                       2
  TOTAL                                                      7
training and liaison aircraft:
  BAC-167 Strikemaster Mk.83                                 8
  Hawk                                                      12
  TOTAL                                                     20
  on order: 16 EMB-312 Tucano from Shorts, Britain
helicopters:
  attack--
    SA-342K Gazelle                                         28
  medium transport--
    AS-332 Super Puma                                        6
    SA-330 Puma                                             10
                               (sub-total            16)
  TOTAL                                                     44
  on order: SA-365N maritime attack
miscellaneous aircraft:
  TTL BTT-3 Banshee RPV/target drone (unconfirmed)
advanced armament:
  air-to-air missiles--
    AIM-9 Sidewinder
    Matra Super R-530
    R-550 Magique
    HOT (unconfirmed)
  air-to-ground missiles--
    AS-11
    AS-12
  on order: AM-39 Exocet air-to-ship missiles,            300
    AGM-64G Maverick AGMs, 200 AIM-7 Sparrow AAMs,         120
    AIM-9 Sidewinder AAMs
anti-aircraft defenses:
  radars--
    French-made radar
    AN/TPS-32
    AR-15
  on order: AN/TPS-63
```

```
    long-range missiles--
      model                                          batteries
        MIM-23B Improved HAWK                            4
    aircraft shelters:
      in both airfields, for combat aircraft
      on order: Shahine 2 (unconfirmed); SA-8
    military airfields:                                   2
      al-Ahmadi (Ahmad al-Jaber AFB), al-Jahra (Ali  al-Salem
      AFB)
Navy:
    combat vessels:                                    number
      MFPBs--
        Lurssen FPB-57                                    2
        Lurssen TNC-45                                    6
        Total                                            8
      patrol craft--
        Halter Marine                                    1
        Vosper Thornycroft 78 ft. (24 meter)            10
        Vosper Thornycroft 56 ft. (17 meter)             5
        Thornycroft 50 ft. (15 meter)                    8
        Vosper Thornycroft 36 ft. (11 meter)             8
        Magnum Sedan 27.3 ft. (8.3 meter)                7
        Seagull class                                    5
        Total                                           44
      on order: 20 Magnum Sedan patrol boats;   5  additional
        Seagull PBs
    landing craft:
      Loadmaster 350 ton LCT                             4
      Vosper 320 ton logistic support                    3
      Vosper Thornycroft 170 ton LCU                     3
      TOTAL                                             10
      on order: 6 SRN-6 hovercraft
    auxiliary vessels:
      tugs (Hayashikane)                                 2
      tugs (Cheverton)                                   2
      launch (Cheverton)                                 6
    advanced armament:
      surface-to-surface missiles--
        MM-40 Exocet
        on order: additional MM-40 Exocet
    special maritime forces:
      Frogmen and divers
    naval bases:
      Kuwait City, Ras al-Qulayah                        2
    ship maintenance and repair capability:
      Kuwait City (Shuwaikh harbor)--190 meter floating dock;
      repair capacity 35,000 DWT
```

# 9. LEBANON

BASIC DATA
Official Name of State: Republic of Lebanon
Head of State: President Amin Jumayyil until September
    1988; position vacant since
Prime Ministers: Dr. Salim al-Houss (recognized by
    Muslims); Lieutenant General Michel Aoun (recognized by
    Christians)
Defense Minister: Adel Ousseiran
Commander-in-Chief of the Armed Forces: Lieutenant General
    Michel Aoun (recognized by Christians); Brigadier General
    Sami al-Khatib (recognized by Muslims)
Commander of the Air Force: Brigadier General Fahim al-Haj
    (loyal to Muslim PM)
Commander of the Navy: Rear Admiral Alberto al-Rharib
    (loyal to Christian PM)
Area: 10,452 sq.km.
Population: (estimate;

| | | |
|---|---|---|
| all data uncertain) | | 3,100,000 |
| ethnic subdivision: | | |
| Arabs | 2,805,500 | 90.5% |
| Armenians | 139,500 | 4.5% |
| Kurds | 46,500 | 1.5% |
| Others | 108,500 | 3.5% |
| religious subdivision: | | |
| Shi'ite Muslims | 992,000 | 32.0% |
| Sunni Muslims | 651,000 | 21.0% |
| Druze | 186,000 | 6.0% |
| Alawis | 31,000 | 1.0% |
| Christians | | |
| Maronites | 651,000 | 21.0% |
| Greek Orthodox | 248,000 | 8.0% |
| Greek Catholic | 155,000 | 5.0% |
| Armenians (Orthodox | | |
| and Catholics) | 124,000 | 4.0% |
| Others | 62,000 | 2.0% |
| nationality subdivision: | | |
| Lebanese | 2,703,200 | 87.2% |
| Palestinians | 350,300 | 11.3% |
| Others | 46,500 | 1.5% |

GDP:
    1976--$3.29 billion
    1977--$3.34 billion (latest year available)
Defense Expenditure:
    1982--$272 million
    1985--$229 million
Foreign Military Aid Received:

financial aid from:
  France--$1.16 million grant  for  trainees  in  France;
  FRG--grant (unconfirmed);  Italy--loan;  Saudi Arabia--
  (at least $7 million); other Arab states--grant
military training:
  foreign instructors/advisors from-- France
  trainees abroad in--USA, France, Italy;  Syria  (Muslim
  officers from army units loyal to Muslim government  of
  Dr. Salim al-Houss)
arms transfers from:
  France (helicopters); FRG (some small arms); Switzerland
  (AAGs, small arms); UAE (vehicles, small arms)
Foreign Forces from:
  Syria (30,000 in Biq'a, Tripoli area and Beirut);  UNIFIL
  (5,800 in South Lebanon); Palestinian organizations  (see
  Part II Chapter 13); limited Israeli observation units in
  the  security  zone  in  South  Lebanon;   1000  Islamic
  Revolution Guards Corps (IRGC) troops in the  Syrian-held
  Biq'a and a few in Sidon, South Lebanon; Libya--observers
  in Beirut until August 1988

INFRASTRUCTURE
  Road Network:
    length:                                           7,370 km
      paved roads                                     6,270 km
      gravel and stone roads                            450 km
      improved earth tracks                             650 km
    main routes:
      Beirut--Sidon--Tyre--Naqurah--Haifa (Israel)
      Beirut--Tripoli--Tartus (Syria)/Homs (Syria)
      Beirut--Zahlah--Ba'albek--Homs
      Beirut--Shtaurah--Damascus (Syria)
      Tyre--Bint J'bail
      Marj Ayoun--Shtaurah--Zahlah
      Marj Ayoun--Jezzin--Sidon
      Ba'albek--Tripoli
  Railway Network:
    length: (partly not in use)                         378 km
      standard gauge                                    296 km
      narrow gauge                                       82 km
    main routes:
      Beirut--Sidon
      Beirut--Tripoli--Homs
      Beirut--Zahlah--Rayaq--Homs/Rayaq--Damascus
        (narrow gauge)
  Airfields:                                               8
    airfields by runway type:
      permanent surface fields                             5
      unpaved fields and usable airstrips                  3
    airfields by runway length:

# LEBANON

```
2440--3659 meters                                       3
1220--2439                                              2
under 1220                                              3
```
international airports: Beirut
major domestic airfields: Rayaq, Kleiat, Khalat  (landing
strip)
Airlines:
  companies:  Middle  East  Airlines  (international);
    Trans-Mediterranean Airways (cargo)
  aircraft:
    Boeing 720B                                         4
    Boeing 707-320C                                    14
    on order: 1 747-200B Combi
Maritime Facilities:
  harbors--Beirut, Juniah, Sidon, Tripoli, Tyre
  anchorages--al-Abde, Chekka, Salata,  al-Minya,  al-Jiya,
    Naqura, Khalde, Sill al-Ouzai, 5 others
  oil terminals--Sidon, Tripoli
Merchant Marine:

| vessel type | number | DWT |
|---|---|---|
| general cargo | 48 | 251,989 |
| bulk carrier | 6 | 146,273 |
| livestock carrier | 8 | 62,835 |
| ro/ro | 2 | 3,922 |
| container | 2 | 4,573 |
| tanker | 2 | 21,960 |
| reefer | 3 | 3,952 |
| bitumen tanker | 1 | 2,049 |
| TOTAL | 72 | 497,553 |

ARMED FORCES
  Personnel:
    military forces (estimate)--
      army                                        34,000
      air force                                      800
      navy                                           400
      TOTAL                                       35,200
    para-military forces--
      gendarmerie                                  7,000
  Army:
    major units:
      infantry  &  special  forces  (partly  skeleton,
      undermanned or disorganized):        10 brigades
        (4-5 brigades loyal to the Christian Prime Minister
        Aoun,  other  brigades  organized  under  Muslim
        Commander in Chief of the Army al-Khatib, loyal  to
        Muslim Prime Minister Dr. Al-Houss)
    small arms:
      personal weapons--
        9mm MAT 49 SMG

211

```
9mm Sterling SMG
7.62mm FAL (FN) SAR
7.5mm M-49/56 SAR
5.56mm CAL (FN) AR (unconfirmed)
5.56mm HK-33 (Heckler & Koch) AR
5.56mm M-16 A1 AR
5.56mm SG-540 AR
```
machine guns--
```
12.7mm (0.5") Browning M2 HMG
7.62mm (0.3") Browning M-1919 MMG
7.62mm MAG (FN) LMG
7.62mm M-60D GPMG
7.5mm AA-52 MMG
7.5mm Chatellerault M-24/29 LMG
```
light and medium mortars--
```
81mm Hotchkiss-Brandt
81mm M-29
60mm Hotchkiss-Brandt
```
light ATRLs--
```
RPG-7
89mm M-65
```

tanks:

| model | number |
|---|---:|
| medium quality | |
| AMX-13/105mm gun | 20 |
| M-48 A1/M-48 A5 | 100 |
| (sub-total | 120) |
| low quality | |
| AMX-13/75mm gun | 30 |
| TOTAL | 150 |

APCs/ARVs:

| model | number |
|---|---:|
| high quality | |
| AMX-VCI | |
| M-113 A1/A2 | |
| VAB | 95 |
| V-150 Commando | |
| (sub-total | 300) |
| others | |
| Saracen/Saladin | 100 |
| TOTAL | 400 |

on order: 85 M-113/M-577 A1; VAB

artillery:
towed guns and howitzers--
```
155mm M-198 howitzer
155mm M-114 howitzer
155mm M-50 howitzer
105mm M-102 howitzer
```
mortars, less than 160mm, but excluding light and
medium--

```
         120mm Brandt M-50 & M-60 mortars
         TOTAL                                          180
   anti-tank weapons:
      missiles--                                   launchers
         BGM-71A TOW
         MILAN
         SS-11
         TOTAL                                      150-200
      guns--
         106mm M-40 A2 recoilless rifle
   army anti-aircraft defenses:
      short-range guns--
         40mm M-42 SP
         30mm Oerlikon
         20mm
Air Force:
   aircraft--general:                                 number
      combat aircraft                                     16
      transport aircraft                                   3
      helicopters                                         33
   combat aircraft:
      interceptors--
         medium quality
            Mirage III BL/EL (grounded)                   10
      strike and multi-role aircraft--
         low quality
            Hawker Hunter F-70/T-66                         6
   transport aircraft:
      Hawker Siddeley Dove                                  1
      Turbo-Commander 690B                                  2
      TOTAL                                                 3
   training and liaison aircraft:
      BAe SA-3-120 Bulldog                                  5
      CM-170 Fouga Magister (some grounded)                 5
      TOTAL                                                10
   helicopters:
      attack--
         SA-342 Gazelle                                     4
      medium transport--
         AB-212                                             8
         SA-330 Puma                                       11
                            (sub-total                     19)
      light transport--
         Alouette II
         Alouette III
                            (sub-total                     10)
      TOTAL                                                33
   advanced armament:
      air-to-air missiles--
         Matra R-530
```

```
military airfields:                                       4
  Rayaq, Kleiat, Khalat (landing strip), Beirut
aircraft maintenance and repair capability:
  routine  repairs  for  existing  models
Navy:
  combat vessels:                                    number
    patrol craft--
      Ch. Navals de l'Esterel 124.7 ft.
        (38 meter)                                        1
      Byblos class 66 ft. (20.1 meter)                    3
      Tracker II class                                    1
      Aztec class (9 meter)                               5
    12 meter PB                                           4
    TOTAL                                                14
    note: additional patrol craft-- see below, Lebanese
      Forces Militia
  landing craft:
    EDIC class LCT                                        2
  naval bases:                                            2
    Beirut, Juniah
  ship maintenance and repair capability:
  a 55-meter slipway for light craft repairs


Non-Government Para-Military Forces in Lebanon:
  military force/organization                         armed
                                                  personnel*
    Lebanese Forces: Combination
      of various Christian militias
      (led by Samir Geagea)                        10,000
                        (8,000 regulars +2,000 reserves)
    Lebanese Forces splinter group
      (led by Elli Hobeiqa,
      under Syrian patronage)             a few hundred
    Druze Community Forces,
      under Walid Jumblatt, and non-Druze
      followers                                    14,000
                       (4000 regulars + 10,000 reserves)
    Al-Amal (Shi'ites)                             10,000
    Hizb Allah (pro-Iran Shi'ites)                   5000
    Tripoli-based pro-Syrian militias
      (Arab  Democratic Party
      Militia, also known as Farsan
      al Arab, or Arab Cavalry)           a few hundred
    Army of South Lebanon (pro-Israeli, commanded
      by Major General Antoine Lahd)                 2500

*All figures are estimates, with wide margins of error.
    Communist Labor Organization         a few hundred
    "Giants" (Franjieh)                             1,000
    Islamic Unification Movement and
```

```
     Islamic Resistance (Tripoli)        a few hundred
   Lebanese Communist Party                        500
   Socialist Arab Ba'ath Party (pro-Iraqi)  a few hundred
   Socialist Arab Ba'ath Party
     (pro-Syrian)                        a few hundred
   Syrian Social Nationalist Party
     (SSNP; pro-Syrian terror
     and suicide squads)                      700-1000
   Independent Nasserites (Murabitun)    a few hundred
   Popular Nasserite Organization (in  Sidon,  led   by
     Mustapha S'aad)
  Palestinian    Organizations    (see    Part    II/Ch.13,
  "Palestinian Military and Para-Military Forces")
Note: 1000 Iranian IRGC men in Lebanon--listed above  under
  foreign forces
```

Tanks, APCs and Artillery in Non-Government Militias

| militia | tanks | APCs | artillery pieces |
|---|---|---|---|
| Lebanese Forces | 100 T-54, a few M-48 AMX-13 & Sherman | 80 inclu- ding M-113 | 100 |
| Al Amal | 50 T-54/T-55, some AMX-13 | a few M-113 | a few 122mm; a few 130mm |
| Druze Community Forces | 50 T-54 | several score includ- ing M-113 | several score including 122mm and 130mm guns, and 122mm BM-21 MRLs |
| Army of South Lebanon | 45 Sherman & T-54 | a few M-113 | 30 |
| Hizb Allah | | several M-113 | several inclu- ding 130mm |

Aircraft:
  Lebanese Forces--3 SA-342 Gazelle helicopters
Militias deploying naval vessels (patrol boats):
  Lebanese Forces-about 25 vessels, including 2 Dvorah patrol
    boats, 1 18 meter patrol craft, 1 tracker II, and  about
    20 small boats of up to 10 meter
Militia contingents in Libya (deployed against  Chad  until
  October 1988):

```
  Druze Community Forces                          300
  Lebanese Communist Party                        250
  Arab Democratic Party                           150
```

## LEBANON

| | |
|---|---|
| Murabitun | 50 |
| Nasserites (Socialist Arab Union) | 50 |
| TOTAL | 800 |

# 10. LIBYA

BASIC DATA
Official Name of State: The Great Socialist People's Libyan
Arab Jamahiriya (Jamahiriya is an Arabic term, meaning
"public" or "polity of the masses")
Head of State (leader; does not hold any other title)
Colonel Mu'ammar al-Qaddafi (in practice also in charge
of the Defense Ministry and Commander-in-Chief of the
Armed Forces)
Deputy Head of State (second in the hierarchy; equivalent
to Prime Minister): Major Abd al-Sallam Jallud
Secretary-General of the General People's Committee
(equivalent to the Cabinet): Zaydallah 'Aziz al-Salihi
Commander-in-Chief of the Armed Forces: Colonel Abu-Bakr
Yunis Jaber
Inspector General of the Armed Forces (equivalent to Chief
of Staff): Colonel Mustapha al-Kharrubi
Commander of the Air Force: Colonel Salih Abdullah Salih
Commander of the Navy: Captain Abdullah al-Latif
al-Shakshuki
Area: 1,759,540 sq. km.

| Population: | | 4,080,000 |
|---|---|---|
| ethnic subdivision: | | |
| Arabs | 3,766,000 | 92.3% |
| Berbers | 163,000 | 4.0% |
| Black Africans | 102,000 | 2.5% |
| Europeans and others | 49,000 | 1.2% |
| religious subdivision: | | |
| Sunni Muslims | 3,958,000 | 97.0% |
| Christians | 122,000 | 3.0% |
| nationality subdivision: | | |
| Libyans | 3,562,000 | 87.3% |
| Egyptians | 339,000 | 8.3% |
| Tunisians | 98,000 | 2.4% |
| Others | 81,000 | 2.0% |

GDP:
1984--$26.76 billion
1986--$20.60 billion
Balance of Payments (goods, services & unilateral transfer
payments):

| year | income | expenditure | balance |
|---|---|---|---|
| 1985 | $10.89 bil. | $ 8.81 bil. | +$2.08 bil. |
| 1986 | $ 6.17 bil. | $ 6.23 bil. | -$60 mil. |

Defense Expenditure:
1986--$1.40 billion (unconfirmed)
1987--$1.30 billion (unconfirmed)
Foreign Military Aid Received:
military training:

foreign advisors/instructors/serving personnel from--
Britain (non-governmental technicians); Cuba; France;
Italy; North Korea; Pakistan; Palestinian personnel
from PFLP-GC; Syria (pilots); USSR and other Soviet
bloc countries (4000, number unconfirmed);
Yugoslavia; Indians and other foreigners residing in
Libya drafted into armed forces; 300 men from
Lebanese Druze Community Forces militia, 250 from
Lebanese Communist Party militia, 150 from the Arab
Democratic Party, 50 from Murabitun, 50 from
Nasserite Popular Organization--participated in
Libyan campaign in Northern Chad until October 1988
trainees abroad in--USSR, other Soviet bloc countries;
France (unconfirmed); Italy; Netherlands (civil
aircraft pilots); Portugal (unconfirmed); Sweden;
Syria; Turkey (unconfirmed); Yugoslavia
(unconfirmed)
arms transfers from:
Austria (artillery pieces, possibly for Iran,
unconfirmed; small arms); Brazil (APCs, ARVs; light
transport aircraft, maritime surveillance aircraft, and
MRLs, unconfirmed); Czechoslovakia (trainer and
transport aircraft); France (combat aircraft,
helicopters, SAMs, tank transporters, ATGMs); FRG
(floating dock); company from FRG: aerial refuelling
systems; Greece (spare parts for American and French
made aircraft, unconfirmed); Italy (electronics, spares
for aircraft) ; Netherlands (transport aircraft); Spain
(recoilless rifles, unconfirmed; ammunition); Sweden
(explosives); Turkey (LST, patrol boats); USSR (combat
aircraft, tanks, SAMs, SSMs, missile corvettes, naval
mines); Yugoslavia (trainer aircraft)
maintenance performed abroad in:
Malta (for corvettes); France (SAMs); Poland (landing
craft); Italy (aircraft, helicopter engines)
construction aid by:
India (airfields)
Foreign Military Aid Extended:
financial aid to:
BR (Italy, unconfirmed); ETA (Basque separatists,
Spain)--grant; IRA (Irish Republican Army); Iran;
various Lebanese militias; M-19 (Colombian
anti-government group); MORO Front (Philippine
Muslims); "Nasserite Egyptian Revolution" (Egyptian
anti-government group); Palestinian organizations
(PFLP-GC and Abu Musa faction of Fatah); Sudan--grant
(money and oil); Syria--grant
military training:
advisors/instructors/serving personnel in--Sudan;
Surinam (100, number unconfirmed); Uganda; Nicaragua

(unconfirmed)
foreign trainees from--Abu Musa faction of Fatah and PFLP-GC groups; ANC and PAC (South African anti-government organizations); Burkina Faso; Chad anti-government rebels; Dominican Republic anti-government rebels; ETA; Kanak (anti-French Socialist National Liberation Front of New Caledonia, unconfirmed); Malta (unconfirmed); MORO Front; Reunion (MIR, Movement for Independence of Reunion, a French-governed island in the Indian Ocean, unconfirmed); SWAPO (Namibian anti-government guerrillas); Syria (pilots); "African Islamic Foreign Legion" (anti-government personnel from Gambia, Senegal, Mali & Niger); Yemeni, Egyptian, Sudanese, Tunisian, and Iraqi anti-government groups

arms transfers to:
Burkina Faso (Brazilian-made ARVs, Italian-made trainer aircraft); Chile anti-government groups (unconfirmed); Iran (APCs, ARVs, other Soviet weapons; Soviet-made SSMs; Austrian artillery, unconfirmed); IRA (small arms, HMGs; SA-7 missiles--unconfirmed); Kurdish rebels in Iraq (small arms); Nicaragua (small arms, unconfirmed); Palestinian military organizations (MRLs, SAMs, artillery pieces); Somali anti-government guerrillas (small arms); SWAPO (small arms); Sudan (small arms, aircraft spares, combat aircraft); Syria (Soviet AAMs); Togo (Brazilian ARVs);

facilities provided to:
Chad anti-government organizations (camps); Palestinian organizations (PFLP-GC, camps); USSR (use of naval bases at Bardiyah & Tobruk, unconfirmed; use of Ouqba ben Nafi AFB, unconfirmed)

forces deployed abroad in:
Chad--troops with the anti-Habre rebels in northern Chad; Lebanon--observers in Beirut, until August 1988); Sudan--a few aircraft supporting Sudanese forces in southern Sudan, and 3,000 soldiers in Western Sudan (Darfur province)

Joint Maneuvers with:
USSR (naval maneuvers)

Cooperation in Arms Production/Assembly with:
companies from FRG and Japan (toxic gas); Italy (assembly of light aircraft, unconfirmed)

INFRASTRUCTURE

Road Network:

| | |
|---|---|
| length: | 19,300 km |
| paved roads | 10,800 km |
| gravel, stone & improved earth roads | 8,500 km |

main routes:
Tripoli--Benghazi--Tobruk--Bardiyah

**LIBYA**

```
    Tripoli--Misratah  (Misurata)--Waddan--Sabha  (Sebha)--
        Marzuq (Murzuq)
    Tripoli--Tunis (Tunisia)
    Tripoli--Ghadams (Ghadames)--Ghat
    Tobruk--Alexandria (Egypt)
    Benghazi--Zighan--Kufra
    Tripoli--Nalut--Sabha
    Sabha--Ghat
    Tobruk--Jaghbud
    Bardiyah--Jaghbud
```

| | |
|---|---|
| Airfields: | 115 |
|   airfields by runway type: | |
|     permanent surface fields | 48 |
|     unpaved fields and usable airstrips | 67 |
|   airfields by runway length: | |
|     over 3660 meters | 6 |
|     2440--3659 | 28 |
|     1220--2439 | 39 |
|     under 1220 | 42 |

international airports: Tripoli, Benghazi (Baninah)
major domestic airfields: Ghadams (Ghadames), Ghat, Kufra, Marsa al-Brega, Misratah, Sabha, Surt (Sidra, Sirt), Tobruk

Airlines:
  companies: Jamahiriya Libyan Arab Airlines (international, domestic, cargo and charter)
  aircraft:

| | |
|---|---|
|     Boeing 727-200 | 10 |
|     Boeing 707-320C | 5 |
|     DHC-6 Twin Otter | 5 |
|     Fokker F-27-600/500/400 | 16 |
|     Fokker F-28-4000 (including a/c on lease) | 3 |
|     Ilyushin IL-76T | 21 |
|     L-100-20 | 4 |

Maritime Facilities:
  harbors--Benghazi, Derna, Misratah, Tobruk, Tripoli
  anchorages--Kasr Ahmed
  oil terminals--Surt (Sidra), Marsa al-Brega, Marsa al-Hairqa (Tobruk), Ras Lanuf, Zawiyah, Zueitinah

Merchant Marine:

| vessel type | number | DWT |
|---|---|---|
|   crude carrier | 8 | 1,032,273 |
|   product tanker | 2 | 61,315 |
|   general cargo | 5 | 28,950 |
|   general cargo/container | 6 | 58,635 |
|   ferry | 3 | 10,807 |
|   ro/ro | 4 | 12,059 |
|   chemical tanker | 1 | 5,390 |
|   TOTAL | 29 | 1,209,429 |

Defense Production:

220

# LIBYA

```
    army equipment: toxic gas (unconfirmed)
ARMED FORCES
  Personnel:
    military forces--
                  regular          reserves           total
      army        85,000            30,000           115,000
      air force    9,000                               9,000
      navy         6,500                               6,500
      TOTAL      100,500            30,000           130,500
    para-military forces--
    "People's Resistance"--one battalion
Army:
  major units:
    unit type      divisions       brigades      independent
                                                  battalions
      armored/tank     2-3             2                3
      mechanized/
        infantry       2-4             2                8
      paratroop                                        13
      Republican Guard                 1
      TOTAL            5-7             5               24
  small arms:
    personal weapons--
      9mm Model 12 Beretta SMG
      9mm L-34 A1 SMG
      7.62mm AK-47 (Kalashnikov) AR
      7.62mm SKS (Simonov) SAR
      7.62mm FAL (FN) SAR
      5.45mm AK-74 (Kalashnikov, unconfirmed) AR
    machine guns--
      12.7mm D.Sh.K. 38/46 (Degtyarev) HMG
      7.62mm MAG (FN) LMG
      7.62mm PK/PKS (Kalashnikov) LMG
      7.62mm RPD (Degtyarev) LMG
      7.62mm SGM (Goryunov) MMG
    light and medium mortars--
      82mm M-43
    light ATRLs--
      RPG-7
  tanks:
    model                                           number
      high quality
        T-72                                          300
      medium quality
        T-62                                       800-1000
        T-55                                      1500-1700
                             (sub-total           2300-2700)
      TOTAL (including about 1500 in storage)      2600-3000
  APCs/ARVs:
    model                                           number
```

```
    high quality
      BMP-1                                                 800
      Engesa EE-9/11                                        300
      Fiat Type 6614/6616
      M-113 Al
    others
      BTR-50/60
      BRDM-2
      OT-62
      OT-64
      Saladin
    TOTAL (approximately 2/3 high quality, about
                            half in storage)      2000
    on order: EE-9/11
  artillery:
    self propelled guns and howitzers--
      155mm M-109 SP howitzer                               18
      155mm Palmaria SP howitzer
      152mm M-1973 SP howitzer
      122mm M-1974 SP howitzer
    towed guns and howitzers--
      155mm GHN-45 howitzer   (possibly  transferred  to
        Iran, unconfirmed)
      152mm M-1943 howitzer
      130mm M-46 gun
      122mm D-30 howitzer
      122mm M-1938 howitzer
      105mm M-101 howitzer
    mortars, over 160mm--
      240mm mortar
      160mm mortar
    mortars, less than 160mm, but excluding light and
      medium--
      120mm mortar
    TOTAL                                                2000
  MRLs--
    140mm
    130mm M-51
    122mm BM-21/RM-70
    107mm Type 63
  on order:  155mm  Palmaria  SP  howitzer;  180mm  SS-40
    Astros II MRL
AFV transporters:                                        1000
anti-tank weapons:
  missiles--                                       launchers
    AT-3 (Sagger)
    AT-4 (Spigot)
    BRDM-2 carrying AT-3 (Sagger) SP
    MILAN
    Vigilant
```

```
    TOTAL                                  2000
  guns--
    106mm recoilless rifle
  surface-to-surface missiles and rockets:
    model                                launchers
      FROG-7
      SS-1 (Scud B)
      TOTAL                                 100
  army anti-aircraft defenses:
    missiles--                           launchers
      Crotale                                30
      SA-6  (Gainful) SP                     36
      SA-7  (Grail)
      SA-8  (Gecko)                          10
      SA-9  (Gaskin) SP                      60
      SA-13 (Gopher) SP
      SA-14 (Gremlin)
    short-range guns--                     number
      57mm
      40mm Bofors L-70
      30mm 30x2 M-53/59 SP
      23mm ZSU 23x4 SP (Gun Dish)
      23mm ZU 23x2
      TOTAL                                 450
    on order: 30mm Artemis (unconfirmed)
  CW capabilities:
    personal protective equipment, Soviet type
    decontamination units, Soviet type
    ABC protection of SSM sites
    stockpile of gases, including Sarine and  Mustard
    (unconfirmed)
Air Force:
  aircraft--general:                       number
    combat aircraft (some in storage)        543
    transport aircraft                       139+
    helicopters                              177
  combat aircraft:
    interceptors--
      high quality
        MiG-25 and MiG-25R (Foxbat)           80
      medium quality
        MiG-21 bis (Fishbed)                  50
      Total                                  130
    strike and multi-role aircraft--
      high quality
        Su-24 (Fencer C)                       6
      medium quality
        MiG-23/27 (Flogger, incl. MiG-23G)   190
        Su-20/22 (Fitter C)                  100
        Mirage F-1                            30
```

```
     Mirage 5                                            80
                                    (sub-total        400)
  Total                                                406
  on order: 9 Su-24 (Fencer C; total order 15)
  bombers--
   Tu-22 (Blinder)                                       7
transport aircraft:
  An-26 (Curl)                                          36
  Boeing 707                                             1
  C-130H Hercules/L-100-20/L-100-30                     10
  C-140 Jetstar                                          1
  DHC-6 Twin Otter                                      10
  Fokker F-27-600                                        8
  Fokker F-28 (unconfirmed)                         a few
  G-222L                                                20
  IL-76 (Candid)                                        28
  L-410 UVP                                             19
  Mystere Falcon 20                                      6
  TOTAL                                               139+
  on order: 25 EMB-121
training and liaison aircraft (some in storage):
  G-2AE Galeb/J-1 Jastreb                              150
  L-39 Albatross                                       120
  SIAI--Marchetti SF-260 M/L                           150
  TOTAL                                                420
helicopters:                                        number
  attack--
   Mi-24/Mi-25 (Hind, number unconfirmed)              40
  heavy transport--
   CH-47C Chinook                                       18
   SA-321 Super Frelon (also
     employed in ASW role)                               8
                                    (sub-total         26)
  medium transport--
   AB-212                                                5
   Mi-2 (Hoplite)                                       35
   Mi-8/Mi-17 (Hip)                                     25
                                    (sub-total         65)
  light transport--
   Alouette III                                         12
   AB-206 JetRanger                                      5
                                    (sub-total         17)
  ASW--
   Mi-14 (Haze)                                         29
  TOTAL                                                177
advanced armament:
  air-to-air missiles--
   AA-2 (Atoll)
   AA-6 (Acrid)
   AA-7 (Apex)
```

```
   AA-8 (Aphid)
   R-550 Magique
 air-to-ground missiles--
   helicopter-mounted AT-2 (Swatter)
anti-aircraft defenses:
 radars--
   Square Pair
 long-range missiles-- (some in storage)
   model                               batteries
     SA-2 (Guideline) & SA-3 (Goa)          93
     SA-5 (Gammon)                           4
     TOTAL            (unconfirmed)          97
 aircraft shelters--
   for some combat aircraft
military airfields:                          18
   al-Adem , al-Bayda, Benghazi (Baninah), Beni Walid,
   al-Bumbah, Ghurdabiyah, Jufra, Kufra, Ma'atan al-Sarra,
   Misratha, Ouqba ben Nafi , Sabhah, Surt (Sirte),
   Tripoli (Mu'atiga), al-Watiyah, Zawiyah, 2 additional
aircraft maintenance and repair capability:
   foreign technicians employed for all models
Navy:
 combat vessels:                             number
   submarines--
     F class (Foxtrot)                        6
   MFPBs--
     Combattante II                           9
     Ossa II                                 12
     Susa (Vosper 100 ft.)                    3
     Total                                   24
   missile frigates--
     Vosper Thornycroft Mk.7                  1
     Koni (with SS-N-2C SSMs;
       usually in ASW role)                   2
                             (sub-total      3)
   missile corvettes--
     Assad class (formerly Wadi class)        4
     Nanuchka class                           3
     Total                                    7
   gun corvettes--
     Vosper Thornycroft Mk.1B (Tobruk)        1
   mine warfare vessels--
     Natya class minesweepers                 8
   patrol craft--
     Garian class                             4
     Poluchat                                 1
     Thornycroft 100 ft. (30.5 meter)         3
     Thornycroft 78 ft. (23.5 meter)          1
     SAR-33                                   14
   Total                                      23
```

on order: 4 Rade Koncar MFPBs
landing craft:
  C-107 LCT                                        2
  PS-700 class LST                                 2
  Polnochny class LCT                              3
  TOTAL                                            7
auxiliary vessels:
  LSD-1 class logistic support ship               1
  maintenance & repair craft, ex-British LCT      1
  Mala midget submarine                           6
  remotely controlled explosive
    motor craft                              50-125
  ro/ro transport ship, 3100 ton                  1
  Yelva diving-support ship                       1
advanced armament:
  surface-to-surface missiles--
    OTOMAT Mk.2
    SS-N-2 Styx
    SS-12
  surface-to-air missiles--
    Seacat
    Aspide
    SA-N-4
  mines--
    Soviet-made acoustic mines
naval bases:                                       5
  al-Khums, Benghazi, Derna, Tobruk, Tripoli
ship maintenance and repair capability:
  facilities at Tripoli with foreign technicians for
  repair of vessels up to 6000 DWT; a 3200 ton lift
  floating dock; and floating docks at Benghazi and
  Tobruk

# 11. MOROCCO

BASIC DATA
 Official Name of State: Kingdom of Morocco
 Head of State: King Hassan II (also Minister of Defense,
   Commander-in-Chief of the Armed Forces and Chief of the
   General Staff)
 Prime Minister: Azzedine Laraki
 Inspector General of the Armed Forces: General Idriss
   Bin-Issa
 Commander of the Air Force: Major General Muhammad Kabaj
 Inspector of the Navy: Captain Lahcen Ouhirra
 Area: 622,012 sq. km., including the former Spanish Sahara
   (409,200 sq. km. excluding this territory)
 Population:                                    23,310,000
   ethnic subdivision:
     Arabs                  13,893,000            59.6%
     Berbers                 9,207,000            39.5%
     Europeans and others      210,000             0.9%
   religious subdivision:
     Sunni Muslims          23,007,000            98.7%
     Christians                256,000             1.1%
     Jews                       47,000             0.2%
 GDP:
   1985--$11.86 billion
   1986--$14.76 billion
 Balance of Payments (goods, services & unilateral transfer
   payments):
   year    income         expenditure        balance
   1986    $5.13 bil.     $5.34 bil.         -$210 mil.
   1987    $5.96 bil.     $5.79 bil.         +$170 mil.
 Defense Expenditure:
   1986--$750 million
   1987--$850 million
 Foreign Military Aid Received:
   financial aid from:
     Saudi Arabia--grant; Kuwait, Qatar, UAE--grants,
     finance of purchase of 24 Mirage 2000s from France and
     various arms from Spain; USA--$52 million grant and
     loan
   military training:
     foreign advisors/instructors from--USA, Belgium,
       France; Egypt (unconfirmed)
     trainees abroad in--USA, Belgium, France, Spain; Egypt
       (unconfirmed)
   arms transfers from:
     Austria (recovery vehicles, tanks); Brazil (APCs);
     Britain (artillery pieces); Canada (jeeps); Egypt
     (mortars; APCs on order, unconfirmed); France (ATGMs,
     combat aircraft, naval SSMs, naval vessels, tank

transporters); FRG (light transport aircraft); Italy (helicopters, land mines, shipborne SAMs); South Africa (APCs); Spain (AFVs, mortars, MRLs, naval vessels, electronic equipment, night vision devices, communications equipment); Switzerland (trainer aircraft); USA (ATGMs, SAMs, tanks, tank transporters)
construction aid by:
USA (improving airfields)
Foreign Military Aid Extended:
military training:
advisors/instructors/serving personnel in--Iraq (unconfirmed), UAE
foreign trainees from--Angola (UNITA, anti-government group in Angola, unconfirmed)
facilities provided to:
USA (use of Sidi Slimane, Ben Guerir [Marrakech] and Casablanca airfields in emergencies; permission for space shuttle to land at Benguerir AFB; use of communications center at Kenitra; storage and use of naval facilities at Mohammedia)
Joint Maneuvers with:
Belgium (joint training of pilots in both countries), France, Spain, USA
Cooperation in Arms Production/Assembly with:
Portugal (aircraft industry, overhauls and production of a light trainer aircraft, unconfirmed)

INFRASTRUCTURE
Road Network:
| | |
|---|---|
| length: | 58,000 km |
| paved roads | 25,750 km |
| gravel, crushed stone roads and earth tracks | 32,250 km |

main routes:
Rabat--Tangier
Tangier--Tetouan--Nador--Oran (Algeria)
Ceuta--Tetouan--Kenitra--Rabat
Rabat--Meknes--Fez--Oujda--Oran
Oujda--Bouarfa--Bechar (Algeria)
Rabat--Casablanca--Marrakech
Casablanca--Safi--Agadir--Tarfaya--L'Ayoun--Bir Moghreim (Mauritania)
Railway Network:
length (standard gauge): 1,891 km
main routes:
Rabat--Casablanca--Marrakech
Rabat--Sidi Kacem--Tangier
Rabat--Sidi Kacem--Meknes--Fez--Oujda--Sidi-bel-Abbes (Algeria)
Airfields: 71

airfields by runway type:
  permanent surface fields                          26
  unpaved fields and usable airstrips               45
airfields by runway length:
  over 3660 meters                                   2
  2440--3659                                        14
  1220--2439                                        28
  under 1220                                        27
international airports: Agadir, Casablanca (Nouasseur),
  Fez, Marrakech, Oujda, Rabat (Sale), Tangier
major domestic airfields: L'Ayoun, Casablanca (Arfa),
  Ouarzazate, Sidi Ifni, Smara-Ferduja, Tantan, Tarfaya
Airlines:
  companies: Royal Air Maroc (international & domestic);
    Royal Air Inter (domestic)
  aircraft:
    Boeing 757                                       2
    Boeing 747-200 Combi/747SP                       2
    Boeing 737-200/737-200C                          7
    Boeing 727-200                                   8
    Boeing 707-320C                                  2
    Fokker F-27-600                                  2
    on order: 10 Boeing 737, delivery 1990-94; 3 ATR-42
Maritime Facilities:
  harbors--Agadir, L'Ayoun (Fousbucra Port), Casablanca, El
    Jedida/Jorf al-Asfar, Kenitra, Mohammedia, Nador, Safi,
    Tangier
  anchorages--Essaouira (Mogador), Larache, Martil
    (Tetouan)
  oil terminals--Agadir, Kenitra, Mohammedia, Safi
Merchant Marine:

| vessel type | number | DWT |
| --- | --- | --- |
| crude carrier | 1 | 6,211 |
| small tanker | 2 | 12,254 |
| chemical tanker | 14 | 216,742 |
| general cargo | 3 | 7,421 |
| bulk carrier | 4 | 163,291 |
| reefer | 13 | 75,999 |
| passenger/cargo | 1 | 1,398 |
| ferry | 1 | 3,180 |
| ro/ro | 3 | 11,082 |
| general cargo/container | 6 | 20,627 |
| TOTAL | 48 | 518,205 |

Defense Production:
  army equipment:
    small arms ammunition; assembly of trucks
  aircraft and air ammunition:
    trainer aircraft

```
ARMED FORCES
  Personnel:
    military forces--
      army                                      170,000
      air force                                  15,000
      navy and marines                            7,000
      Total                                     192,000
    para-military forces-
      gendarmerie--8000; internal security forces--3,000
  Army:
    major units:
```

| unit type | brigades/ regiments | indep. battalions | indep. companies |
|---|---|---|---|
| armored | | 5 | |
| mechanized | 4 | 1 | |
| infantry | 4 | | |
| camel corps | | 10 | |
| desert cavalry | (unconfirmed) 1 | | |
| paratroops | 1 | | |
| commando | | 3 | |
| armored car | | | 4 |
| TOTAL | 9 | 20 | 4 |

```
    small arms:
      personal weapons--
        9mm MAT 49/56 SMG
        9mm Model 38/49 Beretta SMG
        7.62mm AK-47 (Kalashnikov) AR
        7.62mm G-3 AR
        7.5mm MAS 49/56 SAR
      machine guns--
        14.5mm ZPU 14.5x4 HMG (in anti-aircraft role)
        14.5mm ZPU 14.5x2 HMG (in anti-aircraft role)
        12.7mm (0.5") Browning M2 HMG
        7.62mm M-60 D GPMG
        7.62mm MAG (FN) LMG
        7.62mm RPD (Degtyarev) LMG
        7.5mm AA-52 MMG
        7.5mm Chatellerault M-24/29 LMG
      light and medium mortars--
        82mm M-43
        81mm ECIA
        81mm M-29
        60mm M-2
      light ATRLs--
        RPG-7
        89mm Strim-89
        3.5" M-20 (Bazooka)
    tanks:
```

## MOROCCO

| model | | number |
|---|---|---|
| medium quality | | |
| M-48 A5 | | 110 |
| SK-105 (Kurassier) | | 80 |
| | (sub-total | 190) |
| low quality | | |
| AMX-13 | | 50 |
| T-54 | | 10 |
| | (sub-total | 60) |
| TOTAL | | 250 |

on order: 108 M-60 A3; M-48 A5; SK-105 (Kurassier)

APCs/ARVs:

| model | | number |
|---|---|---|
| high quality | | |
| AMX-10 RC | | 37 |
| Engesa EE-9/EE-11 (unconfirmed) | | 60 |
| M-113 A1/A2 | | 460 |
| M-3 (Panhard, unconfirmed) | | |
| Ratel 20/90 | | 60 |
| Steyr 4K 7FA (unconfirmed) | | |
| VAB | | 394 |
| | (sub-total | +1011) |
| others | | |
| AML-90/AML-60 | | 200 |
| EBR-75 | | 25 |
| Eland | | + |
| M-3 half-track | | 100 |
| M-8 ARV | | 55 |
| OT-62 | | 50 |
| UR-416 | | 15 |
| | (sub-total | 445) |
| TOTAL | | 1456+ |

on order: 140 M-113, AMX-10RC; Fahd (unconfirmed)

| artillery: | number |
|---|---|
| self propelled guns and howitzers-- | |
| 155mm M-109 A1 SP howitzer | 56 |
| 155mm Mk. F-3 (AMX) SP howitzer | 48 |
| 105mm Mk. 61 SP howitzer | 24 |
| 100mm SU-100 SP gun | |
| towed guns and howitzers-- | |
| 155mm M-114 howitzer | 70 |
| 152mm howitzer | 12 |
| 130mm M-46 gun | 12 |
| 105mm Light Gun | 36 |
| 105mm M-101 howitzer | |
| 85mm M-1945/D-44 field/AT gun | |
| mortars, less than 160mm, but excluding light and medium-- | |
| 120mm mortar | |
| TOTAL | 410 |

```
    MRLs--
      140mm Teruel
      122mm BM-21                                         36
    anti-tank weapons:
      missiles--
        BGM-71A TOW
        HOT/HOT Commando
        M-47 Dragon                                      480
        MILAN                                             82
        TOTAL                                           1000
      guns--
        106mm M-40 A2 recoilless rifle
        90mm recoilless rifle
    army anti-aircraft defenses:
      missiles--                                    launchers
        MIM-72A Chaparral                                 36
        SA-7 (Grail)
      short-range guns--                               number
        57mm M-1950 (S-60)
        37mm M-1939                                       35
        23mm ZU 23x2                                     200
        20mm M-163 Vulcan SP                              55
        20mm
        TOTAL                                           290+
Air Force:
  aircraft--general:                                   number
    combat aircraft                                       68
    transport aircraft                                    48
    helicopters                                          156
  combat aircraft:
    strike and multi-role aircraft--
      medium quality
        Mirage F-1/F-2B                                   35
      others
        F-5E/F-5F                                         20
        F-5A/B                                            10
        RF-5E                                              3
                                    (sub-total           33)
        TOTAL                                             68
      on order: 10 Mirage F-1
  transport aircraft:
    Beechcraft King Air                                    9
    C-119                                                  5
    C-130H Hercules (including C-130H with  SLAR,  employed
      for electronic surveillance)                        17
    DC-3 Dakota (C-47)                                     8
    Dornier DO-28 D-2                                      3
    Gulfstream                                             1
    KC-130 refuelling                                      3
    Mystere Falcon 20                                      2
```

```
TOTAL                                              48
training and liaison aircraft:
  Alpha Jet                                        22
  AS-202/18A Bravo                                 12
  Beechcraft T-34C                                 12
  Broussard                                         9
  CM-170 Fouga Magister                            22
  TOTAL                                            77
  on order: 20 Gepal IV; Bragg ultra-light aircraft
     (unconfirmed)
helicopters:
  attack--
    SA-342 Gazelle                                 30
  heavy transport--
    CH-47C Chinook                                 12
  medium transport--
    AB-212                                         11
    AB-205                                         30
    Kaman HH-43B Huskie                             4
    SA-330 Puma                                    36
                                 (sub-total        81)
  light transport--
    Alouette III                                    8
    AB-206 JetRanger                               23
    SA-315B Lama                                    2
                                 (sub-total        33)
  TOTAL                                           156
  on order: SA-342; AB-206; 24 500MG or 530MG
miscellaneous aircraft:
  OV-10 Bronco counter-insurgency                   4
advanced armament:
  air-to-air missiles--
    AIM-9J Sidewinder                             320
    R-530 (unconfirmed)
    R-550 Magique
  air-to-ground missiles--
    AGM-65 Maverick                               380
anti-aircraft defenses:
  radars--
    AN/TPS-43                                      16
    AN/TPS-63
  long-range guns--
    100mm M-49 (possibly no longer in service)
military airfields:                                13
  Agadir, Ben Guerir, Boulhout, Casablanca (Nouasseur),
  Fez, Kenitra, Khouribga, Larache, Marrakech, Meknes,
  Oujda, Rabat, Sidi Slimane
aircraft maintenance and repair capability:
  for all existing models
Navy:
```

## MOROCCO

| combat vessels: | number |
|---|---:|
| MFPBs-- | |
| Lazaga | 4 |
| missile frigates-- | |
| Descubierta | 1 |
| mine warfare vessels-- | |
| Sirius class | 1 |
| gunboats/MTBs-- | |
| PR-72 class | 2 |
| patrol craft-- | |
| P-32 | 6 |
| P-200D Vigilance (Cormoran) | 3 |
| VC large patrol craft | 1 |
| Le Fougeux (modified), 53 meter | 1 |
| CMN 40.6 meter | 1 |
| Acror 46 (with customs) | 18 |
| Osprey | 2 |
| Total | 32 |

on order: 2 additional Osprey (Fredrickshavn Vaerft) gunboats ; 4 P-32 patrol boats/ gunboats; an additional Descubierta missile frigate (unconfirmed) and 3 additional P-200D Vigilance

| landing craft: | |
|---|---:|
| Batral LSL | 3 |
| EDIC LCT | 1 |
| TOTAL | 4 |
| auxiliary vessels: | |
| Cargo ship, 1500 GRT | 2 |

advanced armament:
  surface-to-surface missiles--
    MM-40 Exocet
    MM-38 Exocet

| naval bases: | 5 |
|---|---:|

Agadir, Casablanca, Kenitra, Dakhla, Tangier

ship maintenance and repair capability:
  at Casablanca--156 meter dry-dock, repairs up to 10,000 DWT; at Agadir--minor repairs

# 12. OMAN

BASIC DATA
  Official Name of State: Sultanate of Oman
  Head of State: Sultan Qabus bin Sa'id (also Prime Minister
    and Minister of Defense)
  Deputy Prime Minister for Security and Defense: Fahr ibn
    Taymur al-Sa'id
  Minister of State for Defense: al-Muatassam Ibd Hamud
    al-Bu-Saidi
  Chief of the General Staff: Lieutenant General Hamad Ibn
    Sa'id al-Aufi
  Commander of the Army: Major General Khamis Ibn Hamid
    al-Zabani
  Commander of the Air Force: Major General Erik P. Bennett
    (unconfirmed); Acting Commander of the Air Force:
    Brigadier General Talib Bin Marin
  Commander of the Navy: Rear Admiral H.M. Balfour
  Area: 212,200 sq.km.
  Population:                                        1,330,000
    ethnic subdivision:
      Arabs                     1,205,000              90.6%
      Others (Africans, Persians, Southeast
      Asians)                     125,000               9.4%
    religious subdivision:
      Ibadi Muslims
        (Kharadjites)             998,000              75.0%
      Sunni Muslims               250,000              18.8%
      Shi'ite Muslims, Hindus      82,000               6.2%
  GDP:
    1984--$ 9.19 billion
    1985--$10.35 billion
    Balance of Payments (goods, services, & unilateral
      transfer payments):
    year    income           expenditure         balance
    1985    $5.35 bil.       $5.26 bil.          +$ 90 mil.
    1986    $3.50 bil.       $4.47 bil.          -$970 mil.
  Defense Expenditure:
    1986--$1.56 billion
    1987--$1.51 billion
  Foreign Military Aid Received:
    financial aid from:
      Saudi Arabia--grant; USA--$150,000 grant for military
      education and training, $40 million loan
    military training:
      foreign advisors/instructors/serving personnel from--
        Britain (1000 officers and NCOs, 200 of whom are
        seconded from the British forces, the balance hired
        on a personal basis); Egypt; Jordan; Pakistan; USA
        trainees abroad in--Britain, France, FRG, Jordan, Saudi

Arabia
arms transfers from:
Austria (small arms, trucks); Britain (tanks, artillery
pieces, combat aircraft, training aircraft, aircraft
radars and navigation systems, MFPBs, landing ship,
radars, trucks); Egypt (jeeps, APCs); France (ATGMs,
naval SSMs); USA (AAMs, SP guns)
Foreign Military Aid Extended:
financial aid to:
PLO (unconfirmed)
facilities provided to:
USA (airfields at Masirah, Seeb, Khasab, Thamarit;
storage facilities; naval facilities at Masirah and
Jazirat Ghanam; communications center); Britain (use of
airfields)
Joint Maneuvers with:
Britain, Egypt, GCC (members: Bahrain, Kuwait, Oman,
Qatar, Saudi Arabia, UAE)

INFRASTRUCTURE
Road Network:
| | |
|---|---|
| length: | 16,900 km |
| paved roads | 2,200 km |
| gravel, improved earth roads and tracks | 14,700 km |

main routes:
Muscat--Ras al-Khaimah/Dubai--Abu Dhabi (UAE)
Muscat--Izki--Fuhud/Izki--Salalah
Muscat--Sur
Muscat--Fujairah (UAE)
Hajma--Ras al-Daqm
Muscat--Khasab (Mussandam Peninsula)

| | |
|---|---|
| Airfields: | 114 |
| airfields by runway type: | |
| permanent surface fields | 6 |
| unpaved fields and usable airstrips | 108 |
| airfields by runway length: | |
| over 3660 meters | 1 |
| 2440--3659 | 4 |
| 1220--2439 | 55 |
| under 1220 | 54 |

international airport: Muscat (Seeb)
major domestic airfield: Salalah
Airlines:
companies: Gulf Air (international)--jointly owned by
Bahrain, Qatar, UAE and Oman (aircraft listed under
Bahrain); Oman Aviation Service (domestic)
aircraft (excluding Gulf Air):

| | |
|---|---|
| Beechcraft Super King Air 200 | 1 |
| Boeing 727 (Sultan's personal aircraft) | 1 |

```
        Cessna Citation II                                  1
        DHC-6 Twin Otter                                    2
        Fokker F-27-500                                     4
    Maritime Facilities:
      harbors--Mina Qabus, Mina Raysut (Salalah)
      oil terminals--Mina Fahal, Riyam
```

ARMED FORCES
  Personnel:
    military forces--
```
      army                                           17,500
      air force                                       3,000
      navy                                            2,000
      TOTAL                                          22,500
```
    para-military forces--
      tribal force--5,000
      Police/Border   police--7,000   (operating   aircraft,
        helicopters and patrol boats)

  Army:
    major units:

| unit type | brigades | independent battalions |
|---|---|---|
| royal guard | | 1 |
| armored | | 1 |
| armored reconnaissance | | 1 |
| infantry | | |
| (partly motorized) | 2 | 2 |
| paratroop/ | | |
| special forces | | 1 |
| TOTAL | 2 | 6 |

    small arms:
      personal weapons--
        9mm Sterling Mk.4 SMG
        7.62mm FAL (FN) SAR
        5.56mm M-16 Al AR
        5.56mm AUG Steyr AR
      machine guns--
        7.62mm (0.3") Browning M-1919 MMG
        7.62mm MAG (FN) LMG
      light and medium mortars--
        81mm L-16 Al
        60mm Hotchkiss-Brandt
    tanks:

| model | number |
|---|---|
| high quality | |
| Chieftain | 34 |
| medium quality | |
| M-60 Al | 6 |

```
  low quality
    Scorpion                                             30
  TOTAL                                                  70
  on order: 20 Chieftain (unconfirmed)
APCs/ARVs:
  model                                              number
    high quality
      V-150 Commando                                     20
      VAB                                                14
      VBC-90                                              6
                                     (sub-total         40)
    others
      AT-105 Saxon                                       15
      Fahd                                                7
                                     (sub-total         22)
  TOTAL                                                  62
artillery:
    self propelled guns and howitzers--
      155mm M-109 A2 SP howitzer                         12
    towed guns and howitzers--
      155mm FH-70                                        12
      130mm Type 59 gun                                  12
      105mm Light Gun                                    36
      105mm M-102 howitzer                               36
      25 lb. (87mm) howitzer                             18
    mortars, less than 160mm, but excluding light and
      medium--
      120mm mortar                                       12
      107mm (4.2") M-30 SP mortar                        12
  TOTAL                                                 150
  on order: 155mm Palmaria SP howitzer
anti-tank weapons:
  missiles--
  BGM-71A Improved TOW
  MILAN
army anti-aircraft defenses:
  missiles--                                       launchers
    Rapier                                             24
    Tigercat (unconfirmed)
    Blowpipe
  short-range guns--
    40mm Bofors L-60 (unconfirmed)                     12
    23mm ZU 23x2
    20mm VDAA SP                                         9
  on order: Rapier
Air Force:
aircraft--general:                                   number
  combat aircraft                                       39
  transport aircraft                                    41
```

238

OMAN

```
  helicopters                                      32
combat aircraft:
  strike and multi-role aircraft--
    medium quality
      SEPECAT Jaguar S(O) Mk.1/Mk.2/T2             22
    others
      Hawker Hunter FGA-6/FR-10/T-67               17
    TOTAL                                          39
  on order: 8 Tornado strike/multirole aircraft
transport aircraft:
  BAe-111                                           3
  Britten-Norman BN-2 Defender/Islander             6
  C-130H Hercules                                   3
  DC-8                                              1
  DC-10                                             1
  DHC-5D Buffalo                                    4
  Dornier Do-228-100 (used by police
    air wing for maritime
    surveillance & border patrols)                  2
  Gulfstream                                        1
  Learjet (in police service)                       1
  Merlin IV                                         2
  Mystere Falcon 20                                 1
  Mystere Falcon 10                                 1
  Short Skyvan Srs 3M (some employed in
    maritime patrol role)                          15
  TOTAL                                            41
  on order: 1 C-130H; additional DHC-5D
training and liaison aircraft:
  BAC-167 Strikemaster Mk.82                        12
  AS-202 Bravo                                      2
  Hawk                                              8
  PC-6 Turbo-Porter
  TOTAL                                           22+
helicopters:                                    number
  medium transport--
    AB-205                                         19
    AB-212B/Bell 212                                3
    AB-214                                          5
    AS-332 Super Puma                               2
                               (sub-total         29)
  light transport--
    AB-206 JetRanger                                3
  TOTAL                                            32
  on order: Westland HAS Mk.1 Sea King ASW helicopters
    (unconfirmed)
miscellaneous aircraft:
  TTL BTT-3 Banshee RPV/target drone
advanced armament:
  air-to-air missiles--
```

239

```
       R-550 Magique
       AIM-9P Sidewinder
     bombs--
       BL-755 CBU
   anti-aircraft defenses:
     radars--
       AR-15
       Marconi S713 Martello 3D                      2
       S-600
       Watchman
     aircraft shelters--
       for all combat aircraft, at Masirah and Thamarit
   military airfields:                               6
       Khasab (Musandam Peninsula), Masirah, Muscat (Seeb),
       Nizwa, Salalah, Thamarit
Navy:
   combat vessels:                            number
     MFPBs--
       Province class                               3
     gunboats/MTBs--
       Brooke Marine 123 ft. (37.5 meter)           4
     patrol craft (police service):
       CG 27 87.6 ft. (26.7 meter)                  2
       Vosper Thornycroft 75 ft. (22.9 meter)       5
       Watercraft & Shoreham 45.6 ft.
         (13.9 meter)                               3
       P-2000                                       1
       P-1903                                       1
       Vosper 25 meter (with the Navy)              4
       Cheverton 27 ft. (8.2 meter)                 8
       Total                                       24
     on order: P-2000 patrol boats; 1 Province MFPB
   landing craft:
     Brooke Marine 2000 ton landing
       ship-logistics/tank                          1
     Brooke Marine 2200 ton landing
       ship-logistics/tank                          1
     Lewis Offshore 85 DWT LCU                       1
     Impala Marine 75 DWT LCU                        1
     Cheverton 45 DWT LCU                            2
     Cheverton 30 DWT LCU                            1
     TOTAL                                           6
     on order: Skima 12 hovercraft (unconfirmed)
   auxiliary vessels                          number
     Brooke Marine 900 ton royal yacht              1
     Conoship Groningen 1380 DWT
       coastal freighter                            1
     survey craft, 23.6 ton                         1
   advanced armament:
     MM-38 Exocet SSM
```

## OMAN

MM-40 Exocet SSM
naval bases:                                                    5
  Jazirat Ghanam, Mina Raysut (Salalah), Khasam,  Muscat,
  al-Masna'a/Wudam Alwa (Sa'id Ibn Sultan Base)
ship maintenance and repair capability:
  Muscat

# 13. PALESTINIAN MILITARY AND PARA-MILITARY FORCES

On November 15, 1988, in Algeria the PNC proclaimed an independent Palestinian state, which has in reality no control over territory. For all intents and purposes this has not altered the status of Palestinian forces, which remain as diverse and devoid of central autority as ever. The Chairman of the PLO Executive Committee and designated president of the state is Yasir Arafat, who also heads Fatah, the largest constituent organization. All Palestinian military and para-military forces, except the Abu Nidal faction, 15th May Organization and PFLP-SC (see below), are nominally subordinate to the Executive Committee of the Palestine Liberation Organization. The PFLP (GC), Fatah rebels, and the PLF faction headed by Abd al-Fateh al-Ghanem, are not represented on the Executive Committee of the PLO, and for all practical purposes are also not controlled by the PLO Executive Committee.

At the Palestine National Council meeting of April 1987 in Algeria, the PFLP and DFLP both returned to the PLO, and obtained seats on its Executive Committee, which grew from ten to fifteen members so as to allow representation of the returning organizations. The small Palestinian Communist Party also became a formal member of the PLO, with a representative on the Executive Committee. The anti-Arafat Palestine National Salvation Front was left with only four members: al-Sa'iqa, Fatah Rebels, PFLP (GC) and PPSF.

Although the PLO attempts to coordinate the activities of its member organizations, it lacks operational control. In practice, the military forces of all organizations are responsible only to their own leadership. In November 1988 Arafat ordered the PLO to refrain from attacking Israel via Lebanon. The DFLP, PFLP and PLF - Tal'at Ya'qub nevertheless continued their attempts to raid Israel from Lebanon.

The PLF (except for the Abd al-Fateh Ghanem faction) is part of the mainstream PLO. The PLF faction led by Tal'at Ya'qub formally merged with the Abu al-Abbas PLF in 1987. Tal'at Ya'qub died in November 1988.

Abu Nidal's organization collaborated with the PLO in the fighting against Amal in the camps in Lebanon. The organization of the Abu Nidal unit in the Biq'a and in the camps in South Lebanon became similar to that of other organizations in the PLO. In addition, Abu Nidal personally held negotiations with PLO and Fatah leaders; in Algeria in April 1987, during the PNC session, he negotiated with Abu

## PALESTINIAN FORCES

Jihad (Khalil al-Wazir), Arafat's deputy.

Palestinian forces may be divided into four categories: a) quasi-regular units of the various organizations; b) terror squads; c) the regular Palestinian Liberation Army (PLA); and d) militias which occasionally supplement the quasi-regular units.

The quasi-regular forces of Fatah have been scattered among a number of Arab countries. Movement back to Lebanon from Tunisia, Algeria, Iraq, Yemen, and PDRY proceeded apace in 1988; we count the members of the various organizations as single entities regardless of their presumed location. Most of the men who came back to Lebanon were senior and junior commanders. All organizations (except for Fatah, the Abu Abbas faction of the PLF and the ALF) were deployed in Syria and Lebanon. Militiamen remained concentrated mainly in Lebanon. Terror squads were based in Lebanon until summer 1982, from where they operated throughout the world. In 1987, some terror squads resumed operations from Lebanon, from where their activity was directed against Israel, and occasionally against targets elsewhere in the world. They also operated from Algeria, Libya, and Syria.

ARMED FORCES
  Personnel:
    quasi-regular forces--

| organization | commander | armed personnel (estimate) |
|---|---|---|
| PLO | | |
| Arafat Loyalist: | | |
| Al-Fatah | Yasir Arafat | 8,000 |
| Palestine Liberation Front (PLF) | Mahmud al-Zaidan, alias Abu al-Abbas | less than 300 |
| Arab Liberation Front (ALF) | Abd al-Rahim Ahmad | 300 |
| Democratic Front for the Liberation of Palestine (DFLP) | Na'if Hawatmeh | 1,000 |
| Popular Front for the Liberation of Palestine (PFLP) | Dr. George Habash | 600-800 |
| Palestine National Salvation Front (pro-Syrian, anti-Arafat): | | |

## PALESTINIAN FORCES

| | | |
|---|---|---|
| Al-Fatah rebels | Muhammad Sa'id Musa, alias Abu Musa | 2,500 |
| Popular Front for the Liberation of Palestine-- General Command (PFLP--GC) | Ahmad Jibril | 600 |
| Al-Sa'iqa | Dr. Issam al-Qadi | 1,000 |
| Palestine Popular Struggle Front (PPSF) | Bahjat Abu Gharbiyah & Dr. Samir Ghusha | 600 |

Organizations belonging neither to the Arafat loyalists nor to the Palestine National Salvation Front:

| | | |
|---|---|---|
| Palestine Libera- tion Front (PLF)/ Abd al-Fateh al- Ghanem faction | Abd al-Fateh al-Ghanem | less than 100 |

Secessionists:

| | | |
|---|---|---|
| Abu Nidal Faction (al-Fatah Revolutionary Council-FRC) | Sabri al-Bana, alias Abu Nidal | 1,000 |
| 15th May Organization | Muhammad al-Amri,alias Abu Ibrahim | about 100 |
| Popular Front for the Liberation of Palestine--Special Command (PFLP-SC) | Salim Abu Salem, alias Abu Muhammad | 100 |
| al-Fatah pro-Jordan secessionists | Atallah Atallah, alias Abu Za'im | 400 |
| TOTAL, all organizations | | 16,800 |

Approximate Deployment, late 1988 (all organizations):

| country | number |
|---|---|
| Lebanon: | |
| Biq'a | 1,500 |
| Mount Lebanon Area | 1,400 |
| Tripoli & northern Lebanon | 800 |
| Beirut & vicinity | 4,000 |
| South Lebanon (Tyre, Sidon & vicinity) | 4,000 |
| (sub-total | 11,700) |
| Syria (excluding PLA) | 2,500 |
| Other: | |
| Algeria | 500 |
| Iraq | 2,000 |

## PALESTINIAN FORCES

```
      PDRY                                            500
      Sudan                                           500
      Tunisia (administrative personnel)              100
      YAR                                           1,500
                                 (sub-total       5,100)
   TOTAL                                          19,300
   terror squads                            about 200
   PLA Force in Jordan                           2,000
   militias                                     10,000+
Ground Forces:
   major units--                   brigades
      PLA
      in Syria & Syrian-
        occupied Lebanon               2
      in Jordan                        1
      in Iraq                          1
      TOTAL                            4
   quasi-regular forces of
     the major organizations
                   brigades     battalions      companies
      Al-Fatah          3
      PFLP                            6
      PFLP-GC                                       5-6
      Al-Sa'iqa                       5
      DFLP                            8
      PLF                                (estimate) 2
      TOTAL, all
        organizations   3             19             7-8
small arms:
   personal weapons--
   9mm P.P.Sh.41 SMG
   7.62mm AK-47 (Kalashnikov) AR
   7.62mm AKM AR
   7.62mm Type 56 AR
   7.62mm SSG-69 sniping rifle
   5.56mm HK-33 Heckler & Koch AR
   5.56mm M-16 Al AR
   machine guns--
   14.5mm  ZPU  14.5x4  HMG  (in  anti-aircraft  role)
   14.5mm  ZPU  14.5x2  HMG  (in  anti-aircraft  role)
   12.7mm D.Sh.K. 38/46 (Degtyarev) HMG
   7.62mm SGM (Goryunov)
   7.62mm RPD (Degtyarev) LMG
   7.62mm RPK LMG
   7.62mm PK/PKS (Kalashnikov) LMG
   light and medium mortars--
   82mm M-43
   light ATRLs--
   M-72 LAW
   RPG-7
```

245

```
tanks:
  model
    medium quality
      T-55/improved T-54
APCs/ARVs:
  model
    high quality
      M-113                                             a few
    medium and low quality                             number
      BTR-152
      BRDM-2 (also an SP ATGM carrying AT-3 Sagger)
      UR-416
    TOTAL                                               a few
artillery:
    towed guns and howitzers--
      155mm M-1950 howitzer
      130mm M-46 gun
      122mm D-30 howitzer
      122mm M-1938 howitzer
      105mm M-102 howitzer
      100mm M-1955 field/AT gun
      85mm M-1945/D-44 field/AT gun
    mortars, over 160mm--
      160mm mortar
    mortars, less than 160mm, but excluding light and
      medium--
      120mm mortar
    TOTAL                     (unconfirmed)               80
  MRLs--
    122mm BM-21
    122mm BM-11
    107mm
    improvised MRLs on light vehicles
    TOTAL                                                 50
anti-tank weapons:
  missiles--                                         launchers
    AT-3 (Sagger)
    MILAN
    TOTAL                                                200
  guns--
    107mm B-11 recoilless rifle
    106mm M-40 A2 recoilless rifle
    82mm B-10 recoilless rifle
    57mm gun
army anti-aircraft defenses:
  missiles--                                         launchers
    SA-9 (Gaskin) SP                                    a few
    SA-7 (Grail)
  short-range guns--
    23mm ZSU 23x4 SP (Gun Dish)
```

```
23mm ZU 23x2
20mm 20x3 M-55 A4
```

Air Units:

The PLO-affiliated organizations have no air force. The so-called "Fatah Air Force" is designated Force 14. About 200 Palestinians have reportedly undergone training as fighter and helicopter pilots in Libya, YAR, Romania, Pakistan, Cuba, North Korea and the USSR. Other PLO members have learned to fly commercial aircraft in civilian flight schools in Romania, Yugoslavia and several western countries. Some are now flying diverse aircraft, including MiG-23 and MiG-21 fighters, in Libya. Two Palestinian pilots were killed flying a MiG-21 and a MiG-23 for the Libyan Air Force in Northern Chad; one of them was identified as belonging to Jibril's PFLP-GC. Helicopters flown include the Mi-24, Mi-8, CH-4 and AS-321. Transport aircraft flown include the Fokker F-27. Some PLO airmen have reportedly flown aircraft and helicopters in Nicaragua for the Nicaraguan government.

PLO terrorists have trained with hot air balloons and hang-gliders equipped with auxiliary motors. Hang-gliders have been used twice in action, in 1981 and in 1987.

A concentration of Palestinian pilots and affiliated personnel is located in YAR and at Kamran Island (an island legally part of PDRY, but practically controlled by YAR, off the shore of Saleef). The PLO has de facto control of an airline company registered in Guinea Bissau, where Palestinians fly commercial aircraft.

Naval Forces:

| | |
|---|---|
| swimmer-delivery vehicles | |
| underwater demolition squads | 50 men |
| small boat units | 200 men |
| | (concentrated in YAR, at |
| | Kamran Island, and |
| | in Annaba in Algeria) |

Foreign Military Aid Received (by all organizations):

financial aid from:

Algeria; Bahrain; Iraq (to al-Fatah, Abu al-Abbas faction of PLF, ALF, 15th May organization); Kuwait; Libya (to PFLP, PFLP-GC, PLF, al-Fatah rebels); Saudi Arabia ($86 million annually to al-Fatah); Syria (to al-Sa'iqa, PFLP-GC, al-Fatah rebels, Abu Nidal, PLF [Abd al-Fateh al-Ghanem and Tal'at Ya'qub factions only], PPSS); UAE

military training:

trainees abroad in--Algeria, Bulgaria, Cuba, Czechoslovakia, GDR, Hungary, Iraq, Libya. North Korea, Pakistan, PDRY, Syria, USSR, Yugoslavia

arms transfers from:
   Algeria (small arms); Iraq (small arms); Libya (MRLs,
   SAMs, artillery pieces); North Korea (artillery
   pieces); PDRY (Soviet arms); PRC (small arms); Saudi
   Arabia (small arms and ammunition, trucks); Syria
   (tanks); USSR and other Soviet Bloc countries (tanks,
   SAMs); Yugoslavia (AAGs; small arms--unconfirmed)
support forces from:
   Japan and various European countries (individual
      volunteers)
Foreign Military Aid Extended:
   military training, sabotage instruction, and cooperation
   extended by the PLO and affiliated organizations to the
   following non-Palestinian organizations:
   ANC and PAC (South Africa, unconfirmed)
   The Nicaraguan government (formerly FSLN--Front
      Sandinista de Liberacion Nacional)
   Hizb Allah in Lebanon
   SWAPO anti-South African guerrillas in Namibia
   Tamil guerrillas in Sri Lanka

# 14. QATAR

BASIC DATA
  Official Name of State: State of Qatar
  Head of State: Amir Shaykh Khalifa ibn Hamad al-Thani (also
    Prime Minister)
  Minister of Defense: Major General Shaykh Hamad ibn Khalifa
    al-Thani (also Heir Apparent and Commander in Chief of
    the Armed Forces)
  Chief of the General Staff: Colonel Shaykh Mubarak Ibn  Abd
    al-Rahman al-Thani
  Commander of the Air Force: Colonel Shaykh Hamad ibn
    Abdullah al-Thani (unconfirmed)
  Commander of the Navy: Captain Azab Saleem
  Area: 10,360 sq. km.
  Population:                                          330,000
    ethnic subdivision:
      Arabs                          132,000            40.0%
      Pakistanis                      59,000            18.0%
      Indians                         59,000            18.0%
      Persians                        33,000            10.0%
      Others (mostly Southeast
        Asians)                       47,000            14.0%
    religious subdivision:
      Sunni Muslims                  232,000            70.3%
      Shi'ite Muslims                 80,000            24.3%
      Others                          18,000             5.4%
    nationality subdivision:
      Qataris                         83,000            25.0%
      Alien Arabs                     66,000            20.0%
      Alien Non-Arabs
        Southeast Asians (Indians,
        Pakistanis, Chinese,
        Thais, Filipinos, others)    112,000            34.0%
      Iranians                        53,000            16.0%
      Others                          16,000             5.0%
  GDP:
    1980--$7.95 billion (estimate)
  Defense Expenditure:
    1983--$166.94 million
  Foreign Military Aid Received:
    military training:
      foreign     advisors/instructors/serving      personnel
        from--Britain, Egypt, France, India, Jordan, Pakistan
        (until August 1988)
      trainees abroad in--Britain, Egypt, France, Jordan,
        Pakistan , Saudi Arabia
    arms transfers from:
      Britain (helicopters, SAMs); Egypt (APCs, MRLs); France
      (tanks, APCs, MFPBs, naval SSMs, combat aircraft,

249

artillery pieces, anti-ship AGMs)
Foreign Military Aid Extended:
  financial aid to:
    Jordan, Syria, Lebanon, Palestinian organizations--
    grants; Iraq--loans
  Joint Maneuvers with:
    GCC members (Bahrain, Kuwait, Oman, Qatar, Saudi Arabia,
    UAE)

INFRASTRUCTURE
  Road Network:
    length:                                                840 km
      paved roads                                          490 km
      gravel roads                                         350 km
    main routes:
      Doha--Umm Sa'id
      Doha--Salwa--al-Hufuf (Saudi Arabia)
      Doha--Dukhan--Umm Bab (oil fields)
      Doha--al-Ruwais--Zubara
  Airfields:                                                    4
    airfields by runway type:
      permanent surface fields                                  1
      unpaved fields and usable airstrips                       3
    airfields by runway length:
      over 3660 meters                                          1
      1220--2439                                                2
      under 1220                                                1
    international airports: Doha
  Airlines:
    companies: Gulf Air--jointly owned by Oman, Qatar,
    Bahrain and UAE (listed under Bahrain)
  Maritime Facilities:
    harbors--Doha
    oil terminals--Halul Island, Umm Sa'id
  Merchant Marine:

| vessel type | number | DWT |
|---|---|---|
| crude tanker | 1 | 137,676 |
| tanker | 1 | 63,132 |
| general cargo/container | 8 | 147,677 |
| bunkering tanker | 1 | 5,390 |
| container | 3 | 95,542 |
| TOTAL | 14 | 449,417 |

ARMED FORCES
  Personnel:
    military forces--
      army                                                6,000
      air force                                             300
      navy                                                  700
      TOTAL                                               7,000

# QATAR

```
Army:
  major units:
    unit type                  regiments          battalions
      armored/tank                                      1
      guard infantry               1
      infantry                                          5
      TOTAL                        1                    6
  small arms:
    personal weapons--
      7.62mm G-3 AR
      7.62mm L-1 A1 SAR
    machine guns--
      7.62mm MAG (FN) LMG
    light and medium mortars--
      81mm
  tanks:
    model                                           number
      medium quality
        AMX-30                                          24
  APCs/ARVs:
    model
      high quality
        AMX-10P                                         30
        VAB                                            158
        VPM 81 mortar carrier                            4
        V-150 Commando                                   8
                                (sub-total           200)
      others
        Fahd                                          6-10
        Ferret                                          10
        Saracen                                         25
                                (sub-total         41-45)
      TOTAL                                            245
      on order: Engesa APCs, ARVs (unconfirmed);  6  French
        armored vehicles (command post, medical  evacuation
        vehicles)
  artillery:
    self propelled guns and howitzer--
      155mm Mk. F-3 (AMX) SP howitzer                    6
    towed guns and howitzers--
      25 lb. (87mm) howitzer                             8
      TOTAL                                             14
      on order: 6 additional 155mm Mk. F-3 SP howitzers
    MRLs--
      122mm BM-21
  anti-tank weapons:
    missiles--
      MILAN
    guns--
      84mm Carl Gustaf light recoilless rifle
```

## QATAR

| | |
|---|---|
| army anti-aircraft defenses: | |
| missiles-- | launchers |
| Blowpipe | 6 |
| FIM-92A Stinger | 12 |
| Rapier | 18 |
| Roland 2 | 9 |
| Tigercat | 5 |
| Total | 50 |

on order: Crotale SAMs (unconfirmed)

| | |
|---|---|
| Air Force: | |
| aircraft--general: | number |
| combat aircraft | 17 |
| transport aircraft | 4 |
| helicopters | 33 |
| combat aircraft: | |
| strike and multi-role aircraft-- | |
| medium quality | |
| Mirage F-1E/B | 14 |
| others | |
| Hawker Hunter FGA-78/T-79 | 3 |
| TOTAL | 17 |
| transport aircraft: | |
| Boeing 707 | 2 |
| Boeing 727 | 1 |
| Britten-Norman BN-2 Islander | 1 |
| TOTAL | 4 |
| training and liaison aircraft: | |
| Alpha Jet | 6 |
| helicopters: | |
| attack-- | |
| SA-342 Gazelle (employed as light helicopter) | 12 |
| heavy transport-- | |
| Westland Commando Mk.2/3 | 12 |
| medium transport-- | |
| Westland Lynx | 3 |
| Westland Whirlwind Series 3 | 2 |
| (sub-total | 5) |
| maritime attack-- | |
| Westland Sea King (in attack role) | 4 |
| TOTAL | 33 |

on order: AS-332 Super Puma
miscellaneous aircraft:
TTL BTT-3 Banshee RPV/target
drone (unconfirmed)
advanced armament:
air to ground missiles--
AM-39 Exocet
anti-aircraft defenses:
long-range missiles--

```
      on   order:   MIM-23B   Improved   HAWK;
  military airfields:                                          1
      Doha
Navy:
    combat vessels:                                      number
      MFPBs--
        Combattante III                                       3
      patrol craft--
        Vosper Thornycroft 110 ft. (33.5 meter)               6
        Whittingham & Mitchell
          75 ft. (22.5 meter)                                 2
        Damen "Polycat 1450"                                  6
        Keith Nelson type 44 ft. (13.5 meter)                 2
        Fairey Marine Spear class                            25
        Fairey Marine Interceptor class
          fast assault and rescue craft                       2
        P-1200                                                7
        Total                                                50
    landing craft:
      48.8 meter LCT                                          1
    advanced armament:
      MM-40 Exocet SSM
    coastal defense: launchers
      MM-40 Exocet coastal defense missiles                 3x4
    naval bases:                                              2
      Doha, Halul Island (under construction)
```

# 15. SAUDI ARABIA

BASIC DATA
Official Name of State: The Kingdom of Ṣaudi Arabia
Head of State: King Fahd ibn Abd al-Aziz al-Sa'ud (also
   Prime Minister)
First Deputy Prime Minister and Heir Apparent: Crown Prince
   Abdullah ibn Abd al-Aziz al-Sa'ud (also Commander of the
   National Guard)
Defense and Aviation Minister: Prince Sultan ibn Abd
   al-Aziz al-Sa'ud (also Second Deputy Prime Minister)
Chief of Staff of the Armed Forces: General Muhammad Salih
   al-Hammad
Commander of the Ground Forces: Lieutenant General Youssuf
   Abd al-Rahman al-Rashid (also Deputy Chief of Staff of
   the Armed Forces)
Commander of the Air Force: Major General Ahmad Ibrahim
   al-Bukheiri
Commander of the Air Defense Forces: Major General Prince
   Khalid ibn Sultan
Commander of the Navy: Rear Admiral Talal Ibn Salem
   al-Mufadhi
Director of the National Guard: General Abd al-Aziz
   al-Tweijari
Area: 2,331,000 sq.km. (approximation; some borders
   undefined or undemarcated)
Population (estimate):                                8,500,000
   ethnic subdivision:
      Arabs                        7,769,000           91.4%
      Afro-Arabs                     425,000            5.0%
      Others                         306,000            3.6%
   religious subdivision:
      Sunni Muslims                7,829,000           92.1%
      Shi'ite Muslims                425,000            5.0%
      Others (mainly Christians)     246,000            2.9%
   nationality subdivision:
      Saudis                       6,681,000           78.6%
      Yemenis                        969,000           11.4%
      Palestinians                    60,000            0.7%
      Americans                       42,000            0.5%
      Others (Thais, Filipinos,
         Chinese, Indians,
         Pakistanis, other Arabs)     748,000           8.8%
GDP:
   1986--$ 77.41 billion
   1987--$ 71.46 billion
Balance of Payments (goods, services & unilateral transfer
   payments):
   year     income          expenditure        balance
   1986     $33.97 bil.     $45.86 bil.        -$11.89 bil.

## SAUDI ARABIA

1987     $36.44 bil.        $46.01 bil.       -$ 9.57 bil.

Defense Expenditure:
  1985--$17.5 billion
  1987--$16.2 billion

Foreign Military Aid Received:
  military training:
    foreign advisors/instructors/serving personnel from--Britain, Egypt, France, FRG, India, Japan, Jordan, Morocco (1000, unconfirmed), Pakistan, PRC, Syria, Turkey, USA (partly civilian)
    trainees abroad in--Britain, France, Jordan, Pakistan, PRC, Switzerland, Turkey, USA
  arms transfers from:
    Austria (small arms); Britain (combat aircraft, trainer aircraft, hovercraft, SSB radio transceivers, helicopters and minesweepers on order); France (APCs, radars, SAMs, SP artillery); FRG (small arms, electronics, EW equipment); Italy (helicopters); Japan (helicopters); PRC (SSMs); Spain (transport aircraft, trucks); Sweden (trucks); Switzerland (trainer aircraft); USA (AAMs, AGMs, ATGMs, artillery pieces, AWACS aircraft, combat aircraft, aircraft engines, SAMs, tanks, transport aircraft, aircraft simulators, trucks)
  support forces from:
    Bangladesh, Pakistan (a few hundred); USA (AWACS and refuelling aircraft, until May 1989); GCC rapid deployment force (10,000 men, mostly from Saudi Arabia, but some from Bahrain, Kuwait, Oman, Qatar, and UAE); Morocco (unconfirmed)
  construction aid by:
    South Korea, USA, Britain
  maintenance of equipment in:
    France (naval vessels)
Foreign Military Aid Extended:
  financial aid to:
    Burundi ($2.8 million for road construction); Jordan ($360 million), Lebanon, Morocco, PLO, Somalia, Sudan, Syria ($500 million), YAR ($1.8 billion annually, including $84 million for PLO); Iraq--grant and loan; Pakistan; Mauritania--grant; Turkey--loan
  military training:
    advisors/instructors/technicians in--YAR
    foreign trainees from--Bahrain, Jordan, Kuwait, Mauritania, Oman, Qatar, Somalia, Sudan, Tunisia, UAE, YAR
  arms transfers to:
    Iraq (Spanish-made APCs); PLO (ammunition, small arms)
  facilities provided to:
    PLO (training camps for youth units)

Cooperation in Arms Production/Assembly with:
  France (electronics); FRG (small arms and ammunition)
Joint Maneuvers with:
  GCC (members: Bahrain, Kuwait, Oman, Qatar, Saudi Arabia,
  UAE); France; Pakistan

INFRASTRUCTURE
  Road Network:
    length:                                      80,000 km
      paved roads                                35,000 km
      gravel and improved earth and roads        50,000 km
    main routes:
      Jiddah--al-Qunfudhah--Jizan--Hodeida (YAR)
      Jiddah--Medina--Tabuk--Ma'an (Jordan)/Yanbu--Wajh--
        Haql--Aqaba (Jordan)
      Tabuk--Sakhakh--Badanah (on TAPline road)
      Jiddah--Mecca
      Mecca--Ta'if--Qal'at Bishah--Khamis Mushayt/Qal'at
        Bishah--Najran
      Mecca--Ta'if--Abha--Khamis Mushayt
      Riyadh--Buraydah--Ha'il/Buraydah--Medina
      Riyadh--al-Hufuf--Dhahran/al-Hufuf--Doha (Qatar)
      Dhahran--al-Dammam--Qatif--Ras Tanura--Jubayl--
        al-Qaysumah--H-5 (Jordan) (TAPline)
      Dhahran--al-Manamah (Bahrain): 25 km bridge causeway
      Riyadh--al-Kharj--al-Sulayyil--Najran
      Najran--San'a (YAR)
      Rafha (on TAPline road)--al-Najaf (Iraq)
  Railway Network:
    length (standard gauge):                        886 km
    route:
      Riyadh--al-Hufuf--Abqaiq--Dhahran--al-Dammam
  Airfields:                                          176
    airfields by runway type:
      permanent surface fields                         62
      unpaved fields and usable airstrips             114
    airfields by runway length:
      over 3660 meters                                 12
      2440--3659                                       29
      1220--2439                                       98
      under 1220                                       37
    international airports: Dhahran, Jiddah, Medina, Riyadh
    major domestic airfields: Abha/Khamis Mushayt, al-Dammam,
      Arrar, Bishah, Gassim, Qurayat, Ha'il, al-Hufuf, Jawf,
      Jizan, Mecca, Najran, al-Qaysumah, Rafha, Sharawra,
      Tabuk, Ta'if, Turayf, Wajh, Yanbu
  Airlines:
    companies: Saudia (international and domestic); Momen Air
      (domestic)
    aircraft:

256

| | |
|---|---|
| Airbus A-300-600 | 11 |
| Beechcraft A-100 King Air | 2 |
| Boeing 747-100/747-300/747-SP/747-200F | 22 |
| Boeing 737-200/737-200C | 19 |
| Cessna Citation II | 2 |
| Gulfstream II | 5 |
| Gulfstream III | 6 |
| Gulfstream IV | 2 |
| Lockheed L-1011-200 Tristar | 17 |
| Mystere Falcon 900 | 1 |

Maritime Facilities:

harbors--al-Dammam (King Abdul Aziz Port), Jizan, Jiddah (Jiddah Islamic Port), Jubayl, Ras al-Mish'ab, Ras Tanura, Yanbu (King Fahd Port); al-Duba (under construction)

oil terminals--Halul Island, Ju'aymah (offshore oil terminal), Ras Tanura, Yanbu

Merchant Marine:

| vessel type | number | DWT |
|---|---|---|
| crude carrier | 12 | 2,279,954 |
| general cargo | 5 | 24,912 |
| bulk carrier | 2 | 83,287 |
| ore/oil | 1 | 264,591 |
| general cargo/container | 7 | 166,005 |
| ro-ro | 14 | 232,262 |
| product tanker | 4 | 138,460 |
| livestock carrier | 5 | 110,183 |
| container | 3 | 75,691 |
| gas tanker (LPG) | 1 | 61,803 |
| cement carrier | 2 | 53,838 |
| reefer | 4 | 24,748 |
| depot tanker | 4 | 158,372 |
| cement storage | 3 | 207,394 |
| bunkering tanker | 29 | 112,870 |
| ferry | 7 | 10,701 |
| passenger/cargo | 1 | 2,494 |
| chemical tanker | 2 | 47,762 |
| small tanker | 1 | 2,440 |
| methanol tanker | 1 | 42,825 |
| storage tanker | 1 | 36,964 |
| TOTAL | 109 | 4,137,556 |

Defense Production:

army equipment:

production under license--G-3 ARs

manufacture--small arms ammunition, electronic components

planned: tanks, under license; tank guns, under FRG license; electronic equipment, under British, French and US license; APCs

# SAUDI ARABIA

ARMED FORCES
  Personnel:
    military forces--

| | |
|---|---:|
| army | 45,000 |
| air force | 15,000 |
| navy (including a marine unit) | 7,500 |
| national guard (regular) | 25,000 |
| royal guards | 2,000 |
| TOTAL | 94,500 |

    para-military forces--

| | |
|---|---:|
| Mujahidun (affiliated with national guard) | 29,000 |
| coast guard | 6,500 |

  Army and National Guard:
    major units:

| unit type | brigades/ regiments | independent battalions |
|---|:---:|:---:|
| armored | 2 | |
| mechanized | 6 | |
| Royal Guard Infantry | 1 | |
| infantry | | 19 |
| marines (unconfirmed) | | 1 |
| airborne/special force | 1 | |
| TOTAL | 10 | 20 |

    small arms:
      personal weapons--
      9mm Model 12 Beretta SMG
      7.62mm FAL (FN) SAR
      7.62mm G-3 AR
      7.62mm SSG-69 sniping rifle
      5.56mm AUG Steyr AR
      5.56mm HK-33 Heckler & Koch AR
      5.56mm M-16 A1 AR
      machine guns--
      7.62mm (0.3") Browning M-1919 A1 MMG
      automatic grenade launchers--
      40mm Mk.19
      light and medium mortars--
      81mm
      light ATRLs--
      M-72 LAW

    tanks:

| model | number |
|---|---:|
| high quality | |
|   M-60 A3 | 100 |
| medium quality | |
|   M-60 A1 | 150 |
|   AMX-30 | 300 |
| (sub-total | 450) |
| TOTAL | 550 |

on order: 150 kits to upgrade M-60 A1 to M-60 A3
    standard, delivery in process

APCs/ARVs:

| model | number |
|---|---|
| high quality | |
|   AMX-10 | 450 |
|   M-113 A1/A2 | 1000 |
|   V-150 Commando | 1000 |
| (sub-total | 2450) |
| others | |
|   AML-60/90 | 200 |
|   BMR-600 (with marines) | 140 |
|   Fox/Ferret | 200 |
|   M-3 (Panhard) | 150 |
|   UR-416 | + |
| (sub-total | +690) |
| TOTAL | 3140+ |

on order: V-150 & V-300; 200 M-2/M-3
    Bradley with BGM-71C Improved TOW

artillery:

| | |
|---|---|
| self propelled guns and howitzers-- | |
|   155mm M-109 A2 SP howitzer | 224 |
|   155mm GCT SP howitzer | 51 |
| towed guns and howitzers-- | |
|   155mm FH-70 howitzer | 72 |
|   155mm M-198 howitzer | 36 |
|   105mm M-56 Pack howitzer | |
|   105mm M-101 howitzer | |
| mortars, under 160mm, but excluding light and medium-- | |
|   107mm (4.2") M-30 mortar | |
| TOTAL | 700 |

on order: 93 M-992 ammunition carriers from the USA

MRLs:
  180mm SS-40 ASTROS
  127mm SS-30 Astros II
  on order: 300mm SS-60 ASTROS II, 180mm SS-40 ASTROS
    II, and 127mm SS-30 Astros II

engineering equipment:
  M-123 Viper minefield crossing system
  bridging equipment

| | |
|---|---|
| AFV transporters: | 600 |

anti-tank weapons:

| missiles-- | launchers |
|---|---|
|   AMX-10P SP (carrying HOT) | |
|   BGM-71C Improved TOW | |
|   M-47 Dragon | |
| TOTAL | 700 |
| guns-- | |
|   90mm Mecar light gun (unconfirmed) | |

```
    on order: BGM-71D (TOW II)
  surface-to-surface missiles and rockets
      CSS-2 SSM (East Wind, IRBM) (number unconfirmed) 20
  army anti-aircraft defenses:
    missiles--                                launchers
      Crotale                                    12+
      Shahine                                     12
      FIM-92A Stinger                            400
      MIM-43A Redeye
    short-range guns--                         number
      35mm Oerlikon-Buhrle 35x2 CD F-002
      30mm AMX DCA 30 (twin 30 mm) SP
      20mm M-163 Vulcan SP                        72
    on order: Stinger SAM; Gepard 35mm SP AAG; 60 30mm 30x2
      Wildcat SP AAGs; Shahine II
  CW capabilities:
    personal protective equipment
    decontamination units
Air Force:
  aircraft--general:                           number
    combat aircraft                               194
    transport aircraft                             73
    helicopters                                   114
  combat aircraft:
    interceptors--
      high quality
        F-15 C/D Eagle                             60
        Tornado ADV                                 4
                                     (sub total   64)
    strike and multi-role aircraft--
      high quality
        Tornado IDS                                20
      medium or low quality
        F-5E/F                                     85
        F-5A/B                                     15
        RF-5E                                      10
                                     (sub-total  110)
    Total                                         130
    on order: 20 Tornado ADV, 28 Tornado IDS, part of the
      Yamama I agreement, 12-14 F-15, additional 48 Tornado
      IDS and Tornado ADV, part of the Yamama II agreement
  transport aircraft:
    Boeing 747                                     1
    Boeing 737                                     1
    Boeing 707                                     2
    C-130E/H Hercules                             34
    CN-235                                         2
    KC-130H tanker (refuelling)                    8
    KE-3/Boeing 707 tanker (refuelling)            8
    L-100/L-100-30HS (unconfirmed)                 9
```

# SAUDI ARABIA

```
Gates Learjet 35 (employed in
  target-towing role)                              3
Gulfstream III                                     1
Mystere Falcon 20                                  2
VC-140 JetStar (equivalent to
  C-140 JetStar)                                   2
TOTAL                                             73
```
on order: 2 CN-235; Super King Air 200
training and liaison aircraft:
```
BAC-167 Strikemaster                              27
BAe Jetstream 31 (employed as cockpit
  training a/c for Tornado pilots)                 2
Cessna 172 G/H/L                                  12
Hawk                                               4
Pilatus PC-9                                       4
TOTAL                                             49
```
on order: 26 Hawk, 26 Pilatus PC-9, additional 30
Hawk, including 20 Hawk-200
helicopters:
maritime attack--
```
AS-365 Dauphin 2                                  24
```
heavy transport--
```
SH-3 (AS-61A)                                      3
KV-107/KV-107 IIA-17                              16
                           (sub-total            19)
```
medium transport--
```
AB-212 (unconfirmed)                              35
AS-365N Dauphin 2 (employed in medical
  evacuation role)                                 6
                           (sub-total            41)
```
light transport--
```
AB-206 JetRanger                                  30
TOTAL                                            114
```
on order: 15 Bell 406 (OH-58D); 12 UH-60A  Black  Hawk;
12 AS-332 Super  Puma,  naval  attack  configuration;
additional 80 British helicopters, reportedly  UH-60A
(WS-70) and other models
miscellaneous aircraft:
```
E-3A AWACS                                         5
```
MQM-74C Chukar II RPV
TTL BTT-3 Banshee RPV/target drone (unconfirmed)
advanced armament:
```
air-to-air missiles--                         number
  AIM-9J/P Sidewinder
  AIM-9L Sidewinder
  AIM-7F Sparrow                                 850
  Red Top
  Firestreak
air-to-ground missiles--
  AGM-65A Maverick                              2400
```

```
    AS-15TT anti-ship missile
    Sea Eagle anti-ship missile
  bombs--
    laser-guided bombs                                    3000
    CBU                                                   1000
    BL-755 CBU
    JP-233 anti-runway bombs
  on order: AS-15TT air-to-sea missile, 100  AGM-84
    Harpoon air-to-sea missile, AIM-9M AAMs,  995  AIM-9L
    AAMs, 671 AIM-9P-4  AAMS,  ALARM  anti-radiation
    missiles, AM-39 Exocet air-to-sea missiles
anti-aircraft defenses:
  radars--
    AN/FPS-117                                              17
    AN/TPS-43
    AN/TPS-63 (unconfirmed)
  long-range missiles--
    model                                             batteries
      MIM-23B Improved HAWK                               15
  aircraft shelters--
    for combat aircraft
military airfields:                                        20
  Abqaiq, al-Sulayil, Dhahran, Jiddah, Khamis Mushayt,
  al-Kharj, Medina, Riyadh, Sharurah, Tabuk, Ta'if (King
  Fahd), 9 additional
aircraft maintenance and repair capability:
  for all models, dependent on foreign technicians
Navy:
  combat vessels:                                      number
    MFPBs--
      PGG-1 class (Peterson Builders)                      9
    missile frigates--
      F-2000                                               4
    missile corvettes--
      PCG-1 class (Tacoma Boatbuilding)                    4
    mine warfare vessels--
      MSC-322 class minesweeper                            4
    gunboats/MTBs--
      Jaguar class MTB                                     3
    patrol craft-- (some serving with coast-guard)
      P-32                                                 8
      USCG-Type 95 ft. (29 meter)                          1
      Skorpion class (with coast guard)                   15
      Rapier class 50 ft. (with coast guard)              12
      Naja 12                                             20
      Total                                               56
    note: coast guard has 125 additional small patrol
      craft
  on order: 2 26-meter (80 ton) Abeking & Rasmussen
    patrol boats; 4 Blohm & Voss 38.9 meter patrol boats;
```

```
     6 Sandown minehunters
landing craft:
  LCM-6 class                                        8
  SRN-6 class hovercraft (with coast guards)        24
  US LCU 1610 class LCU                              4
  26 ton LCM                                         4
  TOTAL                                             40
auxiliary vessels:
  training ship, 350 ton                            1
  royal yacht, 1450 DWT                             1
  royal yacht, 650 ton                              1
  Durance class tanker, 10,500 ton                  2
advanced armament:
  surface-to-surface missiles--
    OTOMAT Mk.2
    RGM-84A Harpoon                                120
  anti-missile guns--
    20mm Vulcan-Phalanx radar-controlled
  advanced torpedoes--
    F-17P
coastal defense:
  OTOMAT coastal defense missile
special maritime forces:
  frogmen and divers
naval bases (including Coast Guard):               12
  al-Dammam, al-Haql (coast guard), Jiddah, Jizan,
  Jubayl, Makna (coast guard), al-Qatif, Ras al-Mish'ab,
  Ras Tanurah, al-Sharma, al-Wajh, Yanbu
ship maintenance and repair capability:
  repair of vessels, dependent on foreign experts; 22,000
  ton and 62,000 ton floating docks at Dammam; 45,000 ton
  and 16,000 ton floating docks at Jiddah; docks work
  mostly for commercial vessels
coast guard:
  small patrol boats                               120
```

# 16. SOUTH YEMEN (PDRY)

BASIC DATA
Official Name of State: The People's Democratic Republic of
  Yemen (PDRY)
Head of State: President Haydar Abu Bakr al-Attas (also
  Chairman of the Supreme People's Council)
Prime Minister: Yasin Sa'id Nu'man
Defense Minister: Colonel Salih Ubayd Ahmad Ali
Chief of the General Staff: Colonel Haytham Qasim Tahir
  (also deputy defense minister)
Commander of the Air Force: Major Ali Muthanna Hadi
Commander of the Navy: Commander Ali Qasim Talib
Area: 287,500 sq. km. (borders with Saudi Arabia, Oman and
  YAR partly undemarcated and/or disputed)

| Population | | 2,440,000 |
|---|---|---|
| ethnic subdivision: | | |
| Arabs | 2,362,000 | 96.8% |
| Somalis | 34,000 | 1.4% |
| Others | 44,000 | 1.8% |
| religious subdivision: | | |
| Sunni Muslims | 2,433,000 | 99.7% |
| Hindus | 5,000 | 0.2% |
| Others | 2,000 | 0.1% |

GDP:
  1980--$667 million (estimate)
Balance of Payments (goods, services & unilateral transfer
  payments):

| year | income | expenditure | balance |
|---|---|---|---|
| 1986 | $459 mil. | $635 mil. | -$176 mil. |
| 1987 | $545 mil. | $667 mil. | -$122 mil. |

Defense Expenditure:
  1983--$171 million (estimate)
  1984--$194 million (estimate)
Foreign Military Aid Received:
  financial aid from:
    USSR (for repair of refineries damaged in January 1986
    coup d'etat); Saudi Arabia--grant
  military training:
    foreign advisors/instructors from--Cuba, GDR, North
    Korea, Syria, USSR (1000)
    trainees abroad in--USSR, other Soviet Bloc countries
  arms transfers from:
    USSR and Soviet bloc countries (combat aircraft, small
    arms, tanks)
Foreign Military Aid Extended:
  military training:
    foreign trainees from--Palestinian organizations,
    PFLP-GC, al-Fatah, PFLP, May 15; ASALA (Armenians);

## SOUTH YEMEN

Japanese Red Army (JRA); West German Red Army Faction
(RAF, unconfirmed);
arms transfers to:
Palestinian organizations (artillery, tanks, small
arms)
facilities provided to:
Palestinian organizations and other terrorist groups
(training camps); USSR (airfields, naval base at
Socotra)

INFRASTRUCTURE
Road Network:
| | |
|---|---|
| length: | 5,600 km |
| paved roads | 1,700 km |
| gravel and stone roads | 63C km |
| earth tracks | 3,270 km |

main routes:
Aden--Shuqra--Lawdar/Shuqra--al-Mukalla
Aden--Musaymir--Ta'iz (YAR)
al-Mukalla--al-Qatn--Tarim
al-Mukalla--al-Riyan--Salalah (Oman)

| | |
|---|---|
| Airfields: | 30 |
| airfields by runway type: | |
| permanent surface fields | 7 |
| unpaved fields and usable airstrips | 23 |
| airfields by runway length: | |
| 2440--3659 meters | 11 |
| 1220--2439 | 11 |
| under 1220 | 8 |

international airport: Aden (Khormaksar)
major domestic airfields: Ataq, Bayhan al-Qasab,
al-Ghaydah, Lawdar, al Mukalla/al-Riyan, Mukayris,
al Qatn, Qishin, Seiyun/Tarim
Airlines:
companies: Alyemda--Democratic Yemen Airlines
(international and domestic)

aircraft:
| | |
|---|---|
| An-26 | 1 |
| Boeing 737-200C | 2 |
| Boeing 707-320C | 2 |
| DHC Dash 7 | 2 |
| Tupolev Tu-154 | 1 |

Maritime Facilities:
harbors--Aden, al-Mukalla, Nishtun (unconfirmed)
oil terminal--Aden
Merchant Marine:

| vessel type | number | DWT |
|---|---|---|
| general cargo | 1 | 1,723 |
| tanker | 1 | 3,184 |
| TOTAL | 2 | 4,907 |

# SOUTH YEMEN

```
ARMED FORCES
   Personnel:
      military forces--
                                    reserves        regular
         army                          ?             24,000
         air force                                    2,500
         navy                                         1,000
         TOTAL                          ?            27,500
      para-military forces--
         popular militia           (unconfirmed)     15,000
   Army:
      major units:   (not all fully operational nor fully
                      organized)
         unit type                                   brigades
            armored                                      1
            mechanized                                   3
            infantry (mostly skeleton
               or undermanned)                          8
            TOTAL                                       12
      small arms:
         personal weapons--
            7.62mm AK-47 (Kalashnikov) AR
            7.62mm SKS (Simonov) SAR
         machine guns--
            12.7mm D.Sh.K. 38/46 (Degtyarev) HMG
            7.62mm PK/PKS (Kalashnikov) LMG
            7.62mm RPD (Degtyarev) LMG
            7.62mm SG-43 (Goryunov) MMG
         light and medium mortars--
            82mm M-43
         light ATRLs--
            RPG-7
      tanks:
         model                                        number
            medium quality
               T-62
               T-55
            low quality
               T-54
            TOTAL                                      470
   APCs/ARVs:
      model                                           number
         high quality
            BMP-1
         others
            BTR-40/50/60
            BTR-152
            Ferret (possibly phased out)
            Saladin (possibly phased out)
```

```
    TOTAL                                          450
artillery:
    towed guns and howitzers--
        130mm M-46 gun
        122mm D-30 howitzer
        122mm M-1938 howitzer
        100mm M-1955 field/AT gun
        85mm M-1945/D-44 field/AT gun
    mortars, over 160mm--
        160mm mortar
    mortars, less than 160mm, but excluding light and
        medium--
        120mm mortar
    TOTAL                                          350
    MRLs--
        122mm BM-21
anti-tank weapons:
  missiles--
        AT-3 (Sagger)
  guns--
        85mm M-1945/D-44 field/AT gun  (see artillery)
        107mm B-11 recoilless rifle (unconfirmed)
    TOTAL                                          220
surface-to-surface missiles and rockets:
    model                                      launchers
        FROG-7                                        12
        SS-1 (Scud B)                                  6
    TOTAL                                             18
army anti-aircraft defenses:
  missiles--
        SA-6 (Gainful)
        SA-7 (Grail)
        SA-9 (Gaskin, unconfirmed) SP
    short-range guns--
        57mm ZSU 57x2 SP
        57mm
        37mm
        23mm ZSU 23x4 SP (Gun Dish)
        23mm ZU 23x2
Air Force:
  aircraft--general:                             number
    combat aircraft                                 130
    transport aircraft                               18
    helicopters                                      69
  combat aircraft:                               number
    interceptors--
      medium quality
        MiG-21 (Fishbed)                             45
    strike and multi-role aircraft--
      medium quality
```

## SOUTH YEMEN

```
    MiG-23/27 (Flogger B/D)                              25
    Su-20/22 (Fitter C)                                  40
                                      (sub-total         65)
  others
    MiG-17 (Fresco)                                      10
    MiG-15 UTI                                            5
                                      (sub-total         15)
    Total                                                80
  bombers--
    IL-28 (Beagle)                                        5
transport aircraft:
  An-24/26 (Coke/Curl)                                   10
  DC-3 Dakota (C-47)                                      4
  IL-14 (Crate)                                           4
  TOTAL                                                  18
training and liaison aircraft:
  L-39 Albatross (unconfirmed)                        a few
helicopters:
  attack--
    Mi-24 (Hind)                                         20
  medium transport--
    Mi-4 (Hound)                                          4
    Mi-8/Mi-17 (Hip)                                     45
                                      (sub-total         49)
  TOTAL                                                  69
advanced armament:
  air-to-air missiles--
    AA-2 (Atoll)
anti-aircraft defenses:
  long-range missiles--
    model                                         batteries
      SA-2 (Guideline)                                    6
      SA-3 (Goa)                                          3
      TOTAL                                               9
military airfields:                                     14+
  Aden (Khormaksar), al-Anad, al-Ansab (Nisab), Ataq,
  Bayhan al-Qasab, al-Dali, Ghor Ubayd, Ir-Fadhl, Lawdar,
  al-Mukalla, Mukayris, Perim Island, Socotra, Zamakh
Navy:
  combat vessels:                                    number
    MFPBs--
      Ossa II                                            6
    ASW vessels--
      SO-1 class 2
    gunboats/MTBs--
      P-6 MTB                                            2
    patrol craft--
      Fairey Marine Spear                                3
      Fairey Marine Interceptor                          1
      Fairey Marine Tracker 2                            1
```

| | |
|---|---|
| Zhuk class | 2 |
| Total | 7 |
| landing craft: | |
| Ropucha class LST | 1 |
| Polnochny class LCT | 2 |
| T-4 LCM | 3 |
| TOTAL | 6 |
| advanced armament: | |
| SS-N-2 Styx SSM | |
| coastal defense: | |
| land-based SS-N-2C Styx | |
| naval bases: | 4 |
| Aden, al-Mukalla, Perim Island, Socotra | |
| ship maintenance and repair capability: | |

National Dockyards, Aden (4,500-ton floating dock and 1,500-ton slipway)

# 17. SUDAN

Official Name of State: The Republic of Sudan
Head of State: President (Chairman of Sovereignty Council)
Ahmad Ali al-Mirghani (deposed June 30, 1989)
Prime Minister: Sadiq al-Mahdi (deposed June 30, 1989)
Minister of Defense: Major-General Mubarak Uthman Rahmah
(deposed June 30, 1989)
Commander in Chief of the Armed Forces: General Fathi Ahmad
Ali (deposed June 30, 1989)
Head of the Revolutionary Command Committee: Brigadier
General Omar Hassan al-Bashir (since June 30, 1989)
Chief of the General Staff: Lieutenant General Mahdi Abu
Nimr
Commander of the Air Force: Major General Ahmad Arabi
Area: 2,504,530 sq. km.

| Population: | | 23,130,000 |
|---|---|---|
| ethnic subdivision: | | |
| Arabs | 9,715,000 | 42.0% |
| Nilotics, Negroes and others | 13,410,000 | 58.0% |
| religious subdivision: | | |
| Sunni Muslims | 16,191,000 | 70.0% |
| Animists | 4,626,000 | 20.0% |
| Christians (Coptic, Greek Orthodox, Catholic, Protestant) | 1,157,000 | 5.0% |
| Not known | 1,157,000 | 5.0% |
| Refugees: | 1,200,000 | |
| Ethiopians | 800,000 | |
| Chadians | 150,000 | |
| Ugandans | 250,000 | |

GDP:
1983--$7.68 billion
Balance of Payments (goods, services & unilateral transfer
payments):

| year | income | expenditure | balance |
|---|---|---|---|
| 1986 | $ 889 mil. | $ 910 mil. | -$ 21 mil. |
| 1987 | $ 785 mil. | $1.03 bil. | -$245 mil. |

Defense Expenditure:
1987--$420 million (unconfirmed)
1989--$235 million
Foreign Military Aid Received:
financial aid from:
Egypt--$42 million grant (given in arms); Kuwait;
Libya--grant, oil shipments; PRC--$30 million loan
(possibly civilian); Saudi Arabia--grant
military training:
foreign advisors/instructors from--Egypt, Britain, USA
(including aircraft maintenance personnel)

## SUDAN

trainees abroad in--Egypt, Jordan, Saudi Arabia, USA,
FRG
arms transfers from:
Brazil (transport aircraft); Canada (transport
aircraft); Egypt (ATGMs, APCs); France (artillery
pieces); Iraq (artillery pieces, MRLs, ammunition,
small arms); Jordan (obsolete weapons); Libya (small
arms, aircraft spares, trucks; combat aircraft,
unconfirmed); PRC (combat aircraft, tanks); Romania
(helicopters); USA (tanks, SP AAGs) ; Spain/FRG
(helicopters)
support forces from:
Egypt (engineering units); Libya (two or more aircraft
flying close air support missions; troops in Western
Sudan)
construction aid from:
USA
maintenance of equipment in:
USA (aircraft); Jordan (civil aircraft)
Foreign Military Aid Extended:
military training:
advisors/instructors in--
UAE
foreign trainees from--
Eritrean rebels; Kuwait, Jordan, Qatar, UAE; Egypt
(unconfirmed, part of an exchange program)
arms transfers to:
Eritrean rebels
facilities provided to:
Eritrean rebels (camps, unconfirmed); Palestinian
organizations (al-Fatah forces evacuated from Lebanon,
camps)
Joint Maneuvers with:
Egypt

INFRASTRUCTURE
Road Network:
| | |
|---|---:|
| length: | 47,000 km |
| paved roads | 2,000 km |
| gravel and crushed stone roads | 4,000 km |
| earth tracks | 41,000 km |

main routes:
Khartoum--Shendi--Atbara--Suakin--Port Sudan
Atbara--Wadi Halfa (Egyptian border)
Atbara--Merowe--Wadi Halfa
Khartoum--Kassala--Asmara (Ethiopia)
Khartoum--Wad Medani--Gedaref--Gondar
(Ethiopia)
Kosti--Malakal--Juba--Kampala (Uganda)/Juba--Niangara
(Zaire)

```
        Khartoum--al-Dueim--Rabak/Kosti
        Kosti--Gedaref--Kassala--Port Sudan
        Kosti--al-Obeid--al-Fasher--al-Geneina--Abeche (Chad)
        Port Sudan--Hurghada (Egypt)
```

Railway Network:
  length:                                           5,516 km
    narrow gauge (1.067 meter)                      4,800 km
    1.6096 meter gauge (plantation line)              716 km
  main routes:
    Khartoum--Wadi Halfa
    Khartoum--Atbara--Port Sudan
    Khartoum--Sennar--Kosti--El Obeid
    Khartoum--Wad Medani--Sennar--Damazin/Sennar--
      Kosti--Babanusa
    Babanusa--Nyala
    Babanusa--Wau
Airfields:                                               78
  airfields by runway type:
    permanent surface fields                              8
    unpaved fields and usable airstrips                  70
  airfields by runway length:
    2440--3659 meters                                     4
    1220--2439                                           31
    under 1220                                           43
  international airport: Khartoum
  major domestic airfields: Atbara, Dongola, El Fasher,  El
    Geneina, Juba, Kassala, Malakal, Merowe, Myala,  El
    Obeida, Port Sudan, Wadi Halfa, Wau
Airlines:
  companies:  Sudan  Airways  (international,  charter,
    domestic), Trans Arabian Air  Transport  (cargo).  Nile
    Safaris Cargo (cargo charter)
  aircraft:
    Boeing 737-200C/737-200                               2
    Boeing 707-320C                                       8
    DC-8                                                  1
    Fokker F-27-200/600                                   3
    on order: 4  Fokker  F-50
Maritime Facilities:
  harbor--Port Sudan, Suakin
Merchant Marine:
```

| vessel type | number | DWT |
| --- | --- | --- |
| general cargo | 4 | 38,694 |
| multi-purpose | 2 | 25,810 |
| general cargo/container | 5 | 60,555 |
| TOTAL | 11 | 125,059 |

```
ARMED FORCES
  Personnel:
    military forces--
```
```

# SUDAN

```
    army                                          50,000
    air force (including air defense)              5,500
    navy                                             700
    TOTAL                                         56,200
  para-military forces--
    popular defense units                          3,500
    border guards                                  2,500
    Sudan People's Liberation Army
      (SPLA), anti-government
      rebels in control of parts
      of Southern Sudan    (estimate)             30,000
Army:
  major units:
    unit type              division HQ        brigades
      armored                    1                2
      infantry                   4               10
      airborne                                    1
      republican guard                            1
      TOTAL (partly skeleton
        or undermanned)          5               14
  small arms:
    personal weapons--
    9mm Sterling SMG
    7.62mm AK-47 (Kalashnikov) AR
    7.62mm G-3 (Heckler & Koch) AR
    7.62mm SKS (Simonov) SAR
    machine guns--
    12.7mm D.Sh.K. 38/46 (Degtyarev) HMG
    7.62mm RPD (Degtyarev) LMG
    7.62mm SGM (Goryunov) MMG
    light and medium mortars--
    82mm M-43
    light ATRLs--
    RPG-7
  tanks:
    model                                       number
      high quality
        M-60 A3                                     20
      medium quality
        T-55/Type 59                                90
      low quality
        T-54                                        70
        M-47                                        15
        M-41                                        55
        Type 62                                     70
                               (sub-total         210)
      TOTAL                                        320
  APCs/ARVs:
    model                                       number
      high quality
```

273

```
M-113                                                    80
V-150 Commando                                           54
AMX-VCI                                               a few
                              (sub-total             134+)
others
  al-Walid                                             20+
  AML-90                                                 6
  BTR-50
  BTR-152                                              200
  Ferret                                                60
  M-3 (Panhard, unconfirmed)
  OT-64
  OT-62
  Saladin                                               50
                              (sub-total              616)
     TOTAL                                            750+
  on order: M-113;  100  Egyptian  APCs  (al-Walid);  9
  V-150 Commando
artillery:
  self propelled guns and howitzers--
  155mm Mk. F-3 (AMX) SP howitzer                       11
  towed guns and howitzers--
  155mm M-114                                           12
  122mm M-1938 howitzer
  105mm M-101 howitzer
  100mm M-1955 field/AT gun
  25 lb. (87mm) howitzer
  85mm M-1945/D-44 field/AT gun
  mortars, under 160mm, but excluding light and
    medium--
    120mm mortar
    TOTAL                                              250
  MRLs--
    122mm Saqr
anti-tank weapons:
  missiles--
    BGM-71C Improved TOW (unconfirmed)
    Swingfire
    AT-3 (Sagger)
army anti-aircraft defenses:
  missiles--
    SA-7 (Grail)
    MIM-43A Redeye
  short-range guns--                                number
    40mm Bofors L-60                                    80
    37mm M-1939                                         80
    20mm M-163 A-1 Vulcan SP                             8
    20mm M-167 Vulcan (number unconfirmed)             32
    TOTAL                                              200
Air Force:
```

## SUDAN

```
aircraft--general:                                number
  combat aircraft                                      59
  transport aircraft                                   30
  helicopters                                          67
combat aircraft:
  interceptors--
    medium and low quality
      F-6 Shenyang                                     23
      MiG-21 (Fishbed)                                  8
      Total                                            31
  strike and multi-role aircraft--
    medium and low quality
      F-5E/F                                            5
      MiG-23 (Flogger)                                  3
      MiG-17 (Fresco)/Shenyang F-5                     20
      Total                                            28
transport aircraft:
  An-24 (Coke)                                          5
  C-130H Hercules (some being
    overhauled in USA)                                  5
  CASA C-212 (some employed in maritime
    surveillance role)                                  6
  DHC-5D Buffalo                                        3
  DHC-6 Twin Otter                                      1
  EMB-110 P-2                                           6
  Fokker F-27                                           4
  TOTAL                                                30
  on order: 2 C-212
training and liaison aircraft:
  BAC-145 Jet Provost                                   5
  BAC-167 Strikemaster                                  3
  TOTAL                                                 8
helicopters:                                      number
  medium transport--
    Mi-4 (Hound)                                        3
    Mi-8 (Hip)                                         14
    SA-330 Puma/IAR-330 Puma                           24
    Bell 212/AB-212                                     4
                               (sub-total            45)
  light transport--
    MBB BO-105 (possibly serving police)              22
  TOTAL                                                67
advanced armament:
  air-to-air missiles--
    AIM-9 Sidewinder
    AA-2 (Atoll)
anti-aircraft defenses:
  long range missiles--
    model                                       batteries
      SA-2 (Guideline)                                  5
```

## SUDAN

military airfields:                                                13

    Atbara, Dongola, El Fasher, El Geneina, Juba, Khartoum, Malakal, Merowe, El Obeid, Port Sudan, Wad Medani, Wadi Sayidina (under construction), Wau

Navy:

  combat vessels:                                    number

    patrol craft--

      PBR (Yugoslav) 115 ft. (35 meter)          3

      Abeking and Rasmussen 75.2 ft.

        (22.9 meter)                             3

      Sewart class                               4

      Total                                     10

on order: six 11 meter patrol boats from Spain (unconfirmed)

landing craft:

  DTM-221 LCT                                  2

naval base:

  Port Sudan

# 18. SYRIA

BASIC DATA
Official Name of State: The Arab Republic of Syria
Head of State: President Hafez al-Assad
Prime Minister: Mahmoud al-Zu'ebi
Defense Minister: Lieutenant General Mustafa al-Tlass
Chief of the General Staff: General Hikmat Shihabi
Commander of the Air Force: Major-General Ali Malkhafji
Commander of the Navy: Rear Admiral Mustafa Tayara
Area: 185,680 sq. km.
Population: 10,970,000

| | | |
|---|---|---|
| ethnic subdivision: | | |
| Arabs | 9,654,000 | 88.0% |
| Kurds | 878,000 | 8.0% |
| Armenians and others | 438,000 | 4.0% |
| religious subdivision: | | |
| Sunni Muslims | 7,514,000 | 68.5% |
| Alawis | 1,426,000 | 13.0% |
| Shi'ite Muslims | 165,000 | 1.5% |
| Druze | 329,000 | 3.0% |
| Christians (Greek Orthodox, Gregorian, Armenian Catholics, Syrian Orthodox, Greek Catholics) | 1,426,000 | 13.0% |
| Others | 110,000 | 1.0% |

GDP (figures unreliable; calculated according to the official rate of exhange of 3.925 Syrian pounds per US dollar):
1985--$21.20 billion
1986--$25.06 billion
Balance of Payments (goods, services & unilateral transfer payments):

| year | income | expenditure | balance |
|---|---|---|---|
| 1985 | $3.68 bil. | $4.54 bil. | -$860 mil. |
| 1986 | $2.62 bil. | $3.15 bil. | -$530 mil. |

Defense Expenditure:
1986--$3.47 billion
1987--$3.35 billion
Foreign Military Aid Received:
financial aid from:
joint Arab fund--about $1 billion grant of which $500 million from Saudi Arabia; Iran--grant, oil shipments (until August 1988; later--unconfirmed); Libya--loan
military training:
foreign advisors/instructors from--USSR (2000), Bulgaria, Cuba, Hungary, GDR, North Korea
trainees abroad in--USSR, other Soviet bloc countries, France, Libya
arms transfers from:

Austria (trucks); France (ATGMs, helicopters, survey
vessels); USSR (SP artillery, combat aircraft, coastal
defense SSMs, naval vessels, SAMs, SSMs, tanks,
submarines)
Foreign Military Aid Extended:
financial aid to:
Palestinian organizations (al-Fatah rebels, al-Sa'iqa,
PPSF, PLF and PFLP-GC)--grants
military training:
advisors/instructors/serving personnel in--Iran, Libya
(pilots), Palestinian units (al-Sa'iqa), Saudi
Arabia, al-Amal militia in Lebanon
foreign trainees from--Palestinian organizations,
Libya, ASALA, Amal Lebanese militia, Lebanon (Shi'ite
Army officers)
arms transfers to:
Palestinian military forces (tanks, artillery pieces,
small arms); Iran (SAMs, ATGMs, ammunition); ASALA
(small arms); al-Amal militia in Lebanon (various
items)
facilities provided to:
USSR (use of Latakia and Tartus harbor, T-4 airfield);
al-Fatah rebels, PPSF, PFLP-GC, PFLP, DFLP, al-Sa'iqa
and PLF (camps)
forces deployed abroad in:
Lebanon--30,000, in Beqa, northern Lebanon (Tripoli
area), and Beirut

INFRASTRUCTURE
Road Network:
| | |
|---|---|
| length: | 27,000 km |
| paved roads | 21,000 km |
| gravel and crushed stone roads | 3,000 km |
| improved earth tracks | 3,000 km |

main routes:
Damascus--Homs--Hama--Aleppo
Tartus--Banias--Latakia
Latakia--Aleppo--Dir e-Zor--Qusaybah (Iraq)
Tartus--Homs--Palmyra--Qusaybah
Banias--Hama
Damascus--Beirut (Lebanon)
Damascus--Palmyra--Dir e-Zor--al-Hasakah-- al-Qamishli
Damascus--al-Rutbah (Iraq)
Damascus--Dar'a--Ramtha (Jordan)
Damascus--Kuneitra--Rosh Pina (Israel)
Tartus--Tripoli (Lebanon)
Railway Network:
| | |
|---|---|
| length: | 1,997 km |
| standard gauge | 1,686 km |
| narrow gauge | 311 km |

main routes:
    Aleppo--Adana (Turkey)
    Aleppo--Latakia
    Aleppo--Hama--Homs--Tripoli    (Lebanon)/Homs--Zahlah
    (Lebanon)/Homs--Damascus
    Aleppo--al-Qamishli--Mosul (Iraq)
    Aleppo--Dir e-Zor--al-Qamishli
    Damascus--Dar'a--Ramtha (Jordan)
    Damascus--Beirut (Lebanon)
    Latakia--Tartus
    Latakia--Aleppo
    Tartus--Homs
    Dir e-Zor--Abu Kemal

Airfields:     94
  airfields by runway type:
    permanent surface fields   24
    unpaved fields and usable airstrips   70
  airfields by runway length:
    2440--3659 meters   21
    1220--2439   4
    under 1220   69
  international airports: Aleppo, Damascus, Latakia
  major domestic airfields: Dir e-Zor, Palmyra, al-Qamishli, al-Hasakah

Airlines:
  companies: Syrian Arab Airlines (international and domestic)
  aircraft:
    An-24   1
    An-26   5
    Boeing 747 SP   2
    Boeing 727-200   3
    Caravelle 10B (Super Caravelle)   2
    Ilyushin IL-76   4
    Mystere Falcon 20F   3
    Tupolev Tu-134   7
    Tupolev Tu-154   3
    Yakovlev Yak-40   6

Maritime Facilities:
  harbors--Latakia, Tartus
  anchorages--Arwad, Jablah, Banias
  oil terminals--Banias, Latakia, Tartus

Merchant Marine:

| vessel type | number | DWT |
|---|---|---|
| general cargo | 11 | 51,290 |

Defense Production:
  army equipment:
    ammunition; toxic gases; chemical warheads for SSMs (unconfirmed); upgrading of tanks

**SYRIA**

```
ARMED FORCES
  Personnel:
    military forces--
                           regular      reserves         total
        army              306,000       300,000        606,000
                                       (unconfirmed)
        air force
          & air defense    80,000        37,500        117,500
        navy                4,000         2,500          6,500
        TOTAL             390,000       340,000        730,000
    para-military forces--
      Workers' Militia                                 400,000
  Army:
    major units:
      unit type          army         divisions      independent
                         corps                        brigades/
                         HQ                           groups

        all arms            2
        armored                           6               1
        mechanized                        3
        infantry/
          special forces                  1
        airborne/
          special forces                                  7
        TOTAL               2            10               8
      note: 2 new divisions being organized
    small arms:
      personal weapons--
        9mm Model 23/25 SMG
        7.62mm AK-47 (Kalashnikov) AR
        7.62mm AKM AR
        7.62mm SKS (Simonov) SAR
        5.45mm AK-74 (Kalashnikov, unconfirmed) AR
      machine guns--
        12.7mm D.Sh.K. 38/46 (Degtyarev) HMG
        7.62mm PK/PKS (Kalashnikov) LMG
        7.62mm RPD (Degtyarev) LMG
        7.62mm SG-43 (Goryunov) MMG
        7.62mm SGM (Goryunov) MMG
      light and medium mortars--
        82mm M-43
      light ATRLs--
        RPG-7
    tanks:
      model                                            number
        high quality
          T-72/Improved T-72                             1000
        medium quality
          T-62                                           1000
```

```
        T-55                                                    2100
                                        (sub-total       3100)
        TOTAL                                                   4100
        on order: Improved T-72
APCs/ARVs:
  model
    high quality
      BMP-1                                                     1800
    others
      BTR-152
      BTR-40/50/60
      BRDM-2
                                        (sub-total       2000)
        TOTAL                                                   3800
artillery:
    self propelled guns and howitzers--
      152mm M-1973 SP howitzer
      122mm M-1974 SP howitzer
      122mm ISU SP howitzer
    towed guns and howitzers--
      180mm S-23 gun
      152mm M-1943 howitzer
      130mm M-46 gun
      122mm D-30 howitzer
      122mm M-1938 howitzer
    mortars, over 160mm--
      240mm mortar
      160mm mortar
    mortars, under 160mm, but excluding light and
      medium--
      120mm mortar
      TOTAL                                                     2300
  MRLs--
      240mm BM-24
      140mm BM-14-16
      122mm BM-21
engineering equipment:
  MTU-55 bridging tanks
  MT-55 bridging tanks
  tank-towed bridges
  mine-clearing rollers
AFV transporters:                                               800
anti-tank weapons:
  missiles--                                          launchers
      AT-3 (Sagger)
      AT-4 (Spigot)
      BRDM-2 carrying AT-3 (Sagger) SP
      MILAN
      TOTAL                                                     2000
  guns--
```

SYRIA

```
      73mm SPG-9 recoilless gun
surface-to-surface missiles and rockets:
   model                                    launchers
      FROG-7                                      24
      SS-1 (Scud B)                               18
      SS-21 (Scarab)                              18
      TOTAL                                       60
      on order: additional SSMs, including M-9 from PRC
army anti-aircraft defenses:
   missiles--
      SA-6  (Gainful) SP
      SA-7  (Grail)
      SA-8  (Gecko) SP
      SA-9  (Gaskin) SP
      SA-13 (Gopher) SP
      SA-14 (Gremlin)
      SA-16
   short range guns--                            number
      57mm ZSU 57x2 SP
      57mm M-1950 (S-60)
      37mm M-1939
      23mm ZSU 23x4 SP (Gun Dish)
      23mm ZU 23x2
      TOTAL                                     1000
CW capabilities:
   personal protective equipment, Soviet type
   unit decontamination equipment
   stockpiles of nerve gas, including Sarin
   chemical warheads for SSMs
biological warfare capabilities:
   biological weapons and toxins (unconfirmed)
Air Force:
   aircraft--general:                           number
      combat aircraft                              650
      transport aircraft                            32
      helicopters                                  290
   combat aircraft:
      interceptors--
         high quality
            MiG-25 and MiG-25R (Foxbat)            45
            MiG-29 (Fulcrum, multi-role,
               employed as interceptor)            20
                                   (sub-total      65)
         others
            MiG-21 MF/S/bis/U (Fishbed)           280
            Total                                 345
      strike and multi-role aircraft--
         medium quality
            MiG-23 S/U/G (Flogger)
            MiG-27 (unconfirmed)
```

282

```
    Su-20/22 (Fitter C)
                                    (sub-total        215)
        others
        MiG-17 (Fresco)
        Su-7B (Fitter A)
                                    (sub-total         90)
      Total                                           305
      on  order:   additional   MiG-29   (Fulcrum);   Su-24
        (Fencer)
transport aircraft:                                number
    An-24/26 (Coke/Curl)
    IL-14 (Crate)
    IL-18 (Coot)
    IL-76 (unconfirmed)
    Mystere Falcon 20
    Yak-40 (Codling)
    TOTAL                                            32
training and liaison aircraft:
    L-29 Delfin                                      60
    L-39 Albatross                                  100
    MBB 223 Flamingo                                 48
    Piper Navajo                                      2
    Yak-11 (Moose)
    Yak-18 (Max)
    TOTAL                                           210+
helicopters:
    attack--
      Mi-24/Mi-25 (Hind)                             60
      SA-342 Gazelle                                 55
                                    (sub-total       115)
    medium transport--
      Mi-8 (Hip)/Mi-17 (Hip H)                      130
      Mi-4 (Hound)                                   10
      Mi-2 (Hoplite)                                 10
                                    (sub-total       150)
    ASW--
      Kamov Ka-25 (Hormone)                           5
      Mi-14 (Haze)                                   20
                                    (sub-total        25)
    TOTAL                                           290
    on order: SA-342 Gazelle
miscellaneous aircraft:
    Tu-126  (Moss)  AEW,  operated  with  Soviet  aid
      (unconfirmed)
    Soviet-made RPVs
advanced armament:
    air-to-air missiles--
      AA-2 (Atoll)
      AA-6 (Acrid)
      AA-7 (Apex)
```

```
    AA-8 (Aphid)
  air-to-ground missiles--
    AS-12
    HOT
anti-aircraft defenses:
  radars--
    Long Track
    Spoon Rest (P-12)
    Square Pair
  long-range missiles--
    model                                    batteries
      SA-2 (Guideline) & SA-3 (Goa)              65
      SA-5 (Gammon)                               3
      TOTAL                                      68
  aircraft shelters--
    in all airfields, for combat aircraft only
military airfields:                               21
  Aleppo, Blay, Damascus (international), Damascus
  (Meze), Dir e-Zor, Dumayr, al-Suweida, Hama, Khalkhala,
  Latakia, Nassiriyah, Palmyra, Sayqal, T-4,    7
  additional
aircraft maintenance and repair capability:
  for all models in service
Navy:
  combat vessels:                               number
    submarines
      R class (Romeo)                             3
    MFPBs--
      Komar                                       5
      Ossa I                                      6
      Ossa II                                    10
      Total                                      21
    ASW vessels--
      Petya II submarine chaser frigate           2
    mine warfare vessels--
      T-43 class minesweeper                      1
      Vanya class minesweeper                     2
      Yevgenia class minesweeper                  4
      Total                                       7
    patrol craft--
      Zhuk class                                  6
      Natya (formerly a minesweeper)              1
      Total                                       7
  landing craft:
    Polnochny B class LCT                         3
  auxiliary vessels:
    training ship (al-Assad)                      1
    Poluchat torpedo recovery vessel              1
  advanced armament:
    SS-N-2 Styx SSM
```

coastal defense:
  SSC-1B Sepal coastal defense missile
  SSC-3 coastal defense missile
naval bases:                                          3
  Latakia, Minat al-Baida, Tartus
ship maintenance and repair capability:
  minor repairs at Latakia
note: ASW helicopters listed under Air Force

# 19. TUNISIA

BASIC DATA
  Official Name of State: The Republic of Tunisia
  Head of State: President General Zine al-Abedine Ben Ali
    (also Defense Minister)
  Prime Minister: Hedi Backoush
  Secretary-General for National Defense (with the rank of
    Minister): Abdullah Kallil
  Commander of the Armed Forces: General Muhammad Sa'id
    al-Katib
  Commander of the Ground Forces: Lieutenant General Yousuf
    Barakat
  Commander of the Air Force: Major General Riva Atar
  Commander of the Navy: Vice Admiral Habib Fadhila
  Area: 164,206 sq. km.
  Population:                                         7,260,000
    ethnic subdivision:
      Arabs/Berbers                  7,115,000            98.0%
      Europeans                         58,000             0.8%
      Others                            87,000             1.2%
    religious subdivision:
      Sunni Muslims                  7,115,000            98.0%
      Christians                        73,000             1.0%
      Others, including Jews            72,000             1.0%
  GDP:
    1986--$8.85 billion
    1987--$9.67 billion
  Balance of Payments (goods, services & unilateral transfer
    payments):
    year    income          expenditure          balance
    1986    $3.15 bil.      $3.77 bil.           -$620 mil.
    1987    $3.89 bil.      $3.95 bil.           -$ 60 mil.
  Defense Expenditure:
    1986--$417 million
    1987--$520 million (unconfirmed)
  Foreign Military Aid Received:
    financial aid from:
      Saudi Arabia--grant; USA--$27 million grant and loan
    military training:
      foreign advisors/instructors from--USA; France
        (unconfirmed)
      trainees abroad in--Algeria, Egypt, France, Saudi
        Arabia, USA
    arms transfers from:
      Austria (light tanks, small arms); Belgium (small
      arms); Brazil (APCs, ARVs); Britain (artillery pieces,
      patrol craft, target drones); France (helicopters);
      Italy (trainer aircraft, APCs); USA (artillery pieces,
      SAMs, tanks, transport aircraft)

# TUNISIA

Foreign Military Aid Extended:
  military training:
    foreign trainees from--Algeria (part of an exchange
      program)
  arms transfers to:
    Palestinian organizations (unconfirmed)
  facilities provided to:
    France (radar station); PLO/Fatah (camps)
Joint Maneuvers with:
  France, USA; Spain (unconfirmed)

INFRASTRUCTURE
  Road Network:
    length:                                              17,700 km
      paved roads                                         9,100 km
      gravel roads and improved earth tracks              8,600 km
    main routes:
      Tunis--Bizerta
      Tunis--Annaba (Algeria)
      Tunis--Kairouan--Gafsa--Tozeur--Touggourt (Algeria)
      Tunis--Sousse--Sfax--Gabes--Tripoli (Libya)
      Sousse--Kasserine
      Gabés--Gafsa
  Railway Network:
    length:                                               2,051 km
      standard gauge                                        465 km
      narrow gauge (1.0 meter)                            1,586 km
    main routes:
      Tunis--Bizerta
      Tunis--Annaba (Algeria)
      Tunis--Kasserine--Gafsa--Tozeur
      Tunis--Sousse--Sfax--Gabes
      Sfax--Gafsa--Tozeur
  Airfields:                                                   29
    airfields by runway type:
      permanent surface fields                              13
      unpaved fields and usable airstrips                   16
    airfields by runway length:
      2440--3659 meters                                      6
      1220--2439                                             8
      under 1220                                            15
    international airports: Jerba, Monastir, Sfax, Tabarka,
      Tozeur, Tunis (Carthage)
    domestic airfields: Gafsa
  Airlines:
    companies: Tunis Air (international and domestic),
      Tunisavia (domestic)
    aircraft:
      Airbus A-300 B4-200                                    1
      Boeing 737-200C/737-200                                4

| | |
|---|---:|
| Boeing 727-200/727-100 | 8 |
| DHC-6 Twin Otter | 2 |
| Mystere-Falcon 20C | 1 |
| Piper Cheyenne II | 1 |

on order: 1 Airbus A-300 B4-200, 3 A-320, 2 Boeing 737-500

helicopters:

| | |
|---|---:|
| SA-316B Alouette III | 1 |
| SA-330 Puma | 1 |
| SA-365N/365C Dauphin 2 | 2 |

Maritime Facilities:

harbors--Bizerta, Gabes, La Goulette (Tunis), Sousse, Sfax, Zarzis (under construction)

oil terminals--Ashtart, Bizerta (Menzel Bourguiba), Gabes, La Goulette (Tunis), Sekhira

Merchant Marine:

| vessel type | number | DWT |
|---|---:|---:|
| general cargo | 6 | 42,011 |
| passenger ferry | 1 | 3,372 |
| chemical tanker | 6 | 58,267 |
| crude carrier | 1 | 37,224 |
| small tanker | 1 | 9,976 |
| bulk carrier | 3 | 58,581 |
| gas tanker (LPG) | 1 | 9,996 |
| ro/ro cargo | 2 | 5,296 |
| TOTAL | 21 | 224,723 |

Defense Production:

Army equipment:

production under license--
diesel engines (with Italy and Algeria)

ARMED FORCES

Personnel:

military forces--

| | |
|---|---:|
| army | 30,000 |
| air force | 2,500 |
| navy | 4,500 |
| TOTAL | 37,000 |

para-military forces--

| | |
|---|---:|
| gendarmerie | 2,000 |
| national guard | 5,000 |

Army:

major units:

| unit type | regiments/brigades |
|---|---:|
| armored reconnaissance | 1 |
| infantry/mechanized | 2 |
| commando/paratroops | 1 |
| Sahara Brigade | 1 |
| TOTAL | 5 |

small arms:

# TUNISIA

```
personal weapons--
  9mm Model 38/49 Beretta SMG
  9mm Sterling SMG
  7.62mm FAC (FN) SAR
  5.56mm AUG Steyr AR
machine guns--
  7.62mm (0.3") Browning M-1919 MMG
  7.62mm MAG(FN)LMG
light and medium mortars--
  82mm
  81mm
  60mm
light ATRLs--
  89mm Strim-89
```

tanks:

| model | | number |
|---|---|---|
| high quality | | |
| M-60 A3 | | 54 |
| medium quality | | |
| M-48 A3 | | 15 |
| SK-105 (Kurassier) | | 54 |
| | (sub-total | 69) |
| low quality | | |
| AMX-13 | | 50 |
| M-41 | | 15 |
| | (sub-total | 65) |
| TOTAL | | 188 |

APCs/ARVs:

| model | | number |
|---|---|---|
| high quality | | |
| Engesa EE-11/EE-9 | | 20 |
| Fiat Type 6614 | | 110 |
| M-113 A1/A2/M-125/M-577 | | 100 |
| V-150 Commando | | a few |
| Steyr 4K 7FA (unconfirmed) | | a few |
| | (sub-total | 230+) |
| others | | |
| AML-60/AML-90 | | 25 |
| EBR-75 | | 15 |
| Saladin | | 20 |
| | (sub-total | 60) |
| TOTAL | | 290+ |

```
on order: Fahd
```

artillery:

| | number |
|---|---|
| self propelled guns and howitzers-- | |
| 155mm M-109 SP howitzer | 18 |
| towed guns and howitzers-- | |
| 155mm M-114 howitzer (unconfirmed) | 18 |
| 105mm M-108 SP howitzer | 10 |
| 105mm M-101 howitzer | 50 |

```
      25 lb. (87mm) howitzer
      TOTAL                                            96+
      on order: 57 155mm M-198 howitzers
   AFV transporters:
     on order: US-made AFV transporters
   anti-tank weapons:
     missiles--                                   launchers
       BGM-71A TOW                                    100
       M-901 ITV SP (TOW under armor)                  35
       MILAN
   army anti-aircraft defenses:
     missiles--
       MIM-72A Chaparral
       RBS-70
       SA-7 (Grail)
     short-range guns--                             number
       40mm
       37mm
       on order: 26 20mm M-163 Vulcan SP AAG; Egyptian AD
       (unconfirmed)
Air Force:
   aircraft--general:                               number
     combat aircraft                                  11
     transport aircraft                                8
     helicopters                                      37
   combat aircraft:
     strike and multi-role aircraft--
     medium and low quality
       F-5E/F-5F                                      11
     on order: 4-12 additional F-5E/F-5F
   transport aircraft:
     C-130H Hercules                                   4
     other                                             4
     TOTAL                                             8
   training and liaison aircraft:
     Aermacchi MB-326 B/KT/LT                         18
     Rockwell T-6                                     12
     SIAI-Marchetti SF-260WT/C                        17
     SIAI-Marchetti S-208                              2
     TOTAL                                            49
     on  order:  EMB-312   (unconfirmed),    Alpha   Jet
     (unconfirmed)
   helicopters:
     medium transport--
       AB-205/Bell-205                                18
       SA-330 Puma                                     1
                                   (sub-total        19)

     light transport--
       Alouette II                                     6
       Alouette III                                    6
```

```
      AS-350 Ecureuil                               6
                                 (sub-total        18)
      TOTAL                                         37
```
advanced armament:
  air-to-air missiles--
  AIM-9J Sidewinder
```
military airfields:                                7
```
  Bizerta, Gabes, Gafsa, Jerba, Monastir, Sfax, Tunis
aircraft maintenance and repair capability:
  routine maintenance and repairs
Navy:
  combat vessels:                              number
  MFPBs--
```
    Combattante III                            3
    P-48                                       3
    Total                                      6
```
  gun frigates--
```
    Savage class                               1
```
  ASW vessels--
```
    Le Fougeux class corvette                  1
```
  mine warfare vessels--
```
    Adjutant class minesweeper                 2
```
  gunboats/MTBs--
```
    Shanghai II gunboat                        2
```
  patrol craft--
```
    Vosper Thornycroft 103 ft. (31 meter)      2
    Ch. Navals de l'Esterel
      83 ft. (25 meter)                        6
    Lurssen 23 meter                           4
    Total                                     12
```
auxiliary vessels:
```
  tug                                          3
```
advanced armament:
  MM-40 Exocet
  SS-12
```
naval bases:                                   5
```
  Bizerta, Kelibia, Sfax, Sousse, Tunis
ship maintenance and repair capability:
  4 drydocks and 1 slipway at Bizerta; 2 pontoons  and  1
  floating dock at Sfax. Capability to maintain and
  repair existing vessels.

# 20. UNITED ARAB EMIRATES (UAE)

BASIC DATA
   Official Name of State: United Arab Emirates*
   Head of State: President Shaykh Zayd ibn Sultan al-Nuhayan,
      Emir of Abu Dhabi (also Supreme Commander of the Armed
      Forces)
   Prime Minister: Shaykh Rashid ibn Sa'id al-Maktum, Emir of
      Dubai (also Vice President)
   Minister of Defense: Shaykh Muhammad ibn Rashid al-Maktum
   Commander-in-Chief of the Armed Forces: Brigadier General
      Sultan ibn Zayd
   Chief of the General Staff: Major General Muhammad Sa'id
      al-Badi
   Commander of the Air Force and Air Defense Forces:
      Brigadier General Shaykh Muhammad ibn Zayd al-Nuhayan
   Commander of the Navy: Commodore Hazza Sultan al-Darmaki
   Area: approximately 82,900 sq. km. (borders with Oman,
      Saudi Arabia and Qatar partly undemarcated and/or
      disputed)
   Population:                                        1,450,000
      ethnic subdivision:
         Arabs                          725,000           50.0%
         Southeast Asians               635,000           43.8%
         Others (Europeans, Persians)    90,000            6.2%
      religious subdivision:
         Sunni Muslims                  906,000           62.5%
         Shi'ite Muslims                218,000           15.0%
         Others                         326,000           22.5%
      nationality subdivision:
         UAE nationals                  276,000           19.0%
         Alien Arabs                    333,000           23.0%
         Southeast Asians
            (Indians, Pakistanis,
            Thais, Filipinos)           725,000           50.0%
         Others (Europeans, Iranians)   116,000            8.0%
   GDP:
      1986--$21.33 billion
      1987--$23.15 billion
   Defense Expenditure:
      1985--$1.86 billion
      1986--$1.58 billion

*The UAE consists of seven principalities: Abu Dhabi, Dubai,
   Ras al-Khaimah, Sharjah, Umm al-Qaiwain, Fujairah and
   Ajman.

# UAE

Foreign Military Aid Received:
  military training:
    foreign advisors/instructors/serving personnel from--Britain, Egypt, France, Jordan, Morocco, Pakistan, Sudan, USA
    trainees abroad in--Britain, Egypt, France, Jordan, Pakistan, Saudi Arabia, USA
  arms transfers from:
    Brazil (APCs); Britain (APCs, artillery pieces, mobile workshops, SAMs, trainer aircraft, AFV transporters, trucks); Egypt (APCs, air defense systems, unconfirmed); France (combat aircraft, tanks); FRG (tank transporters); Italy (trainer aircraft, transport aircraft); Spain (transport aircraft); Sweden (SAMs via Singapore); Switzerland (trainer aircraft); USA (aircraft training simulator, transport aircraft, SAMs, light reconnaissance vehicles, radio systems)
  support forces from:
    Morocco (5000, unconfirmed)
  maintenance performed abroad in:
    India (naval vessels)
  construction aid by:
    Britain (naval base)
Foreign Military Aid Extended:
  financial aid to:
    Syria, Morocco, Palestinian organizations; Jordan--grant; Iraq--loan
  military training:
    foreign trainees from--Bahrain, Qatar; YAR (unconfirmed)
Forces Deployed Abroad in:
  Saudi Arabia (part of GCC rapid deployment force)
Joint Maneuvers with:
  GCC (members: Bahrain, Kuwait, Oman, Qatar, Saudi Arabia, UAE)

INFRASTRUCTURE
  Road Network:
    length:   2,000 km
      paved roads   1,800 km
      gravel and improved earth tracks   200 km
    main routes:
    Abu Dhabi--Jebel Dhanna
    Abu Dhabi--Bu Hasa
    Abu Dhabi--Muscat (Oman)
    Abu Dhabi--Dubai--Sharjah--Ajman--Ras al-Khaimah
    Dubai--Muscat
    Ajman--Fujairah--Muscat
    Ajman--Daba al-Bay'ah (Oman)

Airfields:                                                      33
  airfields by runway type:
    permanent surface fields                    19
    unpaved fields and usable airstrips         14
  airfields by runway length:
    over 3660 meters                             7
    2440--3659                                   4
    1220--2439                                   6
    under 1220                                  16
  international airports: Abu Dhabi, Dubai, Fujairah, Ras al-Khaimah, Sharjah
  major domestic airfields: Jebel Dhanna, Mina Khor Fakkan

Airlines:
  companies: Gulf Air (international)--jointly owned by UAE, Oman, Qatar and Bahrain, listed under Bahrain); Emirates Air Services (domestic and international); Emirates Airlines (domestic and international)
  aircraft (excluding Gulf Air):
    Airbus A-300-600R                            1
    Airbus A-310-300                             2
    Boeing 727-200                               2
    DHC-7 Dash-7                                 1
    DHC-6 Twin Otter                             3
    Islander                                     1
  on order: 3 Airbus A-300-600

Maritime Facilities:
  harbors--Mina Zayd (Abu Dhabi), Mina Jebel Ali (Dubai), Mina Rashid (Dubai), Mina Sakr (Ras al-Khaimah), Mina Khalid (Sharjah), Fujairah, Mina Khor Fakkan (Sharjah)
  anchorages--Abu Bukhoosh (Abu Dhabi), Ras al-Khaimah
  oil terminals--Dasa Island (Abu Dhabi), Halat al-Mubarras (Abu Dhabi), Jebel Dhanna (Abu Dhabi), Mina Rashid (Dubai), Fateh Oil Storage Terminal (Dubai), Mubarak Oil Terminal (Sharjah)

Merchant Marine:

| vessel type | number | DWT |
|---|---|---|
| crude carrier | 3 | 330,717 |
| product tanker | 6 | 218,215 |
| general cargo | 7 | 40,162 |
| container | 7 | 211,569 |
| tanker | 5 | 94,659 |
| storage tanker | 1 | 12,125 |
| reefer | 1 | 2,540 |
| GC/container | 5 | 118,536 |
| bunkering tanker | 5 | 108,609 |
| cement carrier | 2 | 26,486 |
| TOTAL | 42 | 1,163,618 |

Defense Production:
  naval: construction of patrol boats at Ajman (with British cooperation)

```
ARMED FORCES
  Personnel:
    military forces--
      army                                        42,000
      air force                                    1,500
      navy                                         1,500
      TOTAL                                       45,000
  Army:
    major units:
      unit type                                  brigades
        armored                                        2
        mechanized                                     1
        infantry                                       3
        TOTAL                                          6
    small arms:
      personal weapons--
        9mm Sterling Mk.4 SMG
        7.62mm FAL (FN) SAR
      machine guns--
        7.62mm (0.3") Browning M-1919 MMG
        7.62mm MAG (FN) LMG
      light and medium mortars--
        81mm L-16 A1
    tanks:
      model                                        number
        medium quality
          AMX-30                                      100
          OF-40 Lion MK.2                              36
                                     (sub-total      136)
        low quality
          Scorpion                                     80
        TOTAL                                         216
    APCs/ARVs:
      model                                        number
        high quality
          AMX-VCI
          AMX-10P
          Engesa EE-11 Urutu                           30
          M-3 (Panhard)
          VAB                                          20
          VBC-90
                                     (sub-total      430)
        others
          AML-60/AML-90
          AT-105 Saxon (unconfirmed)
          Fahd                                         50
          Ferret
          Saladin
          Saracen
```

Shoreland Mk.2

|  |  |  |
|---|---|---|
| | (sub-total | 235) |
| TOTAL | | 665 |

on order: M-113 A2; EE-11; M-998 Hummer light reconnaissance vehicle; 70 VBC-90 (unconfirmed) or 90 VAB

artillery:

guns and heavy mortars--      number

high quality

|  |  |  |
|---|---|---|
| 155mm Mk. F3 (AMX) SP howitzer | | 20 |
| 105mm Light Gun | | 50 |
| | (sub-total | 70) |

others

|  |  |  |
|---|---|---|
| 105mm M-102 howitzer | | 50 |
| 105mm M-56 Pack howitzer | | 12 |
| 120mm mortar | | 12 |
| | (sub-total | 74) |
| TOTAL | | 144 |

anti-tank weapons:

missiles--      launchers

  BGM-71B Improved TOW      24

  Vigilant

guns--

  120mm BAT L-4 recoilless rifle

  84mm Carl Gustaf M-2 light recoilless rifle

army anti-aircraft defenses:

missiles--      launchers

  Blowpipe (unconfirmed)

  Crotale      9

  Rapier

  RBS-70

  SA-7 (Grail)

  Skyguard AA system

  Tigercat

short-range guns--

  2x30mm M-3 VDA SP

  2x20mm GCF-BM2 SP

on order: Crotale SAMs

CW capabilities:

personal protective equipment

Air Force:

aircraft--general:      number

|  |  |
|---|---|
| combat aircraft | 37 |
| transport aircraft | 32 |
| helicopters | 66 |

combat aircraft:

strike and multi-role aircraft--

medium quality

|  |  |
|---|---|
| Mirage V--AD/RAD/DAD | 16 |
| Mirage III | 10 |

|  |  | (sub-total | 26) |
|---|---|---|---|
| others |  |  |  |
| Hawker Hunter |  |  | 11 |
| TOTAL |  |  | 37 |

on order: 36 Mirage 2000

transport aircraft:

| BAe-125 | 1 |
|---|---|
| Boeing 707 | 3 |
| Boeing 737 | 1 |
| Britten-Norman BN-2 Islander | 5 |
| C-130H Hercules/L-100-30 | 6 |
| CASA C-212 (employed in EW role) | 4 |
| DHC-4 Caribou | 3 |
| DHC-5D Buffalo | 5 |
| G-222 | 1 |
| Gulfstream II | 1 |
| Mystere Falcon 20 | 1 |
| VC-10 | 1 |
| TOTAL | 32 |

on order: G-222

training and liaison aircraft:

| Aermacchi MB-326 KD/LD | 8 |
|---|---|
| Aermacchi MB-339 | 5 |
| Cessna 182 Skylane | 1 |
| Hawk | 16 |
| Pilatus PC-7 | 23 |
| SIAI-Marchetti SF-260 WD | 7 |
| TOTAL | 60 |

on order: SF-260; 12 Aermacchi MB-339 (unconfirmed); 12 Hawk (unconfirmed)

| helicopters: | number |
|---|---|
| attack-- |  |
| SA-342K Gazelle | 13 |
| medium transport-- |  |
| AB-205/Bell 205 | 10 |
| AB-212 | 3 |
| AB-214 | 4 |
| AS-332 Super Puma (2 in naval attack role) | 8 |
| SA-330 Puma | 8 |
|  | (sub-total 33) |
| light transport-- |  |
| AB-206 JetRanger/Bell 206L | 6 |
| Alouette III | 7 |
| AS-350 Ecureuil | 1 |
| BO-105 (employed in liaison role) | 6 |
|  | (sub-total 20) |
| TOTAL | 66 |

on order: 30 A-109; A-129 (unconfirmed)

miscellaneous aircraft:

| Beech MQM-107A RPV | 20 |
|---|---|

TTL BTT-3 Banshee RPV/target drone
on order: C-130 EW; E-2C Hawkeye AEW aircraft
(unconfirmed); 2 BN-Defender AEW aircraft
advanced armament:
  air-to-air missiles--
  R-550 Magique
  air-to-ground missiles--
  AS-11
  AS-12
  AM-39 Exocet
anti-aircraft defenses:
  radars--
  AN/TPS-70                                                     3
  Watchman
  long-range missiles--                              batteries
  MIM-23B Improved HAWK                                         7
  aircraft shelters--
  for combat aircraft at Abu Dhabi  and  Jebel  Ali  AF
  bases
military airfields:                                            8
  Abu  Dhabi,  al-Dhafra,  Batin  (Abu   Dhabi),   Dubai,
  Fujairah, Jebel Ali (Dubai), Ras al-Khaimah, Sharjah
Navy:
  combat vessels:
  MFPBs--                                               number
    Lurssen TNC-45                                            6
  patrol craft-- (some with coast guard)
    Vosper Thornycroft type 110 ft.
    (33.5 meter)                                             6
    Camcraft 77 ft.                                          5
    Camcraft 65 ft.                                          16
    Watercraft 45 ft.                                        10
    Cantieri Posillipo 68 ft.                                1
    Keith Nelson type 57 ft. (17.4 meter)                    3
    Cheverton 50 ft. (15.3 meter)                            2
    Keith Nelson (Dhafeer) class 40.3 ft.
    (12.3 meter)                                             6
    Fairey Marine Spear                                      6
    Boghammar (13 meter) police boat                         3
    P-1200                                                   10
    Baglietto GC-23 (serving coast guard)                    4
    Total                                                    72
  on order: 2 Lurssen 62 meter missile corvettes

  landing craft:
    Siong Huat 40 meter landing craft logistics             1
    on order: 2 54 meter LCTs from Vosper QAF, Singapore
  auxiliary vessels:
    Cheverton Type tenders                                   2
    on order: 2 Crestitalia 30-meter diver support vessels

advanced armament:
  surface to surface missiles--
    MM-40 Exocet SSMs
  on order: 30 mm Vulcan-Goalkeeper anti-missile guns
special maritime forces:
  a unit of frogmen, divers
naval bases:                                          13
  Ajman, Dalma (Abu Dhabi), Fujairah, Mina Jebel Ali
  (Dubai), Mina Khalid (Sharjah), Mina Khor Fakkan
  (Sharjah), Mina Rashid (Dubai), Mina Sakr (Ras
  al-Khaimah), Mina Sultan (Sharja), Mina Zayd (Abu
  Dhabi), al-Qaffay Island (under construction), Taweelah
  Samha (under construction)

# 21. YEMEN (YAR)

BASIC DATA
Official Name of State: The Yemeni Arab Republic (YAR)
Head of State: President Colonel Ali Abdullah Salih
Prime Minister: Abd al-Aziz Abd al-Ghani
Chief of the General Staff: General Abdullah Hussayn Busheiri
Commander of the People's Army: Lieutenant Colonel Abdullah Naji Daris
Commander of the Air Force: Ahmad al-Shaykh
Commander of the Navy: Lieutenant Commander Muhammad Oumar
Area: 194,250 sq. km. (borders with Saudi Arabia and PDRY partly undemarcated and/or disputed)
Population: 7,310,000

| ethnic subdivision: | | |
|---|---|---|
| Arabs | 6,579,000 | 90.0% |
| Afro-Arabs | 585,000 | 8.0% |
| Others | 146,000 | 2.0% |

| religious subdivision: | | |
|---|---|---|
| Sunni Muslims | 3,618,000 | 49.5% |
| Shi'ite Zaydi Muslims | 3,509,000 | 48.0% |
| Shi'ite Isma'ili Muslims | 51,000 | 0.7% |
| Others | 132,000 | 1.8% |

GDP:
1985--$3.22 billion (unreliable, due to several rates of exchange)
1986--$2.46 billion (unreliable, due to several rates of exchange)
Balance of Payments (goods, services & unilateral transfer payments):

| year | income | expenditure | balance |
|---|---|---|---|
| 1986 | $893 mil. | $1.01 bil. | -$273 mil. |
| 1987 | $1.07 bil. | $1.52 bil. | -$450 mil. |

Defense Expenditure:
1987--$414 million (unconfirmed)
1988--$620 million (unconfirmed)
Foreign Military Aid Received:
financial aid from:
Libya--grant; Kuwait--grant; Saudi Arabia--grant; USA--$3 million grant
military training:
foreign advisors/instructors from--Cuba, Egypt, USA (60, unconfirmed); USSR (500, unconfirmed); Saudi Arabia
trainees abroad in--Jordan, USA, USSR
arms transfers from:
USSR (tanks, combat aircraft, SAMs, SSMs); Saudi Arabia (US-made arms, in coordination with the USA)
maintenance of equipment in:

USSR (aircraft)
Foreign Military Aid Extended:
  military training:
    foreign trainees from--PLO organizations
  facilities provided to:
    Palestinian Organization/al-Fatah: camps, use of
    airfield and naval facilities at Kamran Island; 15,000
    anti-government troops from PDRY, loyal to former
    President Ali Nasser Muhammad (unconfirmed)

INFRASTRUCTURE
  Road Network:
    length:                                        22,275 km
      paved roads                                   1,775 km
      gravel and stone roads                          500 km
      earth and light gravel tracks                20,000 km
    main routes:
      San'a--Hodeida
      San'a--Ta'iz--al-Mukha (Mocha)
      Hodeida--Zabid--al-Mukha/Zabid--Ta'iz
      Ta'iz--Aden (PDRY)
      San'a--Sa'dah--Abha (Saudi Arabia)
      Hodeida--al Saleef--Jizan (Saudi Arabia)
  Airfields:                                            15
    airfields by runway type:
      permanent surface fields                         4
      unpaved fields and usable airstrips             11
    airfields by runway length:
      2440--3659 meters                                9
      1220--2439                                       3
      under 1220                                       3
    international airports: Hodeida, San'a
    major domestic airfields: Kamran Island, Sa'dah, Ta'iz
  Airlines:
    companies: Yemenia--Yemen Airway Corporation (internatio-
      nal and domestic)
    aircraft:
      Boeing 727-200                                   4
      Boeing 737-200                                   1
      DHC-7 Dash 7                                     2
  Maritime Facilities:
    harbors--Hodeida
    anchorages--al-Mukha (harbor planned); al-Saleef (harbor
      under construction)
    oil terminals--Hodeida

**YEMEN**

```
ARMED FORCES
   Personnel:
      military forces--
                           regular        reserves         total
         army              35,000            ?            35,000+
         air force          1,500                          1,500
         navy                 800                            800
         TOTAL             37,300            ?            37,300+
   Army:
      major  units:  (not  all  fully  operational  nor  fully
      organized)
         unit type                                    brigades
            armored                                        6
            mechanized                                     3
            infantry (mostly skeleton or undermanned)      9
            commando/paratroops                            1
            special forces                                 1
            central guards                                 1
         TOTAL                                            21
      small arms:
         personal weapons--
            7.62mm AK-47 (Kalashnikov) AR
            7.62mm SKS (Simonov) SAR
         machine guns--
            12.7mm D.Sh.K. 38/46 (Degtyarev) HMG
            7.62mm PK/PKS (Kalashnikov) LMG
            7.62mm RPD (Degtyarev) LMG
            7.62mm SG-43 (Goryunov) MMG
         light and medium mortars--
            82mm M-43
         light ATRLs--
            RPG-7
            M-72 LAW
      tanks:
         model                                          number
            medium quality
               T-62                                         50
               M-60 A1                                      64
               T-55                                        450
                                     (sub-total            564)
            low quality
               T-54                                        136
               T-34             (unconfirmed)              100
                                     (sub-total            236)
         TOTAL                                            800
      APCs/ARVs:
         model                                          number
            high quality
               M-113 A1 and its derivatives               100
```

```
        others
          AML-90
          BTR-40/50/60
          BTR-152
          al-Walid
          Ferret
          Saladin
                                   (sub-total      400)
          TOTAL                                    500
      artillery:
        guns and heavy mortars--              number
          high quality
            155mm M-114 howitzer
            122mm D-30 howitzer
          others
            122mm M-1938 howitzer
            105mm M-102 howitzer
            100mm SU-100 SP gun
            76mm M-1942 divisional gun
            120mm mortar
          TOTAL                                    320
        MRLs--
          122mm BM-21                              60
      anti-tank weapons:
        missiles--
          BGM-71A Improved TOW
          M-47 Dragon
          Vigilant
        guns--
          85mm M-1945/D-44 field/AT gun
          82mm recoilless rifle
          75mm recoilless rifle
          57mm gun
        surface-to-surface missiles--        launchers
          SS-21                                     4
      army anti-aircraft defenses:
        missiles--
          SA-9 (Gaskin) SP
          SA-7 (Grail)
        short-range guns--                     number
          57mm S-60
          37mm M-1939
          23mm ZSU 23x4 SP (Gun Dish)             40
          23mm ZU 23x2
          20mm M-163 Vulcan SP                    20
          20mm M-167 Vulcan                       52
Air Force:
  aircraft--general:
    combat aircraft (some in storage)            118
    transport aircraft                            24
```

## YEMEN

```
helicopters                                          43+
combat aircraft:
  interceptors--
    medium quality
      MiG-21 (Fishbed)                                48
  strike and multi-role aircraft--
    medium quality
      Su-20/22 (Fitter C)                             20
    others
      F-5E/B                                          15
      MiG-17 (Fresco)                                 32
      MiG-15 (Faggot/Midget, in training role)         3
                              (sub-total             50)
    TOTAL                                             70
transport aircraft:
  An-12 (Cub)                                          1
  An-24/An-26 (Coke/Curl)                              5
  C-130H Hercules                                      4
  DC-3 Dakota (C-47)                                   3
  Fokker F-27                                          5
  IL-14 (Crate)                                        4
  Short Skyvan Srs. 3                                  2
  TOTAL                                               24
training and liaison aircraft:
  Yak-11 (Moose)                                      18
helicopters:
  attack--
    Mi-24 (Hind)                                   a few
  medium transport--
    AB-212                                            5
    AB-204                                            2
    AB-205                                            2
    Mi-8 (Hip)                                       25
    Mi-4 (Hound)                                      1
                              (sub-total             35)
  light transport--
    AB-206 JetRanger                                  6
    Alouette III/SA-315 Lama (unconfirmed)            2
                              (sub-total              8)
  TOTAL                                              43+
advanced armament:
  air-to-air missiles--
    AIM-9 Sidewinder
    AA-2 (Atoll)
anti-aircraft defenses:
  long-range missiles--
    model                                       batteries
      SA-2 (Guideline)                                4
      SA-3                                             3
      SA-6 (Gainful)                                  5
```

**YEMEN**

```
        MIM-23B Improved HAWK      (unconfirmed)           5
      TOTAL                                               17
   military airfields:                                     3
      Hodeida, San'a; Kamran Island (unconfirmed)
Navy:
   combat vessels:                                    number
      mine warfare vessels--
         Yevgenia class                                    3
      patrol craft--
         Poluchat class (unconfirmed)                      1
         Zhuk class                                        5
         Broadsword class (unconfirmed)                    3
         Total                                             9
   landing craft:
      Ondatra LCU                                          2
      T-4 LCM                                              2
      Total                                                4
   naval bases:                                            2
      Hodeida; anchorage at Kamran Island (unconfirmed)
```

# PART III

# COMPARATIVE TABLES
# GLOSSARY OF WEAPONS SYSTEMS
# LIST OF ABBREVIATIONS
# CHRONOLOGY
# MAPS

# Table   1.   Major Armies of the Middle East

| Country | Year | Personnel (thousands) | | | Divisions | | | Indep.Brigades | | |
|---|---|---|---|---|---|---|---|---|---|---|
| | | Reg. | Res. | Total | Armor | Mech. | Inf. | Armor | Mech. | Inf./ Para. Com./ Terr. |
| Egypt | 1987-88 | 380 | 600 | 980 | 4 | 6 | 2 | 3 | - | 19 |
| | 1988-89 | 320 | 600 | 920 | 4 | 7 | 1 | 3 | - | 16 |
| Iran* | 1987-88 | 1300 | 350 | 1650 | 4 | - | 30 | - | - | 5 |
| | 1988-89 | 700 | 1245 | 1945 | 6 | 1 | 36 | - | - | 5 |
| Iraq** | 1987-88 | 555 | 480 | 1035 | 7 | 3 | 35 | - | - | 14 |
| | 1988-89 | 555 | 480 | 1035 | 7 | 3 | 45 | - | - | 14 |
| Israel | 1987-88 | 130 | 310 | 440 | 12 | - | - | - | - | 20 |
| | 1988-89 | 130 | 365 | 495 | 12 | - | - | - | - | 25 |
| Jordan | 1987-88 | 70 | 45 | 115 | 2 | 2 | - | - | - | 3 |
| | 1988-89 | 80 | 60 | 140 | 2 | 2 | - | - | - | 3 |
| Libya | 1987-88 | 85 | 30 | 115 | 3 | 4 | - | 2 | 2 | 1 |
| | 1988-89 | 85 | 30 | 115 | 3 | 4 | - | 2 | 2 | 1 |
| Saudi Arabia# | 1987-88 | 72 | - | 72 | - | - | - | 2 | 6 | 1 |
| | 1988-89 | 70 | - | 70 | - | - | - | 2 | 6 | 2 |
| Syria | 1987-88 | 306 | 300 | 606 | 5 | 3 | 1 | 1 | - | 7 |
| | 1988-89 | 306 | 300 | 606 | 6 | 3 | 1 | 1 | - | 7 |

Note: Plus sign indicates precise number unknown;
      minus sign indicates no entry.
* army and IRGC, excluding Baseej
** excluding Popular Army
# army and National Guard
For classification of tanks according to quality see introductory note
Part II.

| Indep.Battalions | | | Tanks | | | APCs & ARVs | Guns & Mortars | ATGM Launchers | SSM Launchers |
|---|---|---|---|---|---|---|---|---|---|
| rmor | Mech. | Inf./ Para. Com./ Terr. | High Quality | Others | Total | | | | |
| - | - | - | 850 | 1550 | 2400 | 4100 | 2200 | 1400 | 20 |
| - | - | - | 850 | 1550 | 2400 | 4100 | 2200 | 1600-1800 | 24 |
| - | - | - | + | + | 1100 | 2000 | 1500 | + | + |
| - | - | - | + | + | 700 | 1000 | 1000 | + | + |
| - | - | - | 400 | 5100 | 5500+ | 5000 | 4500 | 1500 | 48+ |
| - | - | - | 1000 | 5000 | 6000 | 5000 | 4700 | 1500 | 48+ |
| - | - | - | 1040 | 2750 | 3790 | 8000 | 1200 | + | 12 |
| - | - | - | 1210 | 2600 | 3810 | 8100 | 1300 | + | 12 |
| - | - | - | 375 | 650 | 1025 | 1465+ | 600 | 550 | - |
| - | - | - | 375 | 740 | 1115 | 1565 | 600 | 550 | - |
| 3 | 8 | 13 | 300 | 2500 | 2800 | 2000 | 2000 | 2000 | 100 |
| 3 | 8 | 13 | 300 | 2500 | 2800 | 2000 | 2000 | 2000 | 100 |
| - | - | 19 | 100 | 450 | 550 | 3140 | 700 | 700 | + |
| - | - | 19 | 100 | 450 | 550 | 3140+ | 700 | 700 | 20 |
| - | - | - | 1000 | 3100 | 4100 | 3800 | 2300 | 2000 | 54-60 |
| - | - | - | 1000 | 3100 | 4100 | 3800 | 2300 | 2000 | 60 |

# Table 2. Major Air Forces of the Middle East

| Country | Year | Personnel (thousands) | | | Interceptors | | Strike & Multi-Role Aircraft | |
|---|---|---|---|---|---|---|---|---|
| | | Reg. | Res. | Total | High Quality | Others | High Quality | Others |
| Egypt | 1987-88 | 110 | 85 | 195 | 100 | 310 | - | 175 |
| | 1988-89 | 107 | 85 | 192 | 98 | 290 | - | 154 |
| Iran | 1987-88 | 35 | - | 35 | 15 | 18 | - | 130 |
| | 1988-89 | 35 | - | 35 | 15 | 18 | - | 130 |
| Iraq | 1987-88 | 40 | - | 40 | 55 | 220 | 40 | 372 |
| | 1988-89 | 40 | - | 40 | 56 | 200 | 15 | 412 |
| Israel | 1987-88 | 30 | 50 | 80 | 173 | - | 24 | 485 |
| | 1988-89 | 30 | 55 | 85 | 171 | - | 24 | 440 |
| Jordan | 1987-88 | 7.5 | - | 7.5 | - | - | - | 107 |
| | 1988-89 | 9.7 | - | 9.7 | - | - | - | 107 |
| Libya | 1987-88 | 9 | - | 9 | 80 | 60 | - | 385 |
| | 1988-89 | 9 | - | 9 | 80 | 50 | 6 | 400 |
| Saudia Arabia | 1987-88 | 15 | - | 15 | 60 | - | 20 | 110 |
| | 1988-89 | 15 | - | 15 | 64 | - | 20 | 110 |
| Syria | 1987-88 | 80 | 37.5 | 117.5 | 65 | 280 | - | 305 |
| | 1988-89 | 80 | 37.5 | 117.5 | 65 | 280 | - | 305 |

Note: plus sign indicates precise number unknown; minus sign indicates no
entry.
For classification of combat aircraft according to quality see introductory
note, part II.
* maritime attack
** classification of long range SAMs has been changed. See introductory note
to part II.

| mbers | Total Combat A/C | Transport Aircraft | Helicopters | | | Military Airfields | Long-Range SAM Batteries ** |
|---|---|---|---|---|---|---|---|
| | | | Attack | Transport +ASW | Total | | |
| 15 | 600 | 47 | 70 | 126 | 196 | 20 | 140 |
| - | 542 | 34 | 80 | 118 | 198 | 21 | 132 |
| - | 163 | 120 | + | + | 253 | 10 | 12+ |
| - | 163 | 120 | + | + | 250 | 13 | 22 |
| 18 | 705 | 86 | 160 | 397 | 557 | 20 | 116 |
| 22 | 705 | 86 | 160 | 425 | 585 | 20 | 60 |
| - | 682 | 91 | 77 | 143 | 220 | 11 | + |
| - | 635 | 91 | 77 | 143 | 220 | 11 | + |
| - | 107 | 15 | 24 | 32 | 56 | 7 | 24 |
| - | 107 | 14 | 24 | 45 | 69 | 6 | 14 |
| 12 | 537 | 123 | 80 | 155 | 235 | 11 | 140 |
| 7 | 543 | 139+ | 40 | 137 | 177 | 18 | 97 |
| - | 190 | 73 | 24* | 86 | 110 | 20 | 27 |
| - | 194 | 73 | 24* | 90 | 114 | 20 | 15 |
| - | 650 | 32 | 115 | 175 | 290 | 21 | 150 |
| - | 650 | 32 | 115 | 175 | 290 | 21 | 68 |

# Table 3. Major Navies of the Middle East

| Country | Year | Personnel (thousands) | | | Sub-Marines | MFPBs | Missile Destroyers, Frigates & Corvettes | SSMs |
|---|---|---|---|---|---|---|---|---|
| | | Reg. | Res. | Total | | | | |
| Egypt | 1987-88 | 23 | 15 | 38 | 11 | 29 | 6 | Harpoon, Otomat, Styx |
| | 1988-89 | 20 | 15 | 35 | 10 | 25 | 4 | Harpoon, Otomat, Styx,HY- |
| Iran | 1987-88 | 20 | - | 20 | - | 10 | 6 | Harpoon Seakille |
| | 1988-89 | 20 | - | 20 | - | 10 | 6 | Harpoon Seakille C-801 |
| Iraq | 1987-88 | 5 | - | 5 | - | 12 | - | Styx |
| | 1988-89 | 5 | - | 5 | - | 8 | - | Styx |
| Israel | 1987-88 | 10 | 10 | 20 | 3 | 26+2 hydro-foils | - | Gabriel, Harpoon |
| | 1988-89 | 10 | 10 | 20 | 3 | 24+2 hydro-foils | - | Gabriel, Harpoon |
| Libya | 1987-88 | 4 | - | 4 | 6 | 24 | 10 | Otomat, SS-12, Styx |
| | 1988-89 | 6.5 | - | 6.5 | 6 | 24 | 10 | Otomat, SS-12, Styx |
| Saudi Arabia | 1987-88 | 4.2 | - | 4.2 | - | 9 | 8 | Harpoon, Otomat 2 |
| | 1988-89 | 7.5 | - | 7.5 | - | 9 | 8 | Harpoon, Otomat 2 |
| Syria | 1987-88 | 4 | 2.5 | 6.5 | 3 | 22 | - | Styx |
| | 1988-89 | 4 | 2.5 | 6.5 | 3 | 21 | - | Styx |

Note: Minus sign indicates no entry.

| Gun Destroyers, Frigates & Corvettes | ASW Vessels | Mine Warfare | MTBs & Gunboats | Patrol Craft | Landing Craft | Hover-Craft | Naval Bases |
|---|---|---|---|---|---|---|---|
| - | 16 | 12 | 38 | 30 | 26 | 3 | 7 |
| 1 | - | 9 | 18 | 36 | 24 | 3 | 8 |
| 2 | - | 5 | - | 163 | 11 | 14 | 8 |
| 2 | - | 5 | - | 131 | 12 | 13 | 9 |
| - | 3 | 8 | 7 | 28 | 2-3 | - | 3 |
| - | 3 | 8 | 6 | 32 | 2-3 | 6 | 3 |
| - | - | - | - | 47 | 13 | 2 | 3 |
| - | - | - | - | 47 | 13 | 2 | 3 |
| 1 | - | 8 | - | 23 | 8 | - | 5 |
| 1 | - | 8 | - | 23 | 7 | - | 5 |
| - | - | 4 | 3 | 38 | 12 | 10 | 10 |
| - | - | 4 | 3 | 56 | 16 | 24 | 12 |
| - | 2 | 6 | - | 7 | 3 | - | 4 |
| - | 2 | 8 | - | 7 | 3 | - | 3 |

# Table 4. The Israel-Syria Military Balance

Army

| Country | Personnel (thousands) | | | Divisions | | | Indep. Brigades | | |
|---|---|---|---|---|---|---|---|---|---|
| | Reg. | Res. | Total | Armor | Mech. | Inf. | Armor | Mech. | Inf./Para./Com./Terr. |
| Israel | 130 | 365 | 495 | 12 | - | - | - | - | 25 |
| Syria | 306 | 300 | 606 | 6 | 3 | 1 | 1 | - | 7 |

Air Force and Air Defense

| Country | Personnel (thousands) | | | Interceptors | | Strike & Multi-Role Aircraft | |
|---|---|---|---|---|---|---|---|
| | Reg. | Res. | Total | High Quality | Others | High Quality | Others |
| Israel | 30 | 55 | 85 | 171 | - | 24 | 440 |
| Syria | 80 | 37.5 | 117.5 | 65 | 280 | - | 305 |

Navy

| Country | Personnel (thousands) | | | Sub-marines | MFPBs | Missile Destroyers, Frigates & Corvettes | SSMs |
|---|---|---|---|---|---|---|---|
| | Reg. | Res. | Total | | | | |
| Israel | 10 | 10 | 20 | 3 | 24 +2 hydro-foil | - | Gabriel Harpoon |
| Syria | 4 | 2.5 | 6.5 | 3 | 21 | - | Styx |

Note: Plus sign indicates precise number unknown; minus sign indicates no entry.
For classification of tanks, long-range SAMs and combat aircraft according to quality see introductory note, Part II.

| Tanks | APCs & ARVs | Guns & Mortars | ATGM Launchers | SSM Launchers |
|---|---|---|---|---|
| 3810 | 8100 | 1300 | + | 12 |
| 4100 | 3800 | 2300 | 2000 | 60 |

| Total Combat | Transport Aircraft | Helicopters | | | Military Airfields | Long-range SAM Batteries |
|---|---|---|---|---|---|---|
| | | Attack | Transport + ASW | Total | | |
| 635 | 91 | 77 | 143 | 220 | 11 | + |
| 550 | 32 | 115 | 175 | 290 | 21 | 68 |

| ASW Vessels | Mine Warfare Vessels | Patrol Craft | Landing Craft. | Hover-Craft | Naval Bases |
|---|---|---|---|---|---|
| - | - | 47 | 13 | 2 | 3 |
| 2 | 8 | 7 | 3 | - | 3 |

# Table 5. Eastern Front-Israel Military Balance

Full participants: Israel, Syria, Jordan, Palestinian forces.
Partial participants: Saudi Army (two brigades) and Air Force (two fighter
squadrons and one transport squadron); Kuwaiti Air Force (one squadron);

Army

| | Personnel (thousands) | | | Divisions | | | |
|---|---|---|---|---|---|---|---|
| | Reg. | Res. | Total | Armor | Mech. | Inf. | Total |
| Eastern Front | 532 | 360 | 892 | 10 | 8 | 2 | 20 |
| Israel | 130 | 365 | 495 | 12 | - | - | 12 |
| Ratio, 1988-89 | 4.1:1 | 1:1 | 1.8:1 | 0.8:1 | * | * | 1.7:1 |
| Ratio, 1987-88 | 3.2:1 | 1.1:1 | 1.7:1 | 0.6:1 | * | * | 1.2:1 |

Air Force and Air Defense

| | Personnel (thousands) | | | Interceptors | | Strike & Multi-Role Aircraft | |
|---|---|---|---|---|---|---|---|
| | Reg. | Res. | Total | High Quality | Others | High Quality | Others |
| Eastern Front | 100 | 37.5 | 137.5 | 135 | 295 | 41 | 507 |
| Israel | 30 | 55 | 85 | 171 | - | 24 | 440 |
| Ratio, 1988-89 | 3.3:1 | 0.7:1 | 1.6:1 | 0.8:1 | * | 1.7:1 | 1.2:1 |
| Ratio, 1987-88 | 3.1:1 | 0.8:1 | 1.6:1 | 0.5:1 | * | 0.6:1 | 0.9:1 |

Navy

| | Personnel (thousands) | | | Sub-marines | MFPBs | Missile Destroyers, Frigates & Corvettes | SSMs |
|---|---|---|---|---|---|---|---|
| | Reg. | Res. | Total | | | | |
| Eastern Front | 11 | 2.5 | 13.5 | 9 | 45 | 10 | Styx,Otomat |
| Israel | 10 | 10 | 20 | 3 | 26** | - | Gabriel, Harpoon |
| Ratio,1988-89 | 1.1:1 | 0.3:1 | 0.7:1 | 3:1 | 1.7:1 | * | |
| Ratio,1987-88 | 1.1:1 | 0.3:1 | 0.7:1 | 3:1 | 1.6:1 | * | * |

Note: The constellation of full and partial participants presented here is
only one of several reasonable possibilities; it reflects neither an
absolute certainty nor the maximum force which all countries involved are
thought to be capable of deploying.

Iraq (five divisions, 20 SSM launchers, 150 combat aircraft, 50 helicopters); various militias in Lebanon; Libyan Army (one mechanized division, three mechanized brigades, 20 SSM launchers), Libyan Air Force (two squadron of combat aircraft, one of attack helicopters), and the entire Libyan Navy.

| Indep.Brigades | | | | Tanks | APCs & ARVs | Guns & Mortars | ATGM Launchers | SSM Launchers |
|---|---|---|---|---|---|---|---|---|
| Armor | Mech. | Inf./ Para./ Com./ Terr. | Total | | | | | |
| 1 | 5 | 18 | 24 | 6765 | 6965 | 3780 | 3200 | 110 |
| - | - | 25 | 25 | 3810 | 8100 | 1300 | + | 12 |
| * | * | 0.7:1 | 1:1 | 1.8:1 | 0.9:1 | 2.9:1 | * | 9.2:1 |
| * | * | 0.6:1 | 0.7:1 | 1.8:1 | 0.8:1 | 2.8:1 | * | 8.3:1 |

| Bombers | Total Combat A/C | Transport Aircraft | Helicopters | | | Military Airfields | Long-range SAM Batteries |
|---|---|---|---|---|---|---|---|
| | | | Attack | Transport +ASW | Total | | |
| - | 978 | 91 | 179 | 260 | 439 | 30 | 97 |
| - | 635 | 91 | 77 | 143 | 220 | 11 | + |
| - | 1.5:1 | 1:1 | 2.3:1 | 1.8:1 | 2:1 | 2.7:1 | * |
| - | 1.4:1 | 1.4:1 | 1.6:1 | 1.6:1 | 1.7:1 | 2.7:1 | * |

| Destroyers, Frigates & Corvettes | ASW Vessels | Gun Mine Warfare Vessels | MTBs & Gunboats | Patrol Craft | Landing Craft | Hover- Craft | Naval Bases |
|---|---|---|---|---|---|---|---|
| 1 | 2 | 16 | - | 30 | 10 | - | 8 |
| - | - | - | - | 47 | 13 | 2 | 3 |
| * | * | * | * | 0.6:1 | 0.8:1 | * | 2.7:1 |
| - | * | * | * | 0.6:1 | 0.8:1 | * | 3.3:1 |

Note: Plus sign indicates precise number unknown, minus sign indicates no entry.
* indicates no basis for calculation
** including 2 hydrofoils
For classification of tanks, SAMs and combat aircraft according to quality see introductory note, Part II.

# Table   6.   Arab-Israel Military Balance (Israel vs.

Full participants: Israel, Syria, Jordan, Palestinian forces, Egypt, Libyan Navy. Partial participants: Saudi Army (two brigades)  and  Air Force (two squadrons); Iraq (five divisions,  20  SSM  launchers,  150 combat aircraft, 50 helicopters); Kuwaiti Air  Force  (one  squadron); Algerian  army  (two brigades)  and  Air Force (2 squadrons of Army

| | Personnel (thousands) | | | Divisions | | | |
|---|---|---|---|---|---|---|---|
| | Reg. | Res. | Total | Armor | Mech. | Inf. | Total |
| Arab Coalition | 863 | 960 | 1823 | 14 | 15 | 3 | 32 |
| Israel | 130 | 365 | 495 | 12 | - | - | 12 |
| Ratio, 1988-89 | 6.6:1 | 2.6:1 | 3.7:1 | 1.2:1 | * | * | 2.7:1 |
| Ratio, 1987-88 | 6.5:1 | 2.3:1 | 3.5:1 | 1.1:1 | * | * | 2.2:1 |

Air Force and Air Defense

| | Personnel (thousands) | | | Interceptors | | Strike & Multi-Role | |
|---|---|---|---|---|---|---|---|
| | Reg. | Res. | Total | High Quality | Others | High Quality | Others |
| Arab Coalition | 209 | 122.5 | 332.5 | 248 | 585 | 41 | 706 |
| Israel | 30 | 55 | 85 | 173 | - | 24 | 440 |
| Ratio, 1988-89 | 7:1 | 2.2:1 | 3.9:1 | 1.5:1 | * | 1.7:1 | 1.6:1 |
| Ratio, 1987-88 | 6.8:1 | 2.4:1 | 4.1:1 | 2.1:1 | * | 0.6:1 | 1.3:1 |

Navy

| | Personnel (thousands) | | | Sub-marines | MFPBs | Missile Destroyers, Frigates & Corvettes | SSMs |
|---|---|---|---|---|---|---|---|
| | Reg. | Res. | Total | | | | |
| Arab Coalition | 31 | 17.5 | 48.5 | 19 | 74 | 14 | Styx, Otomat, Harpoon |
| Israel | 10 | 10 | 20 | 3 | 26** | - | Gabriel, Harpoon |
| Ratio, 1988-89 | 3.1:1 | 1.8:1 | 2.4:1 | 6.3:1 | 2.8:1 | * | * |
| Ratio, 1987-88 | 3.4:1 | 1.8:1 | 2.6:1 | 6.7:1 | 3.4:1 | * | * |

Note: The constellation of full and partial participants presented here is only one of several reasonable possibilities; it reflects neither an absolute certainty nor the maximum force which all countries involved are thought to be capable of deploying.

# Arab Coalition, including Egypt and Iraq)

fighter a/c), Moroccan Army (one brigade) and Air Force (one squadron), Libyan Army (one mech. div., 3 mech. brig., 5 para. battalions) and Air Force (two squadrons of combat a/c and one helicopter squadron).

| Indep. Brigades | | | | Tanks | APCs & ARVs' | Guns & Mortars | ATGM Launchers | SSM Launchers |
|---|---|---|---|---|---|---|---|---|
| Armor | Mech. | Inf./ Para./ Com./ Terr./ | Total | | | | | |
| 7 | 7 | 35 | 49 | 9245 | 11265 | 6040 | 5000 | 134 |
| - | - | 25 | 25 | 3810 | 8100 | 1300 | + | 12 |
| * | * | 1.4:1 | 2:1 | 2.4:1 | 1.4:1 | 4.6:1 | * | 11.2:1 |
| * | * | 1.8:1 | 2.4:1 | 2.1:1 | 1.2:1 | 5:1 | * | 4.5:1 |

| Bombers | Total Combat A/C | Transport Aircraft | Helicopters | | | Military Airfields | Long-range SAM Batteries |
|---|---|---|---|---|---|---|---|
| | | | Attack | Transport +ASW | Total | | |
| 17 | 1597 | 134 | 259 | 390 | 649 | 51 | 235 |
| - | 635 | 91 | 77 | 143 | 220 | 11 | + |
| * | 2.5:1 | 1.5:1 | 3.4:1 | 2.7:1 | 3:1 | 4.6:1 | * |
| * | 2.3:1 | 1.9:1 | 3.1:1 | 2.5:1 | 2.7:1 | 4.5:1 | * |

| Gun Destroyers, Frigates & Corvettes | ASW Vessels | Mine Warfare Vessels | MTBs & Gunboats | Patrol Craft | Landing Craft | Hover- Craft | Naval Bases |
|---|---|---|---|---|---|---|---|
| 2 | 2 | 25 | 18 | 66 | 34 | 3 | 16 |
| - | - | - | - | 47 | 13 | 2 | 3 |
| * | * | * | * | 1.4:1 | 2.6:1 | 1.5:1 | 5.3:1 |
| * | * | * | * | 1.3:1 | 2.9:1 | 1.5:1 | 5.7:1 |

Note: Plus sign indicates precise number unknown; minus sign indicates no entry. The classification of tanks, SAMs and combat aircraft according to quality was changed in 1987 and 1988--see introductory note, Part II.
* indicates no basis for calculation. ** including two hydrofoils.

# Table 7. Arab-Israel Military Balance 1984-1989

Full participants: Egypt, Jordan, Syria, Lebanese militias, Palestinian forces.
Partial participants: Algeria, Kuwait, Libya, Morocco, Saudi Arabia; in 1989--also Iraq

Army

| | Divisions | | | | | | | |
|---|---|---|---|---|---|---|---|---|
| | Armor | | Mech. | | Inf. | | Total | |
| | 84 | 89 | 84 | 89 | 84 | 89 | 84 | 89 |
| Arab Coalition | 10 | 14 | 10 | 15 | 3 | 3 | 23 | 32 |
| Israel | 11 | 12 | - | - | - | - | 11 | 12 |
| Ratio | 0.9:1 | 1.2:1 | * | * | * | * | 2.1:1 | 2.7:1 |

Air Force & Air Defense

| | Interceptors | | | | Strike & Multi-Role Aircraft | | | |
|---|---|---|---|---|---|---|---|---|
| | High Quality | | Others | | High Quality | | Others | |
| | 84 | 89 | 84 | 89 | 84 | 89 | 84 | 89 |
| Arab Coalition | 130 | 248 | 620 | 585 | 496 | 41 | 354 | 706 |
| Israel | 40 | 173 | - | - | 445 | 24 | 185 | 440 |
| Ratio | 3.25:1 | 1.5:1 | * | * | 1.1:1 | 1.7:1 | 1.9:1 | 1.6:1 |

Navy

| | Submarines | | MFPBs | | Missile Destroyers, Frigates & Corvettes | |
|---|---|---|---|---|---|---|
| | 84 | 89 | 84 | 89 | 84 | 89 |
| Arab Coalition | 18 | 19 | 67 | 74 | 8 | 14 |
| Israel | 3 | 3 | 24 | 26 | - | - |
| Ratio | 6:1 | 6.3:1 | 2.8:1 | 2.8:1 | * | * |

Note: Plus sign indicates precise number unknown; minus sign indicates no entry.
* indicates no basis for calculation.

| Independent Brigades | | Tanks | | APCs & ARVs | | GUNs & Mortars | | ATGM Launchers | | SSM Launchers | |
|---|---|---|---|---|---|---|---|---|---|---|---|
| 84 | 89 | 84 | 89 | 84 | 89 | 84 | 89 | 84 | 89 | 84 | 89 |
| 51 | 49 | 8065 | 9245 | 8470 | 11265 | 6050 | 6040 | 5150 | 5000 | 54 | 134 |
| 20 | 25 | 3650 | 3810 | 8000 | 8100 | 1000 | 1300 | + | + | + | + |
| 2.5:1 | 2:1 | 2.2:1 | 2.4:1 | 1.1:1 | 1.4:1 | 6:1 | 4.6:1 | * | * | * | * |

| Total Combat A/C | | Helicopters | | | | | | Military airfields | | Long-range SAM Batteries | |
|---|---|---|---|---|---|---|---|---|---|---|---|
| | | Attack | | Transport &ASW | | Total | | | | | |
| 84 | 89 | 84 | 89 | 84 | 89 | 84 | 89 | 84 | 89 | 84 | 89 |
| 1635 | 1597 | 161 | 257 | 324 | 390 | 485 | 649 | 48 | 51 | 304 | 235 |
| 670 | 635 | 55 | 77 | 133 | 143 | 188 | 220 | 11 | 11 | + | + |
| 2.4:1 | 2.5:1 | 2.9:1 | 3.4:1 | 2.4:1 | 2.7:1 | 2.6:1 | 3:1 | 4.4:1 | 4.6:1 | * | * |

| Gun Destroyers, Frigates & Corvettes | | Landing Craft | | Naval Bases | |
|---|---|---|---|---|---|
| 84 | 89 | 84 | 89 | 84 | 89 |
| 8 | 2 | 36 | 34 | 17 | 16 |
| - | - | 13 | 13 | 3 | 3 |
| * | * | 2.8:1 | 2.6:1 | 5.7:1 | 5.3:1 |

# Table 8. The Iran-Iraq Military Balance

Army

| Country | Personnel (thousands) | | | Divisions | | | Indep.Brigades | | |
|---------|------|------|-------|-------|-------|------|-------|-------|-----------------|
| | Reg. | Res. | Total | Armor | Mech. | Inf. | Armor | Mech. | Inf./ Para./ Com./ Terr./ |
| Iran* | 700 | 1245 | 1945 | 6 | 1 | 36 | - | - | 5 |
| Iraq** | 555 | 480 | 1035 | 7 | 3 | 45 | - | - | 14 |

Air Force and Air Defense

| Country | Personnel (thousands) | | | Interceptors | | Strike & Multi-Role Aircraft | |
|---------|------|------|-------|-----------------|--------|-----------------|--------|
| | Reg. | Res. | Total | High Quality | Others | High Quality | Others |
| Iran | 35 | - | 35 | 15 | 18 | - | 130 |
| Iraq | 40 | - | 40 | 56 | 200 | 15 | 412 |

Navy

| Country | Personnel (thousands) | | | Sub-marines | MFPBs | Missile Destroyers, Frigates & Corvettes | SSMs |
|---------|------|------|-------|------|------|------|------|
| | Reg. | Res. | Total | | | | |
| Iran | 20 | - | 20 | - | 10 | 6 | Harpoon, Seakiller C-801 |
| Iraq | 5 | - | 5 | - | 8 | - | Styx |

Note: Plus sign indicates precise number unknown; minus sign indicates no entry.
* army and IRGC
** excluding Popular Army.
***For classification of tanks, long range SAMs and combat aircraft according to quality see introductory note, part II.

| anks | APCs & ARVs | Guns & Mortars | ATGM Launchers | SSM Launchers |
|------|-------------|----------------|----------------|---------------|
| 700 | 1000 | 1000 | + | + |
| 000 | 5000 | 4700 | 1500 | 48+ |

| ombers | Total Combat a/c | Transport Aircraft | Helicopters | | | Military Airfields | Long-range SAM Batteries*** |
|--------|------------------|--------------------|-------------|-----------|-------|--------------------|-----------------------------|
| | | | Attack | Transport | Total | | |
| - | 163 | 120 | + | + | 250 | 13 | 22 |
| 22 | 705 | 86 | 160 | 425 | 585 | 20 | 60 |

| Gun Destroyers, Frigates & Corvettes | ASW Vessels | Mine Warfare Vessels | MTBs & Gunboats | Patrol Craft | Landing Craft | Hover-Craft | Naval Bases |
|--------------------------------------|-------------|----------------------|-----------------|--------------|---------------|-------------|-------------|
| 2 | - | 5 | - | 131 | 12 | 13 | 9 |
| - | 3 | 8 | 6 | 32 | 2-3 | 6 | 3 |

# Table 9. The USA in the Middle East: Financial Aid

| Country | US Financial Aid ($millions) | | | US Arms (major items) Granted or Sold |
|---|---|---|---|---|
| | Grants | Loans | Total | |
| Algeria | .05 | - | - | air traffic control equipment, radar |
| Bahrain | - | - | - | ATGMs, combat aircraft, helicopters, tanks |
| Egypt | 1,300 | - | 1,300 | tanks, APCs, artillery, RPVs, combat aircraft, SAMS, naval SSMs, early warning aircraft, radars |
| Iraq | - | - | - | helicopters (allegedly civilian) |
| Israel | 1,800 | - | 1,800 | tanks, APCs, artillery, combat aircraft, SAMS, naval SSMs tank transporters, attack helicopters |
| Jordan | 26.5 | - | 26.5 | tanks, APCs, artillery, SAMs, AAGs, helicopters, terminally guided artillery shells |
| Kuwait | - | - | - | SAMs, APCs, patrol boats |
| Lebanon | - | - | - | - |
| Morocco | ? | ? | 52 | tanks, ATGMs, SAMs, tank transporters |
| Oman | 0.1 | 40 | 40.1 | SP artillery, AAMs |
| Saudi Arabia | - | - | - | tanks, APCs, artillery, ATGMs, combat aircraft, transport aircraft, SAMs, AAMs, AGMs, AWACS |
| Sudan | - | - | - | tanks, AAGs |
| Tunisia | - | - | 27.0 | tanks, SAMs, transport aircraft, artillery |
| UAE | - | - | - | transport aircraft, SAMs, aircraft training simulator, light reconnaissance vehicles, radio systems |
| Yemen (YAR) | 3 | - | 3 | spare parts, miscellaneous arms (via Saudi Arabia) |

*unconfirmed

# Military), Arms Sales, Advisors, Trainees and Facilities

| US Advisors Present | Trainees in US | Facilities Provided to US | Joint maneuvers with USA |
|---|---|---|---|
| - | ? | - | - |
| + | + | naval & intelligence facilities | - |
| + | + | use of airfields | + |
| - | ? | - | - |
| - | + | - | + |
| + | + | - | + |
| + | + | - | - |
| - | + | - | - |
| + | + | use of airfields, naval communications and storage facilities | + |
| + | - | use of airfields, naval, communications and storage facilities | - |
| + | + | - | - |
| + | + | - | - |
| + | + | - | + |
| + | + | use of naval facility* | - |
| + | + | - | - |

# Table 10. The USSR in the Middle East: Arms Sales, Advisors, Trainees and Facilities

| Country | Soviet Arms (major items) Granted or Sold | Soviet Advisors Present | Trainees in USSR | Facilities Provided to |
|---|---|---|---|---|
| Algeria | tanks, artillery, combat aircraft, SAMs missile corvette, submarine | + | + | - |
| Egypt | spare parts for Soviet weapons | - | - | - |
| Iran* | APCs, AAGs, small arms, artillery | + | + | ? |
| Iraq | tanks, artillery, SAMs, SSMs, combat aircraft, artillery pieces, helicopters | + | + | - |
| Jordan | SAMs, AAGs, APCs | + | + | - |
| Kuwait | surface-to-surface rockets, SAMs, AAGs | + | + | - |
| Libya | tanks, APCs, artillery, SSMs, combat aircraft, SAMs, naval vessels, naval mines | + | + | use of airfield & naval facilities (unconfirmed) |
| Palestinian Org's. | small arms, tanks, artillery, MRLs | - | + | - |
| South Yemen (PDRY) | small arms, tanks combat aircraft | + | + | use of airfields & naval facilities |
| Syria | small arms, tanks, artillery, SSMs, combat aircraft, helicopters, SAMs naval vessels, coastal defense missiles | + | + | use of airfields & naval facilities |
| Yemen (YAR) | SSMs, tanks, SAMs combat aircraft | + | + | - |

* via North Korea and Soviet Bloc countries

# Table 11. France in the Middle East: Arms Sales, Advisors and Trainees

| Country | French Arms (major items) Granted or Sold | French Advisors Present | Trainees in France |
|---|---|---|---|
| Algeria | ARVs, ATGMs, helicopters | - | + |
| Bahrain | ARVs | + | + |
| Egypt | ATGMs, combat aircraft, helicopters, SAMs, AAMs, radars for AAGs, night vision devices | + | + |
| Iran | artillery ammunition, spare parts for MFPBs, rubber boats | - | + |
| Iraq | ATGMs, combat aircraft, helicopters, AGMs, SAMs, AAMs, artillery pieces | + | + |
| Israel | spares (via intermediaries) | - | + |
| Jordan | combat aircraft, AAMs, AGMs, helicopters, radars, ATRL, artillery fire control sys. | - | + |
| Kuwait | SP artillery, ATGMs, combat aircraft, helicopters, radars | + | + |
| Lebanon | helicopters | + | + |
| Libya | ATGMs, combat aircraft, helicopters, SAMs | ? | ? |
| Morocco | tank transporters, ATGMs, combat aircraft, helicopters, AAMs, naval vessels, naval SSMs | + | + |
| Oman | ATGMs, naval SSMs | - | + |
| Qatar | tanks, APCs, artillery, combat aircraft, helicopters, MFPBs, naval SSMs, anti-ship AGMs | + | + |
| Saudi Arabia | APCs, SP artillery, ATGMs, radars, SAMs | + | + |
| Sudan | artillery pieces | - | - |
| Syria | ATGMs, helicopters, naval survey vessels | - | + |
| Tunisia | helicopters | + | + |
| UAE | tanks, combat aircraft | + | + |

# Table 12. Britain in the Middle East: Arms Sales, Advisors, Trainees, and Cooperation in Arms Production.

| Country | British Arms (major items) Granted or Sold | British Advisors Present | Trainees in Britain | Cooperation in arms production |
|---|---|---|---|---|
| Algeria | radars, target drones naval vessels | + | + | naval vessels |
| Bahrain | naval patrol craft | + | + | |
| Egypt | ATGMs, helicopter spares, radio transceivers | - | + | ATGMs, helicopter parts, tank guns, electronics |
| Iran | workshops, spare parts for tanks, radars | - | - | - |
| Iraq | electronic equipment, land rovers | - | + | - |
| Israel | spare parts | - | + | - |
| Jordan | combat engineering equipment, radars | - | + | upgrading of tanks |
| Kuwait | tanks, APCs, naval vessels, trainer aircraft | + | + | - |
| Libya | - | non gvt. personnel on individual basis | - | - |
| Morocco | artillery pieces | - | - | - |
| Oman | tanks, artillery pieces, combat and training aircraft, ground and a/c radars, MFPBs, landing craft, navigation systems | 1000, some seconded, others hired | + | - |
| Qatar | helicopters, SAMs | + | + | - |
| Saudi Arabia | combat and trainer aircraft, hovercraft, radio transceivers, helicopters, minesweepers on order | + | + | |
| Sudan | - | + | - | - |
| Tunisia | naval patrol craft, target drones, artillery pieces | - | - | - |
| UAE | APCs, artillery pieces, SAMs, workshops, trainer aircraft, tank transporters | - | + | - |

# Table 13.   Surface-to-Surface Missiles and Rockets in Service in Middle Eastern Armies (by Number of Launchers)

| Country | Model | | | | |
|---|---|---|---|---|---|
| | FROG 7/4 | SS-1 Scud | SS-21 Scarab | other | total number |
| Algeria | 24 | - | - | - | 25 |
| Egypt | + | + | - | | 24 |
| Iran | - | + | - | Iran-130 | not known |
| Iraq | 24 | 24+ | + | al-Huss-ein | 48+ |
| Israel | - | - | - | MGM-52C Lance, Jericho* | 12 ? |
| Libya | + | + | - | - | 100 |
| Saudi Arabia | - | - | - | CSS-2 | 20(?) |
| Syria | 24 | 18 | 18 | - | 60 |
| South Yemen (PDRY) | 12 | 6 | - | - | 18 |
| Yemen (YAR) | - | - | 4 | - | 4 |

*according to foreign sources

# Table 14. Major Arms Supply-Recipient Ties

| SUPPLIER | Brazil | Britain | France | FRG | Italy | PRC | Spain | USA | USSR |
|---|---|---|---|---|---|---|---|---|---|
| **RECIPIENT** | | | | | | | | | |
| Egypt | training aircraft | helicopters, ATGMs, tank guns, torpedoes, radio transceivers | combat aircraft, helicopters, SAMs, ATGMs, AAMs, night vision devices | mobile shelters, trucks | helicopters, ECM shipborne SAMs, air def. systems | combat aircraft, submarines, MFPBs, missile frigates, SAMs | APCs, trucks | combat aircraft, SAMs, APCs, tanks, EAV, naval SSMs, ATGMs, radars | spare parts |
| Iran | APCs, ARVs, MRLs | spares for tanks, workshops | artillery ammunition, spares, rubber boats | trucks | helicopters, AAGs, naval guns, ammunition, mines | combat aircraft, tanks, artillery, SAMs, coastal def. SSMs | -- | -- | AAGs, APCs, small arms, artillery (via intermediaries) |
| Iraq | APCs, ARVs, MRLs, trucks, trainer aircraft (via intermediaries) | electronic equipment, vehicles | combat aircraft, SAMs, ATGMs, AGMs, AAMs, spares, artillery | helicopters (with Spain), tank transporters | naval vessels, radars, small arms, artillery, helicopters | combat aircraft, tanks, artillery, antiship AGMs | helicopters (with FRG) | helicopters | combat aircraft, tanks, artillery, SAMs, SSMs, helicopters |
| Israel | -- | spares | spares | tank transporters | naval guns | -- | -- | combat aircraft, helicopters, tanks, artillery, SAMs | -- |

| SUPPLIER RECIPIENT | Brazil | Britain | France | FRG | Italy | PRC | Spain | USA | USSR |
|---|---|---|---|---|---|---|---|---|---|
| Jordan | -- | radars, combat enginee-ring equip-ment | combat aircraft, AAMs, AGMs, heli-copters | -- | -- | -- | trans-port aircraft, trainer air-craft | attack helicop-ters, tanks, artillery, ATGMs | SAMs, AAGs, APCs |
| Libya | APCs, ARVs, MRLs | -- | spares | aerial refue-lling sys-tems | electro-nics, spares | -- | ammu-nition, recoil-less rifles | -- | combat aircraft, tanks, SSMs, SAMs, naval vessels |
| Saudi Arabia | -- | training aircraft, hover-craft, ARVs, combat air-craft, radio trans-ceivers | APCs, SAMs, radar, helicop-ters, S.P. artille-ry | small arms, electro-nics, EW equip-ment | helicop-ters | -- | trans-port aircraft | combat aircraft, trans-port aircraft, AAMs, AWACS, artillery, AGMs, ATGMs | -- |
| Syria | -- | -- | helicop-ters, ATGMs | -- | -- | -- | -- | -- | combat aircraft, SAMs, SSMs, coastal missiles, tanks, subma-rines, artille-ry |

# GLOSSARY OF
# WEAPONS SYSTEMS

# ARMY

AA Guns, Short Range (caliber, designation, NATO codename
if relevant, SP when relevant, tracked or wheeled when
relevant, country of origin)
57mm ZSU 57x2 SP, tracked, USSR
57mm M-1950 (S-60), USSR
40mm M-42 (twin 40mm) SP, tracked, USA
40mm Bofors L-70, Sweden
40mm Bofors L-60, Sweden
37mm M-1939, USSR
35mm Contraves Skyguard, see below, Air Defense Systems
35mm Gepard SP, FRG
35mm Oerlikon-Buhrle 35x2 GDF-002, Switzerland; may be part
of 35mm Skyguard system
30mm AMX DCA 30 (twin 30mm) SP, tracked, France
30mm Artemis (twin 30mm), Greece, based on 30mm Mauser AAG,
FRG
30mm 30x2 M-53/59 SP, wheeled, Czechoslovakia
30mm Oerlikon, Switzerland
30mm 30x2 Wildcat SP, wheeled, FRG
23mm ZSU 23x4 (Gun Dish) SP, tracked, USSR (Soviet
designation Shilka)
23mm ZU 23x2, USSR
20mm TCM-20x2 SP (on M-3 halftrack), France (gun)/Israeli
mounting of gun on US-made halftrack
20mm Oerlikon GAI, Switzerland 20mm Hispano-Suiza, France
20mm M-163 A1 Vulcan SP, USA
20mm M-167 Vulcan, USA
20mm 20x2mm SP (mounted on Panhard VCR 6x6), France
20mm 20x3 M-55 A4, Yugoslavia
20mm VDAA SP (mounted on VAB 6x6), France


Air Defense Systems, short-range (caliber of gun,
designation, missiles, SP when relevant, country of
origin)
35mm Skyguard (Contraves Skyguard) 2x35, Aspide or RIM-7M
Sparrow SAM, SP, Italy (gun--Switzerland, SAM--Italy or
USA, chassis and radar--Italy or Austria; Egyptian
designation Amoun)
23mm Nile 23, 2x23, 4xSA-7, SP, Egypt (gun + SAM--USSR or
Egypt, chassis--USA, radar--France)
23mm Sinai 23, see 23mm Nile 23

<u>Anti-Tank Guns</u>    (caliber,    designation,    recoilless    if
   relevant, country of origin)
120mm BAT L-4 recoilless rifle, Britain
107mm B-11 recoilless rifle, USSR
106mm M-40 A1C/A2 recoilless rifle, USA/Israel
100mm M-1955 gun (field/AT gun), USSR; see    guns    and
   howitzers
90mm light gun, low recoil gun, Belgium; used on AFVs
85mm M-1945/D-44 field/AT gun, USSR; see guns and howitzers
84mm Carl Gustaf light recoilless rifle, Sweden
82mm B-10 recoilless rifle, USSR
73mm SPG-9 recoilless gun, USSR
76mm M-1942 divisional gun (ZIS-3), USSR; (field/AT gun,   see
   guns and howitzers)
75mm M-20 recoilless rifle, USA
57mm AT gun, Czechoslovakia


<u>APCs/ARVs</u> (designation, tracked or  wheeled,  APC  or  ARV,
   amphibious if relevant, ATGM equipped if relevant,   country
   of origin)
al-Walid, wheeled APC, Egypt
AML-60, wheeled ARV, France
AML-90, wheeled ARV, France
AMX-10 R/S/P, tracked, amphibious APC, France
AMX-VCI, tracked APC, France
AT-105 Saxon, wheeled APC, Britain
BMP-1, tracked, amphibious, ATGM-equipped APC, with 73mm gun,
   USSR
BMP-2, tracked, amphibious,  ATGM  equipped  APC,  with  30mm
   cannon, USSR
BMR-600, wheeled, amphibious APC, Spain
BRDM-2, wheeled, amphibious, ATGM-equipped ARV, USSR
BTR-40, wheeled, amphibious ARV, USSR
BTR-50, tracked, amphibious APC, USSR
BTR-60, wheeled, amphibious APC, USSR
BTR-152, wheeled APC, USSR
Cadillac  Gage  Commando   Scout,   ARV   (occasionally
   ATGM-equipped), USA
EBR-75, wheeled ARV, France
Eland,  wheeled  ARV,  South  Africa/licensed  production  of
   French AML-90/AML-60
Engesa EE-3 Jararaca, wheeled ARV, Brazil
Engesa EE-9 Cascavel, wheeled ARV, Brazil
Engesa EE-11 Urutu, wheeled, amphibious APC, Brazil
Engesa EE-17 Sucuri,  wheeled,  amphibious  tank  destroyer,
   Brazil
Fahd, wheeled APC, Egypt (FRG collaboration)
Ferret, wheeled ARV, Britain

Fiat Type 6614, wheeled, amphibious APC, Italy
Fiat Type 6616, wheeled, amphibious ATGM-equipped ARV, Italy
Fox, wheeled, amphibious ARV, Britain
FUG-70, see above, BRDM-2, usually without ATGM, Hungary
  (licensed production of Soviet BRDM-2)
M-2, half-tracked APC, USA
M-3, half-tracked APC--see M-2
M-3 (Panhard, VTT), wheeled, amphibious APC (occasionally
  4xHOT are added, see anti-tank missiles), France
M-8 (WWII Greyhound), ARV USA
M-125, derivative of M-113, 81mm mortar carrier, USA
M-901 ITV (TOW under armor), tracked, amphibious
  ATGM-equipped ARV (tank destroyer) (based on M-113 APC),
  USA; see also under ATGM
M-113 A1/A2, tracked, amphibious APC, USA/Italy (licensed
  production)
M-125, derivative of M-113, 81mm mortar carrier, USA
M-577/M-577 A1, tracked artillery command post vehicle (based
  on M-113 APC), USA
OT-62, APC, Czechoslovakia, see BTR-50
OT-64, wheeled APC, Czechoslovakia
RAM, wheeled ARV, Israel; improvement of RBY-2
Ratel 20, wheeled APC, South Africa
Ratel 90, same as Ratel 20 with a 90mm gun and turret, South
  Africa
RBY/RBY-2, wheeled ARV, Israel
Saladin, wheeled ARV, Britain
Saracen, wheeled APC, Britain
Shoreland Mk.2/Mk.3, wheeled ARV, Britain
Steyr 4K 7FA tracked APC, Austria
Type 77, Chinese copy of Soviet BTR-50, PRC; see BTR-50
UR-416, wheeled APC, FRG
V-150 Commando, wheeled, amphibious ATGM-equipped ARV/APC,
  USA
V-300, wheeled APC, USA
VAB, wheeled amphibious APC, France
VBC-90, wheeled ARV, France; derivative of VAB, with a 90mm
  gun
VCR/TH, wheeled, amphibious, ATGM-equipped APC/tank destroyer
  (see anti-tank missiles), France
YW-531, tracked, amphibious APC, PRC


Army Anti-Aircraft Defenses--missiles (designation, NATO
  codename if relevant, SP when relevant, man-portable if
  relevant, range, country of origin)
Ain al-Saqr (Egyptian-improved version of Soviet SA-7),
  man-portable, 4.4 km, Egypt
Blowpipe, man-portable, Britain
Crotale SP, 9 km, France; see also Shahine 2

FIM-92A Stinger, man-portable, 5.4 km, USA
MIM-43A Redeye, man-portable, 3 km, USA
MIM-72A Chaparral SP, 8 km, USA
Mistral (Matra Mistral), man-portable, 6 km, France
Rapier, 6 km, Britain
RBS-70, 5 km, Sweden
Roland, 6 km, France
SA-6 Gainful, SP, 3-21 km, USSR
SA-7 Grail , man-portable, 3.5 km (Soviet designation Strella), USSR
SA-8 Gecko, SP, 11 km, USSR
SA-9 Gaskin SP, 28 km, USSR
SA-11 Gadfly, SP, 28 km, USSR
SA-13 Gopher SP, 10 km, (Soviet designation Strella 10) USSR
SA-14 Gremlin, man-portable, 6-7 km (unconfirmed), USSR
Shahine 2/Crotale Shahine 2, SP, 13km, France; improvement of Crotale listed above
Shahine 2 ATTS (Air Transportable Towed System); a towed version of Shahine 2
Tigercat, Britain


Artillery ammunition carriers (designation, tracked or wheeled, armored, country of origin)
M-992, tracked USA
MT-LB, tracked, armored, USSR; also serves as prime mover for towed artillery


ATGMs (anti-tank guided missiles, designation, NATO codename if relevant, SP if relevant, range, country of origin)
AT-1 Snapper, 500-2300m., USSR
AT-2 Swatter, 600-2500m., USSR
AT-3 Sagger, 500-3000m. (Soviet designation Malyutka), USSR
AT-4 Spigot, 2000m., USSR
AT-5 Spandrell, USSR
AT-6 Spiral, USSR
BGM-71A TOW/BGM-71C Improved TOW, 65-3750m. (range of Improved TOW), USA
BGM-71D TOW II, USA; improvement of BGM-71C
BRDM-2 carrying AT-3 (Sagger) SP, 500-3000m., USSR
Dragon III, 1500m.,USA; improved M-47A
HOT, 75-4000m., France/FRG
HOT Commando, HOT mounted on a Peugeot P-4 4x4 jeep-like vehicle, France
Israeli BGM-71C Improved TOW SP, 65-3750m; derivative of M-113 APC, USA; missile and APC, USA; mounting and hydraulics--Israel
M-3 (Panhard) carrying HOT SP, 75-4000m., France; see also

APC

M-47A Dragon, 1000m., USA

M-901 ITV SP (TOW under armor), BGM-71A TOW, 65-3750m., derivative of M-113 APC, USA; see also APC/ARV

Mapats, 4500m., Israel; laser-beam riding Israeli improvement of US-made BGM-71A TOW

MILAN, 25-2000m., France/FRG

SS-11, 500-3000m., France

SS-12, 6000m., France (can be employed as ATGM or as anti-ship missile launched from ground, helicopter or ship)

Swingfire 300-4000m., Britain/Egypt

T-1/T-16 SP, ATGM system/tank destroyer (unconfirmed), USSR

Vigilant, 200-1375m., Britain

VCR/TH carrying HOT SP, 75-4000m., France; see also APC


Automatic grenade launchers (caliber, designation, country of origin)

40mm Mk.19, USA


Engineering equipment (designation, type, country of origin)

Bar mine-laying system, Britain

EWK pontoon bridge (Faltschwimmbrucke), FRG

Gilois motorized bridge, France

GSP self-propelled ferry, USSR

M-69 Al bridging tank, USA

M-123 Viper minefield-crossing system, USA

MT-55 bridging tank, USSR

MTU-55 bridging tank, USSR

PMP pontoon bridge, USSR

Pomins II, portable (infantry) mine neutralization system, Israel

PRP motorized bridge, USSR

TLB, trailer launched bridge, Israel


Guns & Howitzers (caliber, designation, SP if relevant, gun or howitzer, range, country of origin)

203mm/8" M-110 Al SP howitzer, 16.8 km, USA

203mm/8" M-115 (M-1) howitzer, 16.8 km, USA

180mm S-23 gun, 32 km, USSR

175mm M-107 SP gun, 32.7 km, USA

155mm Mk. F-3 (AMX) SP howitzer, 18 km, France

155mm FH-70 howitzer, 24 km, FRG

155mm G-5 gun/howitzer, 30 km, South Africa

155mm GCT SP howitzer, 23.5 km, France

155mm GHN-45 howitzer/gun, 17.8 km, Austria

155mm M-198 A1 howitzer, 18.1 km, USA
155mm M-114 A2 howitzer, 14.6 km, USA
155mm M-109 A1/A2 SP howitzer, 18.1 km, USA
155mm M-1950 howitzer, 17.5 km, France
155mm M-71 gun/howitzer, 24 km, Israel
155mm L-33 (Sherman/Soltam) SP howitzer, 21 km, Israel
155mm M-50 (Sherman) SP howitzer, 17.5 km, Israel
  (gun-France; chassis - USA, improved in Israel)
155mm M-44 SP howitzer, 14.6 km, USA
155mm M-59 (Long Tom) gun, 22 km, USA
155mm Palmaria SP howitzer, 24 km, Italy
152mm D-20 howitzer/gun, 18 km, USSR
152mm M-1943 (D-1) howitzer, USSR
152mm M-1973 SP howitzer, 18 km, USSR
130mm M-46 gun, 27.1 km, USSR
130mm Type 59 gun, 27.4 km, PRC; copy of Soviet 130mm M-46
122mm M-1974 SP howitzer, 15.3 km, USSR
122mm M-1938 howitzer, 11.8 km, USSR
122mm D-30 howitzer, 16 km, USSR
122mm D-30 SP howitzer, 16 km, USSR  (gun)/Egypt  (conversion
  to SP with British/US aid)
122mm ISU SP gun, 16 km, USSR
105mm Light Gun, 17.2 km, Britain
105mm M-108 SP howitzer, 11.5 km, USA
105mm M-102 A1 howitzer, 11.5 km, USA
105mm M-101 A1 howitzer, 11.3 km, USA
105mm M-56 Pack howitzer, 10.6 km, Italy
105mm M-52 SP howitzer, 11.3 km, USA
105mm Mk.61 SP howitzer, 15 km, France
100mm M-1955 gun, 21 km (field/AT gun), USSR
100mm SU-100 SP gun, USSR
25 lb. (87mm) howitzer, 12.2 km, Britain
85mm M-1945/D-44 gun, 15.8 km (field/AT gun), USSR
76mm M-1942 divisional gun (ZIS-3), 13.3 km, USSR


Light ATRLs   (designation, effective range, country of
  origin)
APILAS (APILAS Manurhin), 400m., France
LAW-80, 500m., Britain
M-72 A1/A2 LAW, 300m., USA
RPG-2, 150m., USSR
RPG-7, 500m., USSR
89mm M-65, Spain
89mm Strim-89, 360m., France
3.5" M-20 (Bazooka), 110m., USA

Machine Guns (caliber, designation, type, country of origin)

14.5mm KPV HMG, USSR
14.5mm ZPU 14.5x4 HMG, USSR; employed in anti-aircraft role
14.5mm ZPU 14.5x2 HMG, USSR; employed in anti-aircraft role
12.7mm D.Sh.K. 38/46 (Degtyarev) HMG, USSR
12.7mm (0.5") Browning M2 HMG, USA
7.62mm Aswan MMG, Egypt; a copy of Soviet 7.62mm SG-43
7.62mm MAG (FN) LMG, Belgium
7.62mm PK/PKS (Kalashnikov) LMG, USSR
7.62mm PKT (Kalashnikov) LMG, USSR
7.62mm RPD (Degtyarev) LMG, USSR
7.62mm RPK LMG, USSR
7.62mm Suez, Egypt; copy of Soviet 7.62mm RPD
7.62mm (0.3") Browning M-1919 MMG, USA
7.62mm (0.3") BAR (Browning) LMG, USA
7.62mm MG 1A1/1A3 LMG, Iran (licensed production of FRG's MG-3)
7.62mm M-60 D GPMG/LMG, USA
7.62mm SG-43 (Goryunov) MMG, USSR
7.62mm SGM (Goryunov) MMG, USSR
7.5mm AA-52/M2 MMG, France
7.5mm Chatellerault M-24/29 LMG, France
5.56mm Minimi (FN) LMG, Belgium


Mortars, heavy (caliber, designation, SP if relevant, range, country of origin)

240mm M-240, 9.7 km, USSR
160mm M-43/53, 5.1 km, USSR
160mm M-66 SP, 9.3 km, Israel
120mm M-43, 5.7 km, USSR
120mm Brandt M-50/M-60, 6.6 km (unconfirmed), France
120mm M-65, 6.3 km, Israel; also available as SP, mounted on US-made M-2 halftrack
107mm (4.2") M-30 SP/towed (SP on M-106 A2 carrier, a derivative of M-113 APC), 5.6 km, USA


Mortars, light and medium (caliber, designation, range, country of origin)

82mm M-41/43, 2550 m., USSR
81mm Hotchkiss Brandt, 4550 m. (unconfirmed), France
81mm M-29, 4590 m., USA
81mm Soltam, 4100 m. (short barrel), 4900 m. (long barrel), Israel
81mm ECIA, Spain
81mm L-16 A1, 5660 m., Britain
60mm Hotchkiss-Brandt, 2050 m., France

60mm M-2, 2550 m., Israel
60mm M-19, 1810 m., USA
52mm IMI, 420 m., Israel


MRLs (caliber, designation, number of launchers, range, country of origin)
300mm SS-60, 4, 68 km, Brazil
290mm (MAR 290), 4, 25 km (unconfirmed), Israel
262mm Ababil, Iraq
240mm BM-24, 12, 10.2 km, USSR
230mm Oghab, 3, 40 km (unconfirmed), Iran; copy of PRC's Type 83 273mm rocket
180mm SS-40 Astros II, 16, 35 km, Brazil
140mm BM-14-16, 16, 9.8 km, USSR
140mm RPU-14, 16, 9.8 km, USSR
140mm Teruel, 40, 18.2 km, Spain
132mm BM-13-16, 16, 9 km, USSR
130mm M-51 (=130mm RM-130), 32, 8.2 km, Romania/USSR
130mm M-51, 32, 8.2 km, Czechoslovakia
130mm Type 63, 19, 10.4 km, PRC
127mm SS-30 Astros II, 32, 30 km, Brazil
122mm BM-11, 30, North Korea; a variant of Soviet BM-21
122mm BM-21, 40, 20.8 km, USSR
122mm RM-70, 40, 20.4 km, Czechoslovakia; similar to Soviet BM-21
122mm Saqr 30, 22.5 km, Egypt
122mm Saqr 10 and Saqr 18, short range versions of Saqr 30, Egypt
107mm RM-11, 8.1 km, North Korea


Personal Weapons (caliber, designation, type, country of origin)
11mm (0.45") M-3 Al SMG, USA
9mm Aqaba SMG, Egypt (improved Port Sa'id)
9mm Carl Gustaf Model 45 SMG, Sweden
9mm L-34 Al SMG, Britain
9mm MAT 49/56 SMG, France
9mm Mini Uzi SMG, Israel
9mm Model 12 Beretta SMG, Italy
9mm Model 23/25 SMG, Czechoslovakia
9mm Model 38/49 Beretta SMG, Italy
9mm Port Sa'id SMG, Egypt (copy of Swedish Carl Gustaf)
9mm P.P.Sh. 41/42/43 SMG, USSR (also available in 7.62mm caliber)
9mm Sterling Mk.4 SMG, Britain
9mm Uzi SMG, Israel
9mm Vigneron M2 SMG, Belgium
7.62mm AK-47/AKM (Kalashnikov) AR, USSR

7.62mm FAL (FN) SAR, Belgium
7.62mm L-1 Al SAR, Britain
7.62mm FAC (FN) SAR, Belgium; similar to 7.62mm CAL/FAL, above
7.62mm FAL (FN) SAR, Belgium; same as 7.62mm CAL/FAL, above
7.62mm Galil sniper rifle, Israel
7.62mm G-3 (Heckler & Koch) AR, FRG/Iran (licensed production)
7.62mm M-1 Garand SAR, USA
7.62mm M-14 SAR, USA
7.62mm Rashid SAR, Egypt
7.62mm SKS (Simonov) SAR, USSR
7.62mm SSG-69 sniper rifle (Steyr), Austria
7.62mm Type 56 AR, PRC; Chinese copy of Soviet AK-47
7.5mm MAS 49/56 SAR, France
5.56mm AR-180 SAR, USA
5.56mm AUG Steyr AR, Austria
5.56mm CAL (FN) AR, Belgium
5.56mm Galil AR, Israel
5.56mm HK-33 (Heckler & Koch) AR, FRG
5.56mm M-16 Al/A2 AR, USA
5.56mm SG-540 AR, Switzerland


Recovery Vehicles (designation, APC/tank chassis, country of origin)
M-578 Al APC, USA
M-88 Al Recovery Tank, USA
T-55 Recovery Tank, USSR
T-62 Recovery Tank, USSR


Surface-to-Surface Tactical Missiles and Rockets (designation, NATO codename if relevant, range, circular error probability (CEP), payload, country of origin)
al-Hussein (Iraqi modified SS-1), 600-700 km, 180kg (unconfirmed), USSR/Iraq
CSS-2 IRBM, 2500-4000 km, PRC
FROG-4, 45 km, USSR
FROG-7 (Soviet designation Luna), 60 km, 450 kg, 500m, USSR
Iran-130, 130 km, Iran
Jericho I, 450 km (unconfirmed; according to foreign publications), Israel
Jericho II, 800 km (unconfirmed; according to foreign publications), Israel
MGM-52C Lance, 75 km (with conventional warhead), USA
M-9, 600 km (unconfirmed), PRC
Saqr 80, 80 km, 200 kg, Egypt; launched from FROG-7 launcher
SS-1 Scud B, 280 km, 800-1000 kg, 1000m, USSR
SS-21 Scarab, 80 km, 100m, USSR

Tanks (designation, caliber of gun, weight, country of origin)

AMX-13 LT, 75mm/105mm, 14.5 ton, France

AMX-30 MBT, 105mm, 36 ton, France

Centurion MBT, 105mm, 52 ton, Britain

Chieftain Mk.3/Mk.5 MBT, 120mm, 52.3 ton, Britain

Khalid--Jordanian designation for Chieftain; see above

M-41 LT, 76.2mm, 24 ton, USA

M-47 A1/2/5 MBT, 90mm, 44 ton, USA

M-48 A1/5 Patton MBT, 90mm/105mm, 46.6 ton, USA

M-60/M-60 A1/A2/A3 MBT, 105mm, 49 ton, USA

M-77 MBT (improved Soviet T-55), Romania

Merkava Mk.1/Mk.2 MBT, 105mm, 56 ton, Israel

Merkava Mk.3 MBT, 120mm, 59 ton, Israel

OF-40 Lion MBT, 105mm, 43 ton, Italy; heavily reliant on FRG's Leopard 1 in design and components

Osorio (EE-T1) MBT, 105mm/120mm, Brazil

PT-76 amphibious LT, 76mm, 14 ton, USSR

Ramses II MBT, 105mm, 36 ton (unconfirmed), Egypt; a Soviet T-54/T-55 upgraded with USA model gun and USA stabilizer, laser range finder, fire control and night vision

Scorpion LT, 76mm, 7.8 ton, Britain

SK-105 (Kurassier; also Jagdpanzer) LT/tank destroyer, 105mm, 18 ton, Austria

T-34 Medium Tank, 85mm, 32 ton, USSR

T-54 B/C MBT, 100mm, 36 ton, USSR

T-55 B/C/D MBT, 100mm, 36 ton, USSR

T-62 MBT, 115mm, 37.5 ton, USSR

T-72 MBT, 125mm, 41 ton, USSR

Type-59 (=T-55), PRC

Type-62 Medium Tank, 85mm, 21 ton, PRC

Type-69, improved Type-59, above, PRC

Vickers Mk.1 MBT, 105mm, 38.1 ton, Britain

# AIR FORCE

AA Guns, Long Range (caliber, designation, country of origin)
100mm M-49, USSR
85mm M-44, USSR

AAMs (designation, NATO codename if relevant, guidance systems, effective range, country of origin)
AA-1 Alkali, semi-active radar guidance, 6-8 km, USSR
AA-2 Atoll, infra-red homing, 5-6.5 km, USSR
AA-2 Advanced Atoll, active radar homing, 5-6.5 km, USSR
AA-6 Acrid, infra-red guidance, 37 km, USSR
AA-7 Apex, infra-red or semi-active guidance, 27 km, USSR
AA-8 Aphid, 5-7.4 km, USSR
AA-10 Alamo, radar homing, 20-34 km, USSR
AIM-7/AIM-7E/F Sparrow III, semi-active radar guidance, 44 km, USA
AIM-9B Sidewinder, infra-red homing, now obsolete, USA
AIM-9E/F Sidewinder, infra-red guidance, USA; improvement of AIM-9B
AIM-9J Sidewinder, USA; advanced version of AIM-9E with enhanced dogfight capability
AIM-9L Sidewinder, infra-red guidance and active laser fuse, 18 km, USA
AIM-9M Sidewinder, similar to AIM-9L, with improved target acquisition and lock-on capabilities, USA
AIM-9P/P4 Sidewinder, improvement of AIM-9B, USA
AIM-54A Phoenix, semi-active radar guidance and fully active radar during terminal guidance, 44 km, USA
Firestreak, infra-red homing, 1.8 km, Britain
Python 3, infra-red guidance, 15 km, Israel
Red Top, infra-red homing, 12 km, Britain
R-530 (Matra R-530), infra-red guidance version/semi-active radar version, 18 km, France
R-550 Magique, infra-red guidance, 10 km, France
Shafrir, infra-red guidance, 5 km, Israel
Super 530D (improved R-530), semi-active homing radar, 25 km, France

Air-to-Ground Missiles (AGMs) (designation, NATO codename if relevant, function, guidance, range, country of origin)
AGM-45A/B Shrike, anti-radar/SAM sites, radar-guidance, 12-16 km, USA
AGM-62A Walleye, anti-ship/airbase/bridge, TV-guided, USA
AGM-65A/B Maverick, anti-tank/hard target, TV-guided, USA

AGM-65C Maverick (=65A/B guided by Laser designator), USA

AGM-78D Standard ARM anti-radar/⌐AM site, passive radar homing, USA

AGM-84, anti-ship missile, air-launched variant of RGM-84A Harpoon SSM, USA; see Navy

AGM-114 Hellfire, helicopter-borne, ATGM, guidance by Laser designator, USA

ALARM, air-launched anti-radar missile, Britain

AM-39, anti-ship, radio and radar guided, 50-70 km, France; air-launched derivative of the MM-38 & MM-40 Exocet SSMs

Armat, air launched anti-radar missile, homing on radar emission, France; enhanced successor version of French-British AS-37

AS-1 Kennel, anti-ship/hard target, radar guidance, 90 km, USSR

AS-2 Kipper, autopilot command override, active terminal homing, 160 km, USSR

AS-4 Kitchen, inertial guidance with radar terminal homing, 400 km, USSR

AS-5 Kelt, anti-ship and hard target, radar guidance, 160 km, USSR

AS-6 Kingfish, inertial guidance, 240 km, USSR

AS-11, anti-ship, wire-guided (optical/tracked navigation), 3 km, France, helicopter-launched anti-ship & anti-tank version of SS-11 ATGM

AS-12, anti-ship, wire-guided (optical/tracked navigation), 6 km, France; helicopter-launched anti-ship version of the SS-12 ATGM

AS-15TT, anti-ship, radar and radio-guided, 14.4 km, France; helicopter-launched

AS-30, radio-guided, 11.2 km, France

AS-30L, laser-guided, France

LX, anti-ship missile (unconfirmed), USSR

Sea Eagle, anti-ship missile, inertial navigation and radar homing, 100 km, Britain

X-23, anti-radiation missile (unconfirmed), USSR


Aircraft, Bombers (designation, NATO codename, maximum speed, range, armament, country of origin)

H-6 (B-6D), Chinese copy of Soviet Tu-16, PRC IL-28 Beagle, 900 km/h., 2260 km, 2040 kg. bombs, 4x23mm gun, USSR

Tu-16 Badger, 945 km/h., 4800 km, Kelt AGM/9000 kg. bombs, 2x2x23mm gun, USSR

Tu-22 Blinder, Mach 1.4, 2250 km, Kitchen AGM and bombs, 1x23mm gun, USSR

Aircraft, Interceptors (designation, NATO codename if relevant, maximum speed, combat radius, armament, country of origin)

F-6 Shenyang (=MiG-19), PRC; see also aircraft, strike & multi-role, & MiG-19, below

F-7 Shenyang (=MiG-21), PRC; see MiG-21, below

F-14A Tomcat, Mach 2.4, 4xAIM-7 or 4xAIM-54A Phoenix + 4xAIM-9, 1x20mm gun, USA

F-15A/B/C/D Eagle, Mach 2.5+, 1000 km, 4xAIM-7/4xAIM-9, 1x20mm gun, USA

FT-6, PRC; two-seat training version of F-6; also JJ-6, Chinese copy of Soviet MiG-19 UTI

MiG-19 PF/PFM Farmer C/D, 1452 km/h., 685 km, 2xAA-2 Atoll AAM, 2 or 3x30mm gun, USSR

MiG-21 MF/S/U Fishbed, Mach 2.1, 1100 km, 2xAA-2 Atoll AAM/Advanced Atoll, 1x23mm gun, USSR

MiG-23 MF Flogger B/E, Mach 2.3, 1200 km, 5xAA-7 Apex/AA-8 Aphid AAM, 1x23mm gun, USSR

MiG-25 Foxbat A/B/E/U, Mach 2.8, 1450 km, 4xAA-8 Aphid/AA-6 Acrid AAM, USSR

MiG-25R, reconnaissance version of MiG-25

Mirage III C/E/BL/EL, Mach 2.2, 1200 km, 1xR530/2xAIM-9, 2x30mm gun, France

Su-27 Flanker A, Mach 2.3, 1500 km, 6-8xAA-10 AAM, 23mm gun, USSR

Tornado (Panavia Tornado) ADV, Mach 2.2, radius 620 km, AIM-9L, Sky Flash AAM, 1x27mm Mauser cannon, Britain, FRG and Italy (joint production); see also Aircraft, Strike and Multi-Role

Xian J-7, Chinese copy of MiG-21, PRC; export version designated F-7 Shenyang, see above


Aircraft, Maritime Surveillance (designation, jet/turboprop, speed, endurance, range, sonar, radar, country of origin)

EMB-111N Bandeirante, based on EMB-110 transport aircraft, turboprop, 360 km/h., 2940 km, sea patrol radar, Brazil

P-3 Orion, turboprop, 608 km/h., 3 hours on station, 3835 km, sonar (ARR-72), APS-115 radar, USA; may carry depth bombs

Westwind I/Sea Scan/ 1124 Sea Scan, based on Westwind 1124, maritime reconnaissance aircraft, 872 km/h., 6 hrs. 30 min. endurance, equipped with search radar, Israel


Aircraft, Miscellaneous (designation, NATO codename if relevant, derivation if relevant, function, speed, range, radar range, country of origin)

Beechcraft 1900C, derivative of commuter/light transport

aircraft to be employed in Egypt in ELINT and/or maritime
surveillance role, USA; see Aircraft, Transport
E-3A Sentry, AWACS, Boeing 707, 853 km/h., 6 hrs. endurance,
radar range 370 km, USA
E-2C Hawkeye, AEW, 602 km/h., 6 hrs. 6 min. endurance, radar
range 250 km, USA
IA-58/IA-66 Pucara, counter-insurgency/trainer (turboprop),
2x20mm gun, 4x7.62mm MG, 1000 kg. bombs, Argentina
OV-10 Bronco (also Rockwell OV-10 Bronco),
counter-insurgency/surveillance aircraft, FLIR sensor,
laser designator, 272 kg. weapon pods/20mm guns/bombs, 463
km/h., 367 km (combat radius with weapon load), USA
Tu-126 Moss, AWACS, Tu-114, 850 km/h., 12,550 km, USSR


Aircraft, Strike and Multi-Role (designation, NATO codename
if relevant, maximum speed, combat radius/range, armament,
country of origin)
A-4 A/B/D/E/J/KU Skyhawk, 1085 km/h., 3200 km, 2x20mm gun,
4,500 kg. bombs, USA (A-4E data)
F-4 D/E Phantom, Mach 2+, 1145 km, 4xAIM-7 + 4xAIM-9, 1x20mm
gun, 7250 kg. bombs, USA
F-4 Shenyang (=MiG-17), PRC, see MiG-17
F-5 A/B/E/F (Tiger II), Mach 1.64, 890 km, 2xAIM-9, 2x20mm
gun, 3.17 ton bombs, USA (F-5E data)
F-6 Shenyang, PRC (Chinese copy of Soviet MiG-19
interceptor); see MiG-19 under aircraft, interceptors
F-16 A/B/C/D Fighting Falcon, Mach 1.95, 925 km, 2xAIM-9,
1x20mm gun, 6.8 ton bombs, USA
Hawker Hunter FGA-6/F-70/FR-10/T-66/T-67, Mach 0.8, 4x30mm
gun, 0.5 ton bombs, Britain
J-1 Jastreb, light attack version of SOKO G-2 Galeb; see
aircraft, training
Kfir C-2/TC-2/C-7/TC-7, Mach 2.3, 768 km, 2xShafrir AAM,
2x30mm gun, 3150 kg. bombs, Israel
MiG-15 Faggot, 1070 km/h., 1400 km, 1x37mm gun, 2x23mm gun,
USSR; also employed as advanced trainer
Mig-17 Fresco, 1145 km/h., 1400 km, 1x37mm gun, 2x23mm gun,
500 kg. bombs, USSR
MiG-23 S/BN/U Flogger A/F/C/S/G, Mach 2.3, 1200 km, AA-7 Apex
& AA-8 Aphid AAMs, 1x23mm twin barrel gun, USSR; see also
Aircraft, Interceptors
MiG-27 Flogger D, Mach 1.6, ca. 500 km, AA-7 Apex & AA-8
Aphid AAMs, 1x23mm twin barrel gun, USSR
MiG-29 Fulcrum, Mach 2.8 (unconfirmed), USSR
Mirage 5/50, Mach 2.2, 1300 km, 2xAIM-9 AAM/2xR-530, 2x30mm
gun, up to 4000 kg. bombs, France
Mirage F-1 B/C/D/E, Mach 2.2, AIM-9/R-530 and R-550 Magique,
AS-30 AGM, 2x30mm gun, 3600 kg. bombs, France
Mirage F-1 EQ5, same aircraft as F-1E, equipped to fire AM-39

Exocet ASM, France

Mirage 2000, Mach 2.2+, 1480 km with external tanks and bombs, 2xSuper R-530 AAM and 2xR-550 Magique AAM, 2x30mm gun, up to 5000 kg. bombs, France

RF-4E Phantom, reconnaissance version of F-4E

RF-5E Northrop Tiger II, a reconnaissance/photography version of F-5E (unarmed), USA

SEPECAT Jaguar S/E-01, Mach 1.6, 1408 km, 2xR-550 Magique or 2xAIM-9 AAM or AS-37 AGM, 1-2x30mm gun, 3600 kg. bombs, Britain and France

Su-7 BM/U Fitter A/B, Mach 1.6, 480 km, 2x30mm gun, 1 ton bombs, USSR

Su-20/22 Fitter C, Mach 2.17, 630 km, AA-2 Atoll AAMs, 2x30mm gun, 4000 kg. bombs, USSR

Su-24 Fencer C, Mach 2.18, 1800 km, 11,000 kg. bombs/AGMs including AS-7 Kerry AGM, one gun, USSR

Su-25 Frogfoot, 880 km/h., 556 km, AA-2 Atoll/AA-8 Aphid AAMs, 30mm guns, maximum armament and bomb load 4 tons, USSR

TA-4 KU, USA--see A-4; designation of advanced two-seat training aircraft for Kuwait

Tornado (Panavia Tornado) IDS, Mach 2.2, 1390 km with heavy weapons load, AIM-9, AGM-65/AS-30 AGM/CBU-15, 2x27mm gun, maximum armament and bomb load 8.1 tons, Britain, FRG and Italy (joint production); see also Aircraft, Interceptors


Aircraft, Tanker (aerial refuelling) (designation, derivation, fuel load, country of origin)

Boeing 707 Tanker, USA--see KC-135; also a Boeing 707 made in USA, converted to aerial refuelling role in Israel

KC-135A Stratotanker, Boeing 707, USA

KC-130H, C-130H Hercules, 23,923 liter, USA

KE-3A, similar to KC-135A, USA; designation of aircraft for Saudi Arabia


Aircraft, Training and Liaison (designation, jet, turboprop or piston engine, ground attack capability if relevant, country of origin)

Aermacchi MB-326 B/KT/LT, jet, ground attack capability, Italy

Aermacchi MB-339, jet, ground attack capability, Italy

al-Gumhuriya, piston, Egypt (German/Spanish model)

Alpha Jet, jet, ground attack capability, France & West Germany/Egypt-assembly

Alpha Jet MS-2, same as Alpha Jet, licensed production in Egypt with improved ground attack and naval attack capabilities

AS-202/18A Bravo and AS-202/26A, piston, Switzerland

BAC-145 Jet Provost, jet, ground attack capability, Britain
BAC-167 Strikemaster Mk.82/Mk.83, jet, ground attack capability, Britain; development of BAC-145
BAe Jetstream 31, turboprop, Britain; a transport aircraft employed for cockpit training for Tornado aircrews
BAe-SA-3-120 Bulldog series 125/126, piston, Britain (formerly Scottish Aviation B-125 Bulldog and Beagle B-125 Bulldog)
Beechcraft Bonanza F-33A and V-35B, piston, USA
Beechcraft T-34C Turbo Mentor, turboprop, USA
Broussard, piston, France
Cessna 172 G/H/L, piston, USA
Cessna 182 Skylane, piston, USA
Cessna 185 Skywagon, piston, USA; same as Cessna U-206
Cessna 318 (T-37), jet, USA
Cessna U-206 Skywagon, piston, USA
CM-170 Fouga Magister, jet, ground attack capability, France/Israel (assembly)
Embraer EMB-312 (T-27), turboprop, Brazil; produced under license by Egypt and Britain; also designated Tucano T-27
FT-6, trainer, two-seat version of F-6 (interceptor), PRC; see interceptors
Galeb--see SOKO
Gepal IV (AMIN Gepal IV), turboprop, Morocco
Grob G-109B, ultra-light, FRG
Hawk, jet, ground attack capability, Britain
L-29 Delfin, jet, ground attack capability, Czechoslovakia
L-39 Albatross, jet, ground attack capability, Czechoslovakia
MBB-223 Flamingo/MBB-Flamingo, piston, FRG/Spain; produced in FRG by MBB or SIAT, and in Spain by CASA
MiG-15 UTI--see Aircraft, Strike and Multi-Role
Pilatus PC-6 Turbo-Porter, turboprop, Switzerland
Pilatus PC-7 Turbo-Trainer, turboprop, Switzerland
Pilatus PC-9, turboprop, Switzerland
Piper Cub/Piper/PA-18 Super Cub, piston, USA
Piper PA-44, USA
Piper Navajo (PA-31), USA
PZL-104 Wilga 35/80, piston, Poland
Rockwell T-6 (Texan, Harvard), piston, USA
SIAI-Marchetti SF-260M/WT/C/L Warrior, piston, Italy
SIAI-Marchetti S-208A, piston, Italy
SOKO G-2A/G-2AE Galeb, jet, ground attack capability, Yugoslavia; J-1 Jastreb derived from G-2A for light attack roles and advanced training
Strikemaster--see BAC-167 Strikemaster
T-33, jet, ground attack capability, USA
Tzukit, (French) CM-170 Fouga Magister upgraded by Israel (strengthened frame and new avionics)

YAK-11 Moose, piston, USSR
YAK-18 Max, piston, USSR


Aircraft, Transport and Executive    (designation,    NATO
codename if relevant,  piston,  turboprop  or  jet  engine,
maximum   cruising   speed,    range,    load,   accommodation,
paratroop  dropping  capability  if  relevant,  country  of
origin)
An-2  Colt,  piston,  200  km/h.,    905    km,    1240    kg./14
paratroopers, USSR
An-12  Cub,  turboprop,  670  km/h.,  3600  km,  20  ton/100
paratroopers, USSR
An-24 Coke, turboprop,  450  km/h.,   640   km,  5700  kg./  38
passengers or 30 paratroopers, USSR
An-26 Curl, turboprop, 440 km/h., 1100 km,  5500  kg./  38-40
passengers, USSR
Arava (IAI 101/201/202 Arava), turboprop, 319 km/h.,  630  km,
2351 kg./24 passengers/16  paratroopers,  Israel  (IAI  202
data)
BAe-111 (BAC-111), jet, 870 km/h., 3013  km,  10,733  kg./119
passengers, Britain
BAe-125 (also known as HS-125),  jet,  845  km/h.,  5318  km,
1088kg./2 pilots + 14 passengers, Britain
Beechcraft  1900C,  turboprop,  435  km/h.,    1469    km,    19
passengers/EW/CEW  equipment,  USA;  a  commuter  aircraft
employed in EW/CEW and/or  maritime  surveillance  role  in
Egypt
Beechcraft King Air B-100, turboprop, 486 km/h., 2232 km,  13
passengers, USA
Beechcraft Queen Air, turboprop, 370  km/h.,  2520  km,  1599
kg./9 passengers, USA; an executive aircraft
Beechcraft Super King Air, turboprop, 536 km/h., 3,658 km, 14
passengers, USA
Boeing 707/707-200/707-320,  jet,   973   km/h.,  7700  km,  43
ton/180 passengers, USA
Boeing 720/720B/720B-023B,  jet,  897  km/h.,  6690  km,  112
passengers, USA
Boeing 727, jet, 960 km/h., 14,740 kg./131 passengers, USA
Boeing KC-135--see Boeing 707, aerial refuelling aircraft
Boeing 737/737-200, jet,  943  km/h.,  3521  km,  15  ton/115
passengers, USA
Boeing 747/747-200B/747-200C, jet, 967 km/h., 10,562 km,  160
ton/450 passengers, USA
Britten-Norman  BN-2A  Islander/Pilatus  BN-2B  Islander  II,
piston,   251    km/h.,    1530    km,   10    passengers,
Britain/Switzerland
C-47--see DC-3 Dakota
C-119, piston, 315 km/h. 725  km,  10  ton/67  troops,  fewer

paratroopers, USA

C-130H-30, stretched version of C-130H, see L-100-30

C-130 E/H Hercules, turboprop, 621 km/h., 3791 km (maximum payload), 19,685 kg./92 paratroopers, USA

C-140 Jetstar, jet, 885 km/h., 3185 km, 1360 kg./10 passengers, USA

C-212--see CASA C-212 Aviocar

Caravelle Super B, 835 km/h., 2,725 km, 9,265 kg./ 104 passengers, France

CASA C-212-5 series 100/C-212 series 200 Aviocar, turboprop, 365 km/h., 408 km, 2770 kg./24 passengers/23 paratroopers, Spain/Indonesia (licensed production)

CASA/Nurtanio CN-235 (also Airtech CN-235), turboprop, 454 km/h., 796 km, 3,575 kg./39 passengers/30 paratroopers, Spain/Indonesia; Airtech is company jointly owned by CASA (Spain) and Nurtanio (Indonesia)

Cessna 310, piston, 361 km/h., 2842 km, 6 passengers, USA

CN-235--see CASA/Nurtanio CN-235

DC-3 Dakota (C-47), piston, 220 km/h., 500 km, 2.5 ton/24 paratroopers, USA

DC-8, jet, Mach 0.8, 11,410 km, 30,240 kg./ 189 passengers, USA

DC-9, jet, 907 km/h., 3095 km, 14,118 kg./119 passengers, USA

DC-10, jet, 925 km/h.. 7,400 km, 43.3 ton/380 passengers, USA

DHC-4/DHC-4A Caribou, piston, 293 km/h., 2,103 km, 3965 kg./32 passengers/26 paratroopers, Canada

DHC-5/DHC-5D Buffalo, turboprop, 467 km/h., 1112 km, 8,164 kg./41 passengers, Canada

DHC-6 Twin Otter, turboprop, 338 km/., 1297 km, 1940 kg./20 passengers, Canada

Dornier Do-28 D/Do-28 D2 Skyservant, piston, 286 km/h., 2875 km, 1000 kg./13 passengers, FRG

Dornier Do-228-100, turboprop, 432 km/h., 1,970 km, 2.2 ton/15 passengers, FRG

EMB-110/EMB-110 P2 Bandeirante, turboprop, 417 km/h., 1900 km, 1681 kg./21 passengers, Brazil

EMB-121 Xingu, turboprop, 450 km/h., 2,352 km, 1,477 kg./9 passengers, Brazil; an executive aircraft Falcon 20--see Mystere-Falcon 20

Fokker F-27 Mk.400/F-27 Mk.600, turboprop, 480 km/h., 1926/1935 km, 5727/5696 kg/40/44 passengers, Netherlands

Fokker F-27 Mk.400M, military version of F-27 Mk.400, 46 paratroopers, Netherlands

Fokker F-28, jet, 843 km/h., 1900 km, 10,478 kg./85 passengers, Netherlands

G 222L, turboprop, 439 km/h., 2409 km, 9000 kg./53 passengers/42 paratroopers, Italy

Gates Learjet 35, jet, 872 km/h., 4200 km, 8 passengers, USA

Gulfstream II, jet, 0.85 Mach, 6,579 km, 8 passengers, USA; an executive jet

Hawker Siddeley Dove, piston, 338 km/h., 620 km, 670 kg./11 passengers, Britain

IL-14 Crate, piston, 358 km/h., 2600 km, 5.3 ton/18 passengers/paratroopers, USSR

IL-18 Coot, turboprop, 675 km/h., 4,700 km, 13,500 kg./122 passengers, USSR

IL-76 Candid, jet, 800 km/h., 6700 km, 40 ton/over 100 passengers, USSR

L-100-20, turboprop, 581 km/h., 3889 km (maximum payload), 21,130 kg./92 paratroopers (optional), USA; civilian or military stretched Hercules

L-100-30, turboprop, 583 km/h., 3326 km (maximum payload), 23,014 kg./passengers--not less than L-100-20, USA; civilian or military stretched Hercules

L-410 UVP, turboprop, 360 km/h., 540km, 1300 kg./2 crew + 19 passengers, Czechoslovakia

MD-315 Flamant, piston, 147 km/h., 10 passengers, France

Merlin IV (corporate version of Metro III), turboprop, 524 km/h., 1805 km, 13-16 passengers, USA

Mystere Falcon 10, jet, 900 km/h., 3,370 km, 7 passengers, France; an executive jet

Mystere Falcon 20, jet, 855 km/h., 4170 km, 1180 kg./7 passengers, France; an executive jet

Mystere Falcon 50, jet, 800 km/h., 6480 km, 8 passengers, France; an executive jet

Sabreliner 75A, jet, Mach. 0.80, 3,173 km, 10 passengers, USA; an executive jet

Short SC-7 Skyvan Srs. 3M, turboprop, 327 km/h., 1075 km, 2358 kg./22 passengers/16 paratroopers, Britain

Tu-124/Tu-134 Crusty, jet, 885 km/h., 3020 km, 8,200 kg./84 passengers, USSR

Turbo-Commander 690B, turboprop, 532 km/h., 11 passengers, USA

Westwind I/Westwind 1124, jet, 872 km/h., 4490 km, 10 passengers, Israel; an executive jet

Yak-40 Codling, jet, 550 km/h., 2,000 km, 2,720 kg./ 32 passengers, USSR


Bombs, Advanced (designation, function, weight, country of origin)

Belouga Dispenser Weapon (BLG-66) Cluster Bomb Unit (CBU), anti-personnel & AFV, 290 kg., France

BL-755 Cluster Bomb, France

Cardoen CBU, cluster bomb, Chile

CBU-7A Cluster Bomb, USA

CBU-55 Cluster Bomb, anti-personnel, USA

Durandal Penetration Bomb, anti-runway bomb, 195 kg., France

JP-233 anti-runway bomb, Britain
Rockeye Cluster Bomb Mk.20, anti-tank CBU, USA


Helicopters, ASW
A-109/AS-109--see Helicopters, Attack
AB-212/Bell 212--see Helicopters, Medium Transport
Kamov Ka-25 Hormone--see Helicopters, Medium Transport
Mi-14 Haze, USSR
SH-3D (=Westland S-61), USA--see Helicopters, Heavy
  Transport
Westland Sea King HAS Mk.1/S-61A/AS-61A--see Helicopters,
  Heavy Transport
Westland Sea King Mk.47--nearly identical to Westland Sea
  King HAS Mk.1


Helicopters, Attack (designation, NATO codename if
  relevant, max. speed, range, armament, country of origin)
Agusta A-109A, 311 km/h., 583 km, 4-8 BGM-71C Improved TOW,
  2-3x7.62mm MG., 1x12.7mm HMG, 12x68mm rockets, Italy; a
  variant employed in ASW and/or naval attack role
AH-1S/AH-1G/AH-1J/AH-1Q Huey Cobra, 333 km/h., 577 km,
  8xBGM-71C Improved TOW, 2x20mm mini-gun pod/68mm
  rockets/grenade dispensers, USA
AH-64 Apache, 300 km/h., 689 km, 8xAGM-114 Hellfire, 30mm
  gun, 68mm rockets, USA
Alouette III--see Helicopters, Light Transport; armed with
  AS-12 AGMs
Bell 406 (OH-58D), Combat Scout, 222 km/h., 556 km, BGM-71C
  Improved TOW, LMG/or 2 AAMS, USA; derived from Bell 206
  light helicopter
500 MG Defender/ TOW Defender/ Advanced Scout Defender, 244
  km/h., 589 km range, 4xBGM-71C Improved TOW, 30mm chain
  gun, USA (derivative of Hughes 500D light transport
  helicopter, renamed McDonnell Douglas 500MD)
530 MG, armament equivalent to Hughes 500MD, USA (military
  derivative of Hughes 530F, renamed McDonnell Douglas
  530MG); see above and Helicopters, Light Transport
MBB BO-105, 6xHOT--see Helicopters, Light Transport
Mi-24 Hind D/E 330 km/h., 4xAT-2 Swatter ATGM, 1x12.7mm MG,
  4x32 57mm rockets, 8 troops, USSR
Mi-25 Hind--improved version of Mi-24
SA-342/SA-342K/L/M Gazelle, 310 km/h., 360 km,
  4xHOT/6xHOT/4xAS-11/2xAS-12, 2x7.62 mm. MG, France
Westland Lynx, 259 km/h., 630 km, 8xBGM-71C Improved
  TOW/8xHOT/6xAS-11 AGM, 2x20mm gun/7.62mm MG, 18x68mm
  rockets, 10 troops, Britain

<u>Helicopters, Heavy Transport</u>  (designation, NATO codename if relevant, speed, range, accommodation, load, country of origin)

AS-61A/A4, Italy (licensed production of US-made S-61A);  see S-61A

CH-47C Chinook, 304 km/h., 185 km radius  (ferry  range  2142 km), 44 troops/9843 kg., USA/Italy (licensed production)

CH-53/CH-53D, 315 km/h., 413 km, ca. 50 troops/5.9 ton/9  ton external payload, USA

KV-107/KV-107 IIA-17, 270 km/h., 1097  km,  25  passengers/12 passengers and 2268 kg, Japan (licensed production of USA-Boeing Vertol 107, Model II)

Mi-6  Hook,  300  km/h.,  1450  km  ferry  range,  65 passengers/12,000 kg. internal payload/ 9000  kg.  external payload, USSR

S-61 A/S-61 A4 (Sikorsky SH-3 Sea King), 267 km/h., 1005  km, 25 passengers/3630 kg., USA; employed mainly in  ASW  role, and in search and rescue with  sonar,  navigation  Doppler radar

SA-321 Super Frelon (SA-3200--earlier aircraft),  275  km/h., 1020 km, 27-30  troops/5000  kg.  external/internal  load, France; can carry AM-39 Exocet AGM

SH-3 (AS-61A) VIP version of S-61 or AS-61,  Italy;  licensed production of S-61

Westland Commando Mk.2 (=S-61A & Westland Sea King  transport version), 28 troops, Britain

Westland  Sea  King  HAS  Mk.1,  211  km/h.,  1110  km,  22 passengers/2720 kg. internal load/3630 kg.  external  load, Britain; employed mostly in  ASW  role  or  in  search  and rescue  role;  equipped  with  Plessey  dipping  sonar, navigation Doppler radar system and search radar  (licensed production of USA-S-61A)


<u>Helicopters, Light Transport</u>  (designation, NATO codename if relevant, speed, range, accommodation, country of origin)

AB-47G/3B-1,  196  km/h.,  367  km,  pilot  +  3  passengers, USA/Italy; licensed production of Bell 47

AB-206 (=Bell 206), Italy

Alouette II (early versions called Sud-Aviation SE  313/3130; later version called Aerospatiale SA-318), 205  km/h.,  720 km, pilot + 4 passengers/600 kg., France

Alouette III (early version called Sud-Aviation  SE-316/3160; later version called Aerospatiale SA-316/319),  210  km/h., 540 km, pilot + 6 passengers/750 kg., France

AS-350 Ecureuil, 230 km/h., 700 km,  pilot  +  5  passengers, France

Bell 206/206B JetRanger II/III, 225 km/h., 608 km, 2 pilots + 4 passengers, USA

Bell 206L LongRanger, improvement of Bell 206, 2 pilots  +  5 passengers, USA

BK-117 (MBB/Kawasaki BK-117), 248 km/h., 493 km, pilot + 6 passengers, FRG/Japan

Hiller UH-12E, 154 km/h., 565 km, pilot + 3 passengers, USA

Hughes 500D, 282 km/h., 531 km, pilot + 4 passengers, USA (=Hughes 500MD attack helicopter for civilian or observation tasks); renamed McDonnell Douglas 500D

Hughes 530F, improvement of 500D, renamed McDonnell Douglas 530F, USA

Hughes 300C, 169 km/h., 370 km, pilot + 2 passengers, USA

MBB BO-105, 270 km/h., 1112 km, pilot + 4 passengers /ca. 300 kg., FRG (=Nurtanio MBB NBO 105, Indonesia); can be fitted with HOT ATGM and used as attack helicopter; licensed production in Spain and Indonesia


Helicopters, Maritime Attack (designation, maximum cruising speed, range, armament, country of origin)

AS-365 Dauphin--same as SA-365

HH-65A Dolphin, 257 km/h., USA (licensed production of French Aerospatiale SA-366 Dauphin 2)

SA-365N/365F Dauphin 2, 252 km/h., 4xAS-15TT air-to-ship missiles, France

SA-366--improved SA-365


Helicopters, Medium Transport (designation, NATO codename if relevant, speed, range, accommodation, load, country of origin)

AB-205 (=Bell 205), Italy; production under USA license

AB-212 (=Bell 212), Italy; production under USA license

AB-214/214A (Bell 214), 250 km/h., 654 km, 16 passengers, Italy; production under USA license

AS-332 Super Puma, 296 km/h, 644 km, 20 passengers, France

Bell 205, 204 km/h., 511 km, 14 troops/1759 kg., USA (AB-205 in Italy)

Bell 212/212B, 259 km/h., 420 km, 10 troops/2268 kg. external load/1814 kg. internal load, USA (AB-212 in Italy)

Bell 222, 259 km/h., 532 km, 8-10 passengers/3,810 kg. external load/3,742 kg. internal load, USA

Bell 412, 259 km/h., 695 km, 14 troops/2268 kg. external load/1814 kg. internal load, USA; a four blade derivative of the Bell 212

HH-34F (S-58), 158 km/h., 450 km, 16 troops, USA

IAR-330 Puma, Rumania; licensed production of French SA-330 Puma (see below)

Kaman HH-43F Huskie (also Kaman model 600-3/5/43B), 193 km/h., 445 km, 10 passengers/1760 kg., USA; employed as maritime rescue or VIP helicopter

Kamov Ka-25 Hormone, 209 km/h., 650 km, in ASW role--search

radar and dipping sonar, in search and rescue role can
carry 12 passengers, USSR; see helicopters, ASW
Mi-2 Hoplite (also PZL Swidnik), 210 km/h., 580 km, 8
troops/2372 kg., Poland (designed in USSR)
Mi-4 Hound, 210 km/h., 400 km, 14 troops/1740 kg., USSR
Mi-8 Hip, 250 km/h., 425 km, 24 troops/ 4000 kg. internal/
3000 kg. external load, USSR
S-76, 269 km/h., 1112 km, 12 troops/1814 kg. external
payload, USA
SA-330 Puma, 263 km/h., 550 km, 16 equipped troops/3,200 kg.,
France
UH-60A Black Hawk (also designated S-70), 268 km/h., 600 km,
14 troops/3630 kg. external load, USA
Westland Lynx--see Helicopters, Attack
Westland Whirlwind Series 3, 159 km/h., 480 km (ferry
range--834 km), 10 troops/ca. 1000 kg., Britain


Radars (designation, effective range, country of origin)
AN/FPS-110, USA
AN/FPS-117, 350 km, USA
AN/TPS-32, 556 km, USA
AN/TPS-43, 408 km, USA
AN/TPS-59, 370 km, USA
AN/TPS-63, 296 km, USA
AN/TPS-70, 350 km, USA
AR-3 D, 24 km, Britain
AR-15, Britain
ELTA-2220/2206 148 km, Israel
Long Track, USSR
Marconi S713 Martello 3-D, 500 km, Britain
Spoon Rest (P-12) 275 km, USSR
Square Pair, USSR
S-600, Britain
Tiger S (TRS-2100), France
Watchman, Britain


RPVs, Mini-RPVs and Target Drones (designation, type,
country of origin)
Aerospatiale CT-20, target drone, France
Beech AQM-37A, target drone, USA
Beech MQM-107B, target drone, USA
DRC-30, USSR
Mastiff, mini-RPV, Israel
MQM-74C Chukar II (also Northrop MQM-74C), target drone, USA
Pioneer, mini-RPV, Israel
Scout, mini-RPV, Israel
SD-3 RPV, USSR
Skyeye R4E-50, mini-RPV, USA

Teledyne Ryan model 124 Firebee, mini-RPV, USA
Teledyne Ryan model 324 Scarab, RPV, USA
TTL BTT-3 Banshee, target drone, Britain


SAMs, Long Range (designation, NATO codename if relevant,
  SP if relevant, range, country of origin)
HAWK, 35 km, USA
HQ-2J (CSA-1), PRC; copy of SA-2
MIM-23B Improved HAWK, 40 km, USA
SA-2 Guideline, 40-50 km, USSR
SA-3 Goa, 25-30 km, USSR
SA-5 Gammon, 250 km, USSR
SA-7, SA-9, Crotale, Crotale/Shahine, Rapier, Stinger,
  Redeye--see Army, SAMs, Short Range

# NAVY

Advanced Anti-Aircraft and Anti-Missile Guns (caliber,
designation, guidance and task, country of origin)
30mm Vulcan-goalkeeper, radar-controlled AAG and anti-missile
gun, Netherlands (system and radar) and USA (gun)
20mm Vulcan-Phalanx, radar-controlled AAG and anti-missile
gun, USA


Air-to-Surface/anti-Ship Missiles (designation, guidance
system, range, launching aircraft, country of origin)
AM-39 Exocet, inertial + active homing, 70 km, Super Etendard
and Mirage F-1 EQ5 fighters, SA-330, SA-321 helicopters,
France; a derivative of MM-38 Exocet SSM
AS-15TT, radar, 14.8 km, AS-365 helicopter, France
Gabriel 3 AGM, active, 52.9 km, F-4E, Kfir, A-4, Seascan,
Israel; a derivative of Gabriel 3 SSM

See also Air Force AGMs; the following can be employed
against naval targets: AGM-62A Walleye; AGM-65A/B/C
Maverick; AS-11; AS-12; AS-1 (Kennel); AS-5 (Kelt)


Armament, Advanced (excluding missiles) (designation, type
of weapon, guidance system, country of origin)
Mk.37, anti-submarine torpedo, acoustic homing, USA
NT-37E, anti-submarine torpedo, acoustic homing, USA;
improvement of Mk.37
Stingray, anti-submarine torpedo, acoustic homing, Britain


ASW Vessels (designation, standard displacement, full load
displacement, speed, AS weapons, guns, missiles, country of
origin)
Chinese ASW vessel, PRC
Koni class ASW frigate, 1700 ton, 2000 ton, 32 knots, 2x12
barrelled RBU 6000, 4x3", 4x30mm, SA-N4 SAM (in
Algeria)/SS-N-2C SSM (in Libya), USSR
Le Fougeux class, 325 ton, 400 ton, 18.5 knots, 2x
anti-submarine mortar, 1x76mm, 2x40mm, France
Petya II class, 950 ton, 1160 ton, 32 knots, 4x16 barrelled
RBU, 2 depth charge racks, 4x3", USSR
Shanghai III, 120 ton, 155 ton, 30 knots, 8 depth charges and
variable depth sonar, 2x5mm, 1x25mm, PRC; similar to
Shanghai II, see Gunboats/MTBs
Sirius class--see patrol craft
SO-1 class, 170 ton, 215 ton, 28 knots, 4x5 barrelled RBU,
4x25mm, USSR

Auxiliary Vessels (designation, function, displacement, speed, country of origin)

Amphion class, repair ship, 14,490 ton full load, 16.5 knots, USA

Armed fishing vessel, coast guard & fishery protection, Algeria

Brooke Marine, 900 ton, royal yacht, 900 ton, 12 knots, Britain

Cargo vessel (765 DWT), Pakistan

Cargo ship, 1500 GRT, 11 knots, Norway

Cheverton type tender, 3.3 ton, 8 knots, Britain

Conoship Groningen coastal freighter, 1380 DWT, 11 knots, Netherlands

Durance class, tanker/supply ship, 10,500 ton full load, 19 knots, France

Harbor craft, 746 ton, 14 knots (former royal Iraqi yacht)

Harbor tanker, 1700 ton full load, Italy

Jansen research vessel (named Ekteshaf), 1,250 ton, FRG

LSD-1 type, logistic support ship, 2470 ton full load, 15 knots, Britain

Luhring Yard, supply ship, 3250 DWT, 16 knots, FRG

Maintenance and repair craft, ex-British LCT, 900 ton full load, 9 knots, Britain

Mala midget submarine (2-man vessel, 7.6 meter), Yugoslavia

Mazagon Docks, water tanker, 9430 ton, 15 knots, India

Niryat diving tender--see patrol craft

Okhtensky tugs, USSR (assembled in Egypt)

P-6, employed as training vessel--see gunboats and MTBs

PN-17 support tanker, 650 ton full load, Yugoslavia

Poluchat I class--employed as torpedo recovery vessel--see patrol craft

Ro-ro transport ship, 3100 ton full load, Italy

Royal Yacht, 1450 DWT, 22.5 knots, Denmark; carries a helicopter

Royal yacht, 650 ton, 26 knots, Netherlands

Spasilac, salvage ship, 1300 ton, 15 knots, Yugoslavia

Sekstan survey ship (also training ship), 345 ton full load, 10 knots, USSR

Stromboli class, support ship, 8706 ton full load, 20 knots, Italy

Survey craft, 23.6 ton, 13.5 knots, Britain

Survey ship, 240 ton, Yugoslavia

Swan Hunter replenishment ship, 33,014 ton full load, 21.5 knots, Britain

Swimmer delivery vehicles

Training craft, 109 ton full load, 22 knots, FRG

Training frigate, 1850 ton full load, 27 knots, can carry SSM, 1x57mm gun, 2x20mm gun, Yugoslavia

Training ship, 350 ton, FRG

Training ship (former royal yacht), 4650 ton, 16 knots, Britain

Water carrier boat, 125 DWT, Yugoslavia

Water tanker, 9430 ton, 15 knots, India--see Mazagon Docks water tanker

Yelva class, diving support ship, 295 ton, 12.5 knots, USSR

YW-83 water tanker, 1250 ton, 10 knots, similar to Italian harbor tanker, USA

"108" class, target craft, 60 ton full load, 26 knots, Yugoslavia


Gunboats/MTBs (designation, gunboat or MTB, length, speed, torpedo tubes if relevant, guns, country of origin)

Brooke Marine gunboat, 123 ft., 25 knots, 1x76mm, 1x20mm (=Brooke Marine 123 ft. MFPB), Britain

Fredrikshavn Vaerft gunboat, 45.8 meter, 20 Knots, 1x40mm, Denmark

Hainan class gunboat, 59 meter, 30.5 knots, 2x2x57mm, 2x2x25mm, 4xRBU 1200 ASW and depth charges, PRC

Jaguar class MTB, 139.4 ft., 42 knots, 4x21" torpedo tubes, 2x40mm, FRG

Kebir, see Brooke Marine 123 ft; same vessel, licensed production in Algeria, 2x23mm gun instead of 1x20mm

Lurssen FPB/gunboat, 38 meter, 126.3 ft., 32 knots, 1x76mm, 1x40mm, 3x7.62mm MG, FRG

P-4 class MTB, 62.3 ft., 55 knots, 2x21" torpedo tubes, 2x14.5mm, 8x122mm MRL, USSR

P-6 class MTB, 84.2 ft., 43 knots, 2x21" torpedo tubes, 4x25mm, USSR

PR-72 class gunboat, 57.5 meter, 28 knots, 1x76mm, 1x40mm, France

Shanghai II class gunboat, 128 ft., 30 knots, 4x37mm, 4x25mm, PRC

Shershen class MTB/gunboat, 118.1 ft., 40 knots, 4x21" torpedo tubes, 4x30mm, USSR


Gun Corvettes (designation, standard displacement, full load displacement, speed, guns, country of origin)

PF-103 class, 900 ton, 1135 ton, 20 knots, 2x3", 2x40mm, 2x23mm, USA

Vosper Thornycroft Mk.1B (Tobruk), 440 ton, 500 ton, 18 knots, 1x4", 2x40mm, Britain

<u>Gun Frigates</u>  (designation, standard displacement, full load
  displacement, speed, guns, country of origin)
Savage class, 1200 ton, 1490 ton,  19  knots,  2x3",  2x20mm,
  USA


<u>Hovercraft</u>  (designation, gross weight,  disposable  weight,
  speed, guns, country of origin)
BH-7 (Wellington) class, 50 ton, 14 ton, 60 knots, 2 Browning
  MG or 4xRGM-84A Harpoon SSM, Britain
Sealand Mk.2/Mk.3 class, 3 ton,
1 ton, 42 knots, Britain
Skima 12 class, Britain
SRN-6 (Winchester) class, 10 ton, 3.6 ton, 52 knots, 1x7.62mm
  MG, Britain
Tropmire Ltd., 6.4 ton, 4.2 ton, 45 knots, Britain


<u>Landing  Craft,  Logistics  (LCL)</u>  (designation,  full  load
  displacement, speed, country of origin)
Siong Huat 40 meter, Singapore
Vosper 320 ton, 9.5 knots, Singapore


<u>Landing Craft, Mechanized  (LCM)</u>  (designation,  full  load
  displacement, speed, country of origin)
150 ton Fairy Marine, 150 ton, 8 knots, Britain
Loadmaster, 350 ton (max. load 150 ton), 10.5 knots,  Britain
  (also designated as LCT)
LCM-6, 62 ton, 9 knots, USA
T-4, 94 ton, 9 knots (unconfirmed--10 knots), USSR
US type LCM, 60 ton, 11 knots, USA
26 ton LCM, FRG


<u>Landing  Craft,  Tank  (LCT)</u>  (designation,  full  load
  displacement, speed, guns, country of origin)
Ash class, 730 ton, 10.5 knots, 2x20mm, Israel
C-107 class, 600 ton, 8.5 knots, 2x20mm, Turkey
DTM-221 class,  410  ton,  9  knots,  1x20mm,  2x12.7mm  HMG,
  Yugoslavia
EDIC class, 670 ton, 8 knots, 2x20mm, 1x120mm mortar, France
Loadmaster, 150 ton, 10.5 knots, Britain
Polnochny class, 1150 ton, 18 knots, 4x30mm,  2x140mm  rocket
  launchers, USSR
750 ton LCT, 750 ton, 9 knots, Netherlands
48.8 meter LCT, no details

Landing Craft, Utility (LCU) (designation, full load
  displacement, speed, guns, country of origin)
250 ton LCU, Iran
Cheverton 45 ton, 7 knots, Britain
Cheverton 30 ton, 6 knots, Britain
Impala Marine 75 ton, 9 knots, Britain
Lewis Offshore, 85 ton, 8 knots, Britain
Ondatra class, 93 ton, 10 knots, USSR
SMB-1 class, 360 ton, 10 knots, USSR
Swiftships, 390 ton, USA
US LCU 1431 class (similar to LCU 510 class), 320 ton, 10
  knots, 2x20mm, USA
US LCU 1466 class, 360 ton, 10 knots, 2x20mm, USA
US LCU 1610 class, 375 ton, 11 knots, 2x12.7mm HMG, USA
Vosper Thornycroft 170 ton, 10 knots, Britain
Vydra class, 600 ton, 11 knots, USSR


Landing Ship, Logistics (LSL) (designation, full load
  displacement, speed, guns, country of origin)
Batral class, 1409 ton, 16 knots, 2x40mm, 2x81mm mortars,
  France
Brooke Marine, 2000 ton class, 12 knots, 1x76mm, 2x20mm,
  Britain; can be employed as LST;
Brooke Marine, 2200 ton, 15.5 knots, 2x2x40mm, Britain (also
  an LST)
Hengam class, 2540 ton, 14.5 knots, 4x40mm, Britain; can be
  employed as LST


Landing Ship, Mechanized (LSM) (designation, full load
  displacement, speed, guns, country of origin)
LSM-1, 1095 ton, 12.5 knots, 2x40mm, 4x20mm, USA


Landing Ship, Tank (LST) (designation, full load
  displacement, speed, guns, country of origin)
3500 ton, 15.5 knots, Denmark
Bat Sheva class, 1150 ton, 10 knots, 2x20mm, Netherlands
LST (South Korean), South Korea
PS-700 class, 2800 ton, 15.4 knots, 6x40mm, 1x81mm mortar,
  France
Ropucha class, 4400 ton, 17 knots, 4x57mm, USSR


MFPBs (designation, standard displacement, full load
  displacement, speed, missiles, guns, country of origin)
"400" Type, Yugoslavia
Aliya--see Sa'ar 4.5, below

Combattante II, 234 ton, 255 ton, 34.5 knots, 4xRGM-84A
    Harpoon or 4xOTOMAT 2, 1x76mm or 1x40mm, France
Combattante III, 395 ton, 425 ton, 38.5 knots, 8xMM-40
    Exocet, 1x76mm, 2x40mm, 2x30mm, France
Dvora, 47 ton, 36 knots, 2xGabriel 2/3 SSM, 2x20mm, Israel
Hegu, 68 ton, 81 ton, 40 knots, 2 Hai Ying SSM (Chinese SS-N2
    Styx), 2x25mm, PRC; copy of Soviet Komar
Komar, 68 ton, 81 ton, 40 knots, 2xSS-N-2 (Styx),
    2x25mm, USSR
Lazaga (formerly called Cormoran/Lazaga), 355 ton (full
    load), 36 knots, 4xExocet, 1x76mm, 1x40mm, Spain (licensed
    production of FRG's Lurssen Type-143); boats for Sudan to
    be armed with RGM-84 Harpoon SSM
Lurssen FPB-57, 353 ton, 398 ton, 38 knots, 4xMM-40 Exocet,
    1x76mm, 2x40mm, FRG
Lurssen TNC-45, 228 ton (half load), 38 knots, 4xExocet, or
    4xOTOMAT 2, 1x76mm, 1x40mm, FRG
October, 71 ton, 82 ton, 40 knots, 2xOTOMAT, 2x30mm, Egypt
    (electronics installed in Britain)
Ossa I, 160 ton, 210 ton, 36 knots, 2xSS-N-2 (Styx),
    2x2x30mm, USSR
Ossa II--see Ossa I, stronger engine
P-48, 250 ton full load, 22 knots, 8xSS-12, 2x40mm,
    France/Belgium
PGG-1 class (Peterson), 384 ton full load, 38 knots,
    4xRGM-84A Harpoon, 1x76mm, 2x20mm, 2x20mm Vulcan-Phalanx,
    USA
Province class, 311 ton, 363 ton, 40 knots, 6xMM-40 Exocet,
    1x76mm, 2x40mm, Britain
Rade Koncar, 240 ton (full load), 40 knots, 4xSSN-2 (Styx),
    1x76mm, 1x40mm, 2x30mm, Yugoslavia
Ramadan, 262 ton, 312 ton, 37 knots, 4xOTOMAT 2, 1x76mm,
    Britain
Reshef--see Sa'ar 4
Sa'ar 2 & 3, 220 ton, 250 ton, 40 knots, Gabriel 2/3 SSM,
    1x76mm or 2x40mm, France
Sa'ar 4, 415 ton, 450 ton, 32 knots, 4xRGM-84A Harpoon,
    5xGabriel 2/3, 2x76mm, 2x20mm, Israel
Sa'ar 4.5, 488 ton, 31 knots, 4xGabriel, 4xRGM-84A Harpoon,
    1x76mm, Israel; carries a helicopter
Susa, 95 ton, 114 ton, 54 knots, 8xSS-12 (M), 2x40mm,
    Britain


Mine Warfare Vessels (designation, standard displacement,
    full load displacement, guns, mines if relevant, country of
    origin)
Adjutant class minesweeper, 320 ton, 375 ton, 1x20mm, USA
Cape class minesweeper, 180 ton, 235 ton, 1x12.7mm HMG, USA
MSC 292/MSC 268 class, 320 ton, 378 ton, 2x20mm, USA

MSC 322 class, 320 ton, 407 ton, 2x20mm, USA
Natya class minesweeper, 650 ton, 950 ton, 4x30mm, 4x25mm, 10 mines, USSR
Nestin minesweeper, 65 ton (standard), 3x20mm, Yugoslavia
Sirius class minesweeper/patrol craft, 400 ton, 440 ton, 1x40mm, 1x20mm, France
Sonya class, 450 ton (full load), 2x30mm, 2x25mm, 5 mines, USSR
SRN-6--see Hovercraft; may serve as mine-laying vessel
T-43 class minesweeper, 500 ton, 580 ton, 4x37mm, 8x14.5mm, 20 mines, USSR
T-58 minesweeper corvette, 900 ton (full load), 4x57mm, 4x25mm, USSR
T-301 class, 159 ton, 180 ton, 2x37mm, 2xMMG, USSR
Tripartite type minesweeper, 510 ton, 588 ton, 1x20mm, Netherlands, Belgium and France
Vanya class minesweeper, 200 ton, 245 ton, 2x30mm, 5 mines, USSR
Yevgenia class minesweeper, 70 ton, 80 ton, 2x14.5mm HMG, USSR
Yurka class minesweeper, 400 ton, 460 ton, 4x30mm, 10 mines, USSR


Missile-Armed Hydrofoils (designation, displacement, speed, missiles, guns, country of origin)
Flagstaff (=Shimrit), 91.5 ton, 52 knots, 4xGabriel, RGM-84A Harpoon, 2x30mm, USA/Israel (licensed production)


Missile Corvettes (designation, standard displacement, full load displacement, speed, missiles, guns, country of origin)
Assad class, 670 ton full load, 33 knots, 4xOTOMAT, 1x76mm, 2x35mm, Italy; formerly designated Wadi class
Bulgarian-Algerian Nanuchka--same as Nanuchka II, constructed in Algeria with Bulgarian assistance
Lurssen 62 meter, 600 ton, 30 knots, 4xMM-40 Exocet/RGM-84A Harpoon, Aspide/Albatros SAMs (in Bahrain) or Sadral SAMs (in UAE) FRG
Nanuchka II class, 780 ton, 900 ton, 30 knots, 4xSS-N-2 SSM, 2xSA-N4, 2x57mm, USSR; in Syria--4xSS-N-9 SSM (unconfirmed)
PCG-1 class (Tacoma Boatbuilding 245 ft.), 732 ton, 815 ton, 30 knots, 8xRGM-84A Harpoon, 1x76mm, 1x20mm Vulcan-Phalanx, 2x20mm, USA
Wadi class--see Assad class


Missile Destroyers (designation, standard displacement,

full load displacement, speed, missiles, guns, country of origin)

Battle class, 2325 ton, 3360 ton, 31 knots, 4xStandard, 4x4.5", 2x40mm, Britain

Sumner class, 2200 ton, 3320 ton, 34 knots, 4x2xStandard, 4x5", USA


Missile Frigates (designation, standard displacement, full load displacement, speed, missiles, guns, country of origin)

Descubierta, 1233 ton, 1479 ton, 26 knots, MM-38 Exocet or MM-40 Exocet, Aspide SAMs, 1x76mm, 2x40mm, Spain; in Morocco carrying MM-38/MM-40, in Egypt carrying RGM-84A Harpoon SSM

F-2000, 2610 ton full load, 30 knots, 8xOTOMAT 2, 1x100mm, 4x40mm, France; carries a helicopter

Jianghu, 1568 ton, 1900 ton, 26.5 knots, 4xHY-2 (Hai Ying 2), 2x100mm, 4x2x37mm, 2xRBU 1200 ASW rocket launcher, 2 depth charge racks, PRC; planned: RGM-84A Harpoon SSMs

Koni, see ASW Vessels

Lupo class, 2208 ton, 2500 ton, 35 knots, 8xOTOMAT 2, 1x5", 4x40mm, Italy; carries a helicopter

Vosper mk.5 class, 1220 ton, 1540 ton, 34 knots, 5xSea Killer SSM, 3x Seacat SAM, 1x4.5", 2x35mm, Britain

Vosper Thornycroft Mk.7, 1325 ton, 1625 ton, 37.5 knots, 4x OTOMAT, 1x4.5", 2x40mm, 2x35mm, Britain, refitted and modernized in Italy


Patrol Craft (designation, length in feet, speed, guns, country of origin)

Abeking & Rasmussen, 75.2 ft., 27 knots, 3x20mm, FRG

Abeking & Rasmussen, 26.2 meters, 40 knots, FRG

Acror 46, 14.5 meters, 32 knots, 2x12.7mm HMG, France

Aztec (Crestitalia), 9 meters, Italy

Baglietto type Mangusta, 98.4 ft., 32.5 knots, 1x40mm, 1x20mm, Italy

Baglietto type 20 GC, 66.9 ft., 36 knots, 1x20mm, Italy

Baglietto GC-23, 23 meter, 38 knots, 1x20mm, 2x12.7mm HMG, Italy

Bertram class (Egypt), 28 ft., 3x12.7mm, 4x122mm MRL, USA

Bertram class (Enforcer, Jordan), 38 ft., USA

Bertram 20 ft., USA

Bertram (Jordan), 30.4 ft., 1x12.7mm HMG, 1x7.62mm MG, USA

Blohm & Voss 38 meters, FRG

Boghammar, 13 meter, Sweden

Broadsword class, 105 ft., 32 knots, 1x75mm recoilless rifle, 1x12.7mm, USA

Byblos class, 66 ft., 18.5 knots, 1x20mm, 2xMG, France

Camcraft 77 feet, 25 knots, 2x20mm, USA
Camcraft 65 feet, 25 knots, 1x20mm, USA
Cantieri Posillipo, 65 ft., 24 knots, 1x20mm, Italy
Cape class (US Coast Guard)--see Mine Warfare Vessels
CG-27, 87.6 ft., 25 knots, Sweden
CH class, 130.8 ft., 16 knots, 2x20mm, France
Ch. Navals de l'Esterel, 124.7 ft., 27 knots, 2x40mm, 2x12.7mm HMG, France
Ch. Navals de l'Esterel, 104 ft., 30 knots, 1x20mm, France
Ch. Navals de l'Esterel, 83 ft., 23 knots, 1x20mm, France
Cheverton, 50 ft., 23 knots, 1x7.62mm MG, Britain
Cheverton, 27 ft., 8 knots, Britain
CMN, 40.6 meter, 25 knots, 2x40mm, 2xMG, France
Crestitalia, 70 ft., 35 knots, 1x30mm, 1x20mm, Italy
Dabur, 64.9 ft., 21.8 knots, 2x20mm, 2xMG, USA/Israel (licensed production)
de Castro (Nisr class), 1x20mm, Egypt
Damen "Polycat 1450", 14.5 meter, 26 knots, 1x20mm, Netherlands
Fairey Marine Interceptor class, 25 ft., 35 knots, Britain
Fairey Marine Spear class, 29.8 ft., 26 knots, 3x7.62mm MG, Britain
Fairey Marine Sword class, 44.9 ft., 28 knots, 1x7.62mm MG, Britain
Garian class, 106 ft., 24 knots, 1x40mm, 1x20mm, Britain
Hyundai, South Korea
Kedma class, 67 ft., 25 knots, 2 MG, Japan
Keith Nelson, 57 ft., 19 knots, 2x20mm, Britain
Keith Nelson, 44 ft., 26 knots, 1x12.7mm HMG, 2x7.62mm MG, Britain
Keith Nelson (Dhafeer) class, 40.3 ft., 19 knots, 2x7.62mm MG, Britain
Le Fougeux (modified)--see ASW vessels
Lurrsen, 23 meter, FRG/Spain (under license)
Magnum Sedan, 27.3 ft., 60 knots, USA
Naja 12, (Naja-ASD 12) 12 meter, 50 knots, 1x20mm, 2x7.62mm MG, France
Niryat II, 95.1 ft., 12 knots, USSR
Osprey, 55 meter, 20 knots (unconfirmed), Denmark
P-6--see MTB (same craft with torpedo tubes removed, used as patrol craft)
P-32, 32 meter, 29 knots, 2x20mm, France
P-200D Vigilance, 60 meter, similar to Lazaga MFPB, Spain; armed with guns only
P-802 (Watercraft P-802), 30 Knots, Britain
P-1200, 39 ft., 21 knots, Britain
P-1903, 19.2 meter, 30 knots, 2x12.7mm, HMG, Netherlands
P-2000, 20 meter, 40 knots (unconfirmed), 1x20mm, Britain
PBR (Yatush), 32 ft., 25 knots, 2x12.7mm HMG, USA/Israel
PBR (Yugoslavia), 115 ft., 20 knots, 1x40mm, 1x20mm, 2x7.62mm

MG, Yugoslavia
Peterson Mk. II, 50 ft., 28 knots, 4x12.7mm, HMG, USA
PGM-71 (Improved PGM), 100 ft., 1x40mm, 2x20mm, 2x12.7mm HMG, USA
PO-2, 82 ft., 30 knots, 2x25mm or 2x12.7mm HMG, USSR
Police boat, 20 ft.
Poluchat I, 97.1 ft., 20 knots, 2x14.5mm, USSR
Rapier class, 50 ft., 28 knots, 2xMG, USA
SAR-33, 33 meter, 40 knots, 2x40mm, 2xMMG, Turkey (FRG design)
Seagull, 24 meter (aluminum boat), 30 knots, South Korea
Sewart class, 40 ft., 30 knots, 1x12.7mm HMG, USA
Sirius class, 152 ft., 10 knots, 1x40mm, 1x20mm, France
Skorpion class, 55.8 ft., 30 knots, 2x7.62mm MG, FRG
SO-1--see ASW vessels
Swift FPB-20, 65 ft., USA
Swiftships, 28.3 meter, USA/Egypt
Thornycroft 100 ft., 12/18 knots, 1x3.7" howitzer, 2x3" mortar, 4xMG or 1x20mm, Britain (Libyan boats--18 knots, Iraqi boats--12 knots; Iraqi boats built under license in Yugoslavia)
Thornycroft 78 ft., 22.5 knots, 1xMG, Britain
Thornycroft 50 ft., Singapore
Thornycroft 45.5 ft., 23 knots, Singapore (similar to Vosper Thornycroft 46 ft.)
Thornycroft 36 ft., 27 knots, Britain
Thornycroft 21 ft., Britain
Timsah class, 31 meter, 25 knots, 2x20mm Oerlikon, Egypt
Tracker/Tracker II, 64 ft., 29 knots, 1x20mm, Britain
USCG type 95 ft.--see above, Cape class, and Mine Warfare Vessels
VC large patrol craft, 31.5 meter, 30 knots, 2x20mm (can carry SS-12 SSMs), France
Vosper 56 ft., 29 knots, Singapore, similar to Vosper Thornycroft 56 ft.
Vosper 25 meter, 25.8 knots, 1x20mm, 2x7.62mm MG, Singapore
Vosper 36 ft., Singapore; similar to British Thornycroft 36 ft.
Vosper Thornycroft 110 ft., 27 knots, 2x20mm, Britain
Vosper Thornycroft 103 ft., 27 knots, 2x20mm, Britain
Vosper Thornycroft 78 ft.--see Thornycroft 78 ft.
Vosper Thornycroft 75 ft., 24.5 knots, 2x20mm, Britain
Vosper Thornycroft 56 ft., 30 knots, 2xMG, Britain
Vosper Thornycroft 50 ft., Britain/Singapore (identical to Thornycroft 50 ft.)
Vosper Thornycroft 36.4 ft.--see Thornycroft 36 ft.
Wasp 30 meter, 22 knots, 1x25mm chain gun, 2x7.62mm MG, Britain
Wasp 20 meter (65.8 ft.), 37 knots, 2xMG, Britain
Wasp 11 meter, 24 knots, Britain

Watercraft & Shoreham 45.6 ft., 22 knots, 1xMG, Britain;
   boats in UAE-speed 25 knots, 2x7.62mm MG
Whittingham & Mitchell 75 ft., 2x20mm, Britain
Zhuk class, 80.7 ft., 34 knots, 2x14.5mm, 1x12.7mm HMG, USSR


SAMs (Shipborne)   (designation, guidance system, range,
   country of origin)
Aspide (Albatross/Aspide), semi-active radar, 18 km, Italy
Barak--see SSMs (Shipborne)
SA-N-4, radar-guided, 9.6 km, USSR
Sadral, infra red homing, 6km, France; maritime version of
   short range Mistral SAM
Standard, semi-active radar homing, 18.5 km, USA
Seacat, radio-command, radar/TV or visual, 6 km, Britain; can
   be employed as SSM or as shipborne SAM


SSMs (Shipborne)  (designation, NATO codename if relevant,
   guidance system, effective range, country of origin)
Barak (employed as SAM, SSM and anti-missile missile), 10 km,
   Israel
C-801, SSM, PRC; Chinese copy of French MM-38 or MM-40
   Exocet
Gabriel 2, semiactive, 20.4 km, Israel
Gabriel 3, active, 36 km, Israel
Hai Ying-2 (HY-2, Silkworm), PRC; Chinese copy of Soviet
   SS-N-2
MM-38 Exocet, inertial and active homing, 42.6 km, France
MM-40 Exocet, inertial, 70.4 km, France
OTOMAT Mk.1/OTOMAT Mk.2, active homing radar, 183.3 km, joint
   French-Italian manufacture
RGM-84A Harpoon, active radar guidance, 111.2 km, USA
Seacat--see SAMs (Shipborne)
Seakiller, radio command, 25 km, Italy
SS-12, ATGM, France; employed on naval craft as anti-ship
   missile; see Army, ATGMs and Air Force, AGMs
SS-N-2/SS-N-2B (Improved Styx), autopilot, active radar
   homing, 40 km, USSR


SSMs (coastal defense)   (designation, guidance system,
   range, country of origin)
SSC-1B Sepal, radio command and active radar guidance, 250
   km, USSR
SSC-2B Samlet, radar homing, 80 km, USSR
SSC-3, inertial and terminal homing, 80-90 km, USSR; coastal
   defense version of SSN-2 improved Styx shipborne SSM
Hai Ying-2 (HY-2, Silkworm), PRC; identical to Hai Ying-2 SSM
   shipborne


368

C-801, 70Km (unconfirmed), PRC


Submarines (designation/NATO codename if relevant, surfaced displacement, dived displacement, main armament, country of origin)

F class Foxtrot, 1950 ton, 2400 ton, 10x21" torpedo tubes, USSR

IKL type 209, 1260 ton, 1440 ton, 8x21", FRG

IKL/Vickers type 206, 420 ton, 600 ton, 8x21" torpedo tubes, Britain, FRG design

K class Kilo, 2500 ton, 3200 ton, 8x21" torpedo tubes, USSR

R class Romeo, 1400 ton, 1800 ton, 8x21" torpedo tubes, USSR

W class Whiskey, 1080 ton, 1350 ton, 6x21" torpedo tubes, USSR

# CHRONOLOGY

# CHRONOLOGY OF KEY STRATEGIC EVENTS, 1988-89

<u>February-April, 1988</u>  The "War of the Cities" between Iran and Iraq. Hundreds of SSMs and rockets fired by both sides on Tehran, Qum and other cities in Iran, and on Baghdad in Iraq. First operational firing of the Iraqi al-Hussein SSM with a range of 650 km. (all told about 190 such missiles fired at Tehran and Qum). On April 26, 1988, Iraq tests its al-Abbas SSM to a range of 900 km.

<u>March 4, 1988</u>  US Secretary of State George Shultz writes to Israeli Prime Minister Yitzhak Shamir, elaborating a new peace plan (the "Shultz Plan").

<u>March 5, 1988</u>  An IDF unit clashes with a Fatah group heading from Lebanon toward Israel, killing one and wounding two. Fatah fires Katyusha rockets, hitting an Israeli village in the Galilee, wounding seven persons and destroying a house.

<u>March 7, 1988</u>  A team of three Fatah sympathizers infiltrates the Negev from Egypt and hijacks a civilian bus. The hijackers are killed during an Israeli police assault on the bus in which they kill three Israeli civilians and wound eight.

<u>March 16, 1988</u>  Iraqi forces attack with chemical weapons Kurdish civilians in the Iranian-held Iraqi-Kurdish village of Halabja. Fatalities, mostly civilians, estimated between 4,000 and 5,000.

<u>March 26, 1988</u>  US Secretary of State George Shultz meets two American professors of Palestinian origin, Ibrahim Abu Lughod and Edward Sa'id, who are members of the Palestinian National Council.

<u>April 3-7</u>  US Secretary of State George Shultz visits Jordan, Saudi Arabia and Israel to promote his peace initiative.

<u>April 6, 1988</u>  A group of young Israeli settlers are attacked by stones near and within the Samarian village of Beita, while hiking in the Nablus area. Several Jewish youngsters are wounded. An Israeli guard opens fire, and two local Arabs and one Israeli girl are killed. The IDF, in reprisal, blows up 13 houses belonging to Beita villagers who took part in the stone-throwing.

<u>April 16, 1988</u>   Khalil al-Wazir, alias Abu Jihad, commander of the military arm of al-Fatah and deputy to PLO chairman Yasir Arafat, is killed in his home in a suburb of Tunis by a small commando raiding party. Two of his bodyguards are also killed. The PLO claims the raid was launched by Israel.

<u>April 18, 1988</u>   An Iraqi army attack succeeds in recapturing Faw and ousting Iranian forces from territory they held since 1986.

<u>April 21, 1988</u>   The US and Israel sign a Memorandum of Agreement (MOA) on strategic cooperation.

<u>May 2-4 1988</u>   Following several Arab attacks in the Security Zone in South Lebanon and along the Israeli border, an IDF unit attacks PLO and Hizballah terrorist bases in South Lebanon, mainly in the village of Maidoun. Three Israeli soldiers are killed, as well as some 20 terrorists.

<u>May 16, 1988</u>   Algeria and Morocco renew diplomatic relations, partially resolving their feud over the Western Sahara by agreeing to hold a referendum. On August 30, 1988 Morocco and POLISARIO agree to a UN-OAU proposal to end the Sahara War following a referendum.

<u>May 25, 1988</u>   Iraqi attack dislodges Iranian troops from their positions near the outskirts of Basrah. Shalamche area under Iraqi control.

<u>June 10, 1988</u>   Algeria, Libya, Mauritania, Morocco and Tunisia set up a committee to explore the unification of the Maghreb countries.

<u>June 24, 1988</u>   A rocket propulsion expert and three other persons, including two Egyptian Army colonels, are charged in the US with attempting to smuggle out strategic materials needed for the construction of SSMs by Egypt.

<u>June 26, 1988</u>   Iraqi forces retake the island of Majnoon, held by the Iranians for a year and a half. Chemical agents allegedly used in Iraqi attack.

<u>July 3, 1988</u>   US cruiser Vincennes shoots down an Iranian passenger aircraft over the Persian Gulf, with the loss of 269 civilian lives.

<u>July 18, 1988</u>   Iran accepts UN Resolution 598 (specifing a ceasefire and negotiations toward peace between Iran and Iraq).

July 22, 1988    Iraq launches an offensive on the central front, with strong participation of Iranian anti-government Mujahideen Halq forces. Iraqi and Mujahideen forces attack Mehran, inflicting casualties on Iranian forces. Some Mujahideen forces attack Karmanshah, but Iranian defenses prevail. Iraqi and Mujahideen forces pull back to the border.

July 31, 1988    King Hussein of Jordan announces his government's disengagement from the West Bank and Gaza Strip, reduction of formal administrative ties, and acknowledgement of the PLO's sole responsibility for these territories.

August 20, 1988    Cease fire in the Iran-Iraq War becomes effective. Iraq launches an offensive against Kurdish rebels and Kurdish population in northern Iraq, employing large forces and chemical weapons. On August 30 Turkey allows Kurdish refugees to cross the Turkish border. As a result, 60,000 to 100,000 Kurds seek refuge there.

September 14-15, 1988    Ambassador Richard Murphy of the US Department of State visits Damascus and confers with President Assad, in an attempt to reach agreement on the election of a president in Lebanon.

September 18, 1988    IDF combined forces (army, air force and navy) attack bases of the Popular Front for the Liberation of Palestine--General Command, at Nu'eima, near Damour in Lebanon.

September 19, 1988    Israel launches into orbit "Offek 1," its first research satellite.

September 23, 1988    Lebanese presidential elections prove abortive, as Syria obstructs the convening of parliament. President Amin Jumayil ends his presidential term. The government of Lebanon is split into two, with one temporary government led by General Michel Aoun and recognized by part of the Maronites, and another, led by Dr. Salim al-Houss, acknowledged by the Muslim communities and Syria.

September 26, 1988    The US announces that its task force in the Persian Gulf, comprising 28 vessels, will be decreased.

October 7-12, 1988    Unrest in Algeria; state of siege proclaimed. Army restores law and order, causing 150-500 persons deaths and many more wounded.

October 19-21, 1988    A Shi'ite suicide attack by carbomb in

374

the Southern Security Zone in South Lebanon causes the death
of eight Israeli soldiers and many wounded. Israel Air Force
responds by air raid on PLO and Shi'ite terrorist outposts in
the Sidon area, inflicting scores of casualties.

October 30, 1988   Five petrol bombs are hurled at an
Israeli bus passing Jericho, causing nine Israeli casualties,
including the death of a mother and three children.

October 31, 1988   US Defense Secretary Frank Carlucci
visits Egypt, Jordan and Israel. In Cairo he signs an
agreement for Egyptian production under license of M-1 A1
tanks.

November 1, 1988   Israeli general elections held. The
results give a slight advantage to the Likud over Labor--40
seats to 39--with a virtual tie overall between the two large
blocks. Orthodox parties gain in strength.

November 3, 1988   Algerian president's new constitutional
proposal is approved by a 92% majority in a referendum.
President Chadli Bendjedid deposes Prime Minister Brahimi and
appoints Kasdi Merbah as successor. On December 22, 1988
Chadli Bendjedid is reelected president by an 87% majority.

November 2-5, 1988   US Secretary of Defense Frank Carlucci
visits the Middle East.

November 15, 1988   The Palestine National Council (PNC)
meets in Algiers and proclaims an independant state of
Palestine, based on the UN's 1947 partition resolution
(181).

November 15-16, 1988   The Sudanese Popular Liberation Army
(SPLA) and Sudan's ruling party, the Democratic Unionist
Party, meet in Ethiopia and draft a peace agreement. In
reality fighting goes on. On January 27, 1989 the SPLA takes
control of the border town of Nasir. De facto SPLA control
over most of Southern Sudan.

December 9, 1988   The Intifada (Palestinian uprising in the
Israel occupied territories) is one year old.

December 14, 1988   Yasir Arafat, Chairman of the PLO, in a
news conference in Geneva, Switzerland, says he accepts UN
resolutions 242 and 338, accepts Israel's right to exist, and
renounces terrorism. Following this statement, US Secretary
of State George Shultz, on behalf of the outgoing Reagan
administration, agrees to begin a political dialogue with the
PLO.

<u>December 16, 1988</u>   Negotiations between representatives of the PLO and the US begin in Tunis. US is represented by Robert Pelletreau, American ambassador to Tunisia.

<u>December 19, 1988</u>   Following Israeli Nov. 1 elections, and against the backdrop of the US-PLO dialogue, a new Israeli coalition government is formed by Likud and Labor. Yitzhak Shamir and Yitzhak Rabin retain their positions as prime minister and defense minister, respectively, Shimon Peres becomes vice-premier and minister of finance, and Moshe Arens foreign minister.

<u>December 20, 1988</u>   Abortive coup d'etat in Sudan.

<u>January 4, 1989</u>   US and Libya produce conflicting versions regarding large chemical plant at Rabta. The Libyans claim the plant is a pharmaceutical complex, while the US and others claim it produces agents for chemical warfare. A West German company is revealed to be aiding construction of the Libyan plant. As tension mounts between the parties, two US Navy F-14 fighter aircraft shoot down two Libyan MiG-23 fighters over the Mediterranean Sea.

<u>January 7-11, 1989</u>   An international conference in Paris, with 149 countries participating, deals with the use of chemical warfare and production of chemical agents. A unanimous resolution is adopted, deploring the use of CW.

<u>February 8, 1989</u>   The US Department of State's annual report on violations of human rights expresses criticism of Israel's conduct in the occupied territories.

<u>February 17-27, 1989</u>   Soviet Foreign Minister Eduard Shvardnadze visits the Middle East, including stops in Syria, Jordan, Egypt, Iraq and Iran. In Iran, Shvardnadze confers with Ayatollah Khomeini. In Cairo he meets with Israel's new Foreign Minister Moshe Arens as well as with Yasir Arafat, Chairman of the PLO.

<u>February 1989</u>   Egypt, Iraq, Jordan and Yemen (YAR) agree to form an economic and political entity: the Arab Cooperation Council (ACC).

<u>February 1989</u>   Maghreb countries--Algeria, Morocco, Tunisia, Mauritania and Libya--form the Arab Maghreb Federation.

<u>February 28, 1989</u>   Israeli fighter aircraft attack PFLP-GC and DFLP command posts and positions near Beirut, Lebanon,

apparently in retaliation for attempts by two DFLP groups to penetrate and attack Israel in preceding weeks. Several DFLP men killed and wounded, but 23 Palestinian schoolchildren also reportedly injured by a bomb that hit their school.

March 1989    US government temporarily suspends $230 million of its aid to Egypt, demanding that Egypt comply with the economic recommendations of the International Monetary Fund (IMF).

March 1989    General Michel Aoun, prime minister of the Christian government in Lebanon, imposes a naval blockade on ports serving the Muslim militias, and attempts to order Syrian troops to withdraw from Lebanon. Syrian and Christian armies commence shelling each other and civilian targets. Syria imposes an effective maritime and air blockade on the Christian-controlled part of Lebanon.

March 15, 1989    Tabah, a disputed border area near Eilat, is returned by Israel to Egypt after a prolonged arbitration process.

April 7-11, 1989    Prime Minister Yitzhak Shamir of Israel visits the US, confers with President George Bush, and proposes a new four point plan that provides for elections in the occupied terrritories, to be followed by further negotiations with the Palestinians elected. The PLO and Palestinian personalities in the occupied territories initially reject Shamir's proposal.

April 1989    Economic crisis and disturbances in Jordan. Eight persons reportedly killed by security forces. King Hussein cuts short a visit to the US and replaces Prime Minister Zaid al-Rifa'i with Sharif Zaid ben Shaker.

April 1989    The USSR revealed to have sold Libya 15 Su-24 advanced fighter aircraft, six of which have already delivered.

April 15, 1989    President Hosni Mubarak of Egypt relieves Field Marshal Muhammad Abd al-Halim Abu Ghazala from his post as deputy prime minister and defense minister, and appoints General Youssuf Sabri Abu Talib to fill the position.

May 3, 1989    Compromise reached in Lebanese crisis between the Aoun Christian government and Syrian forces and Muslim militias, with Kuwaiti mediation: Aoun lifts Christian naval blockade on anchorages and harbors serving the Muslim militias; Syria ceases the shelling of Christian controlled parts of Lebanon; Kuwaiti general is appointed Arab League mediator between the parties. As of mid-June this ceasefire had been violated from time to time and the Syrian blockade remained in effect.

<u>May 1989</u>  PLO Chairman Yasir Arafat on an official visit to France. Meets President Mitterand and in a press conference declares that the Palestinian National Covenant (which calls for the destruction of Israel) is now "caduque", i.e. obsolete, no longer relevant.

<u>May 5, 1989</u>  General Adnan Khairalla, Iraq's minister of defense and deputy commander in chief of the armed forces, killed in a helicopter crash during a visit to Kurdish areas.

<u>May 14, 1989</u>  The government of Israel approves the Israeli peace initiative, including elections in the occupied territories.

<u>May 23-26, 1989</u>  Arab summit conference convened in Morocco, with all Arab states participating, including Egypt, Libya and Syria. Most heads of state are present. Egypt is readmitted unconditionally to membership in the League of Arab States.

<u>May 28, 1989</u>  Clash between IDF soldiers and men from the PFLP, PLF (Tal'at Ya'qub faction) and Hizballah, trying to infiltrate Israel from Lebanon. Two terrorists are killed and two captured. Terrorist Katyusha rocket hits the Israeli village of Metula, wounding one.

<u>June 3, 1989</u>  Ayatollah Khomeini, Iran's national and religious leader, dies. President Hojatoleslam Ali Khamenei succeeds Khomeini as national leader.

<u>June 1989</u>  Hashemi Rafsanjani, speaker of the Iranian Parliament and candidate for the August 1989 presidential elections, visits the USSR and confers with Soviet leaders. Agreements signed on economic cooperation between Iran and the USSR are estimated to encompass $6 billion. Hints of military cooperation.

<u>June 30, 1989</u>  Successful coup d'etat in Sudan: the army overthrows the government. President al-Mirghani is out of the country, but Prime Minister Sadiq al-Mahdi is arrested. Control is quickly consolidated by the army, led by a Revolutionary Command Committee headed by Brigadier General Omar Hassan al-Bashir.

# ABBREVIATIONS

| | |
|---|---|
| AA | anti-aircraft |
| AAG | anti-aircraft gun |
| AAM | air-to-air missile |
| AEW | airborne early warning |
| AFV | armored fighting vehicle |
| AGM | air-to-ground missile |
| AP | anti-personnel |
| APC | armored personnel carrier |
| AR | assault rifle |
| ARV | armored reconnaissance vehicle |
| ASW | anti-submarine warfare |
| AT | anti-tank |
| ATGM | anti-tank guided missile |
| ATRL | anti-tank rocket launcher |
| AWACS | airborne warning and control system |
| batt. | battalion |
| bil. | billion |
| bty. | battery |
| CBU | cluster bomb unit |
| CW | chemical warfare |
| div. | division |
| DWT | dead weight tons |
| ECM | electronic countermeasures |
| ECCM | electronic counter-countermeasures |
| EW | electronic warfare |
| FLIR | forward-looking infrared |
| ft. | feet |
| GCC | Gulf Cooperation Council |
| GDP | gross domestic product |
| GHQ | general headquarters |
| GRT | gross registered tons |
| GPMG | general purpose machine gun |
| HMG | heavy machine gun |
| h. | hour |
| HQ | headquarters |
| km | kilometer |
| kg. | kilogram |
| IAF | Israel Air Force |
| IAI | Israel Aircraft Industries |
| IDF | Israel Defense Forces |
| km | kilometer |
| laser | light amplification by stimulated emission of radiation |
| LCM | landing craft, mechanized |
| LCT | landing craft, tank |

| | |
|---|---|
| LCU | landing craft, utility |
| LMG | light machine gun |
| LSM | landing ship, mechanized |
| LST | landing ship, tank |
| LT | light tank |
| m. | meters |
| MBT | main battle tank |
| MFPB | missile fast-patrol boat |
| MG | machine gun |
| mil. | million |
| mm | millimeter |
| MMG | medium machine gun |
| MRL | multiple-rocket launcher |
| MTB | motor torpedo boat |
| Naval SSM | sea-to-sea missile |
| NCO | non-commissioned officer |
| PGM | precision-guided munition |
| PLA | Palestine Liberation Army |
| PLO | Palestine Liberation Organization |
| port. | portable |
| reg. | regular |
| res. | reserve |
| RPV | remotely piloted vehicle |
| SAR | semi-automatic rifle |
| SAM | surface-to-air missile |
| SDV | swimmer delivery vehicle |
| SLAR | sideways-looking airborne radar |
| SMG | submachine gun |
| SP | self-propelled |
| sq. | square |
| SSM | surface-to-surface missile |
| STOL | short take-off/landing |
| TOE | table of organization and equipment |

# MAPS

Map no. 1

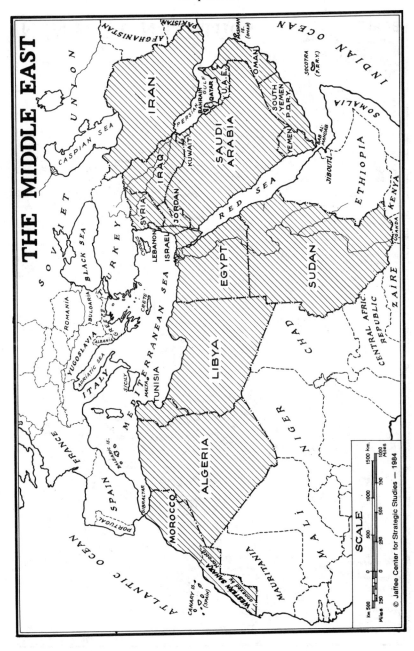

THE MIDDLE EAST

SCALE

© Jaffee Center for Strategic Studies — 1984

Map no. 2

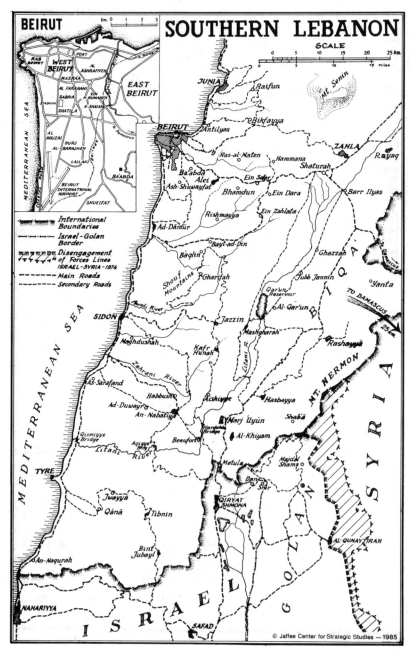

384

Map no. 3

# ISRAEL : NORTHERN FRONT

SCALE

Km. 10 5 0    10    20        50              100 km
Miles 10        0      10      20    30    40    50    60 Miles

●HOMS

├─·──·──·─ International Boundaries
├────── West Bank & Gaza Strip
        Boundaries ("Green Line")
├─·──·──·─ Israel - Golan Border
├─··──··─ Disengagement of Forces
        Lines  ISRAEL - SYRIA - 1974

TRIPOLI

L E B A N O N

BA'ALBEK
            ○ NABEK

JUNIA

BEIRUT
        BA'ABDA  ZAHLA
        ALEI  BEIRUT-DAMASCUS ROAD
        DAMUR

SIDON        JAZZIN        DAMASCUS

        NABATIYA    MARJ
                    UYUN

TYRE

S Y R I A

MEDITERRANEAN SEA

NAHARIYA
ACRE        SAFAD

GOLAN

○ QUNEITRA

HAIFA
        TIBERIAS
        ○ NAZARETH        ○ SUWEIDA

        ○ AFULA    IRBID    ○ DER'A

I S R A E L

HADERA    JENIN        RAMTHA

NATANYA    TULKARM        MAFRAK

HERZLIYA    NABLUS

TEL-AVIV
YAFO    PETAH
BAT-YAM  TIQVA

        ○ LOD
        ○ RAMLE    RAMALLAH    JERICHO    AMMAN    O F
ASHDOD  REHOVOT

ASHQELON            JERUSALEM

                BETHLEHEM        J O R D A N

GAZA        ○ HEBRON        DEAD SEA

K I N G D O M

Jordan River

○ BEERSHEBA        © Jaffee Center for Strategic Studies — 1984

385

Map no. 4

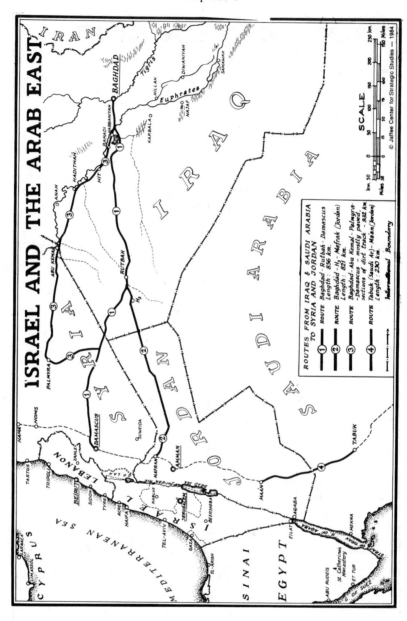

Map no. 5

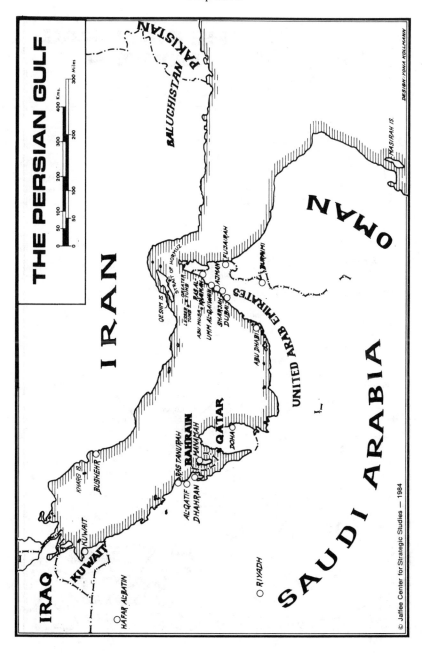

Map no. 6

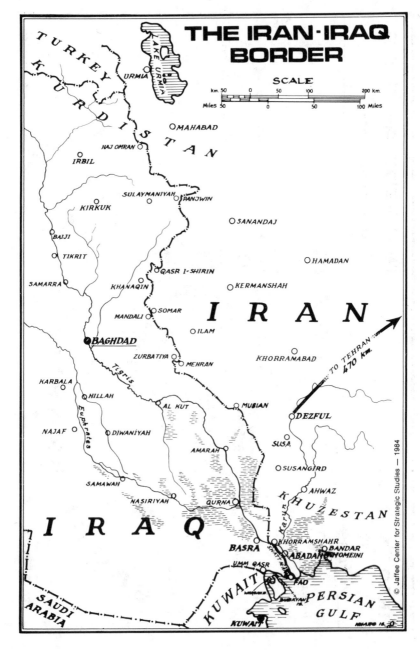

THE IRAN·IRAQ BORDER

Map no. 7

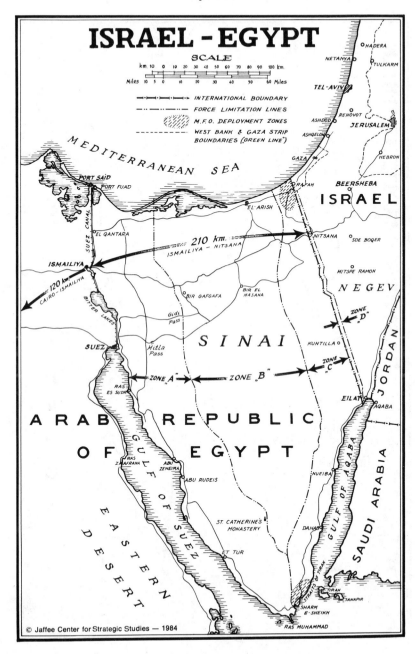

Map no. 8

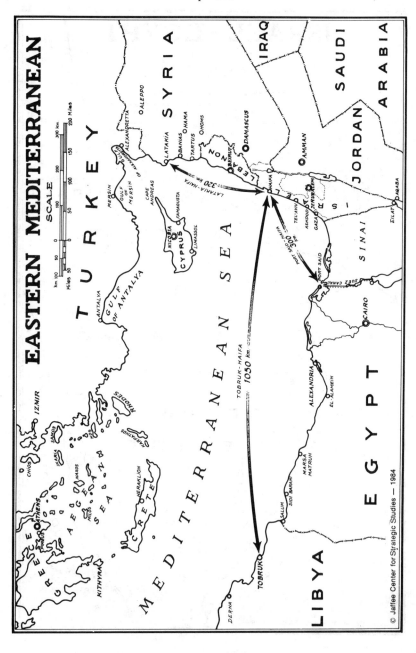

Map no. 9

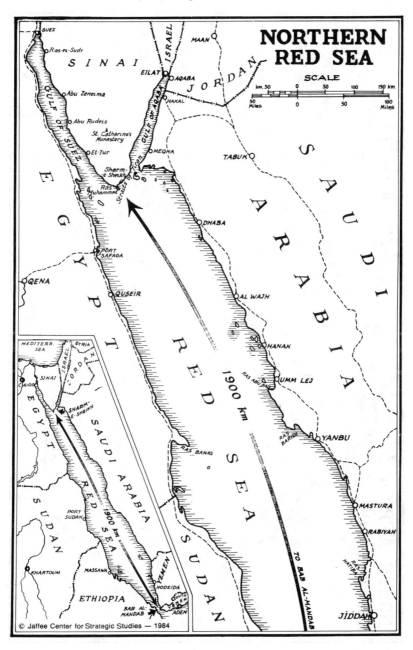

Map no. 10

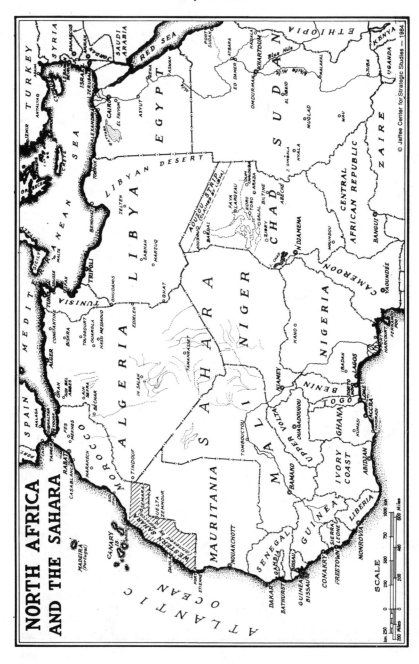